Social Communication and Movement

European Monographs in Social Psychology

Series Editor HENRI TAJFEL

EUROPEAN MONOGRAPHS IN SOCIAL PSYCHOLOGY 4
Series Editor HENRI TAJFEL

Social Communication and Movement

Studies of Interaction and Expression in Man and Chimpanzee

Edited by

MARIO VON CRANACH
Psychological Institute, University of Berne, Switzerland

IAN VINE
Department of Psychology, University of Bristol, England

1973

Published in cooperation with the
EUROPEAN ASSOCIATION OF EXPERIMENTAL
SOCIAL PSYCHOLOGY
by
ACADEMIC PRESS *London and New York*

ACADEMIC PRESS INC. (LONDON) LTD.

24–28 Oval Road
London NW1

US edition published by
ACADEMIC PRESS INC.
111 Fifth Avenue,
New York, New York 10003

Library of Congress Catalog Card Number 72–84351
ISBN: 0-12-724750-5

PRINTED IN GREAT BRITAIN BY
WILLMER BROTHERS LIMITED
BIRKENHEAD

Contributors

Mario von Cranach, *Psychologisches Institut, Universität Bern, Switzerland*

Irenäus Eibl-Eibesfeldt, *Arbeitsgruppe für Humanethologie, Max-Planck-Institut für Verhaltensphysiologie, Starnberg, German Federal Republic*

Johann H. Ellgring, *Max-Planck-Institut für Psychiatrie, Munich, German Federal Republic*

Siegfried Frey, *Max-Planck-Institut für Psychiatrie, Munich, German Federal Republic*
Now at *Psychologisches Institut, Universität Bern, Switzerland*

Nico H. Frijda, *Psychologisch Laboratorium, Universiteit van Amsterdam, The Netherlands*

Ian Hindmarch, *Department of Psychology, University of Leeds, England*

Jan A. R. A. M. van Hooff, *Laboratorium voor Vergelijkende Fysiologie, Rijksuniversiteit Utrecht, The Netherlands*

Adam Kendon, *Project on Human Communication, Bronx State Hospital, New York, USA*

Peter Stringer, *School of Environmental Studies, University College London, England*
Now at *Department of Psychology, University of Surrey, England*

Ernst Timaeus, *Institut für Sozialpsychologie, Universität Köln, German Federal Republic*
Now at *Fachbereich Psychologie, Gesamthochschule Essen, German Federal Republic*

Ian Vine, *Department of Psychology, University of Bristol, England*
Now at *School of Human Purposes and Communication, University of Bradford, England*

Preface and Acknowledgements

In the spring of 1969 a small Working-Group Meeting on Non-verbal Communication was held in Amsterdam under the sponsorship of the European Association of Experimental Social Psychology. It was organized by Nico Frijda and Ian Vine, the other participants being Michael Argyle and Peter Stringer from England, Mario von Cranach and Ernst Timaeus from West Germany, and Jan van Hooff from Holland. The four days of informal papers and discussions were thought to have been fruitful, and consideration was given to publishing these proceedings.

Henri Tajfel suggested that the volume might appear in the present series, and as Nico Frijda was too busy to compile it, the present authors undertook the task of editing contributions. All participants agreed to provide papers, except Michael Argyle, who declined since he was already engaged in publishing his material elsewhere. A further Symposium on Non-verbal Communication, sponsored by NATO and arranged by Michael Argyle and Ralph Exline, took place in Oxford in August 1969, and enabled the editors to put into effect a decision to expand the scope of the work, and to make it more representative of European research on expression and communication at that time. As a result, Adam Kendon, Irenäus Eibl-Eibesfeldt, and Ian Hindmarch agreed to provide contributions based on the research they reported at Oxford; and Johann Ellgring and Siegfried Frey subsequently agreed to collaborate with von Cranach on further papers. Contributors varied somewhat in the speed with which they prepared manuscripts, but the editors must also admit to having been variously distracted by pressures of other work. As a result the final manuscripts were not assembled until three years later. Each, however, although partly based on earlier conference contributions, has been revised especially for this volume.

We must beg indulgence from those contributors whose manuscripts were submitted some time ago; also we must acknowledge the encouragement and patience of Henri Tajfel the series editor, and Mrs Dorothy Sharp of Academic Press. Further thanks are due to the EAESP for supporting the European commuting which the editors found necessary on occasions, and to the Max-Planck-Society, to the University of Berne, and to the University of Bristol for providing direct and indirect support for the editors during the book's preparation.

Permission to reproduce quotations and figures was kindly given by the numerous publishers cited in the text.

Finally we wish to thank all those individuals, too many to mention, who contributed comments and ideas in connection with particular papers or the collection as a whole, who typed manuscripts for ourselves or the authors, or who simply tolerated and encouraged us during the process of preparation—particularly our wives, who sometimes found communication with us difficult and infrequent.

July 1973

MARIO VON CRANACH
IAN VINE

Contents

1

Introduction

Mario von Cranach and Ian Vine

1 The investigation of face-to-face interaction and movement

Until some years ago the scientific study of the field that constitutes the topic of this book was both neglected and fragmented. It no longer seems neglected, but it remains distinctly fragmented. Its diversity can be attributed to a variety of factors. Perhaps the most basic is that its investigators have come from very different disciplines, and this has led to differences of both approach and focus. There are sometimes fundamental disagreements on questions of theory and method which in part reflect these different backgrounds, as may also their particular choices of behaviours to be investigated within the overall area of movement and communication.

The study of face-to-face interaction processes would seem to be fundamental to a variety of disciplines, both "pure" and "applied". So it is scarcely surprising that not only social psychologists, but also social anthropologists and linguists, sociologists, psychiatrists and ethologists should have become involved in this field. What is curious is that systematic research should not have appeared in any quantity until the last decade. It seems that those scientists for whom face-to-face interaction is a basic element in their subject-matter were previously content to take it very much for granted, assuming perhaps that some-

1

thing so commonplace could be understood intuitively with sufficient completeness and precision to eliminate any pressing need for systematic study. It is not easy to pinpoint how the change in attitude which led to a dramatic acceleration of this research came about; but it appears to have occurred more or less simultaneously in several disciplines, and to have taken a variety of directions.

Recently, in conferences and review articles, some efforts have been made to bridge the gaps (e.g. Sebeok *et al.*, 1964; Diebold, 1968; Argyle and Exline, 1969; Duncan, 1969). It is not our intention to attempt to reconcile here the alternative standpoints whose contrast turns out to be fruitful; but in order to locate the contributions of this volume within an overall framework, we must sketch out the main streams of scientific work in this area before we indicate the scope of the book's contents. We do not, however, claim that this book is equally representative of all approaches. In a final section, we shall try to outline what seems to us a possible basis for a more unified theory of communication and movement: one which ideally should permit us to combine the variety of insights which multi-disciplinary interest in a single topic area has already produced.

2 Approaches to the study of communication and movement

2.1 THE ASSESSMENT OF PHYSICAL MOVEMENT DIMENSIONS

In this approach, movement is assessed as a multi-dimensional physical event that is a process of spatio-temporal change (Sainsbury, 1954; Bahrick and Noble, 1966; Webb *et al.*, 1966; Frey, 1971). Change of location of the body and its parts in relation to the physical environment, and the speed and variability of this process, are the objects of investigation. Movement may be related to physiological, psychological or sociological concepts. The validity of the measurements is determined by separate investigations. The approach aims at quantification: it is based on instrumental measurement or systematic observation methods.

The advantage as well as the disadvantage of the approach may be seen in the same characteristic. Since it does not take its point of departure from pre-existing psychological theories but considers movement as a basic behavioural phenomenon, it does not presuppose specific behaviour units prior to empirical investigation. It thus characterizes movement in a general descriptive way, in terms more general than those specifically appropriate to interactional events. On the other hand, it is clumsy and laborious in describing specific signals. The units are in most cases more or less gross descriptions based on spatio-temporal measurements. These characteristics have to be considered in assessing its application and its contribution to a conceptual synthesis.

2.2 THE STRUCTURAL APPROACH

This approach follows explicitly the example of structural linguistics, as adopted in structural anthropology. It is mainly used by social anthropologists (e.g. La Barre, 1947, 1964; and especially Birdwhistell, 1952, 1971) and psychiatrists (particularly Scheflen, 1966, 1968). Its theoretical commitments may be summarized as follows:

1. Communication is a relatively independent behavioural system of multi-channel activity that is governed by "rules" rather than by "laws". These rules are the topic of investigation.
2. The system is holistic and is hierarchically structured so that: (a) the study of behaviour has to proceed with regard to distinct levels of organization and integration; (b) single discriminable structural elements do not possess independent identity, and thus have meaning only in a very restricted sense.
3. Until counter-evidence appears, *all* behaviour is considered to be communicative, with multiple meanings at a variety of levels of integration.
4. The relations between the parts of the system are not probabilistic but deterministic, because the question of whether a rule should be applied is a matter not of probability but of norms.
5. Communicative behaviour is acquired: it originates through socialization in a cultural context, and the meanings of signals are considered as culturally learned, except where the converse can be proved.

From these assumptions the following methodological prescriptions can be derived:

1. Communication should be studied as a total performance in true communicational situations.
2. Research must be based on structural analysis rather than experimental investigation of single variables. Statistical methods are inadequate because of the non-probabilistic nature of communicative

performance and interpretation, the complexity of behaviours, and their intrinsic interdependence.

3. The analysis must be bound to structural levels; ideally, it should proceed from lower to higher levels of integration.

4. In as much as separate communication channels can be distinguished, intra-channel research has to be complemented by inter-channel research, since channels never operate in isolation.

The main achievement of the structural approach is that it has, by research and theoretical discussion, directed attention to important and previously neglected theoretical viewpoints. Its disadvantage may be seen in a certain dogmatism and exaggeration of methodological principles. Even if we agree that communication is based on "rules" rather than "laws", observed instances of communicative behaviour will normally involve deviations from these rules. But this still comes within the general principle, operating in genetics, ethology, learning and culture, that information built into a system only constitutes a statistical norm around which the structure of the system varies, the amount of deviation depending on the extent of its constraints. The amount of constraint necessary to create *strict* observation of the rule is extremely high and rarely reached. This is why the use of statistical inference in analyses is often essential. Besides, experimental research on external variables affecting the operation of the rules has provided fruitful insights into the nature of communicative behaviour.

Closely related to the structural method is a sociological approach that has evolved from Symbolic Interactionism (e.g. Goffman, 1961, 1963, 1971; Garfinkel, 1964). Its object is the description of cultural rules and roles that govern interactive behaviour in a given situational context. The individual adopts a given role and relates to its rules according to his needs and his subjective "definition of the situation". The methods used vary from participant observation to the analysis of biographies and histories, and even to quasi-experiments in field situations. Behaviour is often viewed as a "performance" with affinities to play-acting or game-playing. One major feature of these approaches is that they are well equipped to specify how verbal and non-verbal aspects of interaction are integrated, a task which is essential to the realization of any full theory of communication processes. The relative neglect of verbal interaction in this book should in no way be taken to mean that we are unaware of this crucial requirement.

2.3 THE ETHOLOGICAL APPROACH

In the last decade, biologists have started to apply, under the name of "human ethology" or "social ethology", the methodological and theoretical principles of animal ethology to human behaviour (e.g. Wickler, 1966; Morris, 1967; Eibl-Eibesfeldt, 1967, 1970; Grant, 1968, 1969; Blurton-Jones, 1972). These scientists have worked on the basic assumption that human behaviour depends to a greater or lesser extent on phylogenetically inherited, adaptive predispositions. For this reason, they have as far as possible, considered behaviour as a total performance in its natural environment. Thus they have analysed its structure and function by analogy with related species, taking into account ecological factors. The ontogeny of behaviours is also accorded an important place in their investigations. In this approach, the most suitable methods of research are naturalistic observation and field experiments. Where for instance films are taken, the subjects must be quite unaware of the photographer, and special techniques have been developed for concealed filming (Eibl-Eibesfeldt and Hass, 1967).

The collection of data is directed towards the description of natural behavioural units which together comprise a human "ethogram". This is considered the first and the most important research task. To the material thus obtained, the general comparative methods developed in morphology are applied, and the findings are interpreted in terms of ethological theory, emphasizing functional and adaptive aspects of communicative behaviour.

We cannot overlook the fact, however, that the latter step in particular has met with difficulties. Among these are the absence of living direct ancestors of our own species; the probability that phyletic evolution has occurred; and, perhaps most fundamentally, the substantial change in the human behaviour system brought about by the new dimension of symbolic behaviour gained through the use of language, which makes it necessary to include psychological, social and cultural factors in the analysis. These obstacles are hard to overcome, since an explicit comparative methodology for the treatment of human behaviour has not yet been developed. Methods recently adopted, like cross-cultural comparison and the study of behaviour in isolated cultures (Eibl-Eibesfeldt, 1968; Ekman, 1972), developmental investigation (Blurton-Jones, 1972), and the analysis of abnormal behaviour (Grant, 1968), are mainly used to establish the still widely doubted existence of innate behaviour patterns and a biological substrate on which cultural learning must rest. Studies that provide a full ecological and comparative functional analysis are still awaited.

The potential superiority of the ethological approach consists, of course, in its consideration of man as a biological being. It may be an extremely fruitful component of future more widely based approaches.

2.4 THE EXTERNAL VARIABLE APPROACH

This approach has been so named (Duncan, 1969) because of its basic strategy of attempting to infer the function or meaning in isolated communicative acts from their connection with non-communicative variables (e.g. Argyle, 1969; Ekman and Friesen, 1969a, 1969b). It is mainly followed by social psychologists who stress, besides observational procedures and content analysis, the usefulness of experimental design and statistics. According to Argyle: "The approach, which is recommended here is to carry out rigorously designed experiments, which test hypotheses, but which are carried out in realistic settings with clear meanings and conventions, and which contain all the main ingredients of ordinary social behaviour." (1972, p. 244.)

Since conventional experimental strategies tend to be based on molecular and unsystemic premises, the results of this approach are not easily integrated into a systemic framework. If this step is attempted at all, it arises through secondary interpretation and synthesis of isolated findings. Hopefully, the development of multivariate experimental techniques will lead to an improvement in this area. Another weakness of the method derives from its use of standard research paradigms in which, under more or less severe restriction of the subjects' response dimensions, artificial (e.g. written verbal) reactions are elicited in unnatural situations. This leaves doubts regarding the external validity of the findings. These traditional methods are not inevitable, however, and Argyle (1969) has claimed that a "New Look" is emerging in research on social behaviour. While Argyle's own emphasis on the "skills" aspect of social behaviour can be seen as a subdivision of the "external variable" approach, his particular orientation and emphasis on "feedback" processes (cf. Kendon, 1967) can be seen as one of its more novel and useful features.

The external variable approach has up to now produced the major bulk of readily specified discoveries concerning communication and movement. By taking into consideration novel principles like those proclaimed by Argyle's "New Look", and developing the relevant techniques of experimentation and analysis still further, substantial progress will probably be achieved.

We do not wish to claim that all important research dealing with non-verbal aspects of the communication process can be fitted neatly into one or other of the approaches outlined above, nor that we have referred to even a representative sample of those who have contributed to the present state of the field. A number of important contributions are less easily classified but cannot be left unmentioned. Sommer (1969) and Hall (1966, 1968) show the influence of a variety of approaches in their treatment of the spatial aspects of social behaviour; so also does Sebeok (e.g. 1965) who has been concerned with theoretical questions and has acted as a powerful catalyst in the recent development of communication research (Sebeok, 1968). Nevertheless, in attempting to impose order on a diversified topic we feel that the divisions set out above characterize the main poles of thinking and research on face-to-face interaction to date.

3 The contribution of this volume

The four approaches that we have described constitute a very broad theoretical and methodological classification. As can be seen from this book, the varieties of research performed both within and intermediate between these different orientations may be directed at very different questions. The organization and structure of behaviour in various modalities, the movement of different body parts, the development and psychopathological functioning of behaviour have been investigated, as well as the efficiency of particular communicative modes, methodological questions in the assessment of movement and communication variables, and the methodological impact of these behaviours on psychological research in general. This book, far from showing a unified theoretical orientation, reflects this diversity. We have tried to order the contributions according to their more dominant and obvious common characteristics rather than imposing any more systematic *a priori* classification, leaving them to reveal their own orientations.

3.1 BEHAVIOUR PATTERNS AND COMMUNICATIVE CONSEQUENCES

Half of our contributions have been grouped under this heading. These studies aim at the description of communicative activity and the analysis of its structure, and they all discuss one or more of its many component behaviours and their social effects on recipients.

Kendon's contribution is concerned primarily with how visible behaviour plays an organizing role in the basic cluster of interactive events, which he calls the "encounter". He considers how an interaction is started, maintained and ended; and how, in gatherings of two or more people, agreements can be reached regarding who talks to whom and at what times. An attempt is made to explain why the conduct of face-to-face interactions, in the absence of much conscious effort on the part of the participants, tends normally to exhibit orderly development instead of chaotic disorganization. For this purpose, Kendon makes use of all types of available information, experimental data as well as structural evidence and casual observations. He describes the basic functional characteristics of encounters in order to analyse the requirements they impose upon the behaviour of the participants. He then shows that these requirements are met by interactors acting on various simultaneous levels of behavioural integration, whose spatio–temporal differences reflect their different functions in the organization of the encounter.

Kendon's research illustrates the richness of human interactions, and the significance of micro-behaviours. Nevertheless, in trying to elaborate on the organization of encounters, he is faced with a paucity of firm knowledge regarding many details of what occurs during communication, and he concludes with a plea for the collection of much more descriptive evidence on which we may base a definitive "ethogram" of human communicative behaviour.

The construction and interpretation of an ethogram is the expressed aim of the next chapter. van Hooff is an ethologist, and his contribution is the only one in this book dealing specifically with animal behaviour. The inclusion of his analysis of chimpanzee social behaviour seems appropriate, since chimpanzees are phylogenetically nearer to man than most other species, and with necessary caution a comparison of social behaviour of the two should be instructive. van Hooff himself does not offer such a comparison; instead, he provides a rather detailed and complete description of the social behaviours seen in a colony of captive chimpanzees, the elements of which are grouped under concepts like patterns of locomotion, postures and gestures, body contact, facial display and vocalization. This has been attempted before, though rarely so systematically; but van Hooff goes further by a somewhat novel and intensive application of quantitative methods, involving sequence and multivariate analyses, to his categorized data. This reveals hierarchical structures that are functionally meaningful and give analytic justification for the use of terms more general than his basic observational categories, in higher-order descriptions of the social behaviour of the species.

van Hooff's analytic methods are as yet far from being used as a matter of course in ethology or psychology, but are powerful tools yielding valuable data. Besides its material results, this study may provide the student of human behaviour with good examples and insights regarding the functional differences between structurally related elements in an animal behaviour system. At the same time it shows how the boundaries of communication and general social behaviour, as distinguished in the next section of this Introduction, may be less distinct in a more primitive behaviour system.

Eibl-Eibesfeldt also establishes an ethogram. He describes and classifies the social behaviour of deaf-and-blind-born children at successive stages of their development. Special attention is given to their expressive behaviour. The author, already well known as a proponent of "human ethology", is mainly concerned with the hypothesis that many expressive behaviour patterns of these children are similar to those of normals and are thus most probably innate. His evidence, consisting of observations and film-documents, seemingly gives strong support to this interpretation. This material, on children subject to severe limitations in their opportunities for learned acquisition of communication patterns, seems rather unique and of special interest for the student of human behaviour.

We must recognize, of course, that Eibl-Eibesfeldt's conclusions are controversial, going against the modern psychological emphasis on the role of learning and experience in the development of social behaviour. In fact, this work reinforces the conclusions from recent research on adult expressions of affect in a wide variety of cultures (Eibl-Eibesfeldt, 1968; Ekman et al., 1969; Ekman, 1972) in suggesting that perhaps some expressions are species-characteristic responses to particular affective states and situations, as Charles Darwin long ago argued (Darwin, 1872). Darwin himself was fully aware that this did not imply that social learning could not affect the circumstances in which people of different cultures actually *allow* themselves to exhibit particular expressions (the "display rules" of Ekman and Friesen, 1969a, 1969b). While one might wish that Eibl-Eibesfeldt had provided a more quantitative, controlled, and strictly defined set of data, his results constitute tantalizing leads for future research.

Vine's article also treats communicative behaviours from the developmental viewpoint. He presents no new research material, but discusses instead certain aspects of the immense literature concerned with perception, expression, and mother–infant interaction that is relevant to the development of the sending and receiving of facial-visual signals. He then proceeds to a consideration of their role in socialization.

As an experimental social psychologist by training, Vine is not willing simply to apply the ethological concept of an "Innate Releasing Mechanism" (Tinbergen, 1951) to the "smiling response", as is often done. Instead, he starts with two questions: What are the stimuli that attract the infant's attention, and under what circumstances can one elicit the "smiling response"? In discussing their connection, he finds it necessary to consider in some detail the child's perceptual and cognitive capacities, and the motivation to seek out stimulation. He arrives at the conclusion that, since the cognitive experience provided by facial-visual interaction with the mother is normally rewarding for the child, it must assume an important role in normal infant development, and in establishing early sociability and attachment. Such a hypothesis comes well within the borders of psychology, although Vine emphasizes the use of ethological methods in the investigation of the phenomena concerned, and inclines towards a structural theory.

The final chapter in this section, contributed by Hindmarch, discusses in more detail the expressive significance of one particular class of cues, those associated with the eyes. In particular, he is concerned with the causes and the effects of variations in size of the pupillary aperture in social contexts. After indicating the roles and functions of eye-spots in other species, from butterflies to chimpanzees, he then discusses their significance in human communication, drawing on data from a variety of sources outside the main body of literature on social gazing. Hindmarch finds that the meaning of changes in pupil size is usually ambiguous in the absence of a full contextual specification, though in social situations we often do react differentially to pupillary cues from others. He thus provides further support for the view that communication must be considered as a complex, multi-channel process in which meanings are a function of a total interactive *gestalt*.

3.2   STRUCTURAL ANALYSIS OF FACIAL EXPRESSIONS

The two chapters in this section are closely related; again both their authors have a strong background in experimental psychology. Both deal with the problem of the relation between emotion, expression and the judgement of expression. This judgement shows a structure that is of special concern to them both; its assessment by means of descriptive and analytical quantitative methods is one of their central topics. The reader should notice that the term "structure" is used here in a somewhat different sense to that of our above references to the general "structuralist approach" to communication.

Frijda's chapter, based on a series of experimental investigations, explores the relationship between emotion and facial expression. Frijda starts from the discrepancy between reports of cross-cultural similarities and stable relations between emotion and expression, and the reports of more variable relationships. He proposes a theoretical solution in which emotion embraces more than emotional behaviour: it consists of three components, a situational valence for the subject, an immediate behavioural tendency arising from that valence, and a change in the pattern of probabilities of subsequent behaviours. Expression is seen as the individual behavioural reaction resulting from the external and internal factors that evoke the emotion. Various reasons can thus be given as to why the relationship between emotion and expression is variable. On the other hand, there is a basic structural similarity between the two phenomena. Data from recent studies reveal a hierarchical structure of judgements of emotion that is related to that for expressive features.

While Frijda aims at an appropriate theory of expression and emotion, Stringer's interest lies in the interrelation between concepts, methods and results in research on judgements on facial expressions. He considers that research in this field is often directed by various misconceptions. One of these, involving the inappropriate use of a dimensional approach in the judgement of facial expressions, is selected as a special target. In discussing some of the representative studies in the field, he points out that the dimensional approach is theoretically unjustified. Its properties are clarified in comparison with a cluster-analysis approach, and special attention is given to the interpretation of hierarchical cluster structures.

Stringer argues that "clusters and dimensions are different ways of explaining different types of judgement" (p. 342). Dimensional studies may be very relevant to the analysis of *sequences* of expressions over time. Stringer's type of detailed methodological critique is far from common, and, apart from its importance in the area of judgement of facial expressions, is equally relevant to other problem areas. It will, we hope, encourage more careful considerations of the concepts used in the study of communication and movement, in relation to both the collection of data and its analysis.

3.3   CONCEPTS, STRATEGIES AND METHODS

This last section of the book consists of three chapters, admittedly loosely related. What they have in common is a concern with particular methods of assessment of communicative behaviour, and the relations of these with research concepts and the strategic consequences that they imply. The behaviours chosen for investigation, the levels of analysis adopted, the methodological questions, and their conclusions are, however, very different in each case. All the authors see themselves primarily as social psychologists.

The chapter by Frey and von Cranach reports an attempt to describe quantitatively a general aspect of movement behaviour, namely its variability over a short time period, in terms of three independent characteristics. Empirical data are presented to evaluate the method's validity. These show that, having defined a number of easily discriminable positions for each of a variety of body parts, one can usefully assess movement variability in terms of the number of positions used, their relative frequencies, and their sequential order. Individual differences, and to some extent activity type and social stress factors, were shown to be among the determinants of movement variability. The chapter represents an example of the first type of approach that we outlined (see section 2.1).

The chapter by von Cranach and Ellgring takes its point of departure from empirical findings which suggest that gaze direction can in most circumstances be assessed only very unreliably by observation. These recent findings are in contrast to the conclusions of previous investigators who suggested high judgement validity. In a series of experiments, various factors are identified that influence the perception of gaze direction. When studied more intensively, their interplay turns out to exhibit a simple syntactic organization. Some suggestions are made as to how the important phenomena of social gazing can be empirically assessed more validly and reliably.

In the final chapter, Timaeus deals with methodology on a very different level. Since Rosenthal (e.g. 1966) and his collaborators presented their data on "experimenter-expectancy effects", the question of how the experimenter unintentionally manipulates his subjects' responses and can thus obtain biased data has become salient. Timaeus distinguishes several different strategies by which an experimenter effect can be achieved. Despite a now prodigious literature, one of these, the emission of non-verbal biasing cues by the experimenter, has only rarely been investigated before, and constitutes the main topic of his chapter. Timaeus discusses both the available research from the existing literature and his own findings; he considers experimenter effects in studies of both animals and men, and in areas ranging from perception, through tone discrimination, to suggestibility. This chapter adds to the disquiet currently being voiced about traditional experimental methods; but in making his suggestions on how to resolve problems raised by the findings, Timaeus still considers it possible to stay within the established methodology of experimental social psychology.

4 Some basic requirements for a theory of human communication and movement

The reader who works his way through this book may feel that the various chapters are in some cases so divergent, both in their research topics and in their basic approaches to the phenomena considered, that he cannot detect any common theme. A pluralistic editorial stance such as we have adopted in selecting the chapters can hardly be convincing if the actual phenomena considered do seem to exhibit some natural coherence, and therefore demand some fundamental theoretical unification. On the other hand, it would be dangerous to unify artificially where genuinely different orientations exist side by side. Our aim has been the modest one of bringing together papers which exemplify the best features of the various approaches.

In fact we cannot hope to deal adequately here with the major and essentially unsolved problem of organizing the field systematically and theoretically. Nevertheless, we at least feel obliged to point out what appear to us as some of the basic requirements for a general theory of human communication and movement. The potential significance of the contributions of this volume within such a future structure can then be estimated more readily. These tentative propositions are largely based on considerations which we have published earlier (Vine, 1970; von Cranach, 1971, 1972).

4.1 GENERAL FRAMEWORK

In our proposals we have adopted a framework which synthesizes both a "systems" orientation and a functional-developmental viewpoint that incorporates biological inheritance and cultural tradition as intrinsically significant factors in social and expressive behaviour.

We consider it appropriate to treat behaviour from the overall viewpoint of General Systems Theory (e.g. Buckley, 1968). This necessarily demands an empirical methodology for the investigation of complex systems. Although the feature of hierarchical organization seems to be pervasive in living systems, it is not possible to explore the total behavioural system all at once. We have therefore concentrated on areas predetermined by our specialist interests and training. We have classified these through their divisions into subsystems, and their higher-order relations with super-systems, e.g. the social environment. In our analysis we have endeavoured to take account of the basic viewpoints of structure, function, and history or development.

We consider Man as a biological being and a product of evolution. This, however, still allows us to accept that there is no basic antithesis between nature and culture, but that culture has developed, together with Man himself, as part of the natural environment and thus as an aspect of Man's biological context.[1] Both culture and genotype can themselves be viewed as wider systems which overlap with any particular individual's behavioural systems. Human behaviour systems develop by the integration of both phylogenetic inheritance and cultural tradition with individual experience. This is a special case of the development of systems over time (von Cranach, 1972). In biology it has been found that the connection between the structure and function of a system can best be understood by studying its development and its ecological

---

[1] This viewpoint does not oblige us to assume a basic harmony between nature and culture; their relationship is at present asymmetric and parasitic in that culture draws an increasing amount of energy from nature. This, however, is no rare case in systems–subsystems relationships.

context; and we believe that this principle is also valid in our own problem area.

The elaboration and detailed application of these ideas should lead us to a comprehensive and integrative understanding of human behaviour in general. In this Introduction, however, we shall restrict ourselves to the preliminary treatment of two problems that seem most important in bringing order into our particular field. These are the differentiation and interrelation between certain basic concepts, and the connection between structure, function and history in the organization of human communication and body movement.

4.2 BASIC CONCEPTS

From the standpoint of General Systems Theory, this book's field of interest is the area of overlap between two kinds of behavioural systems: the total behavioural systems of individuals, and the interrelation between the activities of two or more individuals in a *social* system during interaction. All systemic behaviour occurs in temporal and spatial contexts, involving both history and present environment, that together define the interaction situation. We shall now attempt to elaborate on the relationships between these systems and contexts.

4.2.1 *Movement*

To some extent the behaviour systems of interacting individuals can be studied independently. One of their most pervasive aspects is movement, the spatial-temporal change both of the whole body in relation to the environment, and of parts of the body in relation to each other. Movement is often studied directly, as for instance in research on gestures, or else by analysis of some of its immediate consequences, as in the study of speech (i.e. the acoustic consequences of movements of the vocal organs) or of handwriting (as a trace left by movements of the hand and arm). However in studying movement its spatial-temporal quality must always be considered. In the spatial and in the temporal dimensions there are no predetermined levels of analysis defining the conceptual and measurement units; their choice depends on the theoretical presuppositions chosen. The simple units can, of course, be studied descriptively in relative isolation, as Frey and von Cranach have done, or in relation to each other and to larger behavioural units, as Kendon does. But if we wish to gain insight into the total behaviour system, we must consider phenomena in relation to their whole historical and environmental context; only by this means will we be able to understand the significance of particular movements.

4.2.2 *Appearance*

Movement can be contrasted with stasis, in which there is no spatial change in a particular part of the system or subsystem under consideration. Thus some parts of the body may be static in relation to the body as a whole while others are in motion. Alternatively, the body may be static in relation to the environment, yet its components may be in motion in relation to each other. Consequently, what counts as movement and what counts as stasis is, in a sense, arbitrary; it depends upon the spatio-temporal span of our conceptual or measurement focus. In practice most investigations of movement focus on successive static positions rather than on movements *per se*.

Static features can be of interest as a part of behaviour systems, since posture, facial physiognomy, dress and the like can be studied as aspects of the basic framework within which an individual's behaviour system operates. The term "appearance", which includes both static features and a very limited number of dynamic features, such as blushing or blanching, can thus be contrasted with "movement". Taken together these terms encompass the immediately observable aspects or available social cues which indicate the state of an individual's behaviour system. In the wider context, the historical and environmental situation in which the individual operates at a given moment can be described in terms of a combination of both static and dynamic features.

4.2.3 *Interaction*

Social interaction has already been described as the overlap of influence between the behavioural systems of two or more individuals. Interactive behaviours are thus partly patterned by *mutual influence* between individuals, and interaction may be defined by this relationship. It occurs if one individual reacts in an observable way to another who in turn reacts to the first. Its necessary and sufficient conditions are satisfied when there is a mutual influence between any behavioural activities of the individuals involved. This includes reactions to each other's mere presence and appearance, or even attempts to avoid interaction. Intentional or conscious influence is not a necessary feature of interaction, although the verbal components of speech, and some other signals, typically embody this feature.

Interactive behaviour is thus typically the behaviour of an individual involved in interaction, but all behaviour may be treated as interactive if it embodies some reference to a partner, even in the absence of direct face-to-face interaction. Reactions to the imagined behaviour of another person constitute the limiting case of interactive behaviour.

4.2.4 *Communication*

Communication may be defined as the *conventional exchange of messages* between individuals in interaction. It depends on the existence of a system of rules, the code, that is, at least in part, common to both communicating partners and relates specific signs or sign-systems to specific meanings. The communication signals are specific cues or perceptible events, mostly movements, into which normally equivalent and necessarily overlapping meanings are encoded by the sender and decoded by the recipient.[1] It is important to realize that *the code can only come into existence through a phylogenetic and/or ontogenetic history common to the sender and the recipient.* Therefore the overall *communication system*, as constituted by sender, signals, channels, codes and recipient, is the result of a developmental history. It is clear that the encoding as well as the decoding process must include this historical dimension. In Man, the code itself is also likely to contain a cultural and a situational component, in that meanings attached to particular behaviours may be profoundly influenced by the immediate environment and the normative cultural structure in which they occur and are perceived.

Communicative behaviour is thus the encoding or decoding (transmitting or receiving) behaviour of a communication partner. Generally only the encoding behaviour is visible, although the recipient may reveal aspects of the way he decodes by the reply which he in turn encodes.

4.2.5 *Informative behaviour*

Informative behaviour *conveys information* (i.e. data about the state of the individual) to an observer; but here the information is *not* a specifiable part of a common communication code. Behaviour classified as "expressive" may often fall into this category; however, it also encompasses all behavioural cues that constitute immediate information in them-

---

[1] The code itself is sufficient for the definition of communication; there is again no need to assume a communicative intent.

selves, without symbolic or conventional reference to anything which might be represented by them. Informative behaviour may be inter-active but cannot be communicative. Many appearance features are primarily informative.

We should perhaps emphasize that much behaviour that is potentially informative to a fellow interactor may have a quite different principal function, concerned with the smooth operation of the subject's own system of behavioural performance, even when the behaviour is emitted socially. Thus the detailed synchronization and superordinate struc-turing of movements of various body parts during speech production may serve primarily to facilitate the subject's *own* flow of speech and to provide subjective feedback. Much of this complex patterning, as discussed by Kendon in this book for example, may be undetected by the other person. It is thus non-interactive, except in so far as a scientific observer can detect it through intensive observation and use it for higher-order analysis of the subject's performance. It is thus primarily *self*-informative, operating outside the interactive social system of the subjects.

4.2.6 *Summary of concepts*

While movement can be studied on a variety of levels of detail, scope, and integration, the analysis of what constitutes interactive behaviour is restricted to levels determined by the interactors' discriminative performance and perceptual capacities. The analysis of communicative behaviour is still further determined by the structure and complexity of the partners' common conventional codes.

Movement and appearance are the broadest classes of components within an individual's behaviour systems, and can be seen to embrace or form the elements of the other classes of interactive, communicative and informative behaviour. These latter classes may be distinguished in most cases by the following rule of thumb: (a) a behaviour is inter-active if it occurs in reaction to another individual; (b) it is communica-tive if it depends on a common code; (c) it is informative if it conveys information about its bearer without reference to a common code. Most behaviours can be clearly classified, but there are borderline cases which pose difficulties.

It should be borne in mind that these definitions have been developed not from mere logical operations, but from our attempt to order various behaviours according to a basic systemic orientation. Accordingly, our terms only acquire their full intended meanings if this viewpoint is accepted. Since the chapters in this book have not been assembled according to such a criterion they do not necessarily illustrate its utility. It may, however, be interesting to look at how they do fit into the pattern we have proposed. Frey and von Cranach clearly deal with movement on a general level which illustrates the way it may be informative to the scientific observer without necessarily carrying an interactive message. Kendon, van Hooff, Eibl-Eibesfeldt, and also Hindmarch are mostly concerned with interactive and communicative behaviour, but in different species, or in individuals of different ages and developmental histories; and they deal with very different complexes of situational variables. von Cranach and Ellgring investigate the informative details of looking behaviour, but also specify the details of a specific communicative code. Frijda, Stringer, and Timaeus seem to treat their subjects' behaviour mainly as informative, since they do not give much attention to assumptions of a common code; but these chapters also contain more complex viewpoints, as in Timaeus' treatment of "Clever Hans". Vine's paper deals with appearance and movement on a variety of levels, but essentially argues that the behaviours shown in mother–infant interaction during the first year are largely informative rather than truly communicative, since a common code can only be developed gradually. In Man at least, informative behaviour appears to precede communicative behaviour in ontogeny; and in phylogeny a similar trend seems evident.

4.3 STRUCTURE, FUNCTION AND HISTORY OF HUMAN COMMUNICATIVE BEHAVIOUR

Within the systemic framework of general concepts outlined above, communicative behaviour requires further consideration for two reasons. First, we have claimed that the existence and operation of a common conventional code is a prerequisite of true communication. Since the notion of a code postulates specific message-meaning relationships, it implies an underlying psychological *structure*[1] as a necessary feature of encoding and decoding capacities. In consequence, although research on structure must go hand in hand with research on function,

[1] It should be pointed out that the term "structure", as it has been used here, refers to the sender's or receiver's behavioural system, while the same term, as used by structuralist theorists (see section 2.2), refers to the structure of particular communicative acts.

the search for structures should be the first step. The more differentiated a specific code, the more structured the communication system is likely to be. Because human communication is extremely elaborate it has a highly complicated structure. Second, as we have pointed out, the notion of a common code implies historical development. Consideration of the evolutionary and ontogenetic history of the human communicative system seems of special interest in view of the seemingly separate courses of development of the components that contribute to its structural and functional complexity. For this reason, we shall now discuss some ideas about the structure, function and history of communicative behaviour. We shall mainly concentrate on the sender's encoding behaviour, because this is specifically designed to expose a perceptible structure to the recipient, whereas the latter's decoding of the meaning of a message is largely covert, and only revealed in his subsequent interactive behaviours.

Both of us have earlier presented viewpoints on the structure of the face-to-face communicative system (Vine, 1970; von Cranach, 1971) and the general issues have been repeatedly treated elsewhere (e.g. Cherry, 1957; Sebeok, 1965; Hockett and Altmann, 1968; Moles, 1968; Smith, 1968); thus these considerations need not be repeated here. In the present context we are more concerned with problems than with solutions, and will concentrate on exposing these.

The first structural problem the student of human communication is likely to meet is the specification of the basic elements of interaction. A *signal* or display is usually defined as the physical representation of a *message* about the sender's state. If we are to consider single signals as the basic elements of communicative or informative interaction, we should bear in mind that they should be defined not as the smallest units that can be distinguished but as the smallest units that embody differential functions or meanings.[1] Consequently, to identify a signal we must investigate the encoding–decoding process to demonstrate that it is such a small structural unit. It is also necessary to investigate its functions for both sender and recipient in order to prove its relative functional independence.

The first of these tasks has been attempted for gazing signals in the

---

[1] *Meaning* may be understood as a subjective representation of the immediate function of the encoded or decoded message, which is to select appropriate response behaviours from the sender's or recipient's repertoire. It should be noted that the meaning, as distinct from the message, also depends on contextual factors independent of the basic code.

chapter by von Cranach and Ellgring. Vine's consideration of the functions of gazing in mother–child relationships deals in part with the
second. It should be emphasized, however, that in human communication the independent functioning of any single behavioural unit is a
matter of degree. Although structuralists strongly deny the "communicative identity" of single elements, we ourselves consider it appropriate to assume that each one at least has some "semantic nucleus" that
forms the basis for the recipients' decoding. Despite Birdwhistell's
extensive research (e.g. 1971) on body movement units, a great deal of
further work remains to be done on identifying the units which comprise the repertoire of human interactive signals.

The second problem to be solved concerns the higher structures of the
communication system. Here we have to meet the problem of organizational and analytic levels. If communication in general can be understood as a hierarchically organized system, as is already known to be
the case with the language system, then levels of organization have to
be distinguished; and on each level appropriate units must be specified.
Signals, as we have defined them, can be considered as the smallest units
on the lowest syntactic level. However, the specification of higher levels
and their units is far from obvious, and attempts in this direction have
so far achieved little generality. There are proposed structures in
language study which are fairly widely accepted. Vocal signals are subdivided into voice quality, paralinguistic, and prosodic, as well as verbal
features (e.g. Trager, 1958; Crystal and Quirk, 1964); and the structure
of verbal utterances can itself be seen as a hierarchy of levels (e.g.
Chomsky, 1957). Birdwhistell and others have attempted to detect
similar structuring within "kinesic" (body movement) activity, but the
analogy may be misleading; and not all non-verbal signalling is kinesic.
One of the more influential attempts at classifying non-verbal signals
in general (Ekman and Friesen, 1969) unfortunately takes little account
of their hierarchical organization.

We cannot attempt to do more than draw attention to these issues
here, and will mention only one fairly common candidate for specification as a structural level super-ordinate to that which specifies signals as
its units.

Many authors distinguish between various "communication channels" as groupings of units at a higher level than the signal. There is,
however, little agreement as yet on the definition of channels. To give
an example, Vine (1970) suggests: "Nonverbal signals arise from a

number of sources, and are received through several receptor systems. Each distinct source-plus-receiver system may be regarded as a separate communication channel" (p. 280). Thus, according to Vine there exist separate communication channels such as the facial–visual one or the vocal–auditory one. The difficulty with this definition is that without qualification it might allow for an unlimited number of sub-divisions; it does not define a level or precise criteria for distinguishing discrete channels. Obviously, several channels could be identified within the realm of visual reception of social cues alone. Von Cranach (1972), on the other hand, considers a "modality" or channel as being defined by the "interaction of the physical medium (of transmission) with the reception apparatus" (p. 129), and consequently assumes a limited number of channels (optic–visual, acoustic–auditory, kinetic–tactile, etc.). This definition specifies a structural level explicitly and gives a clear basis for its identification. The problem, however, is that a channel thus defined specifies only some of the functional properties of its operation (or "design features" in the sense of Hockett and Altmann, 1968). For functional reasons, a subdivision on a lower level is required, e.g. between verbal and non-verbal aspects of the "acoustic–auditory channel"; and for this purpose von Cranach (1972) has proposed the level of "categories", conceived as systems of signals within a channel, that are coordinated in the encoding and decoding processes by distinct physiological and neurophysiological structures or learned programmes. Thus gestures or spatial behaviour would be separate categories in the "optic–visual channels", while Vine's "facial–visual channel" would become the category of facial cues within the optic–visual system according to this classification. But the above scheme is far from being a complete structural specification. How we integrate different signals, categories and channels into the structure of a full "social performance" (Argyle and Kendon, 1967) is a question involving still further multi-dimensional differentiation of organizational levels.

We are not attempting here to propose a final solution to the problem; but we wish to emphasize that the specification of the structure of communicative behaviour should not be purely a question of taste. In fact, only one appropriate structure can exist if it has to be in accord with the actual functions of the communication system and has to be a product of its phylogenetic and ontogenetic developmental history. Thus, the identification of a category of facial expression in the optical–

visual channel is meaningful only if a basic communicative function, e.g. communication of emotions, and a specific developmental history mediated by cultural rules, can be shown to coincide with its structural properties.

It can now be seen that from this viewpoint most of the critical research on the human communicative behaviour system has yet to be done. Furthermore, this cannot be the task of a single discipline, let alone one school within a discipline. Instead, our propositions imply a need for cooperation between anthropologists, linguists, psychologists, sociologists and ethologists, since human communication is a cultural as well as a psychological phenomenon, while being rooted in a biological history.

Very little work in this field has yet been undertaken on an inter-disciplinary basis, although the long-awaited book by McQuown and associates (see Birdwhistell, 1971) should be a step in the right direction. Certainly the contributions in this volume taken alone or even together do not fully achieve the desired synthesis; but they do, we believe, effectively illustrate the wide range of approaches and phenomena that such a synthesis must attempt to encompass.

References

Argyle, M. (1969). "Social Interaction". Methuen, London.

Argyle, M. (1972). Non-verbal communication in human social interaction. *In* "Non-verbal Communication" (Ed. R. A. Hinde). pp. 243–268. Cambridge University Press, London.

Argyle, M. and Exline, R. (1969). "NATO Symposium on Non-verbal Communica-cation". University of Oxford, Oxford.

Argyle, M. and Kendon, A. (1967). The experimental analysis of social performance. *In* "Advances in Experimental Social Psychology" (Ed. L. Berkowitz), pp. 55–98. Academic Press, New York and London.

Bahrick, H. P. and Noble, M. E. (1966). Motor behavior. *In* "Experimental Methods and Instrumentation in Psychology" (Ed. J. B. Sidowski), pp. 645–676. McGraw-Hill, New York.

Birdwhistell, R. L. (1952). "Introduction to Kinesics: An Annotation System for Analysis of Body Motion and Gesture". University of Louisville Press, Louisville.

Birdwhistell, R. L. (1971). "Kinesics and Context, Essays on Body-Movement Com-munication". Allen Lane, The Penguin Press, London.

Blurton-Jones, N. G. (Ed.) (1972). "Ethological Studies of Infant Behaviour". Cam-bridge University Press, London.

B

Buckley, W. (1968). "Modern Systems Research for the Behavioral Scientist". Aldine, Chicago.

Cherry, C (1957). "On Human Communication". M.I.T. Press, Cambridge, Mass.

Chomsky, N. (1957). "Syntactic Structures". Mouton, The Hague.

Cranach, M. von (1971). Die nichtverbale Kommunikation im Kontext des kommunikativen Verhaltens. In "Jahrbuch der Max-Planck-Gesellschaft", pp. 105–148. Max-Planck Society, Munich. (Also in French (1972) in "La Psychologie Sociale" (Ed. S. Moscovici). Librarie Larousse, Paris).

Cranach, M. von (1972). On the impact of ethology for the understanding of human behaviour. In "The Context of Social Psychology: A Critical Assessment" (Eds J. Israel and H. Tajfel). Academic Press, London and New York.

Crystal, D. and Quirk, R. (1964). "Systems of Prosodic and Paralinguistic Features in English". Mouton, The Hague.

Darwin, C. (1872). "The Expression of the Emotions in Man and Animals". Murray, London.

Diebold, A. R. (1968). Anthropological perspectives. In "Animal Communication" (Ed. T. A. Sebeok), pp. 525–571. Indiana University Press, Bloomington.

Duncan, S., Jr. (1969). Non-verbal communication. Psychol. Bull. **72**, 118–137.

Eibl-Eibesfeldt, I. (1967). "Grundriss der vergleichenden Verhaltensforschung—Ethologie". Piper, Munich.

Eibl-Eibesfeldt, I. (1968). Zur Ethologie des menschlichen Grussverhaltens. I. Beobachtungen an Balinesen, Papuas und Samoanern nebst vergleichenden Bermerkungen. Z. Tierpsychol. **25**, 727–744.

Eibl-Eibesfeldt, I. (1970). "Liebe und Hass". Piper, Munich.

Eibl-Eibesfeldt, I. and Hass, H. (1967). Neue Wege der Human-Ethologie. Homo. **18**, 13–23.

Ekman, P. (1972). Universal and cultural differences in facial expressions of emotion. In "Nebraska Symposium on Motivation", 1971 (Ed. J. Cole), pp. 207–283. University of Nebraska Press, Nebraska.

Ekman, P. and Friesen, W. V. (1969a). The repertoire of non-verbal behavior: categories, usage and coding. Semiotica, **1**, 49–98.

Ekman, P. and Friesen, W. V. (1969b). Non-verbal leakage and clues to deception. Psychiatry, **32**, 88–105.

Ekman, P., Sorenson, E. R. and Friesen, W. V. (1969). Pan-cultural elements in facial displays of emotions. Science, **164**, 86–88.

Frey, S. (1971). "Eine Methode zur quantitativen Bestimmung der Variabilität des Bewegungsverhaltens". Unpublished Ph.D. thesis, University of Regensburg.

Garfinkel, H. (1964). Studies of the routine grounds of every-day activities. Soc. Problems, **11**, 225–250.

Goffman, E. (1961). "Encounters: Two Studies in the Sociology of Interaction". Bobbs Merril, Indianapolis.

Goffman, E. (1963). "Behavior in Public Places". Free Press, New York.

Goffman, E. (1971). "Relations in Public". Allen Lane, The Penguin Press, London.

Grant, E. C. (1968). An ethological description of non-verbal behaviour during interviews. Brit. J. Med. Psychol. **41**, 177–184.

Grant, E. C. (1969). Human facial expression. *Man*, **4**, 525–536.

Hall, E. T. (1966). "The Hidden Dimension". Doubleday, New York.

Hall, E. T. (1968). Proxemics. *Curr. Anthrop.* **9**, 83–108.

Hockett, C. F. and Altmann, S. A. (1968). A note on design features. *In* "Animal Communication" (Ed. T. A. Sebeok), pp. 61–72. Indiana University Press, Bloomington.

Kendon, A. (1967). Some functions of gaze-direction in social interaction. *Acta Psychol.* **26**, 22–63.

La Barre, W. (1947). The cultural basis of emotion and gestures. *J. Pers.* **16**, 49–68.

La Barre, W. (1964). Paralinguistics, kinesics, and cultural anthropology. *In* "Approaches to Semiotics" (Eds T. A. Sebeok, A. S. Hayes, and Mary C. Bateson), pp. 191–220. Mouton, The Hague.

Moles, A. (1968). Perspectives for communication theory. *In* "Animal Communication" (Ed. T. A. Sebeok), pp. 627–642. Indiana University Press, Bloomington.

Morris, D. (1967). "The Naked Ape". Jonathan Cape, London.

Rosenthal, R. (1966). "Experimenter Effects in Behavioral Research". Appleton-Century-Crofts, New York.

Sainsbury, P. (1954). A method of recording spontaneous movements by time-sampling motion pictures. *J. Ment. Sci.* **100**, 742–748.

Scheflen, A. E. (1966). Natural history method in psychotherapy: communication research. *In* "Methods of Research in Psychotherapy" (Eds L. A. Gottschalk and A. H. Auerbach), pp. 263–289. Appleton-Century-Crofts, New York.

Scheflen, A. E. (1968). Human communication: behavioral programs and their integration in interaction. *Behavl. Sci.* **13**, 44–55.

Sebeok, T. A. (1965). Animal communication. *Science*, **147**, 1006–1014.

Sebeok, T. A. (Ed.) (1968). "Animal Communication, Techniques of Study and Results of Research". Indiana University Press, Bloomington.

Sebeok, T. A., Hayes, A. S. and Bateson, Mary C. (1964). "Approaches to Semiotics". Mouton, The Hague.

Sommer, R. (1969). "Personal Space, the Behavioral Basis of Design". Prentice-Hall, Englewood Cliffs, New Jersey.

Smith, W. J. (1968). Message-meaning analyses. *In* "Animal Communication" (Ed. T. A. Sebeok), pp. 44–60. Indiana University Press, Bloomington.

Tinbergen, N. (1951). "The Study of Instinct". Oxford University Press, London.

Trager, G. (1958). Paralanguage: a first approximation. *Studies in Linguistics*, **13**, 1–12.

Vine, I. (1970). Communication by facial-visual signals. *In* "Social Behaviour in Birds and Mammals" (Ed. J. H. Crook), pp. 279–354. Academic Press, London and New York.

Webb, E. J., Campbell, D. T., Schwartz, R. D. and Sechrest, L. (1966). "Unobtrusive Measures: Nonreactive Research in the Social Sciences". Rand-McNally, Chicago.

Wickler, W. (1966). Ursprung und Deutung des Genitalpräsentierens männlicher Primaten. *Z. Tierpsychol.* **23**, 422–437.

PART 1

Behaviour Patterns and Communicative Consequences

2

The Role of Visible Behaviour in the Organization of Social Interaction[1]

Adam Kendon

1   Introduction

Suppose that John wants to talk to Harry about something. If he is to do this successfully, there are a number of conditions which will have to be met. John must make his presence known to Harry, he must identify himself, or be identifiable, and he must make it clear that it is Harry, and not Tom nearby, to whom he wishes to speak. Harry must then agree to be engaged in talk by John, and he must show that he agrees.

Once the conversation is underway, both participants must organize their conduct in accordance with certain rules. Each must continuously

[1] The author is attached to the Project on Human Communication at Bronx State Hospital, Bronx, N.Y. This is sponsored by Albert Einstein College of Medicine and Jewish Family Service, Inc., and supported by the State of New York, NIH Grant No. 15977–02, and the Van Amerigan Foundation. I am very grateful to Dr Albert E. Scheflen, Project Director, for his support and encouragement, and Dr Israel Zwerling, Director, Bronx State Hospital, for granting facilities. Mr Robert McMillan provided valuable comments on an earlier version of this paper. I am also grateful to Drs Aviva Menkes, Andrew Ferber, and C. Christian Beels for useful discussions.

show that he is *with* the other as a co-talker, he must indicate that it is to the conversation, and not to something else, that he is giving his main attention. He must take his turn at talking, and when he speaks he must make it clear to whom he is talking. When he listens, he must indicate to whom he is listening. In speaking, each participant must say things that are appropriately fitted within the prevailing "frame" or "definition" of the conversation, and he must show that he is neither too bored, nor too over-excited by what is being talked about. Furthermore, each must respect the working agreement by which the roles of the participants in the conversation are defined and sustained. In other words, in having a conversation, the participants must cooperate together to maintain a system of relationships, an organization within which the talk, whatever it may be concerned with, can be carried out. We shall say that conversationalists enter into and maintain a "working consensus" which specifies the "ground rules" for their conduct in the conversation.

These features of the organization of face-to-face encounters have been described by Goffman in several essays (1955, 1957, 1961a). In these essays, a fairly detailed analysis is given of the requirements of conversational conduct, but what is not given is any detailed description of the kinds of behaviour that make up this conduct. For instance, Goffman (1957) describes how participants in conversation are often required to be engrossed in its official focus of attention, and he shows what some of the consequences are if this requirement is not met. But he leaves it largely to the reader to fill in the details of what "being engrossed" is like in behavioural terms.

However, while most of us can recognize, with quite remarkable sensitivity, when someone in a conversation is not conducting himself appropriately, it is quite another matter for us to be able to say precisely what it is that he may be doing or not doing. Similarly, while most of us are able to carry out a conversation with some success, if anyone were asked exactly how he did it, he would be unable to say. Yet we must have a systematic and explicit understanding of all the details of conversational behaviour if we are to understand how it is done, how some people fail at it, and how people learn to do it. The ability to converse and thus engage in social interaction is after all the foundation for the complexities of our social life. An understanding of this ability would seem to be essential for any complete theory of the nature of human social behaviour.

In this chapter, we shall attempt to point out those aspects of the behaviour of participants in conversations which appear to organize, establish and maintain conversations. We shall try to indicate, for instance, how people show they are in conversation with one another, how they sustain the "working consensus", and how they achieve a smooth interchange of utterances. We shall be concerned, thus, not with *what* people say to one another, but with how they create and maintain the conditions in which they *can* say things to one another. We are concerned with the nature of face-to-face channels of communication, and not with what these channels are used for. Thus our intention is to emphasize an aspect of interaction that until recently has scarcely been touched on. The classic studies of interaction, such as those initiated by Bales and his colleagues (see, for example, Hare, 1962; Hare *et al.*, 1966), showed an almost exclusive attention to the messages participants in conversational gatherings (so-called "small groups") communicated to one another. And while it was recognized that within gatherings and groups the flow of messages was differentiated along "channels" or "networks" (Bavelas, 1950; Bales *et al.*, 1951; Bales, 1958; Shaw, 1964), almost no attention was paid to how these were organized naturally by the participants. And even today, when there appears to be rather more interest in how people communicate, the emphasis still seems to be upon what messages are exchanged, rather than upon the conditions in which they are exchanged. In studying communication, however, we must be concerned with both channels and messages, though here we shall focus on channels.

Here we shall deal only with *visible behaviour*. This is because almost all the work that is relevant to the question of how conversations are organized has been concerned with this. The organizing functions of speech and other kinds of vocalization, as well as those of such other modes of communication as touch, has so far been left almost completely unexplored.

Visible behaviour, as the term implies, refers to anything an individual does that is visible to another. Thus it includes the way a person moves in space, and the spatial position he may maintain, both in relation to the features of a given site, and in relation to others present. It includes posture, and all kinds of bodily movement, whether highly specialized for communication, such as gestures or facial expressions, or less specialized, such as shifts in posture, or behaviour associated with a task. We also include the individual's appearance—his physiognomy, his dress and style of grooming—though these features will not be dealt with here.

There will be three main sections in the discussion that follows. In the first, we shall deal with those aspects of behaviour in conversations which endure for most of the occasion. We shall describe the kinds of spatial arrangements participants in conversations tend to adopt, the postures they assume, and how these distinguish them from non-partici-pants; we shall also show how these spatial patterns and postures may reflect aspects of the "working consensus" of the occasion. This more or less enduring spatial and postural arrangement will be referred to as the *configuration* of the encounter. It may be thought of as providing a setting for the "business" of the encounter.

In section 2 some features of visible behaviour involved in the organ-ization of the conduct of "business" will be reviewed. The question of how participants signal the identity of the person they are addressing and how changeover to speaker role are smoothly accomplished will also be discussed.

In section 3 attention will be focused upon the behaviour of the individual—particularly on how his social performance is organized.

Although we have tried to refer to the most important of the relevant studies, no comprehensive review of the literature has been attempted. As there is really very little work of direct relevance, many topics have been left unexplored. Thus we can, as yet, say nothing about how conversations are started nor how they are brought to an end, al-though this is an immensely important question. Only Goffman (1963) appears to have given the initiation of encounters systematic attention, and his remarks cover only a few pages.[2] We have also had to leave out any discussion of how social encounters unfold in time. Remarkably little has been done on this, perhaps because it is difficult to make the neces-sary observations. Some provocative ideas and observations have been put forward by Pike (1954) and Scheflen (1968, 1969, 1973). There are also the observations of Bales (1950), Heinicke and Bales (1953), Talland (1955), Lennard and Bernstein (1960), and others who have

[1] For a general review of research into the communicative functions of visible behaviour see Duncan (1969) and Vine (1970). Ray L. Birdwhistell was a pioneer in the systematic study of this area and, while we have made little explicit reference to his work here, since his main concern has been with the relationship of body motion to language, the approach adopted owes much to his thinking. Some representative papers by him are listed in the bibliography.
[2] But see Goffman (1971, Chapter 3), and Kendon and Ferber (1973). These studies have appeared since this chapter was written.

studied psychotherapy groups; but nevertheless it has been necessary to rely more often than one would like upon occasional observations and the analysis of single examples, some of them not yet published elsewhere. However, the intention is to provide an outline sketch of how conversations are organized, and to illustrate the kinds of questions that need to be studied. If solid evidence has not been provided at every turn for what is said here, it is hoped that further investigations may at least be provoked.

There are a few points of terminology which must be settled before proceeding. The term *gathering* will be used for any collection of individuals who are mutually co-present, that is any collection of individuals who are mutually affected in their behaviour by one another's presence. Gatherings typically occur within a more or less well-defined physical space, and we shall use the term *site* to refer to this. Sites are only distinguishable in relation to one another. For instance, for some purposes, the whole of the Great Hall at Euston Station could be considered as a site; for others it would be necessary to treat restricted areas within it as separate sites.

Within a gathering, two basic kinds of units of social organization may be found. These will be known as *solos* and *withs*. A solo is an individual who is not at the time connected with anyone else in any immediate fashion. Thus a man standing by himself waiting for his wife is, for our purpose, a solo. As soon as his wife joins him, however, he becomes a member of a with. Conversational groupings are withs, but so are small groups of people, say a small party of schoolgirls at a railway station, even though they may all be asleep. Within a with, explicit or focused interaction can occur, though members of withs also engage in unfocused interaction, as do, by definition, all solos. *Focused interaction* is said to occur whenever two or more people explicitly acknowledge a jointly maintained focus of attention, as do conversationalists of any kind, card players, or friends waving to one another. But this may not be so with a bootblack and his customer: the customer may be engrossed in his paper while the bootblack is cleaning his shoes; but you cannot have a game of cards with someone who is reading the paper. A collection of individuals engaging in focused interaction is termed a *focused gathering*. Since, for the most part, we shall be dealing only with focused gatherings, the term "gathering" will mainly be used. However, when the more general sense is intended this will be specifically indicated. The term "group" will not be used unless to describe a collection of individuals having an organized relationship to one another, whether or not they are, at the time, collected together in a gathering. This terminology is, of course, taken directly from Goffman (1961, 1963, 1971) and the intention has been to follow his usages as closely as possible.

Throughout we shall be concerned with focused gatherings of adults in which talk is the principal means by which the official focus is sustained. Nothing will be said about children, except in passing, and no attempt will be made at cultural comparisons. Apart from considerations of space, these omissions derive largely from the fact that there is very little data upon which a treatment of these topics can be based. Hall (1959, 1964, 1966) and LaBarre (1964) provide the best summaries on cross-cultural comparisons in visible behaviour. Much of the information they summarize is anecdotal and unsystematized, however. More systematic work in facial expression and gesture has recently been initiated by Ekman (Ekman *et al.*, 1969). Eibl-Eibesfeldt (1968), using an ethological approach, has begun some impressive work on aspects of greeting behaviour in different cultures. The only systematic attempt to check some of Hall's assertions about cultural differences in "personal space" is that of Watson and Graves (1966). The single most impressive cultural comparative study in communicative visible behaviour is still the work of Efron (1941) on patterns of gesticulation. With the exception of the discussion of space, almost all of this cross-cultural work has been concerned with gesture and facial expression, aspects of communicative behaviour with which we are not mainly concerned here. The cultural reference group for the studies described in this chapter is, in fact, Anglo-American and mainly upper-middle class.

2 The configuration

What is the visible difference between a focused and an unfocused gathering? It is evident from Figs 1 and 2 that such a difference exists. In Fig. 1, twenty-nine people, all in the same room, are engaged in eleven separate foci of interaction which are clearly distinguishable from one another. In Fig. 2, nine people are sitting under a tree, but no one is engaged in focused interaction with anyone else. The contrast in the relative arrangement of people in these two pictures is clear. Can any general distinctive features of focused gatherings be specified? Except in settings where there is no freedom of movement (for example

Fig. 1. Focused interactions in a lounge. (Photograph by Paul Byers.)

in a very crowded subway car), the following two conditions in relative spatial arrangements will probably be met:

   a. The participants will be within a certain narrow distance range from one another. The distance depends upon several factors. In

Fig. 2. An unfocused gathering in the open air. (Photograph by Paul Byers.)

crowded or in "open" (public) settings participants are closer to
one another than in "closed" (private) settings. Also, the more
intimate or exclusive the interaction the closer the participants are
likely to be.

b. The participants orient their bodies in relation to one another in
such a way that for each one, the angle through which the head
would have to rotate from its orientation in the saggital plane of
the body to an orientation in which it would be directly facing
another participant is less than ninety degrees. If, to face another,
an individual must turn his head from the saggital plane of orientation through an angle of more than ninety degrees, then it is
highly likely that he is not, at the time of observation, "joined" in
focused interaction with another. Such a spatial and orientational
arrangement will be maintained by the participants for as long as

the encounter lasts, and each individual, by maintaining himself in such an arrangement, marks himself as a participant.

The stable spatial and orientational arrangement of bodies which characterizes a focused encounter will be referred to as the *configuration* of the encounter. It will be our hypothesis that it may be regarded as an overt expression of the "working consensus" of the encounter. It is by maintaining himself in a particular posture, orientation and spatial position relative to others that an individual indicates his continued participation with them. The particular form that the configuration as a whole assumes reflects the type of occasion and the kind of role relationships prevailing in the gathering. If the configuration is fluid or unstable, this reflects a fluidity or instability in the "working consensus" of the occasion. An analysis of the formation of the configuration, involving a detailed examination of the spatial manoeuverings of the participants, should provide some insight into the processes by which the "working consensus" is arrived at.

Again, from Fig. 1 it will be seen that within each of the eleven conversational "knots" the bodies of the participants are oriented towards one another, so that a less than ninety degree head rotation to "facing" is possible. There is a high degree of similarity of posture within each knot, and the distance between people within configurations is less than the distance between people in adjacent configurations. It will also be seen that though, in many cases, the participants are not looking at one another, their heads are turned towards each other and are also tilted forward somewhat.

It will be seen that, by such arrangements, participants in gatherings express their joint engagement, both to each other and to others nearby. Each participant, by maintaining a spatial position, posture and orientation that is appropriate to his role in the gathering, signals to the others that he is committed to joint engagement with them. In doing so he signals that he is claiming certain rights as well as taking on certain obligations. He claims the right to listen and to speak, but he has an obligation also to attend, and to speak when addressed, and to speak in a way that is related to the prevailing "frame" of the gathering.

It may also be seen that the physical arrangement of the members of a gathering has the effect of marking out a region of space that may be called an *interaction territory* (Lyman and Scott, 1967), which, since it tends to be jointly defended against intruding non-participants, is also generally respected by non-participants. Thus, where the focus of the interaction is important or demanding, the participants typically reinforce the bounding functions of their bodies by physical barriers, such as walls. For sustained and demanding conversations, typically, people withdraw into a room. Where focused gatherings are formed in open sites, others normally avoid passing through or near them if they are moving through the site. Non-participants who pass very close to a gathering, as they may be seen to do in rather crowded settings for instance, will be observed to lower their heads markedly as they do so.[1] Gatherings only rarely form in narrow corridors or in other sites that normally function as a passageway where non-participants may be forced to pass through them. Here, in addition to the lowered head, a verbal apology is usually given. Just as it is affronting to the participants in a gathering if non-participants do not respect the space it occupies, so it is affronting to non-participants for people to use as an interactional territory space which is ordinarily open to passers by. Corridor gatherings are, thus, usually quite short-lived.

In discussing configuration studies, *spatial arrangements*, *orientation* and *posture* will be treated separately, although it seems likely that these three aspects are linked systematically. For instance, orientations and postures adopted in a given configuration are probably closely dependent upon the kind of spacing adopted. Another factor of great importance is, of course, the number of participants in the gathering. This we shall not be able to consider, however, for although there have been a good many studies of the effect of gathering size on the interaction process (Thomas and Fink, 1963), no one, to this writer's knowledge at least, has considered the relationship of size to the gathering's physical shape.

2.1   SPATIAL ARRANGEMENTS

Few studies have been concerned with the spatial patterns adopted by gatherings, though there have been some which have dealt with the effect of an individual's position in a gathering upon his performance within it. As Sommer (1967) has pointed out, hardly any investigators have set out to study the effect of space on interaction. Spacing has come to be recognized as important as a result of the re-analysis of data gathered for other purposes.

[1] Observations from a study in progress, in collaboration with Dr A. E. Scheflen.

The present state of our knowledge allows us few general statements. However, one way in which shapes might be examined is to observe how far they approach a circular form. Configurations in which the participants arrange themselves in a circle are probably those in which the participation rights of all the members are defined as equal. In configurations where one or several members are spatially differentiated from the others, so that the pattern approaches a triangular, semi-circular or parallelogrammatic form, participation rights in the inter-action are no longer equal. An extreme form of the non-circular con-figuration would be a lecture in which there is one member at the apex of a triangle, facing all the other members arranged in rows parallel to the base of the triangle. Here the member at the apex typically has the right (and obligation) of sustained speech. Those who are arranged parallel to the triangle's base typically have the right only to listen. Spatial arrangements that are intermediate between this and the circle also tend to be intermediate in the degree to which participation rights are differentiated among the members. Thus the seminar tends to be oval shaped with the leader at the tip of the oval and most of the others facing him in an arrangement that approaches a semicircle. Gatherings that are non-circular tend to have a "head" position at which the member with the most rights to participation is usually located.

Two or three of the studies so far carried out support some of these observations. Thus Sommer (1961) observed that in groups with a leader sitting round a rectangular table, the leader tended to occupy an end position with the other members clustering around and mostly facing him. Two studies can be mentioned which show that where a group member chooses to sit is related to the role he hopes or is expected to play in a gathering. Thus, Strodtbeck and Hook (1961), who re-examined data on mock jury deliberations (where the subjects were real jurors selected from a pool by the usual procedures), found that not only was the man who sat on one or other end of a rectangular table more likely than anyone else to be selected as foreman, but he also tended to be higher in social status and was more likely to play a leading role in the discussion. Similarly, in a re-analysis of data on five-man discussion groups, where the subjects were undergraduates, Hare and Bales (1963) found that some positions at a rectangular table were regularly associated with high participation. These positions were identified as being at either end or at the centre position of a rectangular table, and it was these seats, rather than the two corner ones, that were

C

selected by people who were higher in "dominance" (as measured by a personality questionnaire).

Evidently, then, people who are likely to play a dominant role in the interaction are likely to select appropriate positions from which they can orient to the largest number of others in the gathering. Partly as a consequence of this, it is easier for an occupant of one of these positions to be active, since he can command the attention of others easily. Also, because he can scan every member of the gathering, he is in a better position to pick up cues which tell him when it is appropriate to initiate action. These positions, as a consequence of their characteristics, are traditionally understood to be positions of greatest influence, and are thus assigned to those group members who will exercise the greatest amount of control. The "head" of the table is characteristically occupied by the chairman or leader. That people do perceive table positions in this way was shown in a study by Nancy Felipe (1966) in which subjects were asked to rate table positions on Osgood's semantic differential. "Head" positions were seen as more "active" and "potent" than side positions.

So far we have dealt only with the relationship between spatial arrangement and role differentiation within a focused gathering. There is some evidence to suggest that the kind of interactional task undertaken by the gathering will also be related to the spatial arrangement adopted. Thus Sommer (1965) studied the spatial arrangements in dyadic gatherings, and compared the arrangements adopted when the participants were competing, cooperating, or working separately each upon his own task ("coacting" dyads). He found that for competing pairs, the strongest tendency was for people to sit opposite one another, whereas in cooperative pairs, involved in discussion on a point of mutual interest or in a casual chat, the tendency was for the participants either to sit side by side or, more characteristically, at a diagonal to one another, so that each would have to turn his head through a considerable angle to look directly at the other.

A somewhat similar point, that the distance which separates two members of a gathering is partly related to the type of interaction they are engaging in, is made by Hall (1964, 1966). He has suggested that, at least for Americans of North European cultural influence, a number of distance sets can be distinguished, each appropriate for a different type of interaction. Thus he claims that there is an *intimate distance* where the participants are up to about eighteen inches apart for intimate interactions: a *casual personal distance*, up to about five feet, for casual conversation between friends; a *social–consultative distance*, which varies between five and ten feet and which is used for more formal kinds of interaction, such as discussions or interviews; and *public distance*, upwards of ten feet, adopted when a person formally addresses a group of others. Hall points out that at different distances the senses operate differently, and that this will have consequences for the kinds of communication channels that can be used. At intimate distances, for example, touch, smell and heat senses can all be used in the transmission of information from one individual to another, and each may observe changes in breathing rate in the other, or changes in the state of the epidermal capillaries. At greater distances only vision and hearing can be used, and with increasing distance these become less and less effective for fine detail. Thus with increasing distance there is a greater reliance upon formal language patterns, and a decrease in the reliance of the speaker upon the behaviour of listeners; for instance, head nods and changes in facial expression which, in more intimate types of interchange, play an important part in the interactional process.[1]

Hall's suggestion is, therefore, that there is an appropriate distance for each type of conversation. However, he has given no indication of the *settings* in which these distances are adopted, though there are two studies which suggest this may be a very important consideration (Sommer, 1961; Little, 1965). For example, for casual or social consultative types of conversation much closer distances may be used if the participants are in a public setting (such as a park or street) than if they are in a private one (such as the living room of a house). This is perhaps because the distance adopted in conversation not only reflects something about the mode of interaction employed by the participants but also expresses the relationship between the encounter, as a joint venture, and the other activities that may be in progress at the same site. In public settings closer distances may thus be adopted for conversations because it is necessary for the participants to emphasize their "withness" in a way that it is not within, say, a small living room or office.

It will be evident from above discussion that how an individual places

---

[1] The terms used by Hall for his different interpersonal distances are derived from Joos (1962) who pointed out that there are different linguistic styles for different kinds of transactions. Hall's suggestions, and his integration of Joos' observations, are of great interest but no systematic data have been reported to support them.

himself in relation to the other members of a gathering can be one means by which he may express his position in it. He can choose a *distance* and thus signal the degree of intimacy he hopes to maintain in the interaction. He can choose a *location* (such as a "head" position) to signal his claim to a particular kind of role in the gathering. Clearly, however, the particular location in a gathering that an individual occupies depends upon the particular locations occupied by the other members. Hence, for an individual to maintain a location in a gathering, all members must have agreed to the spatial dispositions of one another. A gathering that is stable in its spatial arrangement, therefore, is one with a stable consensus about the current level of intimacy, relative dominance, and other role relationships of the members. Changes in the spatial arrangement will reflect changes in this consensus. An analysis of the process by which such stable arrangements are arrived at would constitute an analysis of the initial process of negotiation which characterizes the early stages of all focused encounters. No studies have yet investigated how configurations are formed.

2.2 ORIENTATION

We have already suggested that within a focused gathering participants will orient their bodies in such a way that they can rotate their heads to one another by turning through an angle of less than ninety degrees from the saggital plane of orientation. However, within this range there are many possible variations, and we must now examine the significance of some of these.

The principal way in which orientation may vary is in the degree to which the head, shoulders, and hips are brought into alignment with one another, with the individual's ventral surface facing the ventral surface of his co-interactants. The extent to which individuals face each other in this way may be referred to as the extent to which they are *vis-à-vis* one another. In all instances of focused interaction there are moments (though these may be brief) when the heads of the participants are so oriented, but configurations vary a good deal in the extent to which the bodies of the participants are also *vis-à-vis*. These orientations, however, are normally associated with focused interaction between those who are so oriented. Where, in a focused gathering, participants are oriented in *parallel* to one another, the interaction is sustained, not between those who are in parallel but between each individual separately and some common focus. The most obvious example of this kind of arrangement is at a lecture or theatrical performance. Here each member of the audience can be said to be separately facing the lecturer.

In focused gatherings of two participants, the degree to which they are *vis-à-vis* one another is probably related to the intensity of their mutual involvement, and to the amount of distance that separates them. Thus at casual-personal or intimate distances a full *vis-à-vis* orientation would indicate a very large degree of mutual involvement, whereas at a distance of seven feet or so, that of social-consultative interaction, a full *vis-à-vis* orientation is much more common and does not reflect such a high level of mutual involvement.

The above observations on orientation are derived largely from Scheflen (1964). The suggestions concerning the relation between interaction distance and orientation are based mainly on incidental observation. However, Argyle and Dean (1965), in an experiment in which they examined the relations between eye-contact in a social-consultative type of conversation and the distance between the participants reported that at the very close distances imposed on the subjects they exhibited a good deal of turning away of the upper body. Mehrabian has reported several observations on the relation between body orientation in interaction and the attitudes and status differences of the interactors (Mehrabian, 1968a, 1968b, 1969). But these observations were made in an experiment in which subjects were asked to act "as if" they were addressing someone else, where their addressee was an imagined person. He reports that in standing subjects there was no relationship between how directly the subject faced his body to his imagined addressee and his enacted attitude towards him. In female seated subjects, however, Mehrabian found that the more positive the enacted attitude, the more directly was the subject's body faced to the addressee, except for intensely liked addressees, where the directness with which the subject faced the addressee was reduced. Male subjects tended to face their addressee less directly only in the case of intensely liked addressees. For moderately liked, or disliked addressees, there was no relationship between orientation and attitude. These findings are hard to evaluate since the setting in which they were made was so artificial. Naturalistic observations are essential before these factors can be properly assessed.

The only other systematic observations reported on body orientation are those of Sommer (1965). He observed the positions taken at rectangular tables by students in a student cafeteria and found that when pairs of students sat down to have a chat together they would characteristically sit either side of one of the corners. This meant that their upper bodies were at right angles to one another; and for each to turn his head to look directly at the other from the saggital plane of orientation an angle of rotation of forty-five degrees would be demanded. This "forty-five degree" arrangement, as it might be called, appears to be very common in both standing and sitting dyads, where it is probably associated with social-consultative and casual-personal interactions. It will be seen that this arrangement allows considerable flexibility in the extent to which two people may be face-to-face with one another. By head rotation alone each can move to face the other; and they can turn away again without any bodily movement. If they were to sit or stand in a full *vis-à-vis* position a reduction in mutual involvement, as indicated by the extent of mutual looking, would require turning both body and head, and this would mark the change as one of greater magnitude than mere head turning.

Most of the observations we have summarized on orientation have been made with reference to dyadic gatherings. In groups of more than two the phenomenon of body orientation becomes more complex. Scheflen (1964) has pointed to the possibility that a participant may split his orientation. Thus, in a gathering of three persons, while A, say, turns his head and upper body to B, he can also orient his lower body to C, and so still include him in the gathering. In triadic gatherings it is not uncommon to see split orientations of this kind whereby each member orients to the other two simultaneously.

The direction of orientation of the hips and shoulders, and also of the limbs, is relatively slow-changing, and for this reason changes in body orientation may be of greater significance as behavioural events than changes in head–eye orientation. The head and eyes, of course, are highly mobile, and from moment to moment in interaction, especially for the speaker, their direction of orientation changes frequently. Where a person is looking is the mark of his immediate involvement, and if he repeatedly orients his face or eyes towards a specific individual he indicates that this person is a "target" of his attention. We shall see later how head–eye orientation is used in marking the direction of an individual's address, and how in its detailed variation it can play a part in the regulation of utterance exchanges.

Here it is appropriate to refer to the work that has been done on head–eye orientation or *gaze*, as it may more simply be described, in which the principle theme has been how much an individual looks at another, and how this is related to his attitude toward that other. This work has been summarized by Argyle and Kendon (1967), Diebold (1968), Mehrabian (1969), and von Cranach (1968), and we will not discuss it in detail here. In general it appears that in situations where the participants are equal in status and the interaction is cooperative, people look at one another more the more they like one another. However, the amount of eye-orientation another receives will be much less if he is of very low status (Hearn, 1957; Efran, 1968), and Exline (1963) reports that when subjects are in a competitive discussion, if they are low in "need for affiliation" they will look at one another more than they would in a non-competitive interaction. When subjects are high in "need for affiliation" this relationship is reversed. A simple statement of the findings on gaze in relation to attitude does not appear to be possible, since although "looking at" another is always a mark of attention the significance of this attention, and thus the significance of the act of looking, depends upon the context in which it takes place.

All of the studies on gaze so far mentioned have dealt with gatherings of two or three persons only. An unpublished investigation by Weisbrod (1965), represents the only one so far where looking patterns in a gathering of several members have been studied. In this study, who looked at whom was recorded systematically for every member of a seven-member seminar over several sessions. Data on personal preferences among the members of the seminar, on how the members perceived one another in terms of how they contributed to the discussion, and personality data on the participants, was also gathered. It emerged quite clearly from Weisbrod's analyses that who looked at whom was closely related to patterns of power relations in the group. Thus the person who was looked at most when he spoke was perceived by the other group members, and by himself, to be the most influential in the group. It also emerged that sub-groupings of individuals, in terms of perceived mutual support, were marked by patterns of exchanged glances. In this situation personal preferences among members were not marked by mutual looking and whereas studies by others have reported relationships between amount of looking and such personality variables as "affiliativeness" (e.g. Exline, 1963; Exline et al., 1965; Exline and Winters, 1965), this relationship was not found in Weisbrod's study. Her findings indicate that before any generalization can be made about the role of gaze in interaction it will be necessary to investigate how gaze is patterned naturally, and how, as an item of behaviour, it is related to other behaviour in interaction. It must also be examined in a wider range of interactional situations than has been done hitherto.

2.3 POSTURE

In an encounter, participants not only maintain themselves in a particular relative position and orientation, they also tend to assume specific postures which, with some variation, are maintained for most of the time. Variations in posture will be examined later. Here only maintained postures will be considered and their possible significance for understanding the configuration.

In considering posture we must deal with (a) what kinds of postures are adopted in the configuration, and (b) what relationships exist between the postures of the various participants.

1. *Types of postures*
When people gather for interaction they hold their bodies in a particular way. They may stand, sit, kneel, squat or even, at times, lie down. Within these broad categories there are many possible variations, although only some of these are used. Some bodily arrangements are not used because they are physically difficult to maintain for any length of time, but even within the range of possible postures, it appears that there is a considerable limitation on what postures are employed, and it seems likely that for any given type of gathering there is probably a particular postural repertoire that the participants will select from. In some situations, what postures a person may assume is made quite explicit. In parade-ground gatherings, for instance, there are "attention" and "at ease" postures which are specified and assumed upon command. Similarly, in religious ritual posture is made quite explicit. To the extent that there are appropriate postures for types of gatherings, postures may be said to "mark" such differences between gatherings, and are available as signals for others as to what sort of gathering it is. As we shall see, the postures of participants within a given gathering may also differ, and these differences can often be shown to be systematically related to the role of the participant in the gathering, and possibly to more subtle aspects of his attitude towards it or to the other participants.

Remarkably little systematic attention has been given to posture so far. Hewes (1955), who studied the varieties of postures assumed by people in different cultures, found that rather different repertoires are used in different parts of the world. For instance, he found that squatting, though very widespread elsewhere, is little employed in Northern Europe. He found that there were quite wide variations in modes of standing, which were, none the less, consistent within cultures. In certain parts of Africa, for instance, the "nilotic" stance is much used by men. In this stance, one stands on one leg, with the other bent at the knee, the sole of the foot planted against the shin. He found too that there were certain differences in postures assumed by men as compared to women, and these differences were quite widespread. Thus any posture in which the legs are held apart was very rare in women but common in men. Hewes, unfortunately, made no attempt to establish the social contexts in which the various postures he catalogued were found to occur. But we have already indicated there is no doubt that there are systematic relationships between postures assumed and the social context. For example, at conferences or seminars people do not usually sit on the floor or lie down, though they may do this at picnics. At least in some sections of society, there is a "proper" way to sit at the dinner table, and children in such groups are frequently corrected. They are given quite explicit training in what is and is not acceptable. It will be noted too, that in many gatherings the posture rules apply differently to different participants, according to their status. Goffman (1961b) reports, for instance, how in psychiatric staff meetings he has observed lower status participants sat in more upright positions with their limbs drawn together, as compared to higher status participants who more often "lounged". This observation seems to be fairly general. It is as if the posture rules are relaxed selectively for the higher status members of a gathering who usually display a wider range of postures than lower status members.

One or two investigators have reported attempts at an experimental study of the communicative significance of posture. Machotka (1965) presented subjects with drawings of people in various postures and configurational arrangements. He found that female figures in which the limbs are to the side of the body are seen as more "accessible" than those with limbs crossed. However, male figures with exposed chest and arms akimbo are seen as haughty and unapproachable. Machotka's hypothesis was that for a powerful figure to expose himself to others constituted a challenge to others to approach him. By exposing himself, rather than covering himself and seeming defensive, he appeared challenging and thus haughty. Mehrabian (1968a, 1968b, 1969) has reported the results of several studies again based upon the technique of having subjects act as if they were addressing another. He concluded from these that posture would be more relaxed (as measured by degree of asymmetry of limb position and degree of trunk leaning) the lower the status of the addressee. Relaxed postures were also found to be observed with either disliked or liked addressees, but there was less relaxation with addressees to whom the subject was neutral.

Once again it is hard to evaluate the findings of Mehrabian and Machotka until far more is known about what kinds of postures people adopt and the circumstances in which they adopt them. The only way this can be done is to observe systematically the behaviour of people in natural settings. Such an investigation has been started[1] in which a series of sites have been selected which vary in the extent to which they are public. The postures of the individuals present are recorded, together with what they are doing.

Our preliminary results, from the study of three public settings—streets in a small town where people are gathering for a parade, a small town picnic ground, and the open areas of the campus of a large university—suggest that sites differ in the range of types of postures observed in them, and that there are consistent associations between the types of posture assumed by individuals and the type of activity they are engaged in. For example, people in public or semi-public settings who are not involved in any particular attentional focus but are "scanning the scene" typically stand with the weight primarily on one foot rather than on both; characteristically they do not orient their head and torso in the same direction. People who are on the edges of focused gatherings and on the edges of gathering sites more often assume an arms-akimbo posture than those who are full members of focused gatherings or those nearer to the centre of a gathering site. People who are either "scanning" or on the edges of focused gatherings or sites tend to keep their heads erect, or even slightly tilted back, in contrast to people who are full members of focused gatherings who, as we have mentioned before, tend rather to tilt their heads slightly forward. Also, as we have mentioned, people who are passing through or near inter- actional territories (i.e. spaces being used by a gathering) typically bend their heads forward very markedly as they do so.

[1] In collaboration with Dr A. E. Scheflen.

The above observations are quite tentative and have yet to be fully interpreted. They are given here to illustrate the sort of data that are necessary for a systematic study of the significance of postures.

2. *Relations between postures*

Scheflen (1964) has pointed out that the relationship between the postures of participants often depends upon other aspects of the inter-action. Therefore how an individual relates his posture to that of his interlocutor may be an important aspect of his communicative be-haviour. In particular, Scheflen has drawn attention to how the pos-tures of participants may be congruent or non-congruent with one another—that is, members of a gathering may have the same postures or they may show marked differences. Where people are oriented in parallel, as in a lecture or concert, where they are all focusing on the same centre of attention, similarity of posture is very common. This contrasts with the situation when people are not sharing the same focus of attention, in which case greater diversity of posture occurs. When people are engaged in focused interaction, and are thus to some extent *vis-à-vis* one another, it is quite common for them to show similarity of posture, and the degree to which they do so possibly reflects to what extent they are *en rapport*.

The relationship between *rapport* and postural congruence has been studied in a psychotherapy session by Charny (1966). It was found that when the psychiatrist and the patient adopted similar postures the patient talked objectively, whereas when their postures were dissimilar he was more withdrawn and tended to "act out" emotionally. Charny also noted that periods of postural congruence increased as the interview developed in time. After completing the study, Charny learned that the therapist in the film record used in the study, who was of Rogerian persuasion, deliberately sought to be posturally congruent with his patients as part of his technique of gaining *rapport* (Charny, personal communication, 1967). What was not analysed was *which* postures the therapist attempted to mirror. A viewing of the film suggested that the postures adopted by the patient, when she was not congruent with the therapist, were postures that are rarely seen in focused interaction. For instance, during non-congruent periods on the film she would sit with her shoulders hunched together and her head hung forward. It would seem to be worth pursuing the idea that, when somebody is trying to build *rapport* with another, there is only a limited range of postures in the other he may attempt to mirror, since there are only certain kinds of postural relations in interaction within which a jointly oriented exchange can take place.

Where there is marked incongruence in postures, this often reflects sharp differences in role relations within the gathering. Thus in a lecture, for example, the lecturer stands, while all the members of the audience sit, generally in much the same way. Incongruence of posture may also reflect a psychological distancing between the participants. This is perhaps exemplified in Fig. 3, a still taken from a film made

Fig. 3. Drawing from a frame of a film by Kirsch, illustrating postural incongruence.

in 1965 by Sander Kirsch in the women's dormitories of a large urban university where men were waiting to meet their dates. While, in this picture, the girl is turned towards the man, the man remains facing firmly outward with his limbs arranged as if to put a barrier between himself and the girl. He turns his head towards her occasionally as he talks, but he is otherwise quite unchanging in this postural arrangement. This scene lasts for about eight minutes; then another girl is seen to enter and the man gets up and leaves with her. It seems likely that, in his posture, he was expressing the fact that he was not to be linked with the girl he was talking to and that she was not to be seen as his date.

Apart from the work of Charny cited above, Scheflen (1964, 1965) is the main source of observations on postural relations. Detailed systematic observations are still very much needed here, however, before the significance of posture in the configuration is fully understood.

This discussion of configuration, while somewhat speculative in parts, should suggest how spatial arrangement, orientation and posture may reflect a great deal of complex information about how participants are related to one another and to the encounter as a whole. Arriving at the configuration, that is the process by which the bodies of the participants in the gathering come to be arranged so that "business" can begin, often involves quite a complex set of negotiations, conducted for the most part entirely silently. An analysis of these manoeuvres should tell us much about the process of how the "working consensus" of the gathering is arrived at.

3 Encounter dynamics

The configuration, we have suggested, provides a setting within which the business of the encounter can take place. In observing any encounter as it develops in time, one can distinguish a phase during which the participants move about and then find mutually agreeable places to stand or sit; it is our expectation that they will not start to attend to the official purpose of the encounter until the configuration has formed. In formally organized meetings this is quite explicit. Chairmen do not introduce the agenda until the meeting is "in order". Similarly, in less formal settings talk related to the official focus of the gathering does not begin until all the participants are settled in their seats. The details of how, in these less formally organized gatherings, the participants "know" when it is appropriate to begin have yet to be examined. It is possible that each participant assumes a particular posture and orientation to indicate that he is ready.

In this section some features of the organization of the business phase of an encounter will be examined. In particular, we shall consider how speaking turns are arranged and how participants engaged in an address mark the direction of their address.

When a person speaks at a gathering or in some other way actively sends explicit messages, these messages are always *directed*. That is, the speaker always addresses his utterances either to some specific other person in the gathering or to several others, or to the gathering as a whole. As we shall describe, there are aspects of the speaker's behaviour which appear to serve the function of marking the direction of his utterances. If we look at the other participants (those who are not speaking) when the speaker is directing his utterances to a specific other individual it will be observed that the person who is the direct recipient of the speaker's address tends to behave in a different way from the other participants. Indeed, there appears to be a particular relationship between the behaviour of the speaker and the individual he is directly addressing which is not found between the speaker and the other participants present.

It will now be shown how the speaker marks the direction of his utterances and how the behaviour of the direct recipient differs from that of the other participants. An example of the way the relationship between the speaker and the direct recipient is established and further details of the behaviour of speakers and listeners will be given; particular attention will be paid to the question of how speakers and listeners take turns.

3.1 FEATURES OF THE BEHAVIOURAL RELATIONSHIP BETWEEN SPEAKER AND LISTENER

First of all we will describe the case where the speaker is addressing one other individual directly. No effort will be made to give an exhaustive description of the properties of this relationship but we will attempt to highlight the features most commonly observed.

Typically both speaker and direct recipient are oriented towards one another. As a rule they repeatedly scan each other; from time to time their eyes meet. This orientation of head and eyes towards another, with intermittent aiming of the eyes directly at the other, is one of the principle ways in which a person signals to whom his messages are directed. It should be noted that in "aiming the eyes" what we characteristically observe is that the speaker's head repeatedly returns to the same position and then pauses. When not looking at his addressee he looks up or down or to the side, but not at anybody else. When he addresses several others at once, his repeated positioning will be replaced by a repeated scanning of those who constitute the recipients of the address. The movements of his head have a systematic relationship to the organization of his utterances. This will be discussed in a later section.

So far as the *listener* is concerned, if he is the direct recipient of the address, he may be distinguished from the others in the gathering by a heightened congruency of posture with that of the speaker; his head is usually slightly "cocked" to one side, and his visual attention is far more consistent than that of other listeners. Also, the direct recipient, unlike other listeners, tends to exhibit a particular set of gestures, such as head-nods, and also certain changes in facial expression which appear to function at times as comments upon what the speaker is saying. In particular the head-nods, and their vocal equivalent ("I see", "Uh-huh", etc.—sometimes known as "attention signals") are placed at specific points in relation to the speaker's behaviour. Again, the details of this will be described in the next section.

It has also been shown that a speaker and his direct addressee tend to show a coordination of bodily movement that we do not find between speaker and listeners who are not directly addressed. It has been observed that the direct recipient may pick up some aspect of the speaker's movements and move in a similar fashion and in synchrony with him. This may be illustrated by an analysis that was undertaken (Kendon, 1970) of the relationship between the movements of a speaker (T) and his addressee (B) (see Fig. 4.). This was contrasted with the movements of another listener (GI).

In this sequence, B put a question to T, and T replied with a speech lasting about thirty seconds. The group in this study was discussing aspects of British family life, and the discussion was coordinated by B who served as a kind of chairman. When B put his question to T, he faced him and pointed at him with an extended arm. T sat forward. At the precise moment that B finished his question, T leant back, and only two seconds later, when he was sitting with his back against the chair, did he begin to reply. His shift in posture was the immediate response to B's question and B moved as soon as T changed his position: he leant back slightly and lifted his head, then became still and remained so until T began to speak. As T uttered his first two phrases, he moved his left hand leftwards and then back again to his lap; then cocked his head to his left. Precisely in time with these movements, B moved his right arm, which was still extended towards T, out to his right and then back again; he then tilted his head to his right. After this he put his pipe in his mouth and held it there with his right

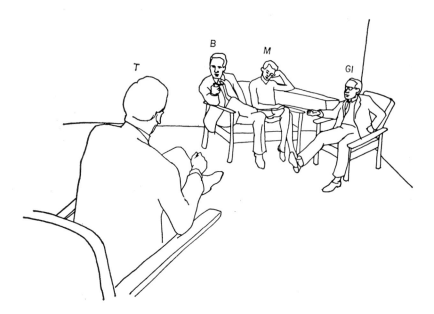

Fig. 4. Drawing from Frame No. 87630 from the film TRD 009 to show the arrangement of people in the sequence in which the relationship between the movements of T and B was studied. (Reproduced from Kendon, 1970.)

hand and remained still until the last two phrases of T's discourse, except that he moved his eyes and his mouth and the fingers of his right hand, and made one multiple head-nod.

It will be seen that from the time T began to respond to B's question until B put his pipe in his mouth B was moving in time with T in a manner that mirrored T's movements. B moved in step with T and in the same fashion: he "danced T's dance".

During the last two phrases of T's speech, B began to move conspicuously again—this time by leaning to his left, then dropping his head forward and leaning again to the left. These movements, although rhythmically coordinated with T's speech, were not related in form to the movements T was making when they were initiated. Thus B leant left and dropped his head forward as T moved his head back and to the left. Thereupon T 's head and body movements became similar to those of **B**: thus T began to dance B's dance—the reverse of what had happened when T began to speak.

These observations, together with other examples reported in more **detail elsewhere (Kendon, 1970),** illustrate further the phenomenon of "interactional synchrony" first reported by Condon and Ogston (1966, 1967). However, we find that the rather conspicuous mirroring of movement described above does not occur continuously. It is usually observed both at the start and again towards the end of an utterance. Our hypothesis is that in matching another's movements the listener signals that he is giving his full attention to the speaker. However, once this has been established the recipient needs only to remain in a "listening posture", and to display intermittent attention signals. Where, as in the case of B and T, the recipient replies next we tend to find conspicuous movement relationships at the end of the interchange as well. This may both signal clearly to the speaker that the listener wishes to speak himself and it may also facilitate the precise timing of the entry of the other into the role of speaker rather as when a musician conspicuously beats time just before it is his turn to play.

It thus seems that there are specific behaviour patterns by which a speaker establishes to whom he is directing his remarks; also there appear to be patterns that distinguish the listener directly addressed from other listeners. Thus the speaker and directly addressed listener exhibit a special relatedness that distinguishes them from other members of the gathering. When this occurs an *axis of interaction* can be said to exist (Watson and Potter, 1962) between the participants. An axis of interaction usually comprises a relationship between two people, a *speaker* and the directly addressed listener, here referred to as the *axial listener*. An axis of interaction between two people may be considered to continue as long as the behavioural relatedness we have described can be observed, though the person occupying the role of speaker and the person occupying the role of axial listener may change. Thus if A addresses B and then B replies addressing A, and so on, an axis of interaction will be said to exist between A and B and it will continue to exist until either stops addressing the other. The exchange of roles within an axis will be referred to as a *pole shift*. When one axis ends and another begins we shall speak of a *change* of interactional axis. Those members of the gathering not participating in a current axis will be referred to as the *non-axial participants*.

It will be seen that the axis of interaction is a public unit of behavioural relatedness. Thus when, at a meeting, each speaker specifically addresses the chairman and there is maintained between speaker and chairman the behavioural relatedness we have described, we shall still assume the axis of interaction is between the speaker and chairman, even though the speaker's remarks are made in such a way as to be a contribution to the discussion of the meeting. The axis of interaction is thus a possible unit for the analysis of the organization of an encounter. In most encounters its integrity is respected by the non-axial participants. It is rare for such a participant to initiate an address to either the speaker or the axial listener. Axes of interaction generally follow one another in succession, and, at least in smoothly running encounters, generally they are not interrupted. Both speaker and axial listener must cease to manifest the behaviour by which they are defined before a new axis can be established.

The next two sections contain examples to illustrate the processes by which axes of interaction can become established; and the behaviour that coordinates the shifts of speaker and axial listener roles within an axis will be discussed.

3.2 MOVEMENT COORDINATION AND THE INITIATION OF INTERACTIONAL AXES

In the preceding section we considered how the movements of the speaker and axial listener were finally coordinated, and how this phenomenon is not observed between the speaker and non-axial listeners. In this section we shall describe an example of how people tend to coordinate their movements immediately before starting a conversation which establishes an interactional axis between them. We shall illustrate how movement coordination can function as an "unofficial" or "non-explicit" exchange of information, making it possible for each participant to know that the other intends to initiate an axis of interaction. It is our contention that the subtle responses observed are a widespread phenomenon in interaction and serve an important function in the coordination of behaviour.

The example is taken from a film of a psychiatric seminar[1] in which five psychiatrists and a social worker meet to discuss a case. One of the psychiatrists (D) serves as chairman, another presents the case, and the social worker (F), a woman, also takes a part in presenting the case. The interchange we are concerned with takes place between D and F. D enters and joins the other participants who are already seated waiting for him. As he sits down he commences with some introductory

---

[1] Taken from an investigation in progress in collaboration with Dr Aviva Menkes. The film was shot at 24 frames per second.

remarks about the object of the meeting and the way it should be conducted which are addressed to the group as a whole. Having done this
he then looks at each member in turn; from each, as he looks at them,
he receives a brief head-nod. Here, each one is presumably confirming
that they have received his remarks, and are at the same time giving
him leave to proceed to the next stage. Having received a head-nod
from the last member of the seminar he looks at, he lowers his head and
leans forward to the coffee table to reach for a cup of coffee. But he is
not engaged in any social address during this action: for the moment
his complete attention is devoted to the coffee cup. However, the
structure of the situation is such that he is expected to be the next to
speak. Moments after his hand has reached the coffee cup and before
he begins to pick it up and lean back in his chair, he rotates his head
to the right to look at F; he then addresses her with a question. It
should be noted that D does not begin to speak to F until his head is
oriented towards her, illustrating a quite general point that the body is
usually first put into the appropriate position for an address before
speech begins. However, what is striking here is that at precisely the
same moment that D begins to rotate his head towards F, F begins the
sequence of movements which result in turning to look at D. Each
orients to the other into an axis of interaction and each begins the
orientation movement simultaneously. It is as if F knew in advance that
she was to be the target of D's next address.

If we examine F's movements, however, and how they relate to
those of D we find that F is moving synchronously with D even before
D begins his orientation towards her. Thus the moment D looks at F,
as he scans the group after his introductory remarks, F slightly raises
her eyebrows, lowers her head and looks to her left, away from D. She
then turns to look at D as he turns to another member of the group.
She moves her head back towards the left and D leans forward and
extends his arm towards his coffee cup. Her head is tilted forward
through this movement and she thus appears to follow D's movements
with her eyes, and, in the movement of her head, she is sharing the
rhythm with which D is moving. Our hypothesis is that in moving
synchronously with D, F shows that she is attentive to him, and this has
the consequence of drawing his attention to her. Perhaps by moving
in rhythm with D, F makes herself available as a person already attentive, thereby increasing the likelihood that D will turn to her in his
next address. Once D chooses to do so, as he does here, the axis between

them can be established simultaneously for F already has acquired, in her movements, D's rhythm. The relationship between D and F's behaviour we have described is illustrated in Fig. 5 (a–d). It will be seen that none of the other participants coordinate their behaviour with D in the way F does here.

(a) D looks at man to his left and F looks at D (frame 05368).

(b) D lowers his head and leans forward to reach for his coffee and F rotates her head as he does so (frame 05403).

The example described above is but one of many we have collected from several different records, in which, prior to the setting up of an explicit axis of interaction, the persons involved move coordinately and, in each case, one individual begins to move coordinately with another. Our hypothesis is that moving into synchrony with another person is one of the devices by which a person can indicate to the other that he wishes to establish an axis with him without making an explicit request. Initiating an axis of interaction with another person is always

(c) F looks down at her coffee as D leans forward to reach for his coffee cup (frame 05433).

(d) D rotates his head to F and she lowers her hand from her coffee cup and rotates her head towards D (frame 05446).

Fig. 5. Sequence of drawings from the film ISP 001 63 to show the relationships between the movements of D and F up to the point where an *interactional axis* is established between them.

a somewhat risky business, since there is the possibility that the other party does not wish to reciprocate. By simply picking up the rhythm of another person's movements one can establish a connection with

him which at the same time does not commit one to an explicit initiation. If, after having joined the rhythm of another, no reciprocal move
is made, it is possible to continue as if no attempt had been made to
initiate an axis.[1]

3.3 FURTHER DETAILS OF THE BEHAVIOUR OF SPEAKERS AND AXIAL LISTENERS

As stated earlier, one of the main features of an interactional axis is that
the axial listener turns his head and eyes towards the speaker and from
time to time nods his head and makes other explicit "attention signals";
the speaker repeatedly returns his head to a position in which he may
be said to be "aiming his eyes" at the axial listener. These phenomena
have been examined in some detail in dyadic gatherings by Kendon
(1967) and since the findings are very pertinent to the coordination of
behaviour within axes of interaction they are discussed in further detail
below.

In this study, seven separate pairs of individuals were filmed as they
talked together in an informal setting. None of the subjects had met
before and they were left together for half an hour to "get acquainted".
The conversations were filmed in such a way that, by the use of mirrors,
it was possible to see both participants full face on the same film. A
detailed analysis was then made of the patterning of head–eye orientation in relation to utterances and their internal structure. This was done
for sixteen minutes of one conversation, and for five-minute stretches of
each of the remaining six.

The main findings can be summarized quite briefly. First it was
found that the time each member of a dyad spent looking at his partner
varied greatly both during conversations within a dyad and from one
dyad to the next. However, it was observed that the person listening
would consistently spend most of the time gazing at the speaker for long
periods, whereas the speaker tended to alternate between looking
towards and looking away from his partner. A detailed examination of
the relation between "looking at" and speaking was undertaken for

---

[1] See Goffman (1963, pp. 91–95) who discusses the function of "catching the eye" in the initiation of focused interaction. He points out how the initiator's glance "can be sufficiently
tentative and ambiguous to allow him to act as if no initiation had been intended, if it
appears that his overture is not desired". We suggest that this is even more the case when the
initiator first signals his wish to engage the other by movement coordination with him.

utterances that lasted for five seconds or more. It was found that the speaker tended to look away from his partner as he began to talk and in many cases somewhat before this, and that he looked back again, usually during the last phrase and continued to look at his partner for sometime after he had finished speaking. It was found that characteristically during the course of a long utterance the speaker would glance at his partner as he came to the end of each phrase, but would always look away just before he resumed speaking. Hesitations were always accompanied by looking away.

It was suggested that this behaviour, although it might have important functions for the speaker, perhaps in relation to his need for information about his interlocutor, or his need to cut out input as he worked out the details of his speech, could also function as a means of communication. It was suggested that by looking away, just in advance of speaking, the speaker could signal his intent to claim the floor. By looking away after the end of each phrase he could signal his intent to continue speaking; while by looking at his partner, and sustaining this look, as he brought his utterance to an end, he could signal his intent to finish. This could thus be a cue to his partner to begin speaking.

An attempt was made to corroborate the last part of this interpretation. To do this, the latency with which A's utterances followed B's was examined for all those cases where A did *not* look up when he came to the end of his utterance and compared with the latencies that occurred where A did look up as he had finished speaking. It was found that of those utterances which ended with an extended look, 29 per cent were followed by either no response or by a delayed response from B; but of those that ended *without* A looking up 71 per cent were followed by either an absence of response or a delay in response from B.

Further analyses were conducted to examine the relationship between the occurrence of B's attention signals and the concurrent behaviour of the speaker. It was found that the highest proportion of attention signals occurred during the pauses in A's speech that occurred between phrases, whereas far fewer occurred during fluent speech, or during hesitation pauses.

In sum, the above findings suggest that the way a speaker patterns his gaze in relation to his speech could function as a cue serving to regulate the behaviour of his interlocutor. In looking away the speaker signals his intention to continue to hold the floor and thereby to forestall any attempt at action by his interlocutor. In looking at his partner, if he does so briefly in mid-utterance, he signals merely that he is going to continue. If he looks at his partner in a sustained fashion as he finishes speaking this acts as a cue to the other to begin speaking.

These findings need to be corroborated by other studies. It is also desirable that studies be made of gaze in other kinds of encounters. Such evidence as we have suggests that while changes in head–eye orientation are regularly patterned in relation to the structure of the speaker's utterances (Kendon, 1967, 1972; Kendon and Cook, 1969; Nielsen, 1962; Scheflen, 1964), what this pattern is will vary according to the situation. Thus in an analysis of a psychotherapy session, Scheflen (1964) has reported how the female therapist regularly looked away as the patient was speaking, but turned to look at him as she spoke. Here, of course, there was a sharp differentiation in role in the situation which was reflected in the kinds of utterances each produced, and this could well be related to differences in the way gazes were patterned. (Some limited data relevant to this point are given in Kendon, 1967, pp. 42–47.) Again, in the unpublished study by Weisbrod (1965) it was found that participants spent 70 per cent of their speaking time looking at others, while listeners spent only 47 per cent of their listening time looking at the speaker. This is related, no doubt, to the finding mentioned earlier that one of the principal means of marking the direction of an address within a gathering is to look at the addressee. In gatherings of more than two, specification of address direction becomes necessary, and so we would expect more looking while speaking in these circumstances. The finding that people, when listening, tended not to look at the speaker as much as they do in dyadic gatherings, may be due to the possibility that most of the addresses in this group were general ones. However, in her analysis, Weisbrod did not distinguish between axial and non-axial listeners. It is our expectation that axial listeners in a multi-person gathering will spend a high proportion of the time looking at the speaker, whereas other listeners may not do so.

3.4   ASPECTS OF THE ORGANIZATION OF THE SOCIAL PERFORMANCE

A participant in a gathering marks his participation, as we have seen, by his physical proximity to the other members, together with a particular pattern of orientation to them. We have noted how he may engage as a speaker, as an active recipient, as a non-axial listener, or how he may temporarily withdraw from the interaction while still remaining a member of the gathering. We have also said something about how his behaviour differs according to how he is participating, and have also said a little, though really much too little, about how participants differ in their roles in gatherings and how these differences are manifested in terms of visible behaviour. In this section we shall try to extend these descriptions somewhat.

Scheflen (1964, 1965) has proposed that an individual's performance in a gathering may be seen to be organized into a set of hierarchically related units. These units are units of communication; Scheflen's particular contribution has been to point out how these units are marked by contrasting bodily positions or postures, and how boundaries between them may be marked by shifts in bodily positions. At the highest level, in terms of the hierarchy proposed by Scheflen, we may distinguish the *presentation*, which comprises the individual's presence in a configuration. This unit is marked by a relatively stable physical location, and it is bounded by substantial changes in this location. The presentation of an individual is roughly equivalent to what is sometimes called his situational role.

Within an individual's presence in a gathering or within his presentation, an individual may be said to enact one or more *positions*. Typically, each participant in a gathering tends to have a limited repertoire of such positions. Each of these positions, Scheflen has observed, are marked by a different postural arrangement, and the change from one position to the next is marked by a shift in posture.

This may best be seen in an illustration (unpublished data, Oxford, 1965). Thus, a lecturer at an informal lecture was observed and his performance could be seen to be made up of four different major units, or positions, as follows: a lecturing position, in which he talked continuously to the audience; a question-asking position, in which he invited people to ask questions; a question-receiving position, in which he listened as a specific question was being asked; and a question-answering position, in which he answered the question. Each of these different positions was distinguished from the other not only in the way the lecturer spoke but also in the postural arrangement he adopted. The change from one to another was marked by, or might be said to be announced by, a change in his posture. For the duration of his presentation, that is for the whole of the time that he was in his role as lecturer, he sat on a table facing the group with his legs swinging clear of the floor. During lecturing, he sat with his spine somewhat curved, his arms resting on his thighs, his hands loosely clasped together. When he finished lecturing, he put his hands under his thighs, palms down on the table and raised his head somewhat, scanning the group with raised eyebrows for questions. In subsequent appearances of the question-asking position, he merely scanned the group with raised eyebrows. As soon as someone began to ask a question he craned his neck forwards, turned his head to one side with it slightly "cocked", raised his brows maximally and looked at the questioner from the corners of his eyes. This was the question-receiving position. At the end of the question, the lecturer turned his head frontally again rapidly, pushed his neck forward, hunched his shoulders and straightened his arms, and generally increased the level of tenseness in his posture. He maintained this posture for the duration of his answer, the posture change and position together characterizing his question-answering position.

Within each position, further units may be discerned which Scheflen identifies as *points*. For instance, when lecturing, a lecturer makes a series of statements which comprise his total discourse. In continuous speech, such as a lecture, the segments probably correspond to the series of points that he might be said to make as he talks. A psychotherapist, in interpreting, may first give a résumé of something the patient has said before giving his interpretation of it. Though a clear definition of the point has yet to be arrived at, Scheflen suggests that one of the ways in which points are distinguished is by a change in the position of the head. Scheflen reports (1964) that interactants in psychotherapy typically show a repertoire of three to five different head positions which occur repeatedly. He gives an example of two points a female therapist was observed to use repeatedly during interchanges with a patient inside an "interpreting" position. While listening to him, her head was slightly lowered, cocked to the right, with averted eyes. At the end of each point she raised her head up, then held it erect, and, looking directly at the patient, produced an interpretative remark. As she ended it, she turned her head to the far right away from the patient, and then resumed the position of the listening point.

So far, no one has attempted to extend Scheflen's notions, or to make systematic observations to confirm them, though a project aimed at doing this is underway.[1] However, one investigation (Kendon, 1972) does bear on some of these observations of Scheflen, though it appears to

[1] By Dr C. Beels and Dr Jane Ferber, Bronx State Hospital.

demonstrate that the hierarchy of communication units he has proposed, though basically sound, is probably more complex than his first formulation indicated. In this study, a detailed analysis was undertaken of the relationship between the speech of an individual and the concurrent movements of his body. The analysis, which was done from a film, was of a man who was talking in a semi-public way within a gathering of about eleven participants. The part of his discourse that was analysed comprised just the first two minutes. The speech was analysed into a number of different units at each of five levels of integration. In this particular discourse forty-eight *phrases* were distinguished, and these were found to be grouped into eighteen groupings, roughly the equivalent of sentences,[1] here called *locutions*. These locutions were further found to be grouped into eleven *locution groups* (or "sub-paragraphs"), and these fell into three *locution group clusters* (or "paragraphs").

For each level of speech organization there was found to be a contrasting pattern of body motion by which each unit at that level was made distinct from those adjacent to it. Thus, for the whole *discourse* (the highest level grouping of speech units used here), the speaker held himself in a different posture from the one he held when listening to someone else before he began to speak. In association with each locution group cluster or "paragraph" of the discourse, the speaker employed his hands and arms in gesticulation differentially. Over the first of these speech units he gesticulated only with his right arm; over the second he gesticulated only with his left arm, while over the third he gesticulated with both arms. So each locution was distinguished by a different pattern of hand and arm movements. Thus, in the second locution group cluster or "paragraph", over the first locution the speaker used broad out-and-out movements of the whole arm; over the second he used movements only in the wrist and fingers; over the third, he flexed his arm from the elbow, then lowered it, and so on. At yet a lower level of organization it was found that each phrase was distinguished from the succeeding one by a different pattern of movement again. Over the first phrase, for instance, the speaker moved his arm out and then moved it in over the second phrase, and so on. Going below the phrase to syllables and even to phones, as Condon and Ogston

---

[1] The reason for the terms "locution" etc. is that the segmentation of the speech was done on a phonetic basis, in terms of intonation patterns, and this does not necessarily result in the same units as a grammatical or semantic analysis. "Sentence" and "paragraph" are syntactic terms and they do not refer to units of speech.

(1966, 1967) have shown, we can again find contrasting changes in body movement.

It was also found that the head moved in a regular, patterned fashion in relation to the units of speech. Thus, at the start of each locution, the head would be either erect or cocked to the right. As the locution progressed the head would be wagged to the left and then lowered, so that by the end of the last phrase the head was now both lowered and rotated to the left. During the pause that followed, between the end of the last and the beginning of the next locution, the head would be moved back to its erect or rightward cocked position. These cyclings of the head in association with successive locutions are clearly closely similar to those described by Scheflen (1964) as markers of points, and are probably closely related to the cyclical patterns of changes in gaze in relation to utterances, as described by Kendon (1967) and above.

To restate what we have been saying, combining the observations of Scheflen (1964) with those of Kendon (1972), if we observe a participant in an interaction we are likely to observe that he will arrange his body in a series of different postures, and that each one of these will be associated with a different mode of activity. He will have a set of postures associated with speaking, another set associated with listening, and for the different ways of speaking, such as questioning, discoursing, commanding, we may expect a distinguishable posture. As he speaks, his speech flow is organized into a series of units at different levels of integration. A repetitive cycling of the head will be observed and this will be seen to mark off, or be associated with, successive speech units at a middle level of organization, probably those units of speech which convey distinct "thoughts" of units of content. If we look in more detail at the flow of speech and how body motion is organized in relation to it, we find that at every level of organization in speech there is a corresponding level at which contrasting patterns of body motion can be distinguished.

What we have described in outlining these observations on posture and posture shifts and patterns of body motion in relation to units of communication enables us to say that one of the ways in which units of communication within an individual are marked is in postural or body position shifts or changes. But we have not dealt with the question of *how* these different units are distinguished from one another. How are we led to label them as "questioning", "commanding", "expounding", and so forth? Are there indeed specific "questioning" postures, "commanding" postures, etc. or is it that postures and movements function merely to show contrasts within conversational sequences in their function? Scheflen's hypothesis is that there is a limited set of modes of presenting to others, though neither he, nor anyone else, has given us a catalogue of what these modes might be. Each mode of presenting is, however, characterized by a number of properties, though it is very doubtful that we could finally characterize any of these properties, since this would always have to be done in terms of the patterning of the behaviours involved and the relation of the unit to its larger context. However, we make the following suggestions.

First of all, it seems likely that there are a number of different postures that "stand for" different modes of presenting. Mehrabian's work, referred to earlier (cf. pp. 43, 48), difficult to evaluate though it is, at least indicated that his subjects had some ideas in common about how they might position themselves in relation to people to whom they held differing attitudes. This is perhaps not surprising, for we all of us have some idea of what a "challenging" posture is like, what a "seductive" posture is like, and so on. What is needed is a criterion by which units of posture might be distinguished. Thus we need to develop careful descriptions of as many different units as can be found, and then do a lot of careful observation to delimit the contexts in which the different units are found to occur. In this way we may quite rapidly learn something more about posture.

Secondly, for a given type of presentation, there may be characteristic accompanying sets of displays. This is suggested by, among other things, the work of Rosenfeld (1966, 1967), who instructed subjects to act towards some other person in a way to make him like them or dislike them, and showed that there were characteristic differences in the amount of smiling, in the amount of gesturing, etc.

Thirdly, there are probably differences in the way in which a person relates his behaviour to that of others, according to his prevailing position. There is the fairly obvious point that someone "lecturing" does all the talking. To give one example of a more subtle sort, one of the characteristics of an individual who is attempting to establish himself in a superordinate position is that he does not accommodate his pace of action to those around him. They rather, are left to accommodate their pacing to his (unpublished data from films of psychotherapy and discussion groups).

Fourthly, different presentations or positions are marked by different speech styles, and indeed by different linguistic forms. There is a considerable body of work on intonation, for example, in which intonation patterns are distinguished in terms of the different attitudes they are said to express (Crystal, 1969). Thus some attempt to list the properties of the distinguishable units of communication is required. This demands an approach involving a great deal of careful description and which recognizes that a communication unit, whatever it may be, is not to be defined in terms of one mode of communication only, but may be manifested in several different ways through several different modes.

4 Conclusions

In studying the organization of behaviour in interaction we may consider, on the one hand, what it is that the interactants convey to each other and, on the other, how people organize themselves into arrangements of communicating individuals and thus make the transmission of contents possible.[1] Thus two adult males of equal social status may engage one another in talk, and they may discuss fishing, or the latest political scandal, or their private lives; but, regardless of what they talk about, they organize themselves into a conversational gathering, and they do this in much the same way in each case. They adopt a spatial, orientational and postural arrangement that is characteristic of conversation, and in conducting the conversation they organize their behaviour into certain units of communicative behaviour which follow one another in a set of patterned relationships irrespective of the topics discussed. It is with these forms of conversational behaviour that we are concerned. An attempt has been made to review how the visible aspects of behaviour function to establish and maintain a conversational occasion. The whole question of how visible behaviour functions in expressing the contents of such conversational occasions has been left aside.

In much of what we have said, we have had to be content with describing regularities of visible behaviour in interaction. That these regularities actually have a communicative function is still largely a

[1] The distinction drawn here is related to the distinction of McBride (1968) between "secondary" and "primary" interaction systems. In these terms, our concern has been entirely with "primary" systems of interaction. "Secondary" systems are mainly comprised of language and make possible conversation about things not immediately present. "Primary" interaction systems deal with the regulation of the immediate relationship of the interacting individuals. I am indebted to McBride for discussions of this issue.

matter of conjecture, though clearly, in so far as the spacing, postures, and movement patterns that people engage in are patterned, we can be sure that they are *available* as a means of communication. Only in the case of the possible "floor-apportioning" function of gaze has the analysis been carried to the point where it can be said that this function is more than a matter of mere conjecture. This criticism has not been stressed, since we have endeavoured to put forward a picture of how the behaviours may function in organizing interaction. It has merely been mentioned here to indicate how much more work there is to be done. Indeed, the work needed for a proper understanding of how interaction is *done* has hardly begun. The reader will realize the paucity of the data so far available.

What kind of research is needed? It is our opinion that a systematic description of interactional behaviour is our primary need at this time. We need to develop techniques for gathering samples of interactional behaviour, as near as possible in natural settings,[1] which must then be approached in the same spirit as an animal ethologist approaches his material when he tries to understand the systems of communication the animals employ. Although, for several species of monkeys and apes, we now have a description of the repertoire of communicative behaviours that is fairly complete, at least so far as vocalization is concerned, and in some few cases, visible behaviour as well (see Altmann, 1968), we do not have even the beginnings of such a repertoire for man, except in the case of language. And even the study of language has been pursued so much in the abstract that, though we now have a considerable knowledge of its structure, we have a relatively poor systematic understanding of its functions.[2]

Our belief is that it is essential for research workers interested in human communication to turn their attention to the task of developing

[1] Dr A. E. Scheflen and Joseph Schaeffer at Bronx State Hospital have pioneered in the development of techniques for gathering visual records of behaviour in natural settings, using video recording. They have been concerned with gathering records of behaviour in households. The use of film as a data-gathering device has been developed by Van Vlack (1964), Eibl-Eibesfeldt (1968) and others. Some account of the relative merits of these media for data gathering and analysis is given in Scheflen, Schaeffer and Kendon (1970), and recommended procedures for filming as a data gathering technique are given in Scheflen (1973). A comprehensive review of the methods referred to here from an anthropological perspective will appear in Schaeffer (Doctoral thesis in preparation, Department of Anthropology, Columbia University).

[2] Dell Hymes has developed this point on several occasions. See, in particular, Hymes (1967). See also Moscovici (1967) and Erving-Tripp (1968).

an "ethogram" of human communicational behaviour. It is probable that this will prove to be a less arduous task than might be supposed, for the repertoire of human communicational behaviour, though complex, is undoubtedly limited. It is already becoming clear that all languages are built up out of the same finite set of basic principles (Lenneberg, 1967; Greenberg, 1969). Universal features in speech have also started to be identified (Lieberman, 1966). Since the other systems of communication employed here are certainly simpler than language, it seems likely that "universals" in them will emerge much more quickly, if only we begin to watch carefully what people do and in the process concern ourselves with what people do in *common* rather than with the subtle ways in which the differences between individuals are expressed.

The rewards of such a description of the systems of communication employed by man will be great. Not only will it provide a firm basis for understanding how interaction is achieved and so enable us to give a much more precise account of socialization and to have a better understanding of socially malfunctioning individuals, but it will also help us to approach the task of a comparative analysis of human behaviour and so understand, more fully than now, the nature of our evolutionary heritage and what is species-specific to *Homo sapiens*.

References

Argyle, M. and Dean, Janet (1965). Eye-contact, distance and affiliation. *Sociometry*, **28**, 289–304.

Argyle, M. and Kendon, A. (1967). The experimental analysis of the social performance. *In* "Advances in Experimental Social Psychology" (Ed. L. Berkowitz), pp. 55–98, Vol. 3. Academic Press, New York and London.

Altmann, S. A. (1968). Primates. *In* "Animal Communication: Techniques of Study and Results of Research" (Ed. T. A. Sebeok), pp. 466–522. Indiana University Press, Bloomington.

Bales, R. F. (1950). Interaction Process Analysis: A Method for the Study of Small Groups". Addison-Wesley, Reading, Mass.

Bales, R. F. (1958). Task roles and social roles in problem-solving groups. *In* "Readings in Social Psychology" (Eds Eleanor Maccoby, T. M. Newcomb and E. L. Hartley), 3rd ed. Holt, New York.

Bales, R. F., Strodtbeck, F. L., Mills, T. M. and Roseborough, Mary E. (1951). Channels of communication in small groups. *Am. Sociol. Rev.* **16**, 461–468.

Bavelas, A. (1950). Communication patterns in task oriented groups. *J. Acoustical Soc. Amer.* **22**, 725–730.

Birdwhistell, R. L. (1952). "Introduction to Kinesics". U.S. Department of State Foreign Service Institute, Washington D.C. (Reprinted 1954, University of Louisville Press, Kentucky.)

Birdwhistell, R. L. (1961). Paralanguage: 25 years after Sapir. *In* "Lectures in Experimental Psychiatry" (Ed. H. W. Brosin), pp. 43–65. University of Pittsburgh Press, Pittsburg.

Birdwhistell, R. L. (1968). Communication without words. *In* "L'Aventure Humaine" (Ed. P. Alexandre), pp. 157–166. Kister, Geneva.

Birdwhistell, R. L. (1966). Some body motion elements accompanying spoken American English. *In* "Communication and Culture" (Ed. A. C. Smith), Holt, Rinehart & Winston, New York.

Birdwhistell, R. L. (In preparation). *In* "Natural History of the Interview" (Ed. N. A. McQuown), Grune & Stratton, New York.

Charny, E. J. (1966). Psychosomatic manifestations of rapport in psychotherapy. *Psychosomat. Med.* **28**, 305–315.

Condon, W. S. and Ogston, W. D. (1966). Soundfilm analysis of normal and pathological behavior patterns. *J. Nerv. Mental Dis.* **143**, 338–347.

Condon, W. S. and Ogston, W. D. (1967). A segmentation of behavior. *J. Psychiat. Res.* **5**, 221–235.

Cranach, M. von (1968). The role of orienting behavior in human interaction. Paper to AAAS, Dallas, Texas.

Crystal, D. (1969). "Prosodic Systems and Intonation in English". Cambridge University Press, London.

Diebold, A. R., Jr. (1968). Anthropological perspectives: anthropology and the comparative psychology of communicative behavior. *In* "Animal Communication: Techniques of Study and Results of Research" (Ed. T. A. Sebeok), pp. 525–571. Indiana University Press, Bloomington and London.

Duncan, S., Jr. (1969). Nonverbal communication. *Psychol. Bull.* **72**, 118–137.

Efran, J. S. (1968). Looking for approval: effect on visual behavior of approbation from persons differing in importance. *J. Pers. Soc. Psychol.* **10**, 21–25.

Efron, D. (1941). "Gesture and Environment". Kings Crown Press, New York.

Eibl-Eibesfeldt, I. (1968). Transcultural patterns of visualized contact behavior. Paper presented at Symposium on Use of Space in Animals and Man, AAAS, Dallas, Texas.

Ekman, P., Sorenson, E. and Friesen, W. V. (1969). Pan-cultural elements in facial displays of emotion. *Science*, **164**, 86–88.

Erving-Tripp, Susan (1968). Sociolinguistics. *In* "Advances in Experimental Social Psychology" (Ed. L. Berkowitz), Vol. 4. Academic Press, New York and London.

Exline, R. V. (1963). Explorations in the process of person perception: visual interaction in relation to competition, sex, and need for affiliation. *J. Pers.* **31**, 1–20.

Exline, R. V., Gray, D. and Schuette, Dorothy (1965). Visual behavior in a dyad as affected by interview content, and sex of respondent. *J. Pers. Soc. Psychol.* **1**, 201–209.

Exline, R. V. and Winters, L. C. (1965). Affective relations and mutual glances in dyads. *In* "Affect, Cognition and Personality" (Eds S. S. Tomkins and C. Izard), pp. 319–350. Springer, New York.

D

Felipe, Nancy (1966). Interpersonal distance and small group interaction. *Cornell J. Soc. Relat.* **1**, 59–64.

Goffman, E. (1955). On face-work: an analysis of ritual elements in social interaction. *Psychiatry*, **18**, 213–31.

Goffman, E. (1957). Alienation from interaction. *Hum. Relat.* **10**, 47–60.

Goffman, E. (1961a). "Encounters: Two Studies in the Sociology of Interaction". Bobbs-Merrill, Indianapolis.

Goffman, E. (1961b). "Asylums: Studies in the Sociology of Total Institutions". Anchor Books, Doubleday, New York.

Goffman, E. (1963). "Behavior in Public Places". Free Press, New York.

Goffman, E. (1971). "Relations in Public". Basic Books, New York.

Greenberg, J. (1969). Language universals: a research frontier. *Science*, **166**, 473–478.

Hall, E. T. (1959). "The Silent Language". Doubleday, Garden City, N.Y.

Hall, E. T. (1964). Silent assumptions in social communication. *Res. Publ. Ass. Nerv. Ment. Dis.* **42**, 41–55.

Hall, E. T. (1966). "The Hidden Dimension". Doubleday, Garden City, New York.

Hare, A. P. (1962). "Handbook of Small Group Research". Free Press, New York.

Hare, A. P. and Bales, R. F. (1963). Seating position and small group interaction. *Sociometry*, **26**, 480–486.

Hare, A. P., Borgatta, E. F. and Bales, R. F. (Eds) (1966). "Small Groups: Studies in Social Interaction", 2nd ed. Knopf, New York.

Hearn, G. (1957). Leadership and the spatial factor in small groups. *J. Abnorm. Soc. Psychol.* **54**, 269–272.

Heinicke, C. and Bales, R. F. (1953). Developmental trends in the structure of small groups. *Sociometry*, **16**, 7–38.

Hewes, G. W. (1955). World distribution of certain postural habits. *Amer. Anthrop.* **57**, 231–244.

Hymes, D. (1967). Models of the interaction of language and social setting. *J. Soc. Issues*, **23**, 8–28.

Joos, M. (1962). The five clocks. *Int. J. Amer. Ling.* **28**, (2), Part V.

Kendon, A. (1967). Some functions of gaze direction in social interaction. *Acta Psychol.* **26**, 22–63.

Kendon, A. (1970). Movement coordination in social interaction: some examples described. *Acta Psychologica*, **32**, 1–25.

Kendon, A. (1972). Some relationships between body motion and speech: an analysis of an example. *In* "Studies in Dyadic Interaction: A Research Conference" (Eds A. Seigman and B. Pope), pp. 177–210. Pergamon Press, New York.

Kendon, A. and Cook, M. (1969). The consistency of gaze patterns in social interaction. *Br. J. Psychol.* **60**, 481–494.

Kendon, A. and Ferber, A. (1973). A description of some human greetings. *In* "Comparative Ecology and Behaviour of Primates" (Eds. R. P. Michael and J. H. Crook). Academic Press, London and New York.

LaBarre, W. (1964). Paralinguistics, kinesics and cultural anthropology. *In* "Approaches to Semiotics" (Eds T. A. Sebeok, A. Hayes and Mary C. Bateson), pp. 191–220. Mouton, The Hague.

Lennard, H. L. and Bernstein, A. (1960). "The Anatomy of Psychotherapy: Systems of Communication and Expectation". Columbia University Press, New York.

Lenneberg, E. (1967). "Biological Foundations of Language". John Wiley, New York.

Lieberman, P. (1966). "Intonation, Perception and Language". M.I.T. Press, Cambridge, Mass.

Little, K. B. (1965). Personal space. *J. Exp. Soc. Psychol.* **1**, 237–247.

Lyman, S. M. and Scott, M. B. (1967). Territoriality: a neglected sociological dimension. *Soc. Problems*, **15**, 236–249.

McBride, G. (1968). On the evolution of human language. *Soc. Sci. Information*, **7**, 81–85.

Machotka, P. (1965). Body movement as communication. (Dialogues: Behavioral Science Research). Western Interstate Commission for Higher Education, Boulder, Colorado.

Mehrabian, A. (1968a). Inference of attitude from the posture, orientation and distance of a communicator. *J. Consult. Clin. Psychol.* **32**, 296–308.

Mehrabian, A. (1968b). Relationship of attitude to seated posture, orientation and distance. *J. Pers. Soc. Psychol.* **10**, 26–30.

Mehrabian, A. (1969). Significance of posture and position in the communication of attitude and status relationships. *Psychol. Bull.* **71**, 359–372.

Moscovici, S. (1967). Communication processes and the properties of language. *In* "Advances in Experimental Social Psychology" (Ed. L. Berkowitz), pp. 226–270, Vol. 3. Academic Press, New York and London.

Nielsen, G. (1962). "Studies in Self-confrontation". Munksgaard, Copenhagen.

Pike, K. L. (1954). "Language in Relation to a Unified Theory of the Structure of Human Behavior". Part I (preliminary ed.). Summer Institute of Linguistics, Glendale, California.

Rosenfeld, H. M. (1966). Instrumental affiliative functions of facial and gestural expressions. *J. Pers. Soc. Psychol.* **4**, 65–72.

Rosenfeld, H. M. (1967). Nonverbal reciprocation of approval: an experimental analysis. *J. Exp. Soc. Psychol.* **3**, 102–111.

Scheflen, A. E. (1964). The significance of posture in communication systems. *Psychiatry*, **27**, 316–321.

Scheflen, A. E. (1965). "Stream and Structure of Communication Behavior: Context Analysis of a Psychotherapy Session". Eastern Pennsylvania Psychiatric Institute, Philadelphia.

Scheflen, A. E. (1968). Human communication: behavioral programs and their integration in interaction. *Behav. Sci.* **13**, 44–55.

Scheflen, A. E. (1969). Behavioral programs in human communication. *In* "General Systems Theory and Psychiatry" (Eds W. Gray, F. J. Duhl and N. D. Rizzo). Little, Brown.

Scheflen, A. E. (1973). "Communicational Structure of a Psychotherapy Transaction". Indiana University Press, Bloomington and London.

Scheflen, A. E., Schaeffer, J. and Kendon, A. (1970). A comparison of videotape and moving picture film in research in human communication. *In* "Videotape Techniques in Psychiatric Training and Treatment" (Ed. M. M. Berger). Brunner. New York.

Shaw, M. E. (1964). Communication networks. *In* "Advances in Experimental Social Psychology" (Ed. L. Berkowitz), Vol. 1. Academic Press, New York.

Sommer, R. (1961). Leadership and group geography. *Sociometry*, **24**, 99–109.

Sommer, R. (1965). Further studies of small group ecology. *Sociometry*, **28**, 337–348.

Sommer, R. (1967). Small group ecology. *Psychol. Bull.* **67**, 145–152.

Strodtbeck, F. L. and Hook, L. H. (1961). The social dimension of a twelve man jury table. *Sociometry*, **24**, 397–415.

Talland, G. A. (1955). Task and interaction process: Some characteristics of therapeutic group discussion. *J. Abnorm. Soc. Psychol.* **50**, 105–109.

Thomas, E. J. and Fink, C. F. (1963). Effects of group size. *Psychol. Bull.* **60**, 371–384.

Van Vlack, J. (1964). Filming psychotherapy from the viewpoint of a research cinematographer. *In* "Methods of Research in Psychotherapy" (Eds L. A. Gottschalk and A. A. Auerbach), pp. 15–24. Appleton-Century-Crofts, New York.

Vine, I. (1970). Communication by facial-visual signals: a review and analysis of their role in face-to-face encounters. *In* "Social Behavior in Birds and Mammals" (Ed. J. H. Crook), pp. 279–354. Academic Press, London and New York.

Weisbrod, Rita M. (1965). Looking behavior in a discussion group. Term paper submitted for psychology 546 under the direction of Prof. Longabaugh, Cornell University, Ithaca, N.Y.

Watson, O. M. and Graves, T. D. (1966). Quantitative research in proxemic behavior. *Amer. Anthrop.* **68**, 971–985.

Watson, Jeanne and Potter, R. J. (1962). An analytic unit for the study of interaction. *Hum. Relat.* **15**, 243–263.

3

A Structural Analysis of the Social Behaviour of a Semi-captive Group of Chimpanzees

Jan A. R. A. M. van Hooff

1 Introduction

The study of primate behaviour started in the laboratory, and, initially, developed largely outside the main stream of ethology. The research centered around classical psychological themes such as learning and intelligence, or was concerned with the variables affecting phenomena such as "sexual" or "social" behaviour (e.g. Yerkes, 1943). The pioneer field study of the chimpanzee by Nissen (1931) testifies, however, that the need for a better understanding of the natural behaviour was felt early. Yet detailed ethograms of most primate species, which would be the basis for further causal analyses (Tinbergen, 1942, 1951; Lorenz, 1960; Kaufman and Rosenblum, 1966) remained lacking. Until 1958, when Carpenter wrote a review on primate field work, this branch of research—and I include here observational studies on zoo colonies like those of Zuckerman (1932), Chance (1956) and Kummer (1957)—

accounted for only a relatively small part of the studies on primate behaviour.

The earliest field work was related primarily to problems concerning ecology, social structure, population dynamics, etc. (e.g. Carpenter, 1934, 1940; Collias and Southwick, 1952). In recent years the number of man-hours devoted to field observations have shown a tremendous increase (Altmann, 1967), and, besides ecological and sociological questions, specifically ethological questions have also attracted interest. More or less detailed ethograms, especially of the social behaviour patterns of several species, have thus been obtained. Outstanding catalogues of social behaviour have been given, for instance, by Kummer (1957), Altmann (1962), Bertrand (1969), Kaufman and Rosenblum (1966), van Lawick-Goodall (1968) and Spivak (1968). However, with respect to the structure of social behaviour and the categorization of social behaviour patterns, most studies are still largely descriptive.

In a review Plutchik (1964) examined the categories that had been set up for primate behaviour by previous authors. The number and types of categories appeared to vary considerably and showed bias towards the particular problem at which research was directed. In most experimental studies he found only a rather small number of categories, each consisting of only a few behavioural acts. Sometimes inferences about concepts like "dominance" or "sex" appeared to be derived from the occurrence of one or a few behavioural acts (e.g. as when dominance is determined from the number of food pellets obtained by the members of a group). Naturalists, on the other hand, tended to set up broad categorial schemes encompassing a large number of behaviour elements. In the rare cases that a rationale for the categorization was given it was practically never of an empirical nature. Since Plutchik's review the same trend remains manifest in primate behaviour research; as yet attempts to reveal empirically the motivational structure underlying social behaviour remain exceptions, for instance for *Macaca mulatta* by Altmann (1968) and for *M. irus* by Thompson (1969).

Anyone who has been observing primates intensively acquires a certain knowledge about the structure of their social behaviour. He appreciates immediately that the elementary patterns of behaviour do not occur fortuitously, but are integrated in "meaningful" systems. Our own success as social beings depends largely on such insight. It permits us to make immediate subtle judgements on social behaviours and attitudes of our fellow men, which can hardly be made rationally explicit. The *Gestalt* perception mechanism which provides this insight is an invaluable aid in making us also aware of the structure of the behaviour of other species (Lorenz, 1959), but it does not exempt us from the obligation to try to present a rationale based on empirical criteria (Altmann, 1967; van Hooff, 1967a).

Especially with respect to human behaviour, our intuitive knowledge seems so self-evident, however, that it may have been an important factor in delaying systematic descriptions of our repertoire of social behaviour and the analysis of our communication processes (Ex, 1969). No doubt an ethological approach can also provide new insights into human behaviour (Tinbergen, 1968) and can be particularly fruitful for the understanding of child behaviour and abnormal behaviour (Ploog, 1963; Grant, 1965a, 1965b, 1968).

It is small wonder that attempts to categorize behaviour empirically have been developed in classical ethology, since initially it was concerned predominantly with non-mammalian species (see Tinbergen, 1942; Hinde, 1966, 1970; Marler and Hamilton, 1966). Here "anthropomorphic" understanding fails so obviously that the detailed description of the behaviour patterns and the analysis of their organization, as first steps in the study of the "machinery" of behaviour, loses the character of forcing an open door which such an approach might seem to have in connection with the study of human and primate behaviour.

Classification of behaviour patterns can be based on different criteria. By its behaviour an organism may adapt to its environment; so a classification in terms of function, the biologically significant consequences, presents itself as meaningful. This presupposes a knowledge of these consequences; detailing our knowledge in this respect is, however, one of the aims of the study of behaviour. For this reason ethologists have warned of the dangers involved in the *a priori* use of functional designations, not only in the classification but also in the description of the behaviour elements (Baerends, 1956; Tinbergen, 1963; Hinde, 1966).

Behaviour is a continuous stream of a finite number of more or less stereotyped, recurring movements and postures. These elementary patterns occur as a result of certain organizing or causal factors, both external and internal. If two elements had exactly the same causal basis, they would occur at the same time and their frequencies of transition with each of the other behaviour elements would be identical. One can thus assess the extent to which the causal bases of any two elements coincide by determining the extent to which their frequencies of occurrence in time or their frequencies of transition with other elements are correlated (Baerends, 1956; Hinde, 1966, 1970). Positive correlation indicates *relatively* similar causal bases, absence of correlation occurs if the causal bases are unrelated and negative correlation indicates inhibitory relations. So the temporal relationships represent a causal organization; the latter ordinarily also reflects a functional organization (Hinde, 1966, 1970).

A structural analysis of the behaviour repertoire and a classification of the behaviour elements on the basis of the temporal relationships presents itself as the logical preliminary to the investigation of the nature and interaction of causal factors and the functional aspects of behaviour. For various species such classifications have been made (for an enumeration, see Hinde, 1966, 1970).

Especially if the number of behaviour elements is large, the interpretation of the great number of correlation coefficients that can be obtained by comparing the temporal relations of the behaviour elements is difficult. A multivariate procedure like factor analysis or cluster analysis can then be the solution. Such a method was used for the first time in ethological research by Wiepkema (1961) in a study of the reproductive behaviour of the bitterling.

The aim of the present study is to reveal the structure of the social behaviour of the chimpanzee by means of similar methods. The analysis is based on the temporal relationships between behaviour patterns as revealed by sequential analysis, namely the patterns of transition frequencies.

2   The chimpanzee colony

After extensive observations on a large number of zoo primates under varying conditions, during which I became familiar with the behaviour characteristics of the chimpanzee, the main quantitative study was carried out at the 6571st Aeromedical Research Laboratory, New Mexico, USA, during the autumn of 1966. In May of the same year a chimpanzee consortium opened (for descriptions see van Hooff, 1967b; van Riper *et al.*, 1967). It was situated in semi-arid desert country, and consisted of a large circular outer enclosure with a diameter of 366 m and a surface of 105,000 m². It was surrounded by a moat about 5 m wide. In the enclosure were a number of concrete windbreak shelters. It supported a growth of native shrubs but was devoid of trees.

Annexed to the outer enclosure was a building which, apart from service and treatment facilities and observation stands, contained two large dormitory rooms of about 16 ×5 ×5 m. The animals could freely commute between each of the dormitories and the outside enclosure most of the day and all night. The animals were fed in the dormitories twice daily. All animals spent the night inside. The building was clearly the living centre of their habitat. Of the spacious outer enclosure only the quadrant nearest to it was used intensively; only during early morning and evening walks would the animals make use of the other quadrants.

The consortium was inhabited by 25 animals, 11 males and 14 females. Their ages, as registered on the official files, are given in Fig. 1.

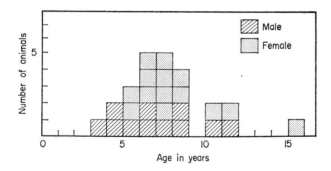

Fig. 1. Distribution of ages and sexes of the chimpanzees of the observation colony.

Comparison of the age and sex composition with data reported from the wild (reviewed by Itani and Suzuki, 1967) suggests that the colony matched the type of group which has been described as a mixed band (Reynolds and Reynolds, 1965) or a mixed nomadic group (Suzuki, 1969). Its average age was probably somewhat lower than that of the usual natural group. It was abnormal in that it contained juveniles which did not have a natural relation with an adult female. However, some of the youngest animals appeared to be relatively closely associated with an adult female which acted rather like a foster-mother (own observations, and Bobkowski, personal communication).

The animals had different origins. Some came from other institutions or menageries while others were imported from the wild; all of them had been kept under conventional zoo or laboratory conditions for some time. The question arises therefore to what extent the behaviour performed under the consortium conditions may deviate from that in a more natural situation; and, more important, to what extent this may have influenced the results of the present study. Comparative studies (Hall *et al.*, 1965; Kummer and Kurt, 1965; Eisenberg and Kuehn, 1966; Southwick, 1967; Bernstein, 1967; Rowell, 1967b) concerning the social behaviour of captive and wild groups suggest that there are hardly any differences with respect to the coordination of the elementary patterns of behaviour and their integration; the different conditions are more likely to affect higher-order phenomena like social organization. Captivity conditions certainly favour intense social interaction and thus an increase in the frequency of occurrence and the intensity of the elementary behaviour patterns, perhaps especially those which may be classified as agonistic patterns (Rowell, 1967b; Gartlan, 1968). The same is undoubtedly true for this colony as well (van Hooff, 1967b) and can be regarded as an advantage for this kind of study (Kaufmann and Kaufmann, 1963; Wickler, 1967). The fact that ecological conditions may differentially affect the frequency of the behaviour patterns has, however, several consequences for the analytical procedures (see below).

3 Determining the behaviour elements

Before the quantitative study at the Holloman consortium was carried out, numerous observations on different species of primates had been made in zoos (van Hooff, 1962, 1967a). Chimpanzees had been observed, notably in the zoological gardens of London, Chester, Arnhem and Rotterdam. These studies, largely of a qualitative nature, during which use was also made of photographic and cinematographic methods, yielded a catalogue of elements of social behaviour which afterwards, when studying the Holloman colony, had to be modified and adapted only at minor points. This similarity of elements under varying conditions can be taken as another argument for the rather stable nature of the elementary patterns of behaviour.

The great problem was what subdivisions of movements and postures should be regarded as behavioural elements. Behaviour is a continuous stream of movement which can be split up in a number of more or less stereotyped recurring elements. The question is, however, how far does

one split up and where does one lump? Most students of primate behaviour have not worried too much about this and have presented
catalogues in a matter-of-fact manner. Especially in experimental
studies, the catalogues are relatively small so that a great deal of lumping and/or selection must have been done (cf. Plutchik, 1964).

Because the purpose of the present study was to reveal empirically
the structure of social behaviour, I have tried to obtain as broad and
representative a selection of elements as possible without *a priori* lumping
of too many movements. However, no two movements performed by a
primate are exactly the same, especially as far as their orientation
component is concerned. It is nevertheless possible to distinguish a
number of typical elements of behaviour each of which has some more
or less stereotyped formal characteristics that distinguish it from other
elements, and which do not seem to be subdivisible into components
that can occur independently. These elements are what Altmann (1965)
calls "the natural units of social behaviour" and which, as he says, can
be empirically determined by dividing up the temporal continuity of
action just as the animals do. Of course an arbitrary decision must be
taken occasionally, but the temporal delimitation is undoubtedly the
least of our problems.

More problematical is the degree to which such units should be
formally distinguished. In the chimpanzee one can observe, for instance,
a number of forms in the way one animal contacts another with its
hand, differing both in intensity and form characteristics. It varies from
a forceful hitting, via a milder slapping to a soft smooth touching. One
can furthermore distinguish hitting with the open hand, or with the fist,
movements of the hand downwards from above, straight forwards, or
upwards from below. These elements, moreover, form a graded range
(cf. Marler, 1959, 1965; Kortlandt, 1967). According to these authors
chimpanzee behaviour is much more graded than that of fishes, birds
and also most lower primates. An indirect indication of this is that
ethologists working with animals like birds and fishes have not appeared
to worry very much about this question.

The instance mentioned may suffice to demonstrate that a catalogue
can be made very extensive indeed. von Cranach and Frenz (1969)
point out that not only can the use of too broadly defined units of
behaviour reduce the validity of the results, but so can the use of too
narrowly defined units. The behaviour catalogue then encompasses an
enormous number of elements, some of which are going to occur

comparatively rarely; this requires disproportionately long observation periods and increased amounts of labour in the analysis. It can, furthermore, lead to data which are less reliable because of the subtle distinctions that have to be made between gradually different elements and which are theoretically uninteresting. This problem presents itself especially in the ethological analysis of the social interaction of our own conspecifics where there are (or where we do more easily notice) many subtle variations in expression (Grant, 1965a).

Obviously a certain amount of lumping is inevitable. It is justified if one uses formal similarity as a criterion. This I have done, admittedly in some cases arbitrarily, and with the risk that some of the lumpings combine elements which may have a different function and meaning. I became aware in the course of the observations that a further splitting might have been desirable in a few cases.

As my object was to determine the structure of social behaviour, my catalogue has been restricted to behaviour elements that typically occur in a social setting, i.e. that are normally released only in the presence of fellows and/or are directed to fellows. Such behaviour patterns are most likely to be primarily communicative, that is their main function is to influence the behaviour of fellows. Elements which do not fulfil the above criterion, and whose function is primarily non-social, can nevertheless have signal value and affect the behaviour of others. This was expected to be the case for the two elements, *gymnastics* [11] and *autogroom* [22], which have therefore been included in the catalogue.[1] Two other such elements, "scratching" and "nose-wiping", have not been included for practical reasons. They occurred commonly both outside and inside interactions. If they have causal factors of a social nature, it is likely that their influence especially manifests itself in the frequency or intensity and duration of the movements. To reveal their social significance one should use scoring methods which preserve the absolute time scale and allow for analytical procedures such as coincidence correlation.

Special attention was given to the description of the vocal behaviour elements. A few types were determined on the basis of normal acoustical distinction. Since it appears difficult to match phonetic descriptions of vocalizations by different authors (Altmann, 1965), and since listeners to a given chimpanzee call give varying phonetic specifications (Nichols, 1954), I also took sound recordings. About 100 sufficiently clear vocal-

[1] The numbers refer to the element catalogue (see Section 5).

izations were analysed by means of Kay B/65 sonagrams. A representative selection is reported here.

Sonagrams can be made in two ways: a "narrow-band" sonagram has a great resolution of frequency (filter bandwidth 45 Hz) but a comparatively low resolution of time (about 1.5 ms); a "broad-band" sonagram, on the contrary, has a bandwidth of 300 Hz and a time resolution of 0.3 ms. Some of the distinctive features of chimpanzee vocalization can only be shown with the optimal resolutions. In contrast to other authors (Reynolds and Reynolds, 1965; Marler, 1969) I have therefore investigated not only the broad-band, but also the narrow-band spectrograms.

4 Methods of observation and recording

A "free" method of observation (von Cranach and Frenz, 1969) was selected with an open system of categories. I attempted to sample as randomly as possible, without a rigid system of rules, however, as to the periods of observation and the individuals to be observed. A similar technique has been used by Chance (1956) and Altmann (1962, 1965). The latter author has extensively discussed its merits and shortcomings.

It was attempted to divide the attention equally between all the individuals. So the number of times that an animal is represented in the protocols should ideally be equivalent to the "intensity" of its social activity. There certainly were deviations from this ideal. As soon as I began to feel that certain animals were predominantly present in my protocols, overcompensation may have occurred.

The group was usually observed between about 7 a.m. and 6 p.m., for periods of 1½ to 2 hours, during September and October 1966. Intervals between observation periods tended to coincide with the "dull" periods when the animals were mainly dozing or grooming. Activity peaks occurred during the first part of the morning and in the afternoon and were to some extent determined by the routine of caretaking. Altogether about 200 hours were spent in active observation.

I regarded as a "social action chain" of an animal any sequence of behaviour elements, classified by me as social ones, that was delimited by periods of non-social activity or non-activity of the order of 10 to 20 seconds, or by a change of social partner. Usually social action chains are part of interactions, that is there are clearly two or more animals involved, of which at least one actively orients itself to another during the chain of social behaviour elements. Usually the social orientation was reciprocal. Kummer (1967) has emphasized the existence of tripartite relations in Hamadryas baboons, where three animals simultaneously "play a different role" in one social engagement. Such relations also exist in the chimpanzee. Yet it is possible usually to distinguish two "main" interactors which are reciprocally oriented, as is apparent from the direction of their glancing and locomotion. As it appeared difficult in many cases to follow more than two individuals, attention was focused on the "main" interactors. In a number of cases this undoubtedly means an oversimplification, imposed by practical limitations.

Although it appears difficult to make the above criteria completely and objectively explicit, I did not experience any uncertainty with it in practice.

Written protocols of the interactions were taken by means of a specially developed shorthand technique. Only the sequence and the relative duration of the behaviour elements of the two interacting apes were scored. Some behaviour patterns which are short but nevertheless distinct may occur in bouts (for instance "hitting" and "biting"). In such cases only the bout itself was scored if the single consecutive acts were each less than 5 to 10 seconds apart.

For fast interactions, records were taken immediately afterwards. Like Chance (1956) I found that a clear picture of the interaction could be maintained in memory for a short stretch of time if attention was not diverted to other things. If interactions proceeded more slowly, records could be taken simultaneously, practically without interrupting observation.

In fast interactions there sometimes was a quick alternation or succession of movements, so that the exact order and the number of times of occurrence of these behaviour elements could not be recorded reliably. Such a phase of interaction was then condensed to a simplified form; the behaviour elements concerned were then scored as each having occurred once simultaneously. Such a decision is in favour of the null-hypothesis, which states that behaviour is a random succession of patterns. In fact, only those interactions were scored about which I felt fully confident and during which the interacting animals were not farther than about 50 m away. At larger distances it became too difficult to observe significant details. At closer distances there also remained the problem that not all the behaviour elements which have been distinguished were equally conspicuous or significant in a physical and perhaps also in a psychological sense (e.g. movements like "screaming" versus "panting").

For the reasons mentioned the scored frequency may, for each behaviour element, represent a different fraction of the frequency of real occurrence. In view of the type of analysis used (see below) this is no serious problem as long as the ratios of the scored frequencies of transition from one behaviour element into another remain representative. Although I feel fairly confident that they are, objective support for this is lacking. The absence of another experienced observer sufficiently familiar with the details of chimpanzee social behaviour precluded a mutual comparison of records in order to obtain some insight into observer reliability. A high degree of agreement between the records of two observers would still not give certainty, however, that the main source of bias, selective perception, is of insignificant influence, especially with observers of the same methodological and theoretical background.

5 The descriptive data: the elements of social behaviour

5.1 INTRODUCTORY REMARKS

Descriptions of social behaviour patterns of the chimpanzee can be found in various sources. They are often rather fragmentary or put in terms which appeal more to an intuitive understanding (e.g. the highly suggestive, but rather anthropomorphic accounts by Köhler, 1922, 1925). In some studies thorough descriptions of particular aspects of social behaviour may be found; thus sexual and parental behaviour have received a great deal of attention from various authors, including, amongst others, the school of Yerkes (see Yerkes, 1943). Until recently behavioural observations on chimpanzees were made in conventional zoo and laboratory settings (van Hooff, 1967b). It is unlikely that the social behaviour could manifest itself in all its aspects under such conditions.

Although Nissen made a pioneer field study in 1931, it was not until the last decade that detailed knowledge on the behaviour of free living chimpanzees began to become available. Many field studies are concerned mainly with ecology, group structure and non-social behaviour, and provide at the most rather general descriptions of social behaviour (e.g. Goodall, 1962, 1963; Kortlandt, 1962; de Bournonville, 1967; Itani and Suzuki, 1967; Suzuki, 1969).

A few other workers provided specific information concerning social behaviour patterns (Goodall, 1965; van Lawick-Goodall, 1967; Reynolds and Reynolds, 1965). The most comprehensive treatment has been given by van Lawick-Goodall (1968) and I shall therefore in particular compare her descriptions and mine. Chimpanzee vocalizations have been treated by Reynolds and Reynolds (1965) and Marler (1969). Kortlandt (1967) has described, among other things, a number of gestures. So there is already quite a substantial basis for comparison.

5.2   PATTERNS OF LOCOMOTION

During social interaction the chimpanzee may perform various types of locomotion, both quadrupedal and bipedal. In this respect this species may be unique, as I have neither observed nor found described such a variety of locomotory patterns in other primates. The following patterns were distinguished:

1. *Smooth approach* This label refers to the normal, free and easy type of locomotion by which an animal may approach a fellow at a walking pace in the knuckle-walking gait typical of the African apes (Tuttle, 1967). An animal walking around in a group may often go in the direction of a partner, though actually aiming at, for instance, food or a sitting corner in that same direction. Therefore, only those approaches have been scored as such which occurred in the context of some social interaction with a partner and led to close proximity.

2. *Hesitant approach* This refers to approach at a walking pace as well; it has, however, a hesitant character in that it is occasionally interrupted or broken off before the actor gets near to the partner. It may be performed occasionally in a more or less crouched manner.

3. *Gallop* The animal moves fast in a trot, often not at full speed but in a restrained manner. The movement may be directed towards or away from a fellow. It lacks the obvious tension and brusqueness of the charge (see below) while it does not share its conspicuous pilo-erection. The same element has been described as the "play chase" by van Lawick-Goodall (1968). The gallop can, however, also occur outside the play context.

4. *Sway walk* A bipedal type of approach, with a varying mode of performance. The animal steps in an exaggerated manner placing its

feet slightly apart, and rocking sideways. Its arms, fully stretched or slightly bent with the elbows outward, are extended laterally at an angle which may approach 90° (Fig. 2). Usually there is strong pilo-erection. This pattern corresponds clearly with the "bipedal swagger" as described by van Lawick-Goodall (1968). The animal may also swing its arms rhythmically in a parallel fashion in front of its body in a lateral plane, or wave them about more or less irregularly above its head. It then keeps its legs in a more normal position, and does not

Fig. 2. Sway walk [4].

always assume the spread stance which is characteristic for the "swag-ger". van Lawick-Goodall (1968) has described an almost identical pattern under the heading "bipedal arm waving and running"; she saw it most frequently in interaction with baboons. Yerkes (1943) noted that the arm-waving display is usually accompanied by "screams, barks or shouts". In our observations this occurred in a minority of cases. The difference between "arm waving" and the "swagger" was of a gradual nature. As I have not consistently distinguished between them, I have lumped both patterns for the purpose of the present analy-sis. Nevertheless, my records suggest that both patterns may represent a slightly different motivation, as is also suggested by van Lawick-Goodall (1968).

5. *Stamp trot* The animal walks or trots along while stamping heavily with its hind feet on the ground. Often this is done in a rhythmical manner in that one foot is placed down gently and the other with force. The head is mostly kept rather low and tucked back between the shoulders which are pulled upwards. The head may make low amplitude vertical rocking movements in a rhythm one or several times as fast as the stamping. In a more intense form the animal may leave the ground with all fours and move along jumping in an undulating fashion (Fig. 3). The pattern may be accompanied by the *rising hoot* [47] or the *scream* [42].

Fig. 3. *Stamp trot* [5] in most intense form.

This spectacular pattern has been described by many authors, most strikingly by Köhler (1921). van Lawick-Goodall (1968) does not set it clearly apart but gives a rather general description under the headings "charging, slapping, stamping, dragging, throwing, and drumming" and "stamping and slapping". She distinguishes explicitly the "quadrupedal hunch": the animal "stands with back rounded and head bent and slightly pulled back between the shoulders". It "may then move forward slowly or in a rapid charge". She interprets this pattern as a high-intensity threat. I have frequently encountered a pattern quite similar to the one described which I at first distinguished as the "stiffgait", but later considered as the lowest intensity form of the stamp trot. The animal walks in a stiff manner with all its hairs on end, sometimes putting down the hind legs with just a bit more force than normal, while its head, tucked down between the pulled up shoulders, makes up-and-down movements of low amplitude.

6. *Brusque rush* This is a tense type of locomotion during which the animal moves towards a partner quadrupedally at full speed, often with the hairs erected (Fig. 4). It corresponds to van Lawick-Goodall's (1968) "attacking charge".

Fig. 4. Adult animal *brusque rushes* [6] after a sub-adult and is about to *trample* [41] it. Sub-adult displays *bared-teeth scream* [42].

7. *Flight* This is said to occur when an animal moves away from another at full speed. It may be accompanied by the *bared-teeth scream* [42] (cf. Fig. 19). An identical definition is given by van Lawick-Goodall (1968). Both Yerkes (1943) and Reynolds and Reynolds (1965) have observed that a fleeing animal might show diarrhoeic defecation and urination.

8. *Avoidance* I considered this to be any locomotion away from a partner during which the animal moved at a trot or at a walking pace. Avoidance may have a very slow and cautious character, and then corresponds obviously with van Lawick-Goodall's (1968) "creeping away". This author moreover distinguishes "hiding", an example of which was also described by Köhler (1922). This pattern has not come to my attention. I have only classified a movement as an *avoidance* when it is manifested by the animal's course and glances that it was directed with respect to some fellow. Thus I have excluded the many locomotions which in a group of animals can be accidentally directed away from a fellow. I suspect though, that some of these "casual walks away" may have been, motivationally, avoiding movements as well.

As a low-intensity form of *avoidance* we may consider the simple movement of turning one's back towards another, for instance, while eating. This movement has not been included in the category of *avoidance*, however.

9. *Flinch, shrink* This may vary from a slight ducking of the head, via more intense withdrawal movements of the upper part of the body, to short momentary actual retreat movements, in that the animal takes

one or more steps backwards. van Lawick-Goodall's (1968) "startle reaction" might be classified under this heading or under my *parry* [16], depending on whether the withdrawal or the shielding element dominates. The causal context of her "startle reaction" is more restricted, however, as it is not typically performed in social interaction but rather in reaction to sudden stimuli like noises, insects, birds, etc.

10. *Squat-bob* An animal may approach a fellow quite closely by shuffling towards it, slowly or rather rapidly, in a squatting position with the hind legs more or less strongly flexed (cf. Fig. 40(b)). The centre of gravity is usually above the animal's feet, as it will occasionally not support itself with its arms (Fig. 5). The body is usually kept in a low

Fig. 5. Sub-adult is *squat-bobbing* [10] in front of *a*-male, meanwhile performing the *rapid ohoh series* [49]. The *a*-male *hoots* [47].

horizontal or oblique position. Close in front of its partner, the animal may bow down by flexing its arms or it may flex and stretch its arm in turn a few times, thus making bobbing movements with the upper body. The animal frequently performs the rapid *ohoh* vocalization [49]. This pattern undoubtedly corresponds with the "bobbing" and "bowing" of van Lawick-Goodall (1968).

11. *Gymnastics* This is probably not a social behaviour pattern in the strict sense because it can also be observed in animals that are alone (Bierens de Haan, 1952). As it may occur, however, in social interactions and as it seems subject to social facilitation, I have included it here. The label unites a variety of exuberant locomotory patterns like climbing, swinging, dangling from arms or feet, pivoting, rolling over, turning somersaults, etc. It may also incorporate various activities with objects like sticks, pieces of cloth, etc. Such patterns have been described

by Köhler (1921) as *Lustige Variationen der Ortsbewegung*, by Reynolds and Reynolds (1965) as "acrobatics" and by van Lawick-Goodall (1968) as "locomotory play".

5.3 POSTURES AND GESTURES NOT INVOLVING BODY CONTACT

12. *Arm sway* Except for the locomotion component it is practically identical to the *sway-walk* [4] (Fig. 6). It combines the "bipedal swagger on the spot" and the "bipedal arm waving" of van Lawick-Goodall. She remarks that the "bipedal arm waving" may be performed "while uttering the 'waa'-bark or screaming". I did not find that this was typically so.

Fig. 6. Successive phases of the *arm-sway* [12].

13. *Stamp* This pattern in turn is practically identical to the *stamp-trot* [5], except for the locomotion component. The animal may stamp with its feet or slam with its hand either on the ground as was most usual in the Holloman colony or on some resounding object. The latter is known both from the wild (Nissen, 1931; Goodall, 1965; Reynolds and Reynolds, 1965) and from zoos.

14. *Vertical head nod* At its lowest intensity form this pattern may consist of a few up-and-down movements of the head, performed at a frequency of roughly 2 to 3 shakes per second. In contrast to the head nodding which is common in humans the head does not pivot upon the neck, but the turning point lies lower in the shoulder region. The pattern may be performed while the actor stands quadrupedally or while he is sitting. In the latter case the movement may be performed in a more intense manner, though the tempo is slower. The turning point may now be as

low as the lumbar region and the animal may rock forward-downward
and backward-upward. At high amplitudes of movement the legs may
come loose from the ground during the backward-upward phase (Fig.
7). This pattern has not been described by van Lawick-Goodall (1968).

Fig. 7. Intense *vertical rocking* [14];
meanwhile the *silent pout face* [53]
is shown.

15. *Upsway* The arm, which in its normal supporting, resting, or man-
ipulatory position is directed more or less downwards, is moved upwards
and forwards in a short jerky movement, usually in a pronated position
(i.e. hand palm downwards). While swinging forwards the hand hangs
down rather limp, its back turned forwards. When the arm stops moving
at a more or less horizontal position the hand may swing out upwards.
The fingers are in the normal semi-flexed position. The pattern is mostly
performed while the animals are out of reach of each other and even
when this is not the case the fellow is only rarely seen to be actually
struck. This pattern probably corresponds with the "hitting away" of
van Lawick-Goodall (1968): "a hitting movement with the back of the
hand directed towards the threatened animal". It is not mentioned
whether the arm is brought forward from below or from above. In the
jungle habitat Kortlandt (1967) never saw this upsway; instead he
observed a gesture during which the bent hand was brought down and
forward from above. The same pattern was called "flapping" by van
Lawick-Goodall. I recorded such a "downsway" only six times in the
Holloman colony. Only once did I see a version in which the arm swung
out to the ipsilateral side, back of the hand in front, in the direction of
an animal behind. I did not observe the "arm raising" of van Lawick-
Goodall in which the palm of the hand is oriented towards a fellow.
16. *Parry* One, or sometimes both arms are raised. The forearm is
kept in a roughly horizontal position over or in front of the head, thus

shielding it off from possible beats from a fellow. van Lawick-Goodall (1968) has described this pattern under the name "startle reaction" and states that it has been incorporated into the repertoire of threat gestures. *Parry* may also correspond with her "bending away".

17. *Hold out hand* A variety of forms were observed. Most common is a form in which the actor, either sitting or standing, extends its arm roughly horizontally towards a fellow. The arm is in a position about midway between pronation and supination (i.e. with the thumb up). The hand may be bent at the wrist so that its back is turned to the partner with the fingers bent or fully stretched (Fig. 8). It is my im-

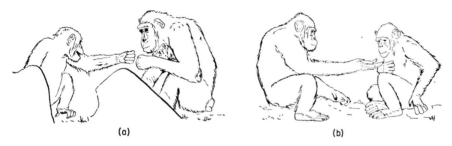

(a)   (b)

Fig. 8. Two common versions of *hold out hand* [17]; (a) with wrist and fingers bent; (b) with hand almost fully stretched.

pression that the first posture occurs more in subordinate animals and the second more in dominant animals; I have not been able, however, to verify this empirically. It has been reported by many authors, e.g. von Allesch (1921), Köhler (1922), Yerkes (1943), Goodall (1963), Kortlandt (1967). Not infrequently seen also is a version in which the arm is in the supinated position with the hand palm up (cf. Fig. 28a); van Lawick-Goodall (1968) observed that during courtship a male might "beckon" by stretching his arm and then making sweeping movements towards himself, the hand making an arc through the air. Such *Winken* has also been reported by Köhler (1922). This form I observed only three times in the Holloman colony and once in the Chester Zoo. I once observed that an adult female made similar "beckoning" movements, looking back while stretching out one arm backwards, parallel to the body axis, during *mount-presenting* [18]. Once I observed how an adolescent male, keeping its arms in the supinated position, "beckoned" by bending and stretching the wrist and simultaneously bending and stretching its four fingers rapidly. Gardner and Gardner

(1969) noted that this gesture occurred naturally in the chimpanzee to which they taught the American Sign Language (ASL), and they pointed out the remarkable coincidence that in ASL there are similar symbols for "give me" and "hurry" (approximately the same pattern, but performed rapidly). These symbols could, therefore, easily be incorporated in the chimp's repertoire. Tervoort (1953), who has made an extensive study of the "esoteric" gesture language that deaf and dumb children develop spontaneously in their interactions, recorded quite similar gestures for the notions "give" and "hurry".

I saw once that an animal, looking back at another individual, stretched out its foot towards it. The same has been observed by Köhler (1922) and Kortlandt (1967).

A remarkable variant is the "stretch over". When assuming the mating position, adult males are commonly seen to stretch one or sometimes both hands forwards and slightly upwards, hand palm down, over the back of a presenting female (Fig. 9a). This fleeting version was not recorded as a separate gesture. On five occasions, however, the "stretch over" was performed towards a female at a distance and may have functioned as a signal indicating the actor's "willingness" to mate (Fig. 9b). In a peculiar version, seen only once, an adult male made

(a)   (b)

Fig. 9. (a) A male stretches one hand over the back of a female while preparing to *mount* [36]. (b) The *stretch over* [17] performed towards a female from a distance.

smooth downward waving movements with both hands towards a female standing in front of him. Thereupon, the female crouch-presented and mating took place.

18. *Mount-present* In accordance with common usage, presenting refers to a behaviour pattern in which an animal orients itself actively or remains oriented more or less passively with its hind-quarters to a

fellow. In the chimpanzee several forms of this presenting can be distinguished. When *mount-presenting*, the animal stands quadrupedally with all its limbs in the normal standing position. It is mostly performed in a rather passive manner. The actor would not actively approach a partner, but would just stop during walking. The behaviour pattern was frequently, but not always, directed to young individuals which might perform the "mount-standing" described under *mount-walking* [37]. van Lawick-Goodall (1967) gives a picture of a mother who stands with one leg placed in a position somewhat extending backwards, thus providing a "step" for the youngster to climb onto its mother's back. In this group, where mothers with offspring were absent, this behaviour was not seen.

19. *Crouch-present* The hind-quarters of an animal are turned towards a partner, mostly in an active manner. The actor may even push itself backwards against the partner. The pattern differs from *mount-presenting* [18] by the marked flexing of the hind legs, so that the genital area may only be a few centimetres above the ground. Often there is flexion of the arms as well; thus the body can be brought into a horizonal position close to or even touching the ground. The animal may then remain resting on its knuckles, either with the arms fully stretched (Fig. 10(b)), or with the strongly bent elbows pointing up backwards (Fig. 10(a)); it may also rest on its elbows, the underarms lying on the substrate. Combination of these postures occurs also. Meanwhile the animal may look backwards over its shoulder or along its arms. The pattern may be occasionally accompanied by low-intensity forms of the *bared-teeth yelp* [43] and *bared-teeth scream* [42] displays. Extensive descriptions of *crouch-presenting* have been given by Yerkes and Elder (1936) and van Lawick-Goodall (1968). It may be done mutually (Fig. 10(c)).

20. *Crouch* The animal lowers its body by flexing its arms and legs until it is in a horizontal position touching the substrate. In extreme cases, moreover, the animal may tuck its head away between its drawn-up shoulders and either look obliquely to its partner from this position or press its face against the ground. The posture may strongly resemble the motor-component of intense *crouch-presenting* [19]. A posture was distinguished as a *crouch* when the hind-quarters of the actor were not directed to the partner, and when it did not contain the locomotion component, directed to the partner, which is characteristic for *squat-bobbing* [10]. It has also been distinguished by van Lawick-Goodall (1968) and Wilson and Wilson (1968).

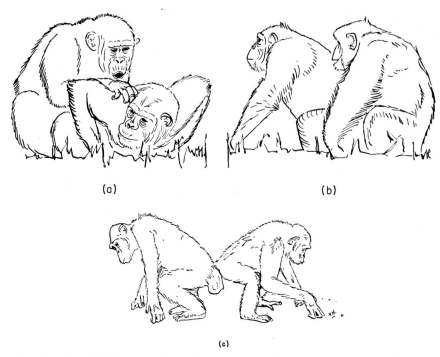

(a)   (b)

(c)

Fig. 10. (a and b) Two versions of the *crouch-presenting* [19] posture; the males *mate* [35] while in the squatting position. (c) Two animals *crouch-present* mutually.

21. *Groom-present* A chimpanzee may adapt this posture after walking up to a partner or after being approached. It is quite variable. The animal may stand, sit or lie down in front of the partner to which it may turn its flanks, back or shoulders. If the partner starts grooming the presenting animal usually keeps rather motionless; it permits the partner to change the position of its limbs or head and it usually then maintains this position at least for a short time even if it seems occasionally somewhat awkward and uncomfortable.

In cases where an animal permitted another to groom it without responding by actively turning some body parts to the groomer, this has not been regarded as *groom-presenting*.

An extensive description of this pattern has been given by van Lawick-Goodall (1968).

22. *Autogroom* This name, adopted from Sparks (1967), designates grooming activity (see [33]) which is directed to the chimpanzee's own body. Only certain parts of the body are accessible to this treatment;

particularly the limbs are favoured. The behaviour pattern has been reported by many authors, e.g. Yerkes (1933, 1943), and van Lawick-Goodall (1968).

23. *Watch* During many of the behaviour elements described here the actor watches its interaction partner. Animals which are not interacting also regularly watch other animals usually with short casual glances. Here *watching* was only counted as such if it occurred in the course of social interaction, but not as part of other behaviour elements and if it lasted for at least a few seconds. There are different forms of looking at a fellow; and these can certainly reflect different motivational states (van Hooff, 1962, 1967a). Thus one can distinguish in the chimpanzee, as in many other primates, between straight, more or less fixed stares, looking obliquely from the corners of the eye, and a quick and repeated shifting of the gaze towards and more or less away from the partner. These forms have not been distinguished here, because their observation was not reliable. van Lawick-Goodall (1968) mentions "glaring", interpreted as a low-intensity threat; it clearly falls into this category but is certainly not identical with it.

5.4 GESTURES AND ACTIVITIES INVOLVING BODY CONTACT

5.4.1 *Simple forms of contact with the hand*
24. *Touch* Any contacting of a fellow's body with the hand which is performed in a smooth or even gentle and "careful" manner. There are a great variety of forms of *touching*; they may be directed, moreover, to different parts of the companion's body. Common is the case in which an animal that performs the *hold-out-hand* gesture [17] finally *touches* the partner; often the region of the partner's mouth is *touched* with the fingers or the knuckles or back of the inward-bent hand. The *touch* may also be directed to the shoulder region or the head. Once an animal was seen to stroke another over the head a few times with the palm of its hand. On seven occasions an animal *touched* the chin of a partner by holding it in the palm of its hand, as if supporting it. On four occasions an animal put one or more fingers in the mouth of the partner and hooked them behind the partner's teeth for some time. The *touch* may also be directed towards the genital area. Thus it was seen four times that an animal took the erect penis of a young male in the palm of its hand for a few seconds. On four occasions an animal

gently patted the scrotum of a large male with the palm of the hand; once this was directed to the anal area of the male. On four occasions an animal *touched* the genital swelling of a female by supporting it from below with the palm of the hand for some time.

On 20 occasions it was seen that an animal gently took the hand of a fellow and brought it into contact with its own body. This occurred nine times while the actor was *groom-presenting* and in all cases the partner reacted by grooming. On seven occasions the hand of the partner was thus led to the mouth of the actor; five times the actor then took the fingers in its mouth for a short while (also reported by von Allesch, 1921), and twice the back of the hand was pressed against its chin. Hand leading was also observed in connection with *clinging* [39].

Many authors have described touching patterns, stroking and leading by the hand, and interpreted these as expressions of friendliness or as signals to alert another chimpanzee (e.g. Köhler, 1922; Nissen, 1931; Yerkes, 1943; van Lawick-Goodall, 1967, 1968). In his experiments on social cooperation Crawford (see Yerkes, 1943) noted how animals might "lead" each other to move or behave in a particular manner by gently pushing the body or limbs. Such gentle "re-positioning" forms also part of the *grooming* pattern [33]. Kortlandt (1967) and van Lawick-Goodall (1968) mention that two chimpanzees may make contact with their hands in a manner that somewhat resembles our hand-shake. In the Holloman colony I never observed this pattern.

25. *Handwrestle* With this activity usually two animals are engaged in it simultaneously while lying or sitting near to each other. One animal may reach out with its hand (occasionally also with its foot) and grasp the other's hand or foot. Then both may try to get a good grip of the other's hand, simultaneously trying to wrest away from the other's grip. This pattern corresponds with van Lawick-Goodall's (1968) "finger-wrestling".

26. *Grasp or poke* This category includes a variety of grasping and poking movements directed at various parts of the partner's body which lack the smooth and gentle character of *touching* [24], but are nevertheless not as brusque and vigorous as *tugging* [29]. They can be of a boisterous character, but remain nevertheless relaxed. van Lawick-Goodall (1968) does not distinguish these movements as a separate category, but mentions "tickling and poking" under the category of play behaviour.

27. *Pull and shake limbs* It was often observed that an animal got hold

of a leg or an arm of a fellow and shook it or pulled at it repeatedly with some force, occasionally dragging the partner along for a short distance. Usually the pattern was performed in a boisterous manner, but without signs of "tension"; only a few times was it performed vigorously in a brusque manner. van Lawick-Goodall (1968) does not describe the pattern in this typical form. Under the heading "attack" she mentions that animals might be dragged along or lifted from the ground by a limb and then be slammed down again, by mature males. I never saw such an intense form. The more relaxed form I observed was, moreover, performed by all age classes.

28. *Hit* Normally the arm is brought down from above and the partner is hit with either the palm of the hand or the knuckles ("slapping"; van Lawick-Goodall, 1968). The movement may be performed, with some or much force, from a bi- (Fig. 11) or tripedal position, but rarely

Fig. 11. The ape on the left is raising its arm to *hit* [28] from a bipedal position.

from a sitting or lying position. Less often the following variations were observed: a hitting movement during which the arm was brought upwards from below, and the partner was struck with the knuckles (three times); a punching movement in which the arm was suddenly stretched forward in a horizontal direction (twice).

Similar to punching is "pushing". Here, force is applied only after the knuckles or back of the hand contact the partner's body. It was reliably observed only five times and is not included in this category.

The category does include "hitting with objects" (seen four times). The objects were a large piece of cloth and sticks. Hitting or near hitting with saplings or sticks has been observed by Kortlandt and Kooij (1963), and by van Lawick-Goodall (1968). Kortlandt (1962, 1967) could release intense forms of this behaviour by presenting a stuffed leopard. "Aimed throwing", also reported by these authors, was observed on three occasions; it is not included in this category.

29. *Tug* This occurs when an animal gets hold of the body, especially the skin or fur of a partner and gives vehement tugs. In doing so the animal may occasionally pull out tufts of hair (see also Kortlandt, 1967). van Lawick-Goodall (1968) describes this pattern under the headings "lifting" and "hair pulling". She also distinguishes "scratching", during which the animal flexes its fingers and draws its nails rapidly across the skin of its fellow; it was performed exclusively by females. I have not recognized this pattern as a separate category.

5.4.2 *Contact with the mouth*

30. *Mouth-mouth contact* An ape may bring its head smoothly near the head of a fellow and bring its lips in contact with those of the partner; occasionally it may contact also other parts of the partner's face or the neck with its lips. Especially if the face of the partner is directed downwards the actor may flex its arms and cock its head before making contact. The partner may do the same or remain passive. On a number of occasions the addressee was observed to chew something, but frequently this was not the case. The lips may be kept more or less together in the normal position or perhaps slightly protruded while the mouth is almost closed; the mouth can also be slightly opened while the lips remain covering the teeth. On a few occasions it was accompanied by the *open-mouth silent bared-teeth* face [52b]. Yerkes (1943) refers to this gesture as a kiss. van Lawick-Goodall (1967, 1968) mentions that mothers "kissed" their infants by lightly putting their lips to some parts of the infant's body.

31. *Gnaw* The actor may make repeated gnawing movements onto the limbs or body of a partner. As an observer may notice when he himself is the partner this *gnawing* may be done with some pressure but never in the jerky and brusque manner which is characteristic for *biting* [32]. The lips are usually not withdrawn; they may even be bent inwards so that they protect the partner's skin from the gnawing teeth (Fig. 12). van Lawick-Goodall (1968) describes "tickling" with the mouth as a

Fig. 12. Gnawing [31] with inwards bent upper lip.

series of "nibbling muzzling movements with the lips pulled inwards over the teeth".

32. *Bite* This category consists of brusque biting and snapping movements (biting intention movements). The biting is done in a jerky and tense brusque manner. After having put its teeth onto the skin of the partner, the actor holds on for a while. In this respect it is usually distinct from the repeated, comparatively smooth movements of *gnawing* [31]. van Lawick-Goodall (1968), who also described this pattern, observed that the only visible after-effect is often a wet spot of saliva on the fur of the other.

I occasionally noticed a bruise or scratch afterwards. Blood was seen to be drawn only on three occasions. Once an adult male inflicted serious wounds upon the hand, head and shoulders of a half-grown female; he kept on "biting" one of the hands for many tens of seconds. Much of the damage may have been caused by the frantic efforts on the part of the screaming female to wrench its hands out of the male's grip.

5.4.3 *Elaborate forms of body contact and allomanipulation*

33. *Groom* This name refers to the "allogrooming" or picking through the fur of another individual which is well known for many primate species (e.g. Yerkes, 1933; Sparks, 1967). It has also received ample attention in the chimpanzee literature (e.g. Köhler, 1922; Yerkes, 1943; Goodall, 1965; van Lawick-Goodall, 1968). Mostly both hands and the lips are used in grooming; one hand mainly pushes the hairs apart whereas dislodged particles may be picked up with the other hand or with the lips (Fig. 13). van Lawick-Goodall (1968) has presented

quantitative data on the partner selection in grooming by chimpanzees. Fully adult males do and receive a great deal of all the grooming. Adult females also do a lot of grooming, mainly to their offspring, but receive less. There is general agreement that the significance of grooming encompasses more than a cleaning function (cf. Sparks, 1967).

Fig. 13. Grooming [33] with both hands and lips.

34. *Genital investigation and manipulation* Males, and occasionally females, would investigate the genital area of other females. It might take the form of a rather casual sniffing at or touching of the labia with the lips (Fig. 14). The labia and vulva might also be manipulated intensively and inspected both olfactorily and visually. van Lawick-Goodall (1968) gave a detailed description of this pattern which fully corresponds with my observations. She reports, moreover, that females were inspected by adult males most frequently at the onset of sexual swelling and immediately after detumescence, whereas infants were interested most in full swellings.

35. *Male mating* General descriptions of the male mating pattern have been given by Yerkes and Elder (1936) and van Lawick-Goodall (1968). I observed most commonly that the male squatted behind a *crouch-presenting* female [19] and bent over her back placing his arms on her shoulders or on the ground next to her (cf. Fig. 10). Next the penis was inserted and pelvic thrusts were given. Whether ejaculation took

Fig. 14.   Genital investigation [34] with lips and nose.

place could not be ascertained reliably and did not count therefore as a criterion. In cases where the female does not crouch sufficiently the male may stand behind the female bipedally with slightly flexed legs (Fig. 15), or stand over the female quadrupedally. Juveniles and half-grown males while squatting often lean backwards on their extended arms. The same has been observed for feral chimpanzees by van Lawick-Goodall (1968) and van Orshoven (personal communication).

Fig. 15.   Male mating [35] in a standing position.

36. *Mount* Both males and females, young and old, may mount another animal by adopting a position similar to the *male mating* [35] posture, in that they stand behind a partner and bring their body more or less over and above that of the partner. In cases where females are the actors or males are interacting with other males this pattern is different from *male mating* by definition. In cases where a male is interacting with a female the pattern was regarded as *mounting* if penis insertion was omitted. Pelvic thrusting was often shown both by females and males. On only one occasion a young male was seen to mount another individual over the head and to thrust onto the other's face. Maldirected mounting has been reported before in the literature, notably for young and inexperienced animals (e.g. Bingham, 1928; Mason, 1965).

37. *Mount-walk* Half-grown and small individuals were often seen to walk bipedally immediately behind the partner (usually an adult female), meanwhile resting their arms on the partner's back or clutching their arms around the thighs (Fig. 16). Such *mount-walking* (occasionally

(a)   (b)

Fig. 16. Mount-walking [37]: (a) common version; (b) rare version in which an adult animal stands over a youngster and both walk along together.

merely *mounting*) might go on for many minutes. Finch (1942) reported "walking in tandem" in infant chimpanzees that were caged together. This behaviour has not been described by van Lawick-Goodall (1968). In her group youngsters 0.5 to 4 years old commonly rode on their mother's back. In the Holloman group, where the youngest individual was 3.5 years old and where no mother-infant relations existed, riding was not observed. The formal similarity suggests that *mount-walking* may be ontogenetically related to "dorsal-riding".

38. *Embrace* An animal thus acting stands or squats in front of the other and clasps it by putting the arms around the partner's body; often this is done reciprocally. A few times one of the pair gently rolled over backwards so that the other came to lie on its belly. The embrace is usually maintained for some seconds and then released. Both Köhler (1922) and van Lawick-Goodall (1968) describe this pattern.

39. *Cling* By putting one or sometimes both arms around the body of the partner from the side or from the rear, bodily contact is made. It is done mainly by young individuals while standing or sitting and especially while walking at the side of another animal (Fig. 17). It is

Fig. 17. A sub-adult *clings* [39] to an adult female.

undoubtedly related to the more intense form of clinging that infants naturally direct to their mothers or a mother substitute (Köhler, 1922; Yerkes and Tomilin, 1935; Yerkes, 1943; van Lawick-Goodall, 1967). The activity can function as a reward (McCulloch, 1939) and is associated with a decrease in sensitivity to aversive stimuli (Mason and Berkson, 1962).

40. *Gnaw-wrestle* Two, sometimes more, animals engage mutually in this boisterous, yet free-and-easy activity. The two bodies may get completely entangled and roll about as one (Fig. 18). Meanwhile the animals keep grasping and gnawing each other at various places. This behaviour is well known and has been described by various authors as social play. It occurs typically, though not exclusively, in the younger

age classes (Köhler, 1922; Bingham, 1928; Yerkes, 1943; Loizos, 1967; van Lawick-Goodall, 1968). Milder forms may be observed between mother and child (Bingham, 1927; Yerkes and Tomilin, 1935; van Lawick-Goodall, 1967).

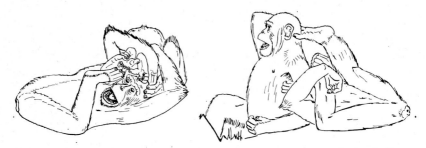

Fig. 18.   Gnaw-wrestling [40]. Note also the *relaxed open mouth* display [50].

41. *Trample* One ape brusquely jumps on top of another (cf. Fig. 4) and stamps vehemently on its back, often simultaneously grasping the hairs on shoulder and back. This usually lasts only a few seconds. The actor typically shows strong piloerection. *Trampling* corresponds with "stamping on the back" of van Lawick-Goodall (1968) and with the "kick and stomp" of Wilson and Wilson (1968).

5.5   FACIAL DISPLAYS AND VOCALIZATIONS

In the chimpanzee, like other primates (Andrew, 1963; van Hooff, 1967a), there appears to be a close association between facial expressions and vocalizations. High-intensity *screaming* [42], for instance, is associated with strong retraction of the lips and some calls derive their typical timbre from a specific mouth posture. During the observations a number of facial-vocal displays were distinguished both on the basis of acoustical properties and facial characteristics. The display categories were chosen in such a manner that easy recognition under the prevailing conditions was possible. This implied that certain subtle distinctions were neglected, because they could only be made when, for instance, an animal was quite close to the observer, or when there was little interference from other sounds. After the observation period a collection of sound recordings was analysed by means of sonagrams, in order to determine objectively the physical characteristics of the display categories. Both sounds that were acoustically representative for the display categories and intermediates have been analysed.

An early attempt to describe chimpanzee vocalizations was made by Yerkes and Learned (1925) who made use of musical notation and phonetic transcriptions. They observed pairs of chimpanzees kept in conventional laboratory cages. Their repertoire of descriptions is certainly not exhaustive. The first survey of chimpanzee facial expressions we owe to Kohts (1935). She observed the interactions of a young individual with human beings and interpreted the expressions in terms referring to human emotional states. Both studies were conducted on animals under rather unnatural conditions. Goodall (1965), Reynolds and Reynolds (1965), and van Lawick-Goodall (1968) presented qualitative data on vocalizations and expressions of feral chimpanzees. They gave short general descriptions of a number of these and an indication of their context. Sonagrams of vocalizations have been given by Reynolds and Reynolds (1965); unfortunately these do not show much detail. The same is true for the sonagrams presented in a preliminary report by Marler (1968). The display categories chosen here closely follow van Hooff (1962, 1967a).

42. *Bared-teeth scream* This is the most intense vocal display, during which the mouth is widely opened and the lips are fully retracted from the teeth and gums (Figs 19 and 22(a)). The vocalizations are usually high-pitched, intense intermittent screams with a sharp timbre (van Hooff, 1962, 1967a). The energy distribution of the expiration phase shows a concentration in three (sometimes four) formant regions, typically situated at $\pm$ 1.6, 3.0 and 4.5 kHz. The highest values measured in each region, occurring especially in *pant-screams* (see below),

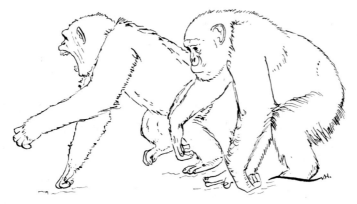

Fig. 19. Female (on the left) *flees* [7] while displaying *bared-teeth scream* [42] after having been hit by male. Note *tense-mouth face* [56] of male.

were 2.0, 3.8 and 5.6 kHz. The lowest values were 1.4, 2.8 and 4.2 kHz; these correspond well with the values recently determined by Lieberman (1968). Both acoustically and in the sonagrams three different types of screams could be distinguished.

a. *Pulse scream* A rasping sound, with a sharp tonal timbre (≪rrra≫). The broad-band sonagram reveals a fast succession of pulses whose energy extends up to 8 kHz with concentrations in the three formant regions. The frequency of the pulses ranges from 60 Hz upwards. The lower pulse frequencies do not yet show up in the narrow-band sonagrams, but higher frequencies manifest themselves as a fine horizontal striping (see the first part of the scream portrayed in Fig. 20).

b. *Double-tone scream* When the frequency of the pulses increases to

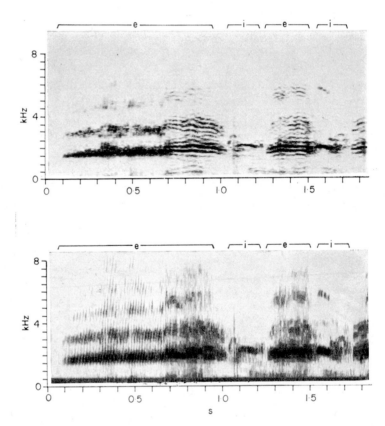

Fig. 20. Transition of a *pulse scream* [42a] into a *double-tone scream* [42b] (e =expiration; =inspiration). Equivalent narrow-band (top) and broad-band (bottom) sonagrams.

about 160 Hz, these become indistinguishable in the broad-band sonagrams as vertical stripes; now, however, they show up clearly in the
narrow-band sonagrams as horizontal lines. This fundamental frequency
may assume values up to 350 Hz. At these higher frequencies the pulses
are no longer detectable as an acoustical rasping, but instead one hears a
usually dissonant double-tone composed of the fundamental and a high-
frequency component representing the formants. Only Yerkes and
Learned (1925) have reported the frequent occurrence of double tones
in chimpanzee screaming, when they rendered a number of these in
musical notation; comparison of frequencies indicates that they have
referred to the same phenomenon.

Figure 20 portrays the sudden transition of a *pulse scream* into a
double-tone scream. This type of scream may also develop gradually out
of low-frequency *hoots* [47], *pout moans* [45] or *ohoh's* [49] via what one
might term "roars". The frequency of the formants gradually increases,
but simultaneously these become higher-order harmonics of lower
fundamentals (see Fig. 32). Both *pulse* and *double-tone screams* last relatively long; the lowest recorded value, the *estimated modal value* and the
highest recorded value are respectively 0.3, *0.5* and 1.2 s. It is remarkable
that both types of screams, which are usually performed loudly, can also
be generated at low intensities. I could record one such instance for each
type of scream.

c. *Pant scream* This is very breathy and is emitted with a rather sharp
timbre (≪a:≫, ≪ae≫). Wide distribution of energy is apparent, up
to 8 kHz, with a tendency of concentration in the highest measured
formant regions. Neither narrow- nor broad-band sonagrams reveal
a further structure. The periodicity of the fundamental has been lost
or its effect is overridden by noise generated by the rapidly expiring air.
Pant screams last for much shorter times than the other screams (0.08 –
0.25 – 0.6 s). The longer calls tend to break up into a few short calls
(0.8 – 0.15 s) without inspirations in between (see Fig. 21). *Pant screams* are
often given while crouching or fleeing ("crouch face": van Hooff, 1962).

In all three *scream* displays the inspirations are usually audible, especially when the pauses between successive screams are shorter than
0.5 s. Inspirations can be noisy or distinctly tonal. In both cases the
major part of the energy is transmitted in the frequency area below
2.5 kHz. Tonal inspirations can have a fundamental between 300 and
1,000 Hz; the frequency does not seem to depend on the characteristics
of the expiration (cf. Fig. 21).

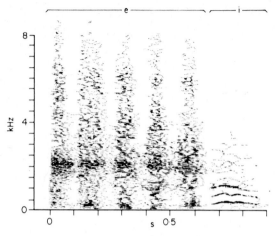

Fig. 21.   Pant scream [42ᶜ].

The "screams" and "roars and growls" of Reynolds and Reynolds (1965), the "screams" (E5 and G) of van Lawick-Goodall (1968) and the "rough scream" of Marler (1969) correspond with the *pulsed scream*. The "pant shriek" of van Lawick-Goodall (1968) corresponds with the *pant scream*.

43. *Bared-teeth yelp* (Fig. 22(b)). This is a high-pitched, moderately loud vocalization of a pure tonal nature without noise or pulses, with rather sharp timbre («ae», «e:»). The fundamental is at 1,500 ± 300 Hz, formants are the first 3 to 5 harmonics, duration is 0.3 – *0.5* – 0.7 s, and

(a)

(b)

Fig. 22.   (a) Bared-teeth scream display [42]. (b) *Bared-teeth yelp* face [43] with covered upper teeth.

pauses in between separate *yelp* expirations are at least 0.5 s. The profile
of the sonagram is level, with a slight tendency to waver; during the
last 0.1 second the profile may, however, bend down rather sharply in a
noisy trail (see Fig. 23). A shorter version of the *yelp* is the *cackle*; the
expiration may become as short as 0.1 s, so that the tonal part is shorter
than the descending noisy trail. *Cackles* may be heard, for instance,
when an animal is feeding; they then alternate with *grunts* [48] (see
Fig. 30(b)). Such short "cackles" clearly correspond to the "fruit word"

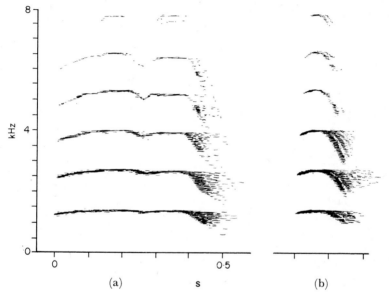

Fig. 23. Bared-teeth yelp [43]: (a) long expiration; (b) short expiration (*cackle*).

described by Yerkes and Learned (1925). A curved profile first ascend-
ing, then descending, forms the transition to the *bared-teeth bark* [46]
(Fig. 24). A lowering of the fundamental and a change in facial expression leads to the *stretched-pout whimper* [44]. Transitions between *yelps*
and the three types of *scream* [42] occur regularly (e.g. Fig. 25). Vocalized inspiration is rare; if it occurs it is a weak tonal sound similar to the
expiration.

   The facial expression of the *bared-teeth yelp* shows the mouth slightly or
half opened, with mouth-corners drawn back; usually the lips are fully
withdrawn baring upper and lower teeth and gums, but occasionally
only the lower teeth are bared (Fig. 22(b)). The display may correspond
with the "squeal" of Reynolds and Reynolds (1965), the "squeak calls"

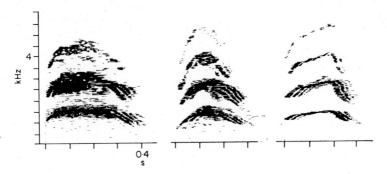

Fig. 24. Gradual change from a *bared-teeth bark* [46ᵃ] into a *cackle* [43].

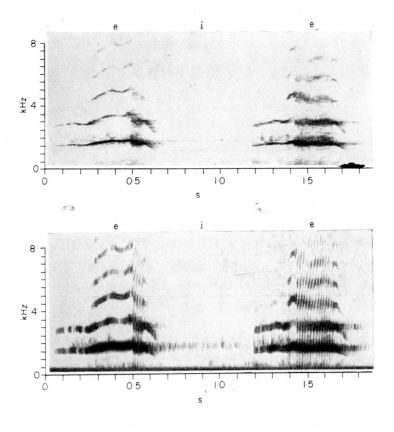

Fig. 25. Transition of a *yelp* [43] into a *double-tone scream* [42ᵇ].
Equivalent narrow-band (top) and broad-band (bottom) sonagrams.

of van Lawick-Goodall (1968) and the "scream without vibrato" of
Marler (1969).

44. *Stretched-pout whimper* Both with respect to its vocal and facial
pattern this display forms an intermediate between the *bared-teeth yelp*
[43] and the *pout-moan* [45]. The vocalization is pure and noiseless. The
fundamental varies between 0.5 and 1 kHz; all harmonics up to ± 4
kHz are about equally strong; at higher frequencies (up to 7 kHz)
weak harmonics may manifest themselves. Occasionally harmonics
around 2 and 3.8 kHz get a slight emphasis. Thus the timbre is still
rather sharp («ae»). The profile of the sonagram is about level
(Fig. (26(a) but there is a strong tendency to waver: both frequency and
intensity oscillations occur, especially in longer calls. Duration of calls
and the pauses in between vary from 0.2 to 1.0 s; short calls tend to
occur in series. The inspirations are not vocalized.

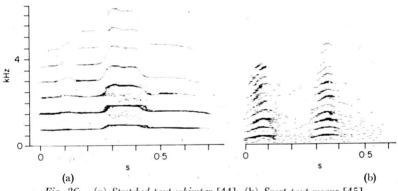

Fig. 26.   (a) *Stretched pout whimper* [44]. (b) *Snort pout moans* [45].

The main characteristic differentiating this display from the *bared-
teeth yelp* [43] and the *pout-moan* [45] is the facial expression. The mouth
is practically closed. The mouth-corners are retracted. The lips are not
retracted but curled outwards and slightly protruding (especially the
upper lip) in a manner that is also characteristic for a sulky or crying
child. This posture has been described under the same name by van
Hooff (1967a) and as "whimpering" by van Lawick-Goodall (1968).

45. *Pout-moan* This is a low-pitched tonal call with melodious timbre
(«o» :, «oe») given at low to moderate intensities. The fundamental
is at 300 – *500* – 700 Hz; harmonics up to 4 or 7 kHz may be present,
but emphasis is on the lower harmonics, often the first two. The duration of calls varies from 0.1 via *0.5* to 0.9s. The frequency profile

undulates slightly in the longer calls; these show also appreciable intensity modulation (Fig. 27). In the short calls the frequency rises initially to level off or even curve down a bit at the end (Fig. 26(b)). Calls are given in series which can last many seconds. The duration of the pauses between calls is proportional to and of the same order of magnitude as the calls. The calls may occasionally develop into *screams* [42].

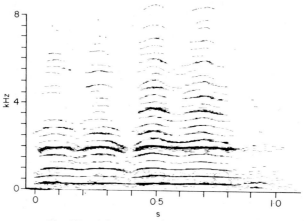

Fig. 27. A long wavering *pout-moan* [45].

The facial posture is characterized by the pouting of the lips which also accompanies the beginning of the *rising hoot* display [47]. The pursed and protruded lips remain in contact near the mouth-corners but they are parted in the middle, showing a round opening (Fig. 28(a)).

The "hoo-wimper" of van Lawick-Goodall (1968) and probably the "moaning-hoots" and "soft moans" of Reynolds and Reynolds (1965) refer to the same display. van Hooff (1962, 1967a) has described it as the "pout-face".

46. *Shrill bark* Intense vocalizations whose main characteristic is that the spectral energy distribution shifts markedly during the call: the areas of maximal density ascend initially, level off in the middle section and descend finally. Two extreme types may be distinguished (see Fig. 29).

a. *Bared-teeth bark* The mouth is hardly or slightly open at the beginning and more widely open during the middle section of the call. The mouth-corners are pulled back and the lips withdrawn from the teeth. The energy distribution is identical to that of the *bared-teeth*

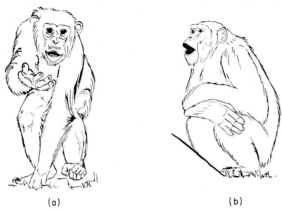

(a)   (b)

Fig. 28.   (a) *Pout moan* [45] and *hold out hand* [17]. (b) *Waow-bark* [46ᵇ].

scream [42]; again it is concentrated into three (sometimes four) formant
zones. For a typical case the formant zones at the start and at the end
of the call were 1.0, 1.9, 2.8 and 3.5 kHz, and in the middle section
1.5, 2.8, 4.2 and 5.5 kHz. The broad-band sonagram (Fig. 29(a)) reveals
a regular pulse structure of 60 to 80 Hz and up. Hence this call, like the
pulse scream [42], has a very rasping quality: it is best rendered phonetic-
ally by ≪wrrraw≫. The duration varied between 0.2 and 0.35 s;
pauses in between calls of a series were of the same order of magnitude.
b. *Waow-bark* At beginning and end of the call the mouth is slightly

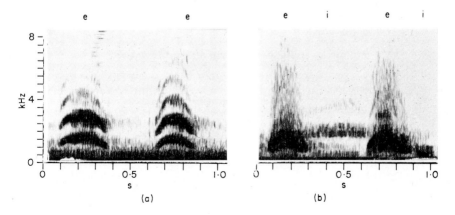

Fig. 29.   (a) *Bared-teeth bark* [46ᵃ]. (b) *Waow-bark* [46ᵇ].

opened and the lips cover the teeth. During the call the mouth is opened
rather widely and in the middle section the teeth may momentarily
be bared slightly (Fig. 28(b)). Here most energy is concentrated in one
region, between 0.8 and 1.8 kHz. A noise column extending up to
±5 kHz is present only in the middle section. The broad-band sonagram (Fig. 29(b)) does not reveal a pulse structure. Hence the call sounds
less rasping, though still rough.

Of the intermediate forms combined with other calls the most curious
is one which trails off into the highly periodic structure of the *pout-
moan* [45] (Fig. 30).

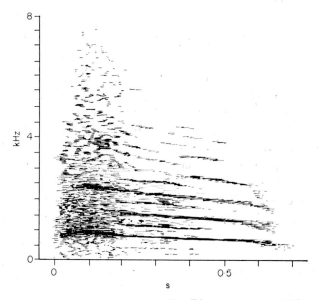

Fig. 30.   A *waow-bark* [46] trails off into a *pout-moan* [45].

This class may correspond with Reynolds and Reynolds's (1965)
"harsh and shrill barks", and the "waa-barks" of Goodall (1965), van
Lawick-Goodall (1968), and Marler (1969).

47. *Rising-hoot* The display starts with a series of low-pitched, moderately loud calls with a very dull timbre (≪u:≫), going on for many
seconds. These become gradually louder and may finally end with one
or more loud *screams* or *waow-barks*. During the initial hooting the lips
may be strongly pursed in a pout; at the end the mouth may be opened
more widely; the teeth may even be bared. The initial low hoots may be

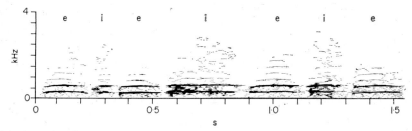

Fig. 31. Vocalizations of the initial phase of the *rising hoot* display [47]; note vocalized inspirations.

coarse and aperiodical, but more often are of a rather periodical nature (Fig. 31). There are only two harmonics, the fundamental one rising slowly from about 250 Hz to about 500 Hz during the hoot-series. The inspiratory phase is almost as strongly vocalized. It can be tonal like the expiration, or rather noisy. The expiratory phase may last from about 0.1 to 0.5 s (typically 0.15). The inspiratory phase is somewhat shorter (0.08 – *0.1* – 0.3 s). Figure 32 represents the end-phase of a *rising hoot* when the energy distribution begins to extend to high frequencies and new fundamentals are "inserted" (see also *double-tone scream* [42b]).

This spectacular display has been mentioned by many authors (e.g. Nissen, 1931; Yerkes, 1943; Goodall, 1965; Reynolds and Reynolds,

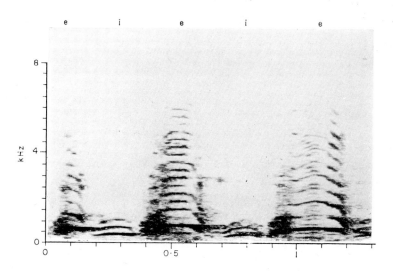

Fig. 32. A *rising hoot* [41]; the last expiration tends towards a *double-tone scream* [42ᵇ].

1965; van Hooff, 1967; van Lawick-Goodall, 1968; Marler, 1969).

48. *Grunt or Grunt-bark* This category consists of a number of low-pitched, low to moderately intense calls with a rather dull timbre (≪ʌ≫ or ≪ɔ≫). Fairly tonal forms were observed in which a steady fundamental periodicity is maintained. The call represented in Fig. 33(a) has a fundamental frequency of about 190 Hz, with emphasis

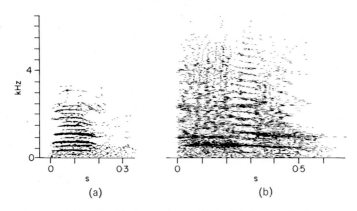

Fig. 33.   (a) A tonal *grunt* [48]. (b) A *groan* [48].

especially on harmonics 4 and 6. Often a sustained periodicity is absent and the calls appear in the broad- and narrow-band sonagrams as columns of noise reaching up to about 2.5 kHz. Concentration of energy occurs often around 0.5, 1.0 and, sometimes, 1.5 kHz (Fig. 34(a)). In

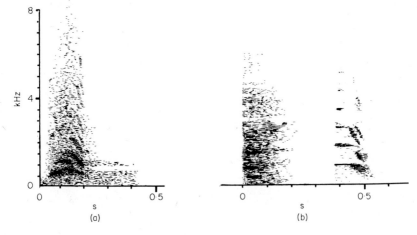

Fig. 34.   (a) A *grunt-bark* [48]. (b) A *cough* [48] followed by a *cackle* [43] during eating.

the broad-band sonagrams an irregular vertical striation can occasionally be seen; it is correlated with a certain acoustical roughness. The frequency profile may be practically horizontal (Fig. 33(a)), or consist of a short phase in which the first formant ascends about 0.3 kHz and then descends again (Fig. 34(a)). This form grades into the *waow-bark* [46b]. Sometimes there is a very sudden onset; such "coughs" can be heard for instance during the initial phase of feeding (Fig. 34(b)) because of the variations of the mouth cavity which are the effect of chewing, these feeding calls vary considerably in timbre (Andrew, 1963; Marler, 1969).

Grunts and *grunt-barks* are rather short, varying from 0.07 via *0.15* to about 0.25 s. Longer *grunts* ("groans"), up to 0.6 s (e.g. Fig. 33 (b)), were noticed only rarely.

The facial expression during the low-intensity grunts is fairly relaxed: the mouth may practically be closed or slightly opened. At higher intensities the mouth may open wider and the lips may be somewhat protruding.

With this class undoubtedly correspond the "grunts", "gruff barks" and "panting barks" of Reynolds and Reynolds (1965) and the "grunts", "groans", and "huu-calls" of Goodall (1965) and van Lawick-Goodall (1968).

49. *Rapid ohoh series* Rather breathy and slightly rough grunts are delivered in rapid rhythmic succession (3 to 4 expirations per second). A series may last one or two seconds. The calls derive their typical hollow timbre (≪o≫ , ≪c≫) from the mouth posture; the mouth is opened fairly wide, the lips cover the teeth and the mouth-corners are drawn forward slightly, thus creating a large, round mouth aperture. Most *ohoh series* are rather stable but occasionally one gradually develops into a *scream* [42], *yelp* [43] or *shrill bark* [45]. Figure 35 portrays such a rising *ohoh series*. The single low-intensity calls contain energy up to ±5 kHz. The main formant regions are at 0.5 ±0.1 kHz and 1 ±0.2 kHz. A less heavy concentration of energy is often found between 2.5 and 3.5 kHz. In a rising series both regions may approach each other and the energy distribution becomes more regular. The inspirations are strongly vocalized, mostly tonal, with formant frequencies of 0.5 ±0.1 kHz and 1 ±0.2 kHz. The display corresponds with the "bobbing pants" of van Lawick-Goodall (1968).

50. *Relaxed open-mouth display* The mouth is kept in a moderate-to-wide open position. The mouth-corners may be slightly withdrawn, but the

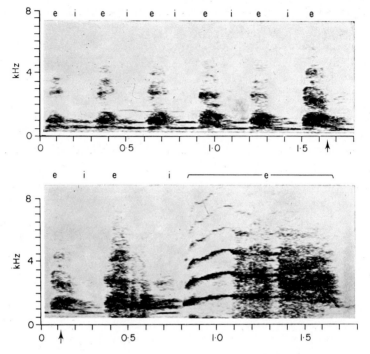

Fig. 35. A rapid *ohoh series* [49] becomes intense and ends with a *yelp* or *scream* [43 or 42] expiration; same moments in successive sonagrams are marked by an arrow.

lips maintain their normal relaxed position, so that the upper teeth remain wholly or partly covered by the upper lip; the lower teeth are slightly bared (Fig. 36). On some occasions the lips may slide farther back, but the gums are hardly ever visible. This facial expression is

Fig. 36.   Relaxed open-mouth face [50].

normally accompanied with a *staccato* rhythmic breathing, which easily develops into rhythmic low-pitched grunting to which the open mouth renders the characteristic ≪ah≫ timbre. The sonagrams (e.g. Fig. 37) show columns of noise extending practically uninterrupted to about 6 kHz. A formant region can be distinguished at 1.0 – 1.2 kHz and also occasionally at 0.4 – 0.5 or 1.8 – 2.0 kHz. The grunts last about 0.1 s and may be given at a rate of 2 to 4 per second. Within one bout of ≪ah≫ -grunts the rate often suddenly accelerates and decelerates again.

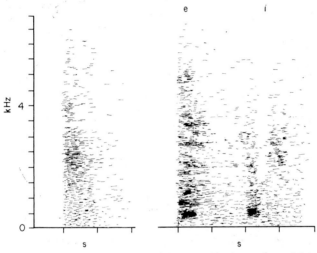

Fig. 37.   Relaxed open-mouth display [50]: (a) unvocalized panting; (b) ≪ah≫ grunt (both expiration and inspiration vocalized).

The facial expression has been described by van Hooff (1962, 1967a), Andrew (1963) and Bolwig (1964), who observed it in other primates as well, and by van Lawick-Goodall (1968) ("playface", "laughing").
51. *Pant* This is identical to the "panting" described by van Lawick-Goodall (1968). It is a fast rhythmic breathing which can amount to five expiration cycles per second. By its normally smooth onset and ending it differs from the panting which may accompany the *relaxed open mouth* display [50]. The mouth is in a relaxed position and jaws and lips are only slightly parted. It often accompanies *mouth-mouth contact* [30] and *embracing* [38]. The occurrence of *panting* can be visually detected from the slight synchronous body shake that accompanies it, even when the sound is not audible because of background noise or the distance of the actor.

52. *Silent bared-teeth display* Three forms can be distinguished.
a. *Horizontal bared-teeth face* The mouth-corners are withdrawn and the lips retracted from teeth and mostly also gums (Fig. 38). The mouth is kept practically closed. This expression is invariably made while the animal is motionless or moving slowly. It has been described for the chimpanzee as well as for other primates as the "grin" by van Hooff (1962), and under the present name by van Hooff (1967a). It corresponds with the "silent grin" of van Lawick-Goodall (1968).

Fig. 38.   Horizontal bared-teeth face [52a].

b. *Open-mouth bared-teeth face* Again mouth corners and lips are maximally withdrawn, baring most teeth and gums, but now the mouth is widely open (Fig. 39). The movement may accompany *embracing* [38], *mouth-mouth contact* [30] and *panting* [51]. It has not been explicitly distinguished before (but see plate VII in van Hooff 1967a).
c. *Vertical bared-teeth face* The lips (mainly the upper one) are retracted but the mouth-corners are at their normal position. The teeth are kept in a closed position. The retraction of the lips without mouth-corner retraction causes these (especially the upper lip) to be slightly protruded (Fig. 40). The demeanour is relaxed and quiet. The expression has not been described by other authors. In 1966 Bobskowski recorded it on film in the Holloman colony (Beckwith, personal communication).
53. *Silent pout face* The lips are strongly pursed and pushed forward in a pout (Fig. 41). The facial expression is not accompanied by vocalization and can be maintained for many tens of seconds. It has not been distinguished before.

Fig. 39.   (a) *Open-mouth bared-teeth* face [52b]. (b) Mother displays [52b] towards her youngster before *embracing* [38] it (after a photograph by H. Albrecht).

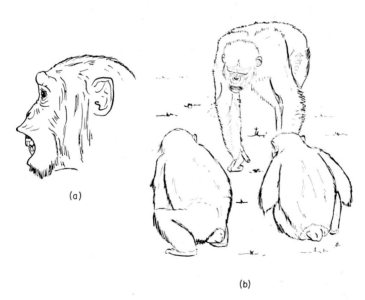

Fig. 40.   (a) *Vertical bared-teeth* display [52c]. (b) Adult male displays [52c] towards a pair of half-grown, individuals who utter *rapid ohoh's* [49] and *squat-bob* [10] in front of him.

The 53 main behavioural elements treated above occurred sufficiently frequently to be included in the following quantitative analysis. Apart from these a few more behavioural elements distinguished which occurred relatively rarely or have been recorded few and far between. 54. *Lip-smack* The mouth is opened rather widely and closed again rhythmically; the teeth may be hard to clap together, the mouth-corners are at the normal position or pulled forward slightly. In contrast to most other primates who may produce *lip-smacking* in a variety

Fig. 41.   *Silent pout* face [53] in an adult male.

of contexts, chimpanzees *lip-smack* almost exclusively during grooming (van Hooff, 1962, 1967a; van Lawick-Goodall, 1968), especially at the beginning or after breaks. Only once did I see it outside such a context, namely while clinging. van Lawick-Goodall noted that a particular male would often "lip-smack" while mating. Once I observed distinct "teeth-chattering", i.e. the same jaw movements as in *lip-smacking*, but now the lips were fully retracted from the teeth. A male did it while holding out his hand when he approached a small female. "Teeth-chattering", common in many monkey species (van Hooff, 1962, 1967a), has so far been observed only in one ape species, namely the gibbon, *Hylobates lar* (own observations).

55. *Splutter* The animal blows air through its compressed lips, thus making a spluttering sound. It occurs in the same context as *lip-smacking* and may be merely an alternative for it. Once I saw an animal *spluttering* intensively, not while grooming, but while observing the grooming interactions of another pair. It is not mentioned by van Lawick-Goodall (1968) and may be a local habit. *Spluttering* has never been seen in monkeys, but is common also in orangs (*Pongo pygmaeus*) (own observations).

56. *Bulging lips* Occasionally chimpanzees that stamp or sway have

tightly compressed lips (van Lawick-Goodall, 1968) and an arching upper lip which suggests that it may be blown up (Fig. 42). But for the fact that the jaws are usually also firmly clenched, it resembles the "attack"-face (van Hooff, 1962) or "tense mouth face" (van Hooff, 1967a). The latter with narrow tense lips (Fig. 19) also occurs in the chimpanzee (Wilson and Wilson, 1968), but it is much less conspicuous. The *bulging lips* expression may also occur during human braving behaviour.

Fig. 42. Bulging lips [56]
in adult male.

57. *Horizontal head shake* This consists of a few movements of the head from side to side (rate about 2 cycles per second). This is achieved by pivoting the head around a point somewhere between the shoulders, but a slight head rotation may also form part of it. Explicitly recorded ten times only during the latter part of the observation period, it may have been more common than my figures suggest. On nine occasions it led to or occurred simultaneously with patterns that will appear to fall into the "play category".

58. *Vacuum thrust* On 24 occasions young males were seen to squat and to support their backward slanting bodies on their arms which were placed behind their back. Their buttocks a few centimetres above the ground, they would perform pelvic thrusting *in vacuo* with their penis fully erect. On 19 occasions a female addressee *crouch-presented* [19] and the male *mated* [35]. The display has been noted by Yerkes and Elder (1936).

59. *Clitoris rubbing* On 13 occasions a female was seen to squat and rub her genital area over the ground. The pattern accompanied *mouth-mouth contact* [30] or *embracing* [38].

60. *Siphoning food* An animal that is chewing food may bulge its lower

lip and drop some food on the lower lip of a partner. This form of food-sharing was observed 22 times. It has been reported by other authors (Köhler, 1921, 1922; Yerkes, 1943; van Lawick-Goodall, 1967, 1968) to occur especially between mothers and offspring. Köhler (1921, 1922) and van Lawick-Goodall (1968) also mention the presentation of food by hand. I saw this only once.

5.6 DISCUSSION ON THE SOCIAL BEHAVIOUR ELEMENTS

As the present study was conducted on chimpanzees living in an atypical environment and having unnatural antecedents, it is of interest to compare the present list with data collected on other and especially feral chimpanzees. Most of the behaviour patterns listed have also been noticed and sometimes described by other authors. As van Lawick-Goodall (1968) has presented the most comprehensive treatment so far, I shall restrict the comparison to this study. My typology of behaviour elements was set up from data collected before her 1968 work became available. However, my observations and criteria were influenced, of course, by previous publications on the subject by her and others.

I have distinguished 60 main elements of social behaviour, some of which can clearly be split up further. It is not possible to say exactly how many types van Lawick-Goodall does distinguish. She treats the different elements of behaviour within the framework of a number of qualitatively defined categories of a "motivational" and/or "functional" nature. In different categories one may encounter descriptions of similar or perhaps identical patterns (e.g. "scream calls" during aggressive behaviour and "screaming" during submissive behaviour and when an animal is frightened). But it is not always clear whether indeed a morphological difference is implied or not. The number of different types of elements is estimated to be about 70.

Of the list presented here, 30 behaviour elements agree well with elements described by van Lawick-Goodall. This is quite probably also true for another 19 elements for which matching is not possible on all points, either because certain details cannot be judged or because there is a difference in emphasis. Both lists also show differences with respect to the degree of differentiation. The following elements of van Lawick-Goodall cannot be placed clearly in my list: "hiding", "play walk", "scratch", "sitting hunch", "branching", "arm raising", "head tipping". Not mentioned by van Lawick-Goodall are my elements:

approach [1], *hesitant approach* [2], *mount-walk* [37], *cling* [39], *vacuum thrust* [58], *clitoris rub* [59], *vertical head nod* [14], *horizontal head shake* [57], *pull limb* [27], *splutter* [55] and *silent pout* [53]. The existence of some of these, (e.g. the first four), is implied in some of van Lawick-Goodall's descriptions. Except for her elements "arm raising", "branching", "tree-leaping", "play walk", and my elements *vertical head nod, horizontal head shake, silent pout, spluttering, vacuum thrust* and *clitoris rub*, the differences mentioned are most likely due to different observational criteria, rather than to peculiarities of both groups. Thus I am inclined to conclude that there is very good agreement on the whole.

Comparison of the vocal repertoires of different species of primates shows that those of at least many higher species are of a "graded" nature. This in contrast to what is found in many other vertebrates, notably many birds, and some other primate species, where the repertoire can be separated into discrete non-overlapping elements (Marler, 1959; Marler and Hamilton, 1966). That the chimpanzee vocal repertoire consists of a set of continuously intergrading signals is indicated by preliminary analyses by Marler (1965, 1969). The present work conclusively supports this. In Fig. 43 a schematic representation of the vocal repertoire is given, with the typical elements that were distinguished during this study; the lines indicate that sonagrams were obtained either of discrete intermediates between the respective elements or of gradual changes between them.

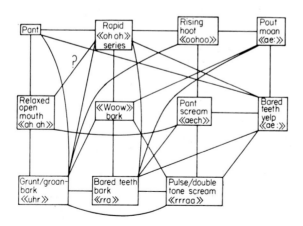

Fig. 43. Schematic representation of the vocal repertoire. The lines indicate that phonetic intermediates or gradual changes between the respective elements were recorded.

6   The quantitative analysis of the structure of social behaviour

6.1   INTRODUCTORY REMARKS

One way to study the relation between the different elements of an animal's behaviour repertoire is to determine to what extent the occurrence of any two behaviour elements in a number of standard time periods is correlated (see section 1). Hinde (1966) has pointed out that the degree of correlation is affected by the choice of the period length. In an established group of primates individual animals need not show any specific social behaviour together for long stretches, but may perform a comparatively short "social action chain" (see p. 83) consisting of a few elements, to a certain partner, to be followed perhaps by a completely different chain to another partner a short while later. They may equally show a particular behaviour, like grooming, for a comparatively long time. Thus variation in the period length for analysis might affect different behaviours differentially. The time scale is complicated by the fact that a certain length might be "right" for one behaviour and "wrong" for another.

For these reasons, which had indeed been empirically found to complicate the issue during preliminary work on the social behaviour of *Macaca fascicularis* (unpublished data), preference was given to sequential analysis. As the basic datum of our analysis of the structure of social behaviour we have taken the patterns of transition frequencies between elements.

In this analysis my first 53 behaviour elements were included, each of which was scored as preceding and/or succeeding other elements at least 30 times. A 53-dimensional matrix of transition frequencies was constructed. For each behaviour element I determined the number of times it was both preceded and succeeded in the behaviour sequence of an actor by each of the other elements.

Although the behaviour elements that I distinguished often occur on their own, it is not uncommon that more than one (occasionally even more than two) occur simultaneously. Instances of common combinations are *pout moan* and *hold out hand*, *crouch* and *bared-teeth scream*, etc. Altmann (1962, 1965, 1968), who was especially interested in the probabilities of occurrence of transitions, regarded any such combinations of two or more elements as new elements. Thus all behaviour elements were mutually exclusive. This of course led to a considerable increase in the number of elements. For the purpose of this study a knowledge of the exact probabilities of transitions was not considered of primary importance. So if two elements *a* and *b* occurred simultaneously they were entered in the matrix as passing into each other once ($a \rightarrow b$ and $b \rightarrow a$). If an element *c*, for instance, preceded the combination of *a* and *b*, *c* was scored in the matrix as preceding both *a* and *b*. Consequently any element can have more than one element preceding or following it.

Some elements like *hold out hand* are occurrences which usually last only a few seconds, and which may be repeated after a short interval in the course of the same interaction. It would not be illogical to assume that the element was preceded and succeeded by itself. Other elements like the *relaxed open mouth* may last an appreciable time and accompany a sequence of other elements, such as *gnaw-wrestling, hit, gnaw, grasp,* etc. Each time such an accompanying element occurs, both are scored as passing into the other once. But now the question arises how to treat the longer lasting element: should it be considered to pass into itself whenever there is a change in accompanying elements? How should we treat elements like *grooming* which can go on for many minutes on their own? As the absolute duration has not been recorded, a solution on the basis of the time parameter was out of the question, and it was decided to disregard the transitions of an element into itself.

6.2   ANALYSIS OF PRINCIPAL PATHWAYS

The behaviour elements differ considerably with respect to the frequency of their occurrence. This is reflected by the numbers of times the elements are involved in a transition. Table 1 gives for each behaviour element the total number of times it preceded and succeeded another element. The values range from about 30 to about 1,400. The Table also shows that some elements more often precede, i.e. tend to occur in the beginning of a social action chain, while others more often follow, i.e. tend to conclude a chain. As a measure for the degree to which the frequencies of preceding and succeeding differ, the χ^2 values have been computed.

If we attribute significance to the values of $\chi^2 > 8$, which would correspond with a level of significance below 1 per cent in the case of completely independent binomially distributed items, we find eight elements which are typical "beginners". Apart from *watching, rising*

TABLE 1

Comparison of the number of times an element is involved in transitions as preceding and succeeding other elements. (Difference expressed in χ^2 values. Positive values: stronger tendency to precede. Negative values: stronger tendency to succeed.)

	Preceding	Succeeding	χ^2
Smooth approach [1]	1466	828	$+177.44$
Watch [23]	1086	640	$+115.25$
Rising hoot [47]	517	266	$+80.46$
Stamp trot [5]	402	284	$+20.30$
Gallop [3]	216	141	$+15.76$
Vertical head nod [14]	235	168	$+11.14$
Squat-bobbing [10]	306	219	$+10.61$
Brusque rush [6]	570	474	$+8.82$
Gymnastics [11]	89	66	$+3.41$
Pout moan [45]	326	286	$+2.61$
Bared-teeth scream [42]	790	732	$+2.21$
Stamp [13]	468	429	$+1.70$
Hold out hand [17]	543	502	$+1.61$
Hesitant approach [2]	616	575	$+1.41$
Trample [41]	171	158	$+0.77$
Sway-walk [4]	139	134	$+0.09$
Arm sway [12]	598	588	$+0.08$
Silent pout [53]	114	110	$+0.07$
Relaxed open-mouth [50]	349	1337	$+0.05$
Pull limb [27]	257	254	$+0.02$
Shrink, flinch [9]	698	706	-0.05
Gnaw-wrestle [40]	496	503	-0.05
Stretched pout whimper [44]	150	157	-0.16
Crouch [20]	210	219	-0.19
Parry [16]	228	245	-0.61
Grasp, poke [26]	520	547	-0.68
Autogroom [22]	37	46	-0.98
Gnaw [31]	353	380	-0.99
Hand-wrestle [25]	224	246	-1.03
Bared-teeth yelp [43]	417	450	-1.26
Flight [7]	426	465	-1.71
Silent bared-teeth [52]	235	270	-2.43
Rapid ohoh [49]	555	618	-3.38
Groom-presenting [21]	218	261	-3.86
Grunt-bark [48]	125	163	-5.01
Pant [51]	120	162	-6.26
Bite [32]	92	132	-7.10
Genital investigation [34]	106	152	-8.20
Shrill bark [46]	212	279	-9.14

TABLE 1—*contd*

	Preceding	Succeeding	χ^2
Mount [36]	78	127	−11.71
Avoid [8]	504	619	−11.78
Upsway [15]	133	203	−14.58
Hit [29]	821	1003	−18.16
Mouth-mouth [30]	180	272	−18.73
Touch [24]	131	225	−24.82
Tug [29]	231	354	−25.86
Mount-presenting [18]	32	82	−27.51
Mount-walking [37]	35	98	−29.85
Male mating [35]	88	178	−30.45
Groom [33]	285	442	−33.91
Cling [39]	36	107	−35.25
Crouch-presenting [19]	139	267	−40.35
Embrace [38]	246	451	−60.29

hoot and *vertical head nod* they are all different types of approach. Of the 16 elements that are typical "finishers", ten involve some form of maintained bodily contact.

These data indicate that the elements tend to occur in a certain sequential order. More or less regular sequences, forming typical chains of elements, have been found in the behaviour of many animals (see Hinde, 1966). Although it is possible sometimes to recognize "ideal" chains, it appears that these are mostly far from rigid in reality. The "ideal" chains can be derived from "principal pathway diagrams", as constructed by a number of authors. For this purpose the most common procedure is to place together those elements which share the highest absolute transition frequencies (e.g. Baerends *et al.*, 1955; Morris, 1958; Grant, 1963; Dane and van der Kloot, 1964).

Against this method of comparing the importance of transitions, it can be objected that the absolute transition frequencies are being used. Thus highly preferential transitions between elements that occur relatively rarely disappear almost completely when compared with the absolutely large transitions between frequently occurring elements, even if the latter hardly exceed the level expected on the basis of a random distribution of transitions. Therefore I used a different measure. For each combination of succeeding elements, the frequencies were computed that would be expected if the transitions were distributed randomly, given the total numbers of precedents and subsequents for every element. (For a particular cell in the transition matrix this frequency is arrived at by multiplying the marginal totals of the respective row and column and dividing this by the sum total of transitions.) The discrepancy between the observed (o) and the expected (e) transition frequencies can be expressed by the quotient o/e, but in order to minimize the effect of random variations I chose to use $q=(o-e)/\sqrt{e}$. This also represents, to some extent, the statistical significance of the preference of the transitions; for it represents one term of the χ^2 formula, and would lead to a slight underestimate of the statistical significance if the transitions were independent. As we were interested in the relative importance of the transitions, this measure was regarded as acceptable. For statistical reasons, when e was less than 5 a minimum value of 5 was specified as the expected frequency.

The preferential pathways are represented diagrammatically in Fig. 44. In order to keep the diagram manageable, I have restricted it to the most important transitions, adopting a very stringent criterion of significance; only quotients greater than 5 (corresponding with a χ^2–value of at least 25) have been considered.

In the bottom left-hand corner a group of elements is centred around the *relaxed open mouth* [50]. Except for *gallop* [3], which tends to occur at the beginning, all the elements appear to pass over into each other rather easily and within the group there is no sequential preference. The group unites boisterous, though relaxed, elements involving bodily contact. It clearly corresponds to what is commonly referred to as "social play".

By the element *hit* [28] this group is connected with a group in the upper left-hand corner. Here, the "beginner", *brusque rush* [6] may lead to rough treatment of the partner. I shall term it the "attack group". To the right of this we find a group of four elements which frequently pass over into "attack" elements, notably via *stamp-trot* [5] which tends to occur at the beginning of sequences; the reversed transitions are obviously much rarer. *Sway walk* [4] and especially *stamp* [13] and *arm sway* [12] have close connections with each other and with *hit* [28]. To the right these elements link to *rising hoot* [47]. The conspicuous nature of these elements and the fact that they do not involve direct body contact suggests that this third set of elements should be termed the "bluff" or "show" group. *Hoot* [47], also often a "beginner", passes over regularly into the closely associated elements *squat-bobbing* [10]

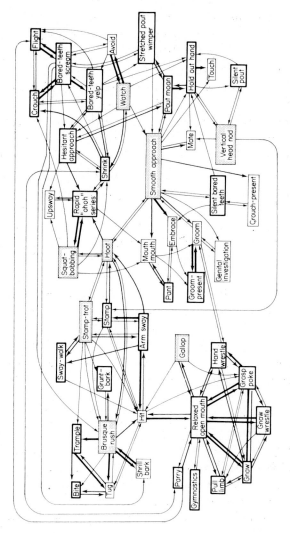

Fig. 44. Principal within-animal transitions during chimpanzee social behaviour. Thick arrows correspond to $q > 15$ (see p. 132); medium to $q > 10$; thin to $q > 5$. Elements that tend to occur at the beginning of sequences (cf. Table 1) are set in a frame with a stippled border; finishers are in a frame with a thin border and elements that are not significantly more often beginners than finishers (and vice versa) are in a frame with a thick black border.

and *ohoh series* [49]. *Upsway* [15] is frequently an end-point here. Via *hesitating approach* [2] and especially *shrink* [9], *bared-teeth yelp* [43] may be reached. This movement often follows *bared-teeth scream* [42] which, moreover, alternates frequently with *crouch* [20] and *flight* [7]. Thus this upper right-hand corner group may be termed the "flight" or "submission" group. It is surrounded by elements like *shrink* [9] and *avoid* [8] which share an element of withdrawal. *Bared-teeth scream* [42] may also lead to "attack" elements.

Via the "beginner", *watch* [23], another large group may be entered, the elements of which centre around and are often preceded by *smooth approach* [1]. There is a general tendency here towards an increase in "affinity", namely towards elements which involve smooth and free and easy bodily contact. There seem to be a few sub-groups of this group: on the left these centre around *mouth-mouth* [30] and *embrace* [38], around *groom* [33] and *genital investigation* [34] and *crouch present* [19]. On the right, linked to the "submissive" group via *stretched pout wimper* [44], there is the rather clear chain from *pout moan* [45] to *touch* [24]. *Male mating* [35] is often reached via *holding out hand* [17]; this can also result from *vertical head nodding* [14]. The latter may lead to elements of the "bluff"- group as well. Due to the stringent criteria used, not all of the 53 behaviour elements appear in this diagram of course.

The existence of regular sequences is only partly manifest in this diagram. It is based on transitions between two elements: a "second-order approximation" in the terminology of Altmann (1965). If higher-order approximations are made the degree of stereotypy exposed will undoubtedly increase, as Altmann has shown to be the case for the Rhesus monkey.

The number of preferential combinations in the diagram constitutes 6 per cent of the total number (2,756) of possible combinations of the matrix of transition frequencies. However, about 61 per cent of this total number actually occurred once or more. So in the above pathway analysis a rather limited use of the available information is made, and it is obvious that a consideration of the total pattern of transition frequencies is desired. Besides, the present simple two-dimensional representation cannot accommodate all the relations properly.

6.3   MULTIVARIATE ANALYSIS OF THE TEMPORAL RELATIONSHIPS

6.3.1   *Methods of analysis*

The more causal factors two behaviour elements a and b have in common, the more b will tend to pass over into each of the other 52 elements to the extent that a's tendency to do so is itself great. They will consequently have patterns of transition frequencies that are correlated positively. After determining these correlations for every pair of elements, the resulting matrix of correlations can be subjected to multivariate analysis. This method has been used by Wiepkema (1961), who applied factor analysis. My method diverges from his at a few points.

As I am interested, at this point, in the degree to which behaviour elements share causal factors, the datum concerning the order in which any two elements are arranged in time has been neglected; only the frequency with which the elements occur as neighbours has been considered. To this end the original matrix of transition frequencies was made symmetrical by adding up the symmetrically situated cells.

In order to compensate for the different frequencies with which the elements are involved in transitions (see Table 1), one can use the quotient o/e instead of the absolute neighbourship frequencies (Wiepkema, 1961). For the reason given on p. 132, one may also use the quotient $(o - e)/\sqrt{e}$. This reduces the amount of error variance that is due to the great influence of random variations when expected values are small. That this is indeed the case has also been verified empirically for the present material: in order to get an insight into the variability of the results, the total number of scored interactions was split into three groups, corresponding to the first, middle and final third of the observation period. For each group of data the component analysis, to be discussed below, was performed. The final results of the three groups were in good agreement if the "eccentricity" quotient $(o - e)/\sqrt{e}$ was used (see van Hooff, 1970). This was less so when o/e was used. Therefore, the results obtained by using $(o - e)/\sqrt{e}$ will be given here.

Since transitions of an element into itself have not been scored, the cells of the principal diagonal of the matrix of eccentricity quotients contain negative values. Our conclusions about the causal relationships of the elements will be based on the relative values of the eccentricity quotients. Since an element is, of course, causally identical with itself, it is justified to replace the negative values in the principal diagonal by

F

the highest values of the respective rows. On average this does lead to an accentuation of significant correlations.

Next the rank correlations between the ranges of eccentricity coefficients were determined for every pair of behaviour elements by means of Spearman's ρ.

It is possible to represent two variables geometrically as vectors in the Euclidian space with a common origin and a length that is equal to one unit, i.e. equal to their variance in standard notation. We can now represent their correlation by making this value equal to the cosine of their angle; so the variables will appear coincident if their correlation coefficient is equal to one, and point in opposite directions if it equals minus one. If we want to represent the correlations between n variables, this can be done, as a rule, only in an n-dimensional space. If a number of variables share to a large extent certain causal factors, so that they are positively correlated strongly with each other, their vectors will form a bundle in this space, which can be conceived to centre around a hypothetical common component or dimension. The projection of the vector on the latter then explains the greater part of the variance of the respective elements.

In our case the question is to what extent such bundles can be distinguished, how many there are, and to what extent the hypothetical common components explain the variance of the elements. By means of principal component analysis, a form of factor analysis, followed by a varimax rotation (Harman, 1967), such an insight can be gained. Each of the n variables is described in terms of n new uncorrelated components. If there is causal linkage between elements this will result in the finding that a (sometimes much) smaller number of components explains the major portion (say more than 80 per cent) of the total variance of the matrix. These components may also be referred to as "systems" or "causal categories", in part according to whether attention is focused on the relations between the behavioural elements or the hypothetical causal factors which control them.

A further method which can be used to acquire an insight into the structure is cluster analysis. I used the hierarchical method of McQuitty (1966), that, according to Bijnen (1969), is the most suited for a purpose like the present one. Whereas component analysis explains the relations between the variables in terms of a certain, preferably smaller, number of independent basic variables, this type of cluster analysis groups the elements together in a structure of concordance in which the hierarchical aspects are emphasized. The elements are joined in categories in such a manner that any one element is correlated more strongly with the elements of its own category than with elements in any other category; the degree to which this is so is expressed in a coefficient of concordance ranging from 0 to +1. First the pair or pairs with the highest correlation coefficients are joined, forming a category. Successively, new elements or other categories are joined, yielding new categories of higher order.

6.3.2 Results of the component analysis

Table 2 presents the results of the component analysis. For each of the 53 behaviour elements the loadings on the respective components are presented in rows. The component loading indicates the degree to which the behaviour element is correlated with the component. The components have been arranged from left to right according to decreasing "importance". For each component this "importance" is expressed as the sum of squares of the loadings on the respective component. This value indicates the amount of the total variance of the correlation matrix (which equals 53 for 53 elements in standard notation), which is explained by the respective components. Here only the seven most important components are presented. The total of their sums of squares amounts to 43.6; this is 82 per cent of the total variance, leaving 18 per cent to be explained by the remaining 46 components.

If we consider loadings greater than 0.35 (corresponding with a p of about 1 per cent for a Pearson's r correlation coefficient) as significant, all elements appear to have significant loadings on at least one of the first five components, and 51 elements have their *highest* loading on one of these components. Each component can be semantically identified by considering the elements that have a high loading exclusively on that component.

Thus there are 19 elements that have their highest loading on the first component and most of these have no appreciable loadings on other components. All those elements which in the preferential pathway diagram (Fig. 44) clustered around *smooth approach* appear in this group as well. We may therefore designate the common element which expresses itself in this component the "affinitive system". It represents a common distribution of both external and internal causal or organizing factors, whose constitution is not, however, revealed here of course.

Amongst the elements that have their highest loading on component

TABLE 2

Component loadings (multiplied by 100)

Component	I	II	III	IV	V	VI	VII
Touch [24]	**90**	8	−9	−12	13	6	−3
Cling [39]	**87**	6	0	−7	4	−11	−2
Hold out hand [17]	**86**	−20	−19	6	1	10	−15
Smooth approach [1]	**86**	−3	−23	−16	12	15	2
Silent pout [53]	**83**	0	7	10	3	18	−12
Groom [33]	**83**	19	−9	−16	−9	−11	**36**
Embrace [38]	**82**	0	−28	−1	8	−16	3
Groom-presenting [21]	**78**	17	−14	−8	9	−10	**45**
Pant [51]	**78**	−15	−18	−16	34	−3	19
Pout moan [45]	**76**	−23	−2	26	8	−8	−*36*
Mount-presenting [18]	**75**	−6	−10	2	0	10	2
Mount-walking [37]	**75**	26	−16	2	5	−11	−11
Male mating [35]	**73**	20	9	−15	−13	**37**	−11
Mouth-mouth [30]	**72**	−13	−30	−25	**35**	−4	31
Genital investigation [34]	**70**	30	−9	−25	−4	24	1
Autogroom [22]	**66**	17	−1	−5	−6	−3	**44**
Silent bared-teeth [52]	**65**	−19	−13	27	25	−1	−13
Stretched pout whimper [44]	**65**	−25	−4	**43**	4	−30	−*38*
Crouch-presenting [21]	**63**	−27	−29	28	25	18	−4
Watch [23]	**45**	−29	−14	6	33	6	5
Relaxed open-mouth [50]	−12	**95**	4	−6	−8	10	−1
Grasp, poke [26]	3	**94**	14	−12	−2	10	−4
Gnaw-wrestle [40]	−10	**93**	2	−2	−14	−4	10
Gnaw [31]	23	**87**	−3	−15	−13	−8	15
Pull limb [27]	16	**85**	8	−19	−26	11	−6
Gymnastics [11]	−9	**81**	14	−16	−10	2	−11
Hand-wrestle [25]	34	**68**	−16	−11	−24	−6	30
Gallop [3]	−23	**62**	13	−3	12	**35**	14
Mount [36]	34	**46**	1	−32	22	3	−26
Trample [41]	2	27	**91**	−1	−1	11	9
Tug [29]	−24	−5	**89**	17	4	−11	−4
Brusque rush [6]	−27	−9	**88**	15	5	−3	−1
Bite [32]	−8	6	**84**	30	−10	−19	10
Grunt-bark [48]	−8	−26	**80**	−2	12	5	−24
Sway-walk [4]	−2	**46**	67	−17	0	27	−3
Stamp-trot [5]	−20	27	**65**	−16	−7	**52**	8
Hit [28]	−*49*	55	55	−6	−14	16	−5
Stamp [13]	−*39*	41	54	−7	10	**39**	−5
Shrill bark [46]	−30	−29	**52**	**49**	26	−20	−11
Arm sway [12]	−*62*	30	**50**	−13	15	**36**	3

TABLE 2—*contd*

Component	I	II	III	IV	V	VI	VII
Flight [7]	−23	−13	32	**80**	−8	0	21
Crouch [20]	12	−30	7	**76**	15	−18	6
Avoid [8]	−20	−4	−12	**75**	20	28	−2
Bared-teeth scream [42]	7	−*38*	25	**73**	−8	−28	−20
Bared-teeth yelp [43]	**37**	−*36*	−11	**65**	15	−28	−29
Parry [16]	−33	**42**	−3	**62**	−12	−26	−16
Shrink, flinch [9]	−11	−*64*	7	**59**	28	6	2
Hesitant approach [2]	32	−*58*	−10	**43**	29	13	−16
Squat-bobbing [10]	22	−12	5	18	**86**	−3	−2
Rapid "ohoh" [49]	22	−30	−1	8	**82**	12	4
Rising hoot [47]	17	−22	**40**	−19	**62**	24	−12
Upsway [15]	0	−*40*	8	32	**48**	29	−7
Vertical head nod [14]	**38**	0	4	−17	28	**74**	−4
Portion of variance explained	26%	20%	13%	10%	6%	5%	3%

Note: Positive significant values are **in bold print** and negative ones *in italics*.

II, all those are present that also showed strong association in the bottom left corner of the preferential pathway diagram. The common causal factors which this component represents may be termed the "play system". Component III finds its purest and strongest expression in the elements that in the preferential pathway diagram were classified in the "attack" group and furthermore has high loadings on those that were called the "bluff" elements. This component can therefore be said to represent the "aggressive" system. It may seem remarkable that *flight* has an almost significant loading on this component, but in a fight a fast retreat of even a dominant animal is not rare, especially when other animals join with his adversary.

Amongst the elements that have high loadings on component IV, *flight* and *crouch* excel, and, except for *parry*, the other elements were found to cluster more or less around these two in the pathway diagram. We will therefore call this component the "submissive" system. Remarkably, *bite* scores high on this component. This agrees with the impression that *bite* is the "aggressive" element that is most likely to be used by subordinate individuals in "defense".

Component V expresses itself most purely and strongly in *squat-bobbing* and the *rapid ohoh series*, and furthermore in *rising hoot* and *upsway.* The primary affinitive elements *mouth-mouth* and *panting* reach values around the significance level. These elements take an intermediate place in the pathway diagram between: the "bluff" group, the elements *shrink* and *hesitant approach* of the submissive system, and the element *mouth-mouth* belong to the affinitive system. The elements involved moreover often have an "agitated" appearance; this component was therefore given the neutral designation "excitement" system.

Component VI manifests itself mostly, though not very purely, in only one element, the *vertical head nod.* It reaches moderately high values in the elements that we classified before in the "bluff" group. In the pathway diagram *vertical head nod* was the element that formed the link between the "affinitive" group and the "bluff" group. Also the elements *gallop* and *mate* share to some extent the causal factors that this component represents. The conspicuous character of the most representative elements suggests the designation "show" system.

Three elements that belong to the affinitive system, namely *groom-presenting*, *autogroom* and *groom*, distinguish themselves by the fact that these share specific causal factors represented by component VII. One may call it the "comfort" system.

The remaining components reach appreciable values only in one or a few elements. The interpretation of these components is difficult, and the consideration of elements that have fairly high values on them but do not reach our criterion of significance is not of much help. Therefore they have not been presented in the Table. They may represent causal factors that are rather specific to a certain element; besides, the influence of error variance will not be negligible in such cases.

If elements have significant loadings on more than one component this can mean that the causal factors of both components are simultaneously of influence, and that the element therefore reflects a certain balance of both systems. Instances of behaviour patterns which are influenced by two or more independent systems have been described for various species (see Hinde, 1966, 1970). It can also mean that a particular element can be mobilized independently by two different systems. (A trivial instance of such a case is the pattern of biting, which in many species can occur within the framework of both feeding and agonistic behaviour.) Of course the two possibilities are not mutually exclusive.

The component analysis does not provide conclusive evidence on this point, although it is suggestive. Thus the element *parry* shares causal factors with both the submissive system and the play system. However, *all* other elements united by the "submissive" system have sometimes strong, negative loadings on the "play" component, whereas the "play" elements have negative loadings on the "submissive" system. The fact that *parry* occurs easily in connection with elements of both systems suggests, therefore, that there are two motivationally different forms of this element.

An instance of the other possibility could be found in the vocal-facial displays, *silent pout, pout moan, silent bared-teeth, stretched-pout whimper, bared-teeth yelp, bared-teeth scream*. Not only do these constitute a range of formally intergrading elements, but these can also be arranged correspondingly according to decreasing influence of the "affinitive" and increasing influence of the "submissive" component (Fig. 45). A similar range of facial-vocal displays with decreasing "submission" and increasing "aggression" can be distinguished (Fig. 46).

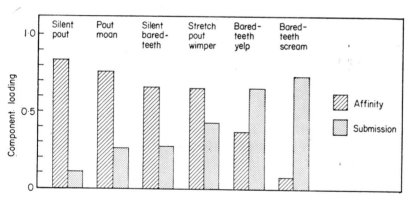

Fig. 45. A range of facial-vocal displays, progressively differing with respect to their loadings on the "affinitive" and "submissive" systems.

A group that distinguishes itself by the mixed nature of its causation is the bluff group. Apart from high "aggressive" loadings these elements have also appreciable loadings on both the "play" component (notably *sway-walk, stamp* and also *hit*) and on the "show" component (notably *stamp trot, stamp* and *arm-sway*).

In judging the theoretical significance of the structure which is revealed by the present method it is of the utmost importance to realize that it is to a large extent determined by the selection of the variables. Of course the test battery, i.e. the collection of variables selected, should represent the total domain that one wants to study; in other words one

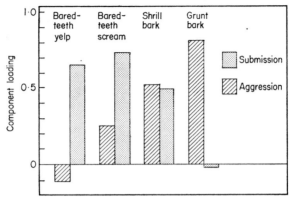

Fig. 46. Facial-vocal displays graded with respect to their loadings on the "submissive" and "aggressive" systems.

should ensure that all social behaviour elements are present. Apart from this seemingly trivial consideration, it is also necessary to realize to what extent the lumping and splitting of variables is of importance. A specific component that only explains a fraction of the total variance can manifest itself as a more important common component if it is further split up into a number of elements that have positive correlations amongst each other. If these new elements are in a similar way correlated with all the other elements, the result will be that the other elements will also tend to be more strongly correlated amongst each other, and that the degree of differentiation between these other elements will decrease. Conversely, if one lumps the elements that are united by a common component, this component may, in effect, disappear, and the degree of differentiation among the remaining elements will increase. Thus, elements that were the expression of a common component may now split up into sub-groups, provided that the component does not reflect a rather unitary set of causal factors. These aspects will now be partially investigated for the present material.

First we will investigate the "affinitive" elements. To that end we lump together those elements that have significant loadings on the first four of the other components, but have no significant loadings on the "affinitive" component, into four new variables, "play", "aggression", "submission" and "excitement". These lumped variables replace the original elements in the transition matrix, which is then treated as before. Table 3 shows the results. The affinitive causal factors now differentiate over a number of new components. Nine elements have a

TABLE 3
Component analysis of the elements of the "affinitive" system

Component	AI	AII	AIII	AIV	AV	AVI	AVII	AVIII	AIX	AX
Groom [33]	**90**	12	03	06	-06	04	-12	29	11	-01
Groom presenting [21]	**86**	01	08	17	-06	08	-01	04	**37**	-05
Mouth-mouth [30]	**84**	08	-10	-21	06	21	**36**	-01	-15	-11
Pant [51]	**81**	12	-12	-12	34	05	30	00	-11	-15
Autogroom [22]	**71**	**41**	04	07	-22	-18	-16	18	31	01
Embrace [38]	**69**	-01	34	-06	**41**	26	-12	-12	-12	-09
Mount-presenting [18]	**57**	18	31	07	08	**56**	-05	03	-05	-05
Vertical head nod [14]	-05	**88**	-23	-01	-01	12	33	03	03	13
Silent pout [53]	08	**85**	34	11	09	-02	-03	-15	21	-05
Male mating [35]	19	**83**	10	15	-01	08	-06	**37**	12	-02
Hold out hand [17]	06	**82**	32	-13	27	08	-18	14	-07	15
Touch [24]	23	**75**	30	06	16	00	14	23	-06	-31
Pout moan [45]	-04	33	**91**	-04	03	06	01	06	-00	-04
Stretched pout whimper [44]	-07	13	**90**	-22	22	04	-00	-00	-04	15
Bared-teeth yelp [43]	-04	-06	**71**	-20	**54**	09	05	-02	09	30
Cling [39]	**49**	31	**70**	19	-16	14	-05	-14	-07	-11
Mount walk [37]	25	-11	**61**	18	-23	**56**	00	-02	-23	03
«Play»	15	05	-00	**84**	-08	-02	-10	**37**	01	-23
«Aggression + Bluff»	-24	19	-22	**81**	-12	-08	22	-17	-16	04
Silent bared-teeth [52]	15	34	17	-09	**82**	10	14	-02	19	01
Crouch-presenting [19]	11	28	08	-27	**40**	**68**	21	12	-02	20
Smooth approach [1]	**40**	24	26	-11	06	**50**	16	16	12	*-40*
«Excitement»	09	03	06	07	11	07	**95**	00	17	08
Genital investigation [34]	15	**38**	-03	13	-03	13	02	**82**	11	-22
Watch [23]	25	16	-19	-19	21	02	28	11	**80**	05
«Submission»	-26	04	28	-23	09	07	19	-24	08	**76**
Portion of the variance explained	19%	17%	15%	7.2%	6.9%	6.2%	6.2%	5.1%	4.9%	4.6%

Note: Positive significant values are **in bold print** and negative ones *in italics*.

significant loading, and seven elements their highest loading, on component AI. Its most specific representative is *grooming* and it furthermore comprises a number of gentle contact movements like *embrace, mouth-mouth* and *mount-presenting*; we could designate it the "groom and contact" system. Component AII can quite clearly be designated as the "male-mating" system.

Component AIII encompasses elements that, except for *clinging*, are typically performed by the younger animals. The *pout moan* which scores the highest loading is in a number of other species an almost exclusive juvenile expression (van Hooff, 1962, 1967a). In the chimpanzee it belongs to the first elements to occur during ontogeny (von Allesch, 1921) and seems to be especially effective in re-establishing contact between mother and child (van Lawick-Goodall, 1967, 1968). Here the group includes a form of contact, *mount-walking*, that tends to end a sequence (see Table 1) and is in form related to "dorsal riding". We shall therefore designate this component as the "juvenile contact" system.

Silent bared-teeth represents rather specific causal factors (component AV) which are also of significant, though secondary, influence in *embrace, bared-teeth yelp* and *croach-presenting*. The component AVI emphasizes common aspects of both presenting postures (*crouch-* and *mount-presenting* and *approach*). Genital investigation is a strong representative of rather specific factors that to a certain extent are shared by "play" and *male mating* (component AVIII). The categories "excitement" (component AVII) and "submission" (component AX) manifest themselves now in specific components. "Play" and "aggression" even go together in that they appear to share causal factors and that their specific aspects do not show up any more (component AIV).

In contrast to the differentiation that is brought about in the "affinitive" category, by lumping the elements of the other categories, is the similarity of the general structure obtained after the same procedure has been applied to the "play" category (Table 4). Five components explain almost the total amount of variance, and the first four reflect aspects we were familiar with already. The present results, however, show a stronger accentuation of the specific differences revealed earlier. The elements that represented the play component most purely again represent one component. Those that had appreciable loadings on other systems share high loadings on specific components with the variables representing the lumped systems; for instance, *stamp, sway-*

TABLE 4

Component analysis of the elements of the "play" system

Component	PI	PII	PIII	PIV	PV
Grasp, poke [26]	**97**	−02	−16	−01	06
Gnaw [31]	**94**	−11	−13	15	03
Hand-wrestle [25]	**94**	−11	−10	17	−12
Gnaw-wrestle [40]	**94**	02	−19	−10	15
Pull limb [27]	**90**	04	−25	02	12
Relaxed open mouth [50]	**90**	03	−25	−10	21
Gymnastics [11]	**75**	27	−04	05	**48**
Sway-walk [4]	07	**93**	−09	14	−01
Stamp [13]	−14	**90**	06	−14	20
«Aggression +Bluff »	−18	**90**	08	−05	−06
Hit [28]	26	**82**	−27	−24	30
«Submission »	−27	−06	**92**	04	06
«Excitement »	−52	27	**72**	−18	−09
Mount [36]	06	09	−32	**85**	21
«Affinity »	−01	−29	**35**	**78**	−29
Gallop [3]	**60**	33	08	03	**68**
Portion of the variance explained	41%	22%	12%	10%	7%

Note: Positive significant values are **in bold print** and negative ones *in italics*.

walk, and *hit* with "aggression", and *mount* with "affinity". The only new component is the fifth, expressing common factors of two elements that have large loadings on the first component as well, namely *gymnastics* and *gallop*. These clearly have a certain "acrobatic" aspect in common and do not necessarily involve direct social interaction. It is, furthermore, of interest that "excitement" and "submission" are united on the basis of common characteristics that contrast them very strongly with "play"; note the negative loading of "excitement" on component PI of "play" and the negative loadings of the "play" elements on component PIII.

Table 5 shows the results for the aggressive system. Five components explain more than 90 per cent of the variance. The grouping obtained is for the greater part a stronger accentuation of differences suggested already by the results of the general matrix.

The first component can be identified again as the "bluff" component, since common aspects of *rising hoot*, "play" and *hitting* with the

TABLE 5

Component analysis of the elements of the "aggression and bluff" system

Component	ABI	ABII	ABIII	ABIV	ABV
Stamp [13]	**96**	11	−05	−03	04
Stamp-trot [5]	**93**	19	−07	14	01
Arm-sway [12]	**92**	05	02	−30	16
Sway-walk [4]	**80**	**38**	−22	−22	−22
Rising hoot [47]	**67**	−07	22	**52**	14
«Play »	**54**	−05	−14	*−47*	*−61*
Hit [28]	**53**	24	−20	*−72*	*−12*
Tug ⌊29]	20	**95**	05	−09	13
Bite [32]	−08	**93**	20	−18	14
Trample [41]	**35**	**92**	−08	−03	−05
Brusque rush [6]	20	**69**	23	−07	**56**
«Submission »	−21	26	**90**	01	18
«Excitement »	13	−18	**85**	**36**	−10
Shrill bark [46]	−10	**37**	**79**	−25	**36**
«Affinity »	00	−10	−03	**94**	−05
Grunt bark [48]	**49**	**41**	25	−09	**67**
Portion of the variance explained	30%	24%	16%	14%	9%

Note: Positive significant values are **in bold print** and negative ones *in italics*.

typical "bluff" elements are emphasized. The second component sets the "attack" elements apart. The fourth component represents the "affinitive" system with which *rising hoot*, and to a lesser extent "excitement", show similarity, but which, in this configuration, appears to be incompatible with "play" and *hitting*. "Excitement" again has much in common with "submission", as is revealed by component ABIII. These systems share their common causal factors with *shrill bark*, which has also loadings on the "attack" component and component ABV. The latter component has not manifested itself before; it combines both types of *bark* and *brusque rush*, and represents factors that specifically exclude "play" altogether. All three have appreciable loadings on "attack" as well, but since they do not involve direct body contact we shall call them "threat" elements.

Investigation of the "submissive" elements in relation to the other four lumped systems (Table 6) hardly reveals any further differentiation than was apparent already, although less overtly, from the results

TABLE 6

Component analysis of the elements of the "submissive" system

Component	SI	SII	SIII	SIV	SV
Bared-teeth scream [42]	**93**	*−04*	06	08	15
Crouch [20]	**92**	*−04*	25	05	*−01*
Flight [7]	**90**	17	06	17	33
Bared-teeth yelp [43]	**80**	*−35*	25	*−19*	13
Stretched pout whimper [44]	**56**	*−63*	*−09*	*−45*	07
«Play »	*−03*	**88**	*−29*	04	*−02*
Parry [16]	**66**	**67**	*−04*	*−04*	*−16*
«Excitement »	03	*−07*	**96**	05	*−01*
Hesitant approach [2]	**40**	*−30*	**81**	00	*−10*
Shrink-flinch [9]	10	*−68*	**61**	*−14*	16
Shrill bark [46]	20	*−25*	21	**88**	*−05*
«Aggressive+Bluff »	*−16*	**56**	*−07*	**76**	08
Avoid [8]	**44**	*−12*	*−07*	*−18*	**83**
«Affinity »	*−08*	*−31*	32	*−78*	31
Portion of the variance explained	31%	20%	17%	16%	7.2

Note: Positive significant values are **in bold print** and negative ones *in italics*.

of the general matrix. The notable exception is *avoidance*, which appears to have rather specific causal factors that would seem to a limited extent to influence the "affinitive" system and *flight* as well. Already, in the results of the total matrix (Table 2), it distinguished itself from the other elements of the category by its relatively high, though not significant, loading on the "show" component. This corresponds with the intuitive judgement that avoidance is not necessarily accompanied by the subjective element of fear, which is a regular attribute of the other elements of the group. In the present configuration the combined "aggressive" and "bluff" elements on the one hand, and the combined "affinitive" elements and *stretched pout whimper* on the other, share a bipolar component, indicating that their causal factors mutually exclude one another. A similar case holds for the combined "play" elements on the one hand and *stretch pout whimper* and *hesitant approach* on the other.

6.3.3   Results of the cluster analysis

The cluster analysis yields a visual representation of the relational structure of the elements. Figure 47 gives this for the general matrix

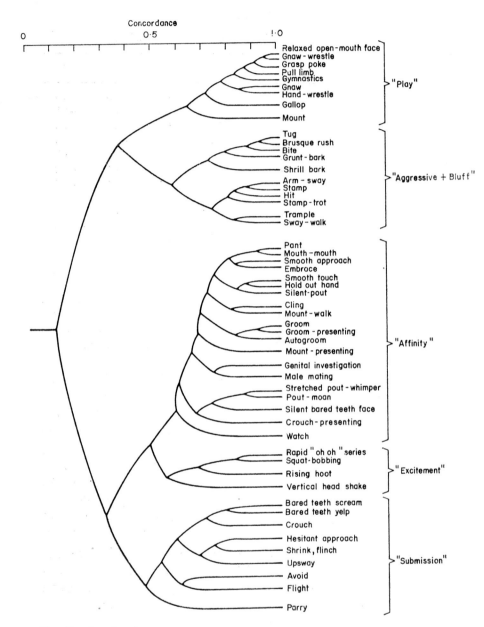

Fig. 47. Results of the cluster analysis. The behavioural elements are placed in a hierarchical structure of concordance.

in which all elements are present individually. On the ordinate the elements have been arranged in such a manner that those that are most concordant are placed next to each other. The point where their lines unite on the abscissa indicates their concordance, as expressed in a coefficient that ranges from 0 to 1 (McQuitty, 1966). When two elements are found to unite in a cluster, the element or other cluster with which it is most concordant is placed next, forming a new cluster, and so on. The distance between adjoining elements or clusters on the ordinate is greater if their coefficient of concordance is lower.

The diagram reveals a hierarchical structure. The same five main groups which were determined by means of component analysis can again be distinguished. From top to bottom respectively we find: "play"; "aggression", consisting of two distinct sub-groups (namely "attack" and "bluff"); "affinity", showing no clear differentiation here; "excitement" (without *upsway*, but instead loosely associated with *vertical head nod*); and finally "submission", the elements of which (notably *parry*) are least strongly associated. The differences between this and the component analysis are a matter of detail rather than of principle. In agreement with the previous results it is also found that the clusters "play" and "aggression" show some concordance, while the same is true for "affinity" and "excitement" and for both of these and "submission".

We can again lump the elements belonging to particular systems into new "compound" elements in the transition matrix, in order to emphasize the specific aspects of the remaining elements (see pp. 68–69). Thus, for example, the differentiating aspects of the "affinitive" elements gain emphasis by lumping the other elements into four "compound" elements: "aggression", "submission", "play" and "excitement". The differentiation is in accordance with the results of the component analysis of Table 3 (see Fig. 48).

Other combinations of selective lumping lead to similar results and these have not therefore been presented here.

7 Discussion and conclusions

Both component and cluster analysis of the transition frequency patterns of the social behaviour elements reveal that these are integrated in a clear structure. The nature of the structure depends, however, to a considerable extent on the choice of the elements and the extent to

which these are split or lumped. If all the 53 main behaviour elements
that have been distinguished are individually represented in the matrix
of transition frequencies, five main components emerge that have a
significant influence on all the elements. If one consequently joins the
elements that are united by one component (this has been done for four

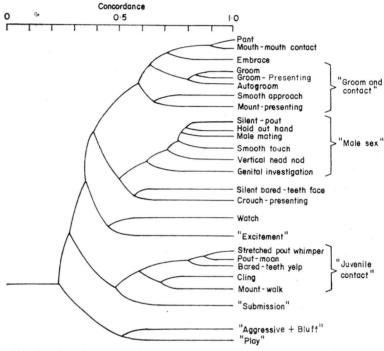

Fig. 48. Results of the cluster analysis. The "affinitive" elements are represented
individually. The elements of each of the four remaining categories have been lumped
together, and are represented in the respective "category variables".

of the five main components), the elements that have not been lumped
may further differentiate; and the existence of common characteristics
specific to more limited groups of elements may be revealed. This
appears to be especially so when the "affinitive" elements are further
investigated. On the other hand, variables that have arisen from the
lumping of elements which represent the same component may now
appear to have certain aspects in common as well. Thus the variables
"aggression and bluff" and "play", when compared with the "affinitive" elements (Table 3) appear to have much in common. This is also
true, though less so, when these variables are compared with the "sub-

missive" system. The variables "excitement" and "submission" behave in a similar way when compared with the "aggression and bluff" elements and with the "play" elements. However, they do not do so when compared with the "affinitive" elements.

The relations that become manifest are, therefore, dependent on the level of analysis. The structure is clearly of a hierarchical nature; at one level the specific aspects and at another the common aspects of groups of elements are emphasized.

The hierarchical organization of causal influences is well portrayed by the cluster analysis. First it shows how all the elements represent a collection of the individual types, and, as more individual types are classified together, higher and higher orders of hierarchical types are revealed. By contrast the component analysis can be considered to "cut through" the hierarchical tree at a certain level.

An advantage of the component analysis is that it can more appropriately represent variables that have appreciable loadings on more than one of the independent components. In cluster analysis such a variable is joined to only one of the categories. Thus the element *parry* in Table 2 appears to have significant loadings on both the "play" (0.62) and the "submission" (0.42) component. The cluster analysis places it next to the "submissive" group, with which it is concordant at 0.45 (Fig. 7).

Examples of a hierarchical behaviour organization can be found elsewhere in the ethological literature. Most well-known is Tinbergen's (1942, 1951) representation of the reproductive activities of the male three-spined stickleback in a hierarchical motivation model. Tinbergen's model suggests that there are quite distinct levels of integration, and it has been assumed that these correspond to a hierarchical system of discrete neural mechanisms. For many other species, mainly birds and fishes, it has been shown that behaviours, especially courtship activities, can be arranged in groups, each element representing a specific balance of the influences of three main motivational components or tendencies, which have been identified as the "attack", "flight", and "sexual" systems. In many of these studies one particular activity was defined to represent one of the respective tendencies; in other words the tendencies were assessed in terms of only one behavioural variable. Such methods can easily lead, as they have done, to a conception of a certain group of activities being the expression of a restricted number of unitary drives, the correlates of distinct neural mechanisms. However, on a narrower time scale the correlations become less absolute, and the influence of different experimental variables on the members of a group may be quite diverse, so that it is necessary to postulate more specific causal factors (for an extensive discussion of these aspects see Hinde, 1970).

On the basis of such considerations Andrew (1962, 1963) regarded an explanation of the causation of primate displays in terms of the usual three-drive model as misleading. Moreover, as it became clear that all primate social behavioural elements cannot be accommodated into the flight-aggression-sex model, one had to "create new drives". It would seem, however, that his alternative of explaining the causation of primate displays in terms of "stimulus contrast" can lead to a misunderstanding similar to that which the "drive" concept has given rise to. Besides, it may lead to circular arguments, since the degree of stimulus contrast is inferred from the "intensity" of the animal's reaction (for an extensive discussion see van Hooff, 1967a).

The present data appear to leave few opportunities for the controversy referred to above. On the one hand they offer a clear case of an empirical categorization of behaviour elements based on analysis of their causal similarities, i.e. by means of a "classical" ethological method. On the other hand the hierarchical nature of the structure revealed does not leave room for unwarranted deductions about unitary causal mechanisms. Moreover, it goes almost without saying that one cannot solely on the basis of these statistically defined factors make inferences as to the physiological nature of the underlying mechanisms. The components refer to causal or organizational systems, consisting of both internal and external factors controlling and integrating the occurrence of a certain number of behaviour elements. To reveal the nature of such factors and separate the external and internal influences, one has to do research specifically aimed at those questions (Baerends, 1956; Wiepkema, 1961; Blurton-Jones, 1968). A categorization like the present one can form a comprehensive framework on which such directed research can be based.

In the classical "courtship" studies the elements of social interaction could be attributed partly or wholly to three main motivational categories, namely a "flight", an "attack" and a "sexual" category (the "FA" system, Morris, 1956). The first two may be taken together on the basis of their function as "agonistic" (Scott and Fredericson, 1951) or "distance increasing" (Tinbergen, 1959) behaviour. It depended on the scope of the research whether one termed the third category the "sexual" one, or felt inclined to use a wider term, implicating other social contact behaviour besides sexual behaviour. In the latter case the existence of a "social drive" has been debated (Stamm, 1962; Tembrock, 1964), i.e. whether there are other "attracting" forces besides those leading to sexual and parental behaviour. With respect to primates, Zuckerman's (1932) original view that sexual factors almost exclusively accounted for the social coherence has not been acceptable to recent investigators (see Marler, 1968). Emphasis is placed also on other cohesive factors, such as the attraction between the infant and, in the first place, the mother and other group members (see also Chance, 1963; Hall, 1965; Wickler, 1967).

In those cases where students of primate behaviour gave a classification of the social behaviour patterns—usually without an empirical rationale or with one of only a qualitative nature—sexual behaviour can often be distinguished from non-sexual social behaviour. Thus Hall (1962) distinguishes in *Papio* baboons the categories "agonistic", "sexual" and "social" behaviour; the latter category also includes "play". Kaufman (1967) divides the social behaviour patterns of the Rhesus monkey into two main groups, "non-agonistic" and "agonistic", the latter being subdivided into "aggressive" and "submissive" categories. In the same species Freedman and Rosvold (1962) distinguish "aggressive", "anxiety", "sexual", and "affinitive" or "social succouring" behaviours. They do not mention "play"; but it may not have occurred in the laboratory set-up they employed. A similar categorization is made by Alexander and Harlow (1965), who, moreover, do distinguish a fifth category, namely "play". Rowell (1966, 1967a, 1969) uses a similar categorization, admitting that it involved some arbitrary decisions, and pointing out the difficulty that is encountered with "play", as it appears to involve motor patterns that also form part of the category of "aggression". Loizos (1969), who noted that in the chimpanzee also the "aggressive" and "playful" motor patterns have much in common, found that "aggression" and "play" can also be distinguished by the different temporal patterning of these formally similar elements in interaction.

The same major motivational systems tend to emerge, then, as were found in our study. These classifications clearly have, therefore, a general validity. The differences, particularly with respect to the categories of "affinity" and "play", are in some cases a reflection of the author's specific interest; in others they reflect the observational conditions.

The latter undoubtedly played a role in a study by Thompson (1969), who set out to determine empirically the basic motivational tendencies underlying the social behaviour shown in dyadic confrontations between macaques, in order to get an insight into the motivations that are responsible for the structure of natural groups. Pairs of animals met each other twice, during two 10-minute periods, two months apart. The frequencies of eight different behaviours (*fighting, chasing, mounting, atypical mount, genital inspection, genital presenting, grooming* and *tail up*), the individual's weight, and the inter-individual distance were correlated. On the basis of these correlations and the relative frequencies of the behaviours Thompson infers the existence of three basic motivations: a grooming tendency, influencing the behaviour of males and especially females; a mounting tendency, specific to males; and a spacing tendency, excited by the sight of another animal and proportional in strength to that animal's proximity and size. *Fighting, atypical mounting* and *chasing* would result when the mounting tendency is thwarted by the partner.

From our own studies on *Macaca irus* (unpublished material) we know that there are other frequently occurring macaque behaviour patterns than the eight listed by Thompson. Perhaps the inclusion of variables like "lip-smacking", "teeth-baring", "flight", etc. might have given a more direct indication of the "spacing tendency". In contexts other than a 10-minute confrontation, "fighting" and "chasing" may well appear to represent more than a thwarted mounting tendency, namely a more general aggressive tendency, functioning also as part of the "spacing tendency". Thus the original spacing tendency might differentiate into an "aggressive" and a "submissive" one.

In our own research a few behaviour patterns like *gnaw-wrestling* and *relaxed open-mouth face* are clustered in what might be called a "play" group. This motivational system undoubtedly plays an important role in natural groups (Loizos, 1967), but is unlikely to manifest itself in short-lasting confrontations.

The most representative picture of the motivational components that determine the group structure is therefore undoubtedly obtained by selecting a broad repertoire of behaviour patterns and studying their occurrence in a variable setting or in conditions near to the natural ones.

An empirical categorization under such conditions has been made recently by Altmann (1968), in his study of the social behaviour of the rhesus monkeys of Cayo Santiago Island. It differs fundamentally from mine in that it is based not on the transition frequencies between neighbouring elements of *the actor itself* but on the transition frequencies obtained by establishing in what manner each behaviour element is responded to by *the partner*. Thus dyads of interaction are obtained. More than half of the patterns fell into a group termed "primarily agonistic signals". Furthermore there are groups of "primarily affinitive and mild tactile signals" (comprising, amongst others, "grooming"); "primary sexual signals of males"; "primary sexual signals of females"; "play"; "suckling and weaning"; "aggressive chases" (comprising "chase" and "flee", etc.); "carrying of infants"; and finally two "agonistic patterns". As these groups are based on quite different criteria, more than a superficial correspondence with our categories cannot be expected.

The most comprehensive classification of chimpanzee social behaviour has been given by van Lawick-Goodall (1968). It is essentially qualitative and comprises the following headings: (a) "calls, facial expressions and autonomic behaviour"; (b) "flight and avoidance"; (c) "frustration"; (d) "aggressive behaviour"; (e) "submissive behaviour"; (f) "reassurance behaviour"; (g) "greeting behaviour"; (h) "communication patterns occurring in the context of feeding, sexual behaviour, mother-offspring relationships, social play and grooming". The classes may refer primarily to common causal aspects of the context, or to functional similarities, or even to common effector mechanisms. So the classes overlap and a number of behaviour patterns are discussed under more than one heading (e.g. "stamping" under both aggressive behaviour and frustration, and "swagger" under both aggression and courtship).

In a number of cases such a plural representation does, however, reflect the fact that the stimulus value of a certain display depends on the characteristics of the context, for instance the social status, and, in connection with this, the preceding behaviour of both actor and reactor. Thus the "swagger" (corresponding with our *arm-sway*) may in some contexts have a repulsive and in others an attractive effect. This indeed is also suggested by the results of my Table 2. *Arm-sway* shares independent common causal factors with both the "attack" elements on the one hand and with a number of "show" elements that include *male mating* on the other.

The different nature of the two categorizations only permits a superficial comparison; but such differences as there seem to be are probably not of a fundamental nature. Thus, van Lawick-Goodall distinguishes "submissive" touching from holding out the hand. In my case both *touching* and *hold out hand* appear not to be correlated with what we called the submissive component (Table 1). However, Table 3 shows that both these elements, apart from possessing large loadings on the "male mating system" (component AII), also have nearly significant loadings on the "juvenile contact system" (component AIII). Though both elements again do not share the causal factors that are specific for the typical "submissive" elements (component AX), they are connected with the "submissive" elements, albeit weakly, by component AIII. Whether there is agreement between the studies may therefore in part depend on what is meant by terms such as "submissive". Furthermore, the criteria used for assessing the relative importance of relationships between the elements of social behaviour may be of influence.

The present study was intended to show the *typical* relationships of the elements. I selected a method, therefore, that emphasizes those relationships that are outstanding because they are based on mutual transition frequencies occurring either more or less frequently than would be expected on the basis of a random distribution of behaviour elements. By using the quotient $(o - e) / \sqrt{e}$ the absolute magnitude of both observed and expected transition frequencies is of some influence as well; it is commensurate with the greater significance that should be attributed to a similar ratio of deviation, according to whether the expected value is greater. If, for instance, the absolute transition frequencies had been used, or, as in a qualitative study, had implicitly been accentuated, a different picture would certainly have been obtained (see p. 58).

By its nature a quantitative analysis reveals the general aspects of a certain set of frequently occurring phenomena; however, the specific aspects of rather unique occurrences, though possibly theoretically significant, find no expression. The chance of encountering such unique occurrences, which are due to an exceptional combination of the causal variables, is likely to increase the higher on the phyletic scale one gets, as the system of variables that affect behaviour then becomes more complex. With increasing plasticity in the patterning of behaviour elements, there is also an increasing complexity in the mechanisms of perception and integration, with experience and insight gaining importance, especially in the highest primates. This undoubtedly also affects the social, notably communicative, behaviour, as is clearly manifest in our own species. In the chimpanzee it is especially tactile communication and the hand gestures that show an increasing variability. For, although learning has been shown to play a possible, albeit moderate, role in the control of vocalization (Hayes, 1951; Randolph and Brooks, 1967; Randolph and Mason, 1969), it is especially the gestures that can be elaborately conditioned (Gardner and Gardner, 1969). In agreement with this is the high variability of the hand gestures observed in nature (Kortlandt, 1967; van Lawick-Goodall, 1967, 1968a), a variability that is also manifest in this study. The "down movement", a version of the "overstretch" described under *hold out hand* [17], is an instance of such a unique, but probably highly meaningful variant. This and other gestures may be gestural pictograms that owe their functionality to the contextual insight of both interacting partners.

This emphasizes McKrioch's (1967) and Mason's (1970) recommendations that our attempts to develop and apply adequate quantitative methods should not lead to disregard of the qualitative account and of the anecdotal narrative, which can so clearly elucidate "the illuminating particular" (Mason, 1970).

References

Alexander, B. K. and Harlow, H. F. (1965). Social behavior of juvenile Rhesus monkeys subjected to different rearing conditions during the first six months of life. *Zool. Jb. Physiol.* **71**, 489–508.

Allesch, J. G. von (1921). Bericht über die drei ersten Lebensmonate eines Schimpansen. *Sber. Preuss. Akad. Wiss.* **39**, 672–685.

Altmann, S. A. (1962). A field study of the sociobiology of Rhesus monkeys, *Macaca mulatta. Ann. N.Y. Acad. Sci.* **102**, 338–435.

Altmann, S. A. (1965). Sociobiology of Rhesus monkeys. II: Stochastics of social communication. *J. Theor. Biol.* **8**, 490–522.

Altmann, S. A. (1967). The structure of primate social communication. *In* "Social Communication among Primates". (Ed. S. A. Altmann), pp. 325–362. University of Chicago Press, Chicago.

Altmann, S. A. (1968). Sociobiology of Rhesus monkeys. IV. Testing Mason's hypothesis of sex differences in affective behaviour. *Behaviour*, **32**, 49–69.

Andrew, R. J. (1962). The situations that evoke vocalization in primates. *Ann. N.Y. Acad. Sci.* **102**, 296–315.

Andrew, R. J. (1963). The origin and evolution of the calls and facial expressions of the primates. *Behaviour*, **20**, 1–109.

Baerends, G. P. (1956). Aufbau des tierischen Verhaltens. *Handb. Zool. Berlin*, **8**, 1–32.

Baerends, G. P., Brouwer, R. and Waterbolk, H. Tj. (1955). Ethological studies on *Lebistes reticulatus* (Peters). *Behaviour*, **8**, 249–334.

Bernstein, I. S. (1967). A field study of the pigtail monkey (*Macaca nemestrina*). *Primates*, **8**, 217–228.

Bertrand, M. (1969). "The Behavioral Repertoire of the Stumptail Macaque". (*Bibl. Primatol.* Vol. 11). Karger, Basel.

Bierens de Haan, J. A. (1952). Das Spiel eines jungen solitären Schimpansen. *Behaviour*, **4**, 144–146.

Bingham, H. C. (1928). Sex development in apes. *Comp. Psychol. Monogr.* **5**, 23.

Blurton-Jones, N. G. (1968). Observations and experiments on causation of threat displays of the Great Tit (*Parus major*). *Anim. Behav. Monogr.* **1**, 75–158.

Bolwig, N. (1964). Facial expression in primates with remarks on a parallel development in certain carnivores. *Behaviour*, **22**, 167–193.

Bournonville, D. de (1967). Contribution à l'étude du chimpanzé en Republique de Guinée. *Bull. Lust. Fond. Afr. Noire*, **29**, 1188–1269.

Bijnen, E. J. (1969). "Cluster-analyse. Overzicht en Evaluatie van Technieken". Doctoral Thesis, Tilburg.

Carpenter, C. R. (1934). A field study of the behavior and social relations of Howling Monkeys (*Alouatta palliata*). *Comp. Psychol. Monogr.* **10**, 1–168.

Carpenter, C. R. (1940). A field study in Siam of the behavior and social relations of the Gibbon (*Hylobates lar*). *Comp. Psychol. Monogr.* **16**, 169–182.

Carpenter, C. R. (1958). Soziologie und Verhalten freilebender nichtmenschlicher Primaten. *Handb. Zool. Berlin*, **8**, 1–32.

Chance, M. R. A. (1956). Social structure of a colony of *Macaca mulatta*. *Br. J. Anim. Behav.* **4**, 1–13.

Chance, M. R. A. (1963). The social bond of the primates. *Primates*, **4**, 1–22.

Collias, N. E. and Southwick, C. H. (1952). A field study of population density and social organization in Howling Monkeys. *Proc. Amer. Phil. Soc.* **96**, 143–156.

Cranach, M. von and Frenz, H. G. (1969). Systematische Beobachtung. *In* "Handbuch der Psychologie" (Ed. C. F. Graumann), Vol. 7, pp. 269–331. Verlag für Psychologie, Göttingen.

Dane, B. and Kloot, W. G. van der (1964). An analysis of the display of the Goldeneye Duck (*Bucephala clangula* G.). *Behaviour*, **22**, 283–325.

Eisenberg, J. F. and Kuehn, R. E. (1966). The behaviour of *Ateles geoffroyi* and related species. *Smithson Misc. Coll.* **151**, 1–63.

Ex, J. (1969). "Communicatie van gezicht tot gezicht". Dekker and van der Vegt, Nijmegen.

Finch, G. (1942). Chimpanzee frustration responses. *Psychosom. Med.* **4**, 233–251.

Freedman, L. Z. and Rosvold, H. E. (1962). Sexual aggressive and anxious behavior in the laboratory Macaque. *J. Nerv. Ment. Dis.* **134**, 18–27.

Gardner, B. T. and Gardner, R. A. (1969). Teaching sign language to a chimpanzee. *Science*, **165**, 664–672.

Gartlan, J. S. (1968). Structure and function in primate society. *Folia Primat.* **8**, 89–120.

Goodall, Jane (1965). Chimpanzees of the Gombe Stream Reserve. *In* "Primate Behavior" (Ed. I. DeVore), pp. 425–473. Holt, Rinehart & Winston, New York.

Grant, E. C. (1963). An analysis of the social behaviour of the male laboratory rat. *Behaviour*, **21**, 260–281.

Grant, E. C. (1965a). The contribution of ethology to child psychiatry. *In* "Modern Perspectives in Child Psychiatry" (Ed. J. G. Howell), pp. 20–37. Oliver & Boyd, London.

Grant, E. C. (1965b). An ethological description of some schizophrenic patterns of behaviour. *In* "Proceedings of the Leeds Symposium on Behavioural Disorders", pp. 3–14. May and Baker, Dagenham.

Grant, E. C. (1968). An ethological description of non-verbal behaviour during interviews. *Br. J. Med. Psychol.* **41**, 177–184.

Hall, K. R. L. (1962). The sexual, agonistic and derived social behaviour patterns of the wild Chacma baboon (*Papio ursinus*). *Proc. Zool. Soc. Lond.* **139**, 283–327.

Hall, K. R. L. (1965). Social organization of the old world monkeys and apes. *Symp. Zool. Soc. Lond.* **14**, 265–289.

Hall, K. R. L., Boelkins, R. C. and Goswell, M. J. (1965). Behaviour of Patas monkeys, *Erythrocebus patas*, in captivity, with notes on the natural habitat. *Folia Primat.* **3**, 22–49.

Harman, H. H. (1967). "Modern Factor Analysis". University of Chicago Press, Chicago.

Hayes, C. (1951). "The Ape in our House". Harper, New York.

Hinde, R. A. (1966). "Animal Behaviour, a Synthesis of Ethology and Comparative Psychology". McGraw-Hill, New York. (Also 2nd edition, 1970.)

Hooff, J. A. R. A. M. van (1962). Facial expressions in higher primates. *Symp. Zool. Soc. Lond.* **8**, 97–125.

Hooff, J. A. R. A. M. van (1967a). The facial displays of the catarrhine monkeys and apes. *In* "Primate Ethology" (Ed. D. Morris), pp. 7–68. Weidenfeld & Nicolson, London.

Hooff, J. A. R. A. M. van (1967b). The care and management of captive chimpanzees with special emphasis on the ecological aspects. Tech. Rep. ARL-TR-67-15, 6571st Aeromed. Res. Lab., N. Mexico.

Hooff, J. A. R. A. M. van (1970). A component analysis of the structure of the social behaviour of a semi-captive Chimpanzee group. *Experientia*, **26**, 549–550.

Itani, J. and Suzuki, A. (1967). The social unit of chimpanzees. *Primates*, **8**, 355–381.

Kaufman, I. C. and Rosenblum, L. A. (1966). A behavioural taxonomy for *Macaca nemestrina* and *Macaca radiata*. *Primates*, **7**, 205–258.

Kaufman, J. F. (1967). Social relations of adult males in a free-ranging band of Rhesus monkeys. *In* "Social Communication among Primates" (Ed. S. A. Altmann), pp. 73–98. University of Chicago Press, Chicago.

Kaufmann, J. H. and Kaufmann, A. (1963). Some comments on the relationship between field and laboratory studies of behaviour, with special reference to *Coatis*. *Anim. Behav.* **11**, 464–469.

Köhler, W. (1921). Aus der Anthropoïdenstation auf Teneriffa. V. Zur Psychologie des Schimpansen. *Sber. Preuss. Akad. Wiss.* **39**, 686–692.

Köhler, W. (1922). Zur Psychologie des Schimpansen. *Psychol. Forsch.* **1**.

Köhler, W. (1925). "The Mentality of Apes". Routledge & Kegan Paul, London.

Kohts, N. (1935). Infant ape and human child. *Trudy Zoopsikhol. Lab. Gos. Darvin. Muz.* **3** (Sci. Mem. Mus. Darwin., Moscow).

Kortlandt, A. (1962). Chimpanzees in the wild. *Sci. Amer.* **206**, 128–138.

Kortlandt, A. (1967). Handgebrauch bei freilebenden Schimpansen. *In* "Handgebrauch und Verständiging bei Affen und Frühmenschen" (Ed. B. Rensch), pp. 59–102. Huber, Bern.

Kortlandt, A. and Kooij, M. (1963). Protohominid behaviour in primates. *Symp. Zool. Soc. Lond.* **10**, 61–88.

Kummer, H. (1957). Soziales Verhalten einer Mantelpaviangruppe. *Beih. Schweiz. Z. Psychol.* **33**, 1–91.

Kummer, H. (1967). Tripartite relations in Hamadryas baboons. *In* "Social Communication among Primates" (Ed. S. A. Altmann), pp. 63–71. University of Chicago Press, Chicago.

Kummer, H. and Kurt, F. (1965). A comparison of social behaviour in captive and wild Hamadryas baboons. *In* "The Baboon in Medical Research" (Ed. H. Vagtborg), pp. 65–80. University of Texas Press, Austin.

Lawick-Goodall, Jane van (1967). Mother-offspring relationships in freeranging Chimpanzees. *In* "Primate Ethology" (Ed. D. Morris), pp. 287–346. Weidenfeld & Nicolson, London.

Lawick-Goodall, Jane van (1968). The behaviour of free-living chimpanzees in the Gombe Stream Reserve. *Anim. Behav. Monogr.* **1**, 161–311.

Lieberman, P. (1968). Primate vocalizations and human linguistic ability. *J. Acoust. Soc. Amer.* **44**, 1574–1584.

Loizos, Caroline (1967). Play behaviour in higher primates: a review. *In* "Primate Ethology" (Ed. D. Morris), pp.176–218. Weidenfeld & Nicolson, London.

Loizos, Caroline (1969). An ethological study of chimpanzee play. *In* "Proc. 2nd Intern. Congr. Primatol. Atlanta, 1968", Vol. 1, pp. 87–93. Karger, Basel.

Lorenz, K. (1959). Gestaltwahrnehmung als Quelle wissenschaftlicher Erkenntniss. *In* "Uber tierisches und menschliches Verhalten", Vol. 2, pp. 255–300. Piper, München.

Lorenz, K. (1960). Prinzipien der vergleichenden Verhaltensforschung. *Fortschr. Zool.* **12**, 265–294.

Marler, P. (1959). Developments in the study of animal communication. *In* "Darwin's Biological Work" (Ed. P. R. Bell), pp. 150–206. Cambridge University Press, Cambridge.

Marler, P. (1965). Communication in monkeys and apes. *In* "Primate Behavior" (Ed. I. DeVore), pp. 544–584. Holt, Rinehart & Winston, New York.

Marler, P. (1968). Aggregation and dispersal: two functions in primate communication. *In* "Primates. Studies in Adaptation and Variability" (Ed. Phyllis C. Jay), pp. 420–438. Holt, Rinehart & Winston, New York.

Marler, P. (1969). Vocalizations of wild chimpanzees, an introduction. *In* "Proc. 2nd Intern. Congr. Primatol. Atlanta, 1968", Vol. 1, pp. 94–100. Karger, Basel.

Marler, P. and Hamilton, W. J. (1966). "Mechanisms of Animal Behavior". John Wiley, New York.

Mason, W. A. (1965). The social development of monkeys and apes. *In* "Primate Behavior" (Ed. I. DeVore), pp. 514–543. Holt, Rinehart & Winston, New York.

Mason, W. A. (1970). Chimpanzee social behavior. *In* "The Chimpanzee" (Ed. G. H. Bourne), Vol. 2, pp. 265–288. Karger, Basel.

Mason, W. A. and Berkson, G. (1962). Conditions influencing vocal responsiveness of infant chimpanzees. *Science*, **137**, 127–128.

McCullogh, T. L. (1939). The role of clasping activity in adaptive behavior of the infant chimpanzee. III. The mechanism of reinforcement. *J. Psychol.* **7**, 305–316.

McKrioch, D. (1967). Discussion of agonistic behavior. *In* "Social Communication among Primates" (Ed. S. A. Altmann), pp. 115–122. University of Chicago Press, Chicago.

McQuitty, L. L. (1966). Similarity analysis by reciprocal pairs for discrete and continuous data. *Educ. Psychol. Measur.* **26**, 825–831.

Morris, D. (1956). The function and causation of courtship ceremonies. *In* "L'Instinct dans le Comportement des Animaux et de l'Homme" (Ed. M. Autuori), pp. 261–284. Masson, Paris.

Morris, D. (1958). The reproductive behaviour of the ten-spined stickleback (*Pygosteus pungitius* L.). *Behav. Suppl.* No. 6.

Nichols, J. W. (1954). The specification of chimpanzee vocalization. *Diss. Abstr.* **20**, 1454.

Nissen, H. W. (1931). A field study of the chimpanzee. *Comp. Psychol. Monogr.* **8**, No. 1.

Ploog, D. (1963). Verhaltensforschung und Psychiatrie. *In* "Psychiatrie der Gegenwart, Forschung un Praxis", Vol. I/1B, Teil B, pp. 292–443. Grundlagen forschung der Psychiatrie.

Plutchik, R. (1964). The study of social behaviour in primates. *Folia Primat.* **2**, 67–92.

Randolph, M. C. and Brooks, B. A. (1967). Conditioning of a vocal response in a chimpanzee through social reinforcement. *Folia Primat.* **5**, 70–79.

Randolph, M. C. and Mason, W. A. (1969). Effects of rearing conditions on distress vocalizations in chimpanzees. *Folia Primat.* **10**, 103–112.

Reynolds, V. and Reynolds, Frances (1965). Chimpanzees of the Budongo Forest. *In* "Primate Behavior" (Ed. I. DeVore), pp. 368–424. Holt, Rinehart & Winston, New York.

Riper, D. C. van, Fineg. J. and Day, P. W. (1967). Development of a primate source. *Lab. Anim. Care*, **17**, 472–478.

Rowell, Thelma E. (1966). Hierarchy in the organization of a captive baboon group. *Anim. Behav.* **14**, 430–443.

Rowell, Thelma E. (1967). Female reproductive cycles and the behavior of baboons and Rhesus macaques. *In* "Social Communication among Primates" (Ed. S. A. Altmann), pp. 15–32. Chicago University Press, Chicago.

Rowell, Thelma E. (1967). A quantitative comparison of the behaviour of a wild and a caged baboon group. *Anim. Behav.* **15**, 499–509.

Rowell, Thelma E. (1969). Intra-sexual behaviour and female reproductive cycles of baboons (*Papio anubis*). *Anim. Behav.* **17**, 159–167.

Scott, J. P. and Fredericson, E. (1951). The causes of fighting in mice and rats. *Physiol. Zool.* **24**, 273–309.

Southwick, C. H. (1967). An experimental study of intragroup agonistic behaviour in Rhesus monkeys (*Macaca mulatta*). *Behaviour*, **28**, 182–209.

Sparks, J. (1967). Allogrooming in primates, a review. *In* "Primate Ethology" (Ed. D. Morris), pp. 148–175. Weidenfeld & Nicolson, London.

Spivak, H. (1968). "Ausdrucksformen und soziale Beziehungen in einer Dschlelada-Gruppe (*Theropithecus gelada*) im Zoo". Juris Verlag, Zürich.

Stamm, R. A. (1962). Aspekte des Paarverhaltens von *Agapornis personata* Reichenow (Aves, Psittacidae, Loriini). *Behaviour*, **19**, 1–57.

Suzuki, A. (1969). An ecological study of chimpanzees in a savanna woodland. *Primates*, **10**, 103–148.

Tembrock, G. (1964). "Verhaltensforschung. Eine Einführung in die Tier-Ethologie". Gustav Fischer, Jena.

Tervoort, B. Th. M. (1953). "Structurele analyse van visueel taalgebruik binnen een groep dove kinderen". N. Hollandse Uitg. Mij., Amsterdam.

Thompson, N. S. (1969). The motivations underlying social structure in *Macaca irus*. *Anim. Behav.* **17**, 459–467.

Tinbergen, N. (1942). An objectivistic study of the innate behaviour of animals. *Bibliogr. Biotheor.* **1**, 39–98.

Tinbergen, N. (1951). "The Study of Instinct". Oxford University Press, London.

Tinbergen, N. (1959). Comparative studies of the behaviour of gulls (Laridae): a progress report. *Behaviour*, **15**, 1–70.

Tinbergen, N. (1963). On aims and methods of ethology. *Z. Tier-Psychol.* **20**, 410–433.

Tinbergen, N. (1968). On war and peace in animals and man. *Science*, **160**, 1411–1418.

Tuttle, R. H. (1967). Knuckle walking and the evolution of Hominoid hands. *Amer. J. Physic. Anthrop.* **26**, 171–206.

Wickler, W. (1967). Socio-sexual signals and their intraspecific imitation among primates. *In* "Primate Ethology" (Ed. D. Morris), pp. 69–147. Weidenfeld & Nicolson, London.

Wiepkema, P. R. (1961). An ethological analysis of the reproductive behaviour of the bitterling (*Rhodeus amarus* Bloch). *Arch. Neerl. Zool.* **14**, 103–199.

Wilson, W. L. and Wilson, C. C. (1968). Aggressive interactions of captive chimpanzees living in a semi-free-ranging environment. Tech. Rep. ARL-TR-68-9, 6571st Aeromed. Res. Lab., N. Mexico.

Yerkes, R. M. (1933). Genetic aspects of grooming, a socially important behavior pattern. *J. Soc. Psychol.* **4**, 3–25.

Yerkes, R. M. (1943). "Chimpanzees, a Laboratory Colony". Yale University Press, New Haven.

Yerkes, R. M. and Elder, J. H. (1936). Oestrus, receptivity and mating in chimpanzee. *Comp. Psychol. Monogr.* **13**, 5.

Yerkes, R. M. and Learned, B. W. (1925). "Chimpanzee Intelligence and its Vocal Expression". William & Wilkins, Baltimore.

Yerkes, R. M. and Tomilin, M. I. (1935). Mother-infant relations in chimpanzee. *J. Comp. Psychol.* **20**, 321–359.

Zuckerman, S. (1932). "The Social Life of Monkeys and Apes". Kegan Paul, London.

4

The Expressive Behaviour of the Deaf-and-Blind-Born

Irenäus Eibl-Eibesfeldt

1 Introduction

1.1 INBORN PATTERNS OF EXPRESSIVE BEHAVIOUR

Animals communicate in diverse ways by optical, acoustical, chemical, tactile, and even electrical signals, many of which have been shown to be inborn (cf. Eibl-Eibefseldt, 1970). The morphological structures that serve the function of signalling, as well as the motor patterns ("expressive movements") themselves, develop through a process of self-differentiation in the same way as organs develop, i.e. by processing information laid down in the genome of the species. The understanding of these inborn signals is also either learned or inborn. In the latter case receptor mechanisms ("innate releasing mechanisms") which have evolved during phylogeny allow the animals to react appropriately on perception of the signals (Tinbergen, 1951; Sackett, 1966).

The concept of phylogenetic adaptations in behaviour has been discussed in detail by Lorenz (1965) and Eibl-Eibesfeldt (1970). It is often argued that ethologists, when dealing with phylogenetic adaptations, adhere to an antiquated "simple" learning–instinct dichotomy. This assertion is, as will be seen, a rather inadequate representation of modern ethological views. Lorenz's main argument is based upon the

163

fact that behaviour patterns are well adapted to the environment in which they typically occur, and that this adaptedness needs to be explained. In order for adaptation to occur information about the environment to which the animal is adapted must have been fed into the organism. If we observe for example that every male bird of one species produces, in detail, the same type of courtship song, it is reasonable to ask how the information concerning the specific patterning was acquired. Such a question arises wherever we find that a structure or behaviour is "moulded" as if to fit specific features of the environment.[1] There are only limited ways in which htis acquisition of information can take place. For example, the individual may actively interact with the environment, informing, and thus adapting, itself by direct learning. Or it can acquire information via tradition: in a number of birds the song is passed on this way. In some infra-human primates, individually discovered techniques of food manipulation (e.g. potato-washing in Japanese macaques) are "culturally traditioned". Finally, the species can adapt by way of mutation and selection; such an adaptation can be conceived of as trial and error learning at the species level, so to speak. The information thus acquired is stored in the genome of the species and is decoded during ontogeny.

By means of deprivation experiments it is possible to find out how an adaptation came about. If, for example, a bird is hatched and raised in isolation in a soundproof chamber, and if none the less at sexual maturity it starts to sing and court in the same way as all the normally raised members of the species, then we can argue that the information concerning the specific patterning of the song and the courtship movements was contained in the genome, and was decoded during ontogeny through a process of self-differentiation. There is, of course, always an environment acting upon the developing organism; and since Speman's studies, biologists are well aware of self-stimulation processes and the like as important agents in embryonic development (cf. Eibl-Eibesfeldt, 1970). In whatever way environment and self-stimulation contribute, for example during decoding, they certainly do not provide the patterned information about the mould towards which the behaviour is adapted. We have to keep in mind the point that questions referring to an adaptation only make sense when we define the level of integration, so our question must be appropriate to the level we are concerned

---

[1] We could of course avoid the question by assuming a "preformed harmony" to exist between the organism and its environment, as vitalists like to suggest.

with (von Holst and von Saint-Paul, 1960). Neglect of this rule has caused a lot of confusion. For phylogenetic adaptations the terms "inborn", "inherited", "innate", or "instinctive" are used; all serve as shorthand descriptions. If one says a motor pattern is inborn, then that means that the underlying neuronal and other organic structures develop relatively inflexibly through self-differentiation, according to the developmental instructions encoded in the genome.

Occasionally the suggestion that only "differences" are inherited appears in discussion (e.g. Jensen, 1961). This has contributed to the semantic confusion. The phrase is, indeed, meaningless. Differences are abstractions; they lack physical reality. The genetic code, and not any abstraction, is inherited, and we already know from molecular biology quite a lot about how, in principle, this code is read.

The discovery that behaviour patterns of animals are often pre-programmed by phylogenetic adaptation raises the question of whether human behaviour could possibly be partly pre-programmed in similar ways. Charles Darwin as early as 1872 had pointed out a number of cross-cultural similarities in human expressive movements, which he interpreted as originating in a common phylogenetic root. He considered these patterns to be inborn in man, an opinion which has since been challenged repeatedly, recently for example by LaBarre (1947), Birdwhistell (1963, 1968) and Montagu (1968). In a number of cases comparison with other primates has revealed, however, behaviour patterns which are very probably phylogenetically old, as is the case with the expressions of smiling and laughing, for which homologues are found in the "horizontal bared-teeth face" and "relaxed open-mouth face" respectively of the chimpanzee (Fig. 1(a), (b)) and some monkeys (van Hooff, 1971, and see Chapter 3). Kissing is another example of a phylogenetically old behaviour pattern. It derives from the maternal behaviour of mouth-to-mouth feeding. In its ritualized form it serves the function of bonding. Chimpanzees are known to kiss each other (Fig. 1(c), (d)), e.g. during greeting (again see van Hooff, Chapter 3, and van-Lawick-Goodall, 1968).

The comparative approach is able to show phylogenetic adaptations in the expressive behaviour of man; strict proof, however, comes from the study of persons who were, during their ontogeny, deprived of the opportunity to learn the usual expressive behaviour patterns. This is to a great extent the case with deaf-and-blind-born individuals who grow up in eternal darkness and silence, and therefore cannot hear or see expressive behaviour in others. If all means of communication were normally learned during ontogeny, as some environmentalists assume, it should be expected that such deprived persons should deviate substantially from non-deprived individuals in their expressive behaviour. To a certain extent the blind-born should also deviate, although to a lesser degree since they are less deprived.

(a)   (b)

(c)   (d)

Fig. 1. (a, b) The homologues of the human smile—the "horizontal bared-teeth face", and laugh—the "relaxed open-mouth face" (after van Hooff). (c, d) Mouth-to-mouth feeding, and kissing (after van Lawick-Goodall).

1.2 DEAF-AND-BLIND-BORN CHILDREN

The expressive behaviour of blind-born infants has been the subject of various investigations (Thompson, 1941; Fulcher, 1942; Freedman, 1964, 1965). In contrast, very little is known about the expressive behaviour of the deaf-and-blind-born. There are a number of publications which describe case histories and general behaviour of deaf-and-blind-born persons (Wade, 1904; Salmon, 1950; Myklebust, 1956), but to my knowledge only one paper (Goodenough, 1932) presents a more detailed description of the expressive behaviour of a deaf-and-blind-born 10-year-old girl. According to this report the girl laughed whole-heartedly upon finding her doll or when dancing on the tips of her toes, a pattern which she had acquired without instruction. When annoyed she turned her head away, pouting her lips and frowning, and when strongly annoyed she shook her head and showed her clenched teeth.

In 1966 I started an investigation of the behaviour of the deaf-and-blind-born, recording their activities by 16 mm film in slow motion. Three girls and two boys all deaf and blind from birth, and one boy deaf and blind from the age of one-and-a-half years were available. All are still under observation. The subjects and assessments of their brain states are listed in Table 1. The particulars are taken from the files of the institution in which they live.

The children with very marked brain damage showed extremely poor learning ability. They needed to be fed, clothed and cleaned and were not yet toilet trained. They exhibited many stereotypic movements (see description below). The imbeciles did much better in learning. Beatrice and Heiko are borderline cases and it is difficult to tell whether they have slight or extensive brain damage. Their retardation may seem greater owing to the fact that they are very handicapped thalidomide children (both lack arms in addition to their severe sensory deficiencies).

The following account is based on films which are published by our institution as a special archive (HF49–53, Humanethologisches Filmarchiv, Max-Planck-Gesellschaft, Percha). Before we discuss the expressive behaviour patterns of the deaf-and-blind-born, a general account of their behaviour will be presented; but my special attention was focused upon Sabine, whom I have observed since May 1966; I visited her at least twice a year for a couple of days at her institution. The girl was born without any complications. For unknown reasons she has no eyes, and she never reacted even to sounds close to the threshold of pain. Her development was slow. She started to walk at an age of five years and at $6\frac{1}{2}$ years she still drank from the bottle. With assistance the ate pudding and babyfood. She walked only a few paces with evident lack of security. She was not yet accustomed to a day-and-night cycle and was not properly toilet-trained. Toys did not interest her much. She could discriminate between persons familiar and unfamiliar to her by means of her senses of touch and smell.

G

TABLE 1

Details of deaf-and-blind children studied

| Subject | Sex | Born | Neurological assessment | | | Cause of the deficiency* |
			Very extensive brain damage (idiotic)	Extensive brain damage (imbecile)	None or slight brain damage	
Petra	female	1955	yes			Mother had German measles during pregnancy, deficiency from birth
Patrik	male	1964	yes			Mother had German measles during pregnancy, deficiency from birth
Beatrice	female	1960		?		Thalidomide case, deformed limbs
Heiko	male	1961		?		Thalidomide case, deformed limbs
Sabine	female	1959			slight ?	Unknown, deficiency from birth, no eyeballs
Harald	male	1957			intelligence average	Meningitis at 18 months of age

*All the deaf-and-blind children which I have observed so far are highly retarded and it is difficult to determine whether they have been imbeciles from birth or are retarded due to their relative lack of stimulation. Since many cases result from virus infections during pregnancy, congenital brain damage is often a genuine cause of debility. This does not seem to be the case for Sabine and Heiko, since Sabine in particular shows exploratory behaviour.

Frequently she would sit for hours in a bent position. At 6½ years she was admitted to the Landesblindenanstalt in Hannover for education. Within a year she was walking quite well; she adapted to a day-and-night cycle and wet her diapers only during the night. She ate by herself and started to play and explore actively. She had learned to orient herself by touch and she knew her familiar environment well. This was in general terms her behaviour pattern when I met her for the first time. By her inquisitiveness, activity and ability to discriminate persons she contrasted significantly with most of the other deaf-and-blind-born, who, due to their brain damage, showed no exploratory activity at all.[1]

2   Behaviour of the deaf-and-blind

2.1   GENERAL ACCOUNT OF THE BEHAVIOUR OF THE SAMPLE

2.1.1   *Stereotypes and autistic activities*
Stereotypic movements are typical for all deaf-and-blind-born. In the imbeciles, Beatrice and Patrik, a sideways swaying of the head was predominant. Prechtl (1950) also observed similar movement stereotypies in normal but hospitalized children. The movement pattern resembles the automatic breast seeking movements of a baby; the stereotypy, according to Prechtl, is derived from such movements. These movements did not occur in Sabine. She did shake her head strongly and with fast movements from side-to-side occasionally, but this differed markedly from the slow head-swaying of the others. Grinding of the teeth was observed in all of the deaf-and-blind-born. In Sabine the habit declined when, following her teacher's assistance, she became actively engaged in play and other activities. Another common stereotypy was swaying back and forth of the body while sitting, and when sitting alone she often raised and lowered her eyebrows in rhythmic succession.

Sabine used to hit her mouth rhythmically with the palm of one or both hands, or hit her cheeks in a similar manner; otherwise she rhythmically pressed one hand against her chestbone. These and similar behaviour patterns can be interpreted as a way of self-stimulation to overcome the poverty of external stimulation. Blind-born

[1] I am pleased to thank her teachers, Karl-Heinrich Baaske and Miss U. Sigmund, for their hospitality at the Landesblindenanstalt, Hannover; also I thank Dr J. Hahnloser and Miss Heidi Sbrzesny for their assistance.

children often rub their eyes to create phosphenes for retinal stimulation. Sabine, who had no eyeballs, did not show this stereotypy, although the movement pattern of eye-rubbing was regularly used in other contexts, e.g. when crying.

During her phases of activity, kicking fits occurred with great regularity. When walking about, for example, she would suddenly stop, trample her feet rapidly on the spot, and at the same time shake her hands alternately and shake her head in sideways movements. The same pattern occurred when she was operating her four-wheeled trolley. Suddenly, while lying on the trolley on her belly, she would rapidly move all her extremities, kicking in a coordinated fashion akin to that of the quadrupedal vertebrate gait. It resembled an outburst of running activity. When sitting on her trolley she often waved both her raised hands synchronously, at the same time nodding her head in phase. Hand-waving could also be released by disturbing Sabine. It occurred, for example, when Sabine was persistently approached by a stranger with whom she refused to have any contact. Sucking of the fingers or just the thumb is another very common behaviour of the deaf-and-blind-born. It will occur regularly in the deaf-blind when, after social interaction, they are suddenly left alone, or when puzzled by a task which they cannot solve. Sabine showed this behaviour often after she had encountered a person strange to her.

2.1.2   *Play and exploratory behaviour*

During 1966 and 1967 Sabine (at 7 years of age) played and actively explored her environment. She walked around touching the walls and floor with her open hands, letting her palms glide along objects. Small objects were brought to her mouth, touched with the lips, sniffed at, banged against the floor or table, or rolled around for a while in the hands and then often discarded. When given an object she did not like, she would hand it back. She would grasp the object with one hand and hold it away from her body waiting for someone to take it, and only then let it go. She had favourite toys and searched for them. One was a little cart in which she used to sit and glide along. Another was the four-wheeled trolley on which she used to lie down on her belly and push herself along with her feet on the floor. She was skilful at this operation. After hitting an obstacle she would move the whole trolley a few feet backwards, lift the front, and at the same time turn it in a new direction and then proceed again. Her behaviour was quite in contrast to the behaviour of the other deaf-and-blind-born, who did not explore and play in such an elaborate way.

Due to a change of teachers she then lost her reference person, and this was probably the cause of a regression; she stopped playing during 1968, except with her trolley. Objects which she had used for simple construction games, like wooden rings which she put on herself, were taken to the mouth only. This regression has largely persisted until the present (summer 1971), although recently she became attached to a new reference person and is improving again. When out in the open for a walk she likes to pick up little sticks and handle them, placing them on the ground and picking them up again, but shows no sign of using them as tools (e.g. to poke at the ground).

2.1.3 *Social interactions*

Sabine, as well as Heiko, was observed to show clear discrimination between different persons. When someone touched Sabine, she grasped their hand, put it to her nose, smelled it, and if the person was strange to her she pushed the hand away. If the person then continued their efforts to establish contact, Sabine would normally turn around, showing her back, and huddling and sucking her fingers. Sometimes she would act as if angered (see below). Persons well known to her were immediately recognized by touch. She used to grasp one hand and slide her other palm along the arm of the person. She would invite a familiar person to play, for example by assuming a position which was an invitation to help her turn somersaults. Alternatively, she might grasp the hand of the person and guide her to go out for a walk. She would try to embrace a familiar person and would invite being tickled. She liked, in particular, to climb onto her mother's lap and be patted and stroked. She invited her to do so, by pulling her mother's hand down to her cheek (Fig. 2(a–c) and Fig. 3). She would also seek such contact when in distress by clinging to her mother (see page 178, Fig. 6). When contacted by a stranger she would herself try to seek contact with a reference person, grasping a hand and leaning against or even hiding her face in the lap of the reference person. She does this also when in distress. Only persons acquainted with her are addressed when she seeks help, e.g. in unbuttoning her jacket.

The clear discrimination between strangers and friends was of particular interest, since no one ever tried to teach Sabine or Heiko such a discrimination. On the contrary, everyone was kind to these

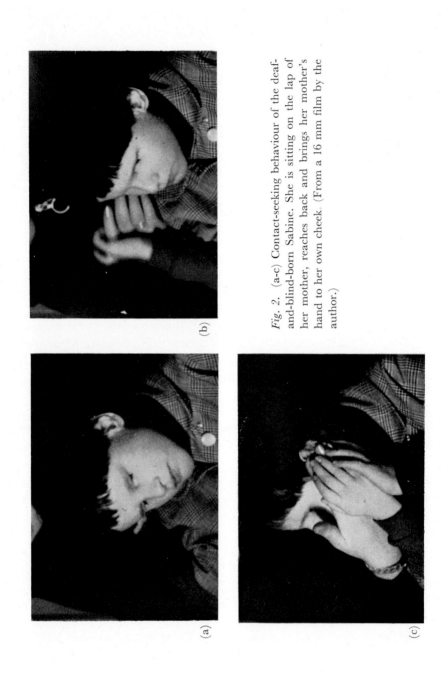

Fig. 2. (a-c) Contact-seeking behaviour of the deaf-and-blind-born Sabine. She is sitting on the lap of her mother, reaches back and brings her mother's hand to her own cheek. (From a 16 mm film by the author.)

children, particularly strangers, although occasionally caretakers mildly punished the children by a pat on the hand in cases of disobedience. Strangers, none the less, released avoidance behaviour. It seems as if the "fear of strangers" so typical for normal children had matured in these deprived ones without the aid of any education. In fact it matures in normal children in a similar way, without the need for any negative experiences with strangers. At first strangers are smiled at, but at an age of 7 to 9 months approaching strangers release fear

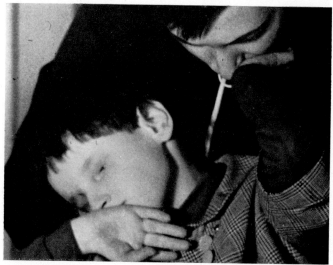

Fig. 3. Contact-seeking behaviour in Sabine. (From a 16 mm film taken by the author.)

responses (Bowlby 1969). It is interesting that fear of strangers was released in Sabine by touch and smell alone. How this reaction matured was not observed. No fear of strangers was observed in the other children. Petra, in particular, when in distress, tried to embrace and climb onto the lap of anyone she came in contact with. (All these deaf-and-blind-born children liked to nestle against a person when in distress or in a tender mood.)

Aggressive behaviour was occasionally observed, although it was not rewarded when it occurred. Sabine aggressively pushed people away with her hands when they were recognized as strangers. She pushed with the open palm or by a sideways sweeping movement using the back of her hand. When the refusal was not accepted, and the person continued to seek contact with her, she often displayed anger fits.

This behavioural syndrome will be described below. Sabine also showed anger fits when repeatedly offered objects she did not like or when she was taken away from her favourite play-cart. She did not, however, defend any of these objects when they were taken away from her. This contrasts with the behaviour of a boy, Harald, who became deaf and blind at the age of $1\frac{1}{2}$ years. This very bright boy—he has already learned to communicate by Lorms' alphabet—was seen to hover over a parcel when it was given to him, and did not allow anyone, even his friends, to assist him in opening it. He simply pushed people away or even pressed them away forcibly with his body. Again, this pattern developed against the efforts of teachers and nurses. As he is now at an age of approximately 11 years and able to communicate, he can be told not to be unkind but to share things, which he actually does.

In play with others Harald sometimes became quite rough, even to the extent of biting, and hair-pulling. In 1970 he repeatedly bit his female teacher. He would grasp her arm with both hands, pull it towards his face and bite into it severely, without letting it go immediately. Aggressive behaviour of this type was released when a promise was not kept, a wish refused, or when he was forced to do something which interfered with some other activity of his. When on vacation on the island of Amrum he was promised to be driven around in a car. This was done on the first day, but on the second day he was told that there would be no excursion this time. On receiving this message by touch language he bit the teacher and afterwards smashed a chair. Only after this was done did his tension seem relieved, and he became friendly again. On another occasion in a field he asked to be driven around by car, but his request was refused. He again bit the teacher, who in self-defence pushed him back. He, however, got hold of her jacket and tore it.

Of great interest were Harald's reactions following such anger fits, since he definitely behaved as if under the stress of a bad conscience. He would quietly stand on the spot sucking his thumb, after a while extending his hand with the palm open—a gesture which he always uses when seeking contact and inviting tactile "talk". He would only relax when contact was granted. Once, after having bitten the lady teacher, he touched the scar on her arm the next morning. He had been laughing before, but stopped immediately, and after a pause signalled by touch alphabet into her hand: "Hurt" (*"weh"*). His movements were very slow as if sad. When she asked in reply "Who has done it?", he replied

"Harald". She then said, "Tomorrow it will be good again", and upon this he immediately brightened up and started a social game which he always uses when in a happy mood: he grasped her, rubbed his forehead against her head, and laughed.

In view of the fact that Harald is not yet able to communicate about any complicated or abstract subject his behaviour is most interesting. He evidently showed conscience, and it is difficult to see how this moral sense could have been acquired. Of course, the teachers try to explain the terms "good" and "bad" in the concrete situations of aggressive misbehaving. "Harald is bad, bites Sabine", he would be told on occasion; yet then one would remove him from his victim without punishment. It is difficult to imagine how this treatment alone could suffice to make Harald emotionally capable of regretting. We may therefore hypothesize an innate disposition for this emotion, but this has not been tested further.

Harald can be very tender, and he is highly discriminating as to whom he shows affection. His little sister is the only person that he kisses spontaneously. In the institution he is particularly fond of a girl aged 10 years. He likes to walk around with her, his arms around her shoulder. Manifestations of sexual interest are not shown, however, to any of the girls he has grown up with. He derives clear reassurance from his beloved teacher. When I invited him to play a game of tugging each other with our hands, he proved to be shy and evidently did not dare to pull me. The moment his female teacher sat beside him he started tugging at me, and laughed at this.

2.2 EXPRESSIVE BEHAVIOUR

2.2.1 *Smiling*

Smiling (Fig. 4(a–d)) was observed in all the deaf-and-blind-born studied so far. It occurred spontaneously during play, and in Sabine when she sat by herself in the sun patting her face with the palms of her hands. Smiling could be released by patting, mild tickling, and engaging in social play. The smiling started with an upward movement of the corners of the mouth. At higher intensities the lips opened wide in front, exposing the teeth in the way sighted persons do; the eye-slits were narrowed, and finally the head was raised and tilted back.

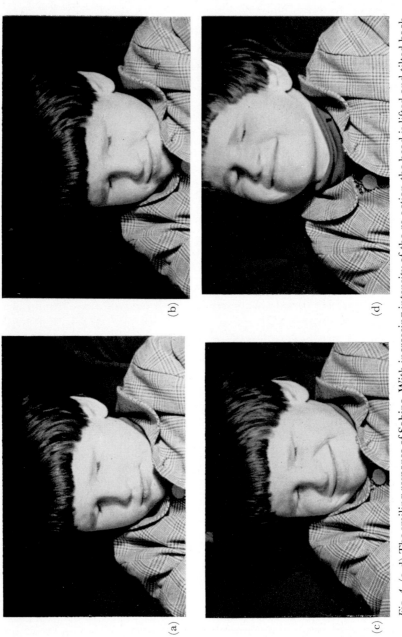

Fig. 4. (a-d) The smiling response of Sabine. With increasing intensity of the re-action the head is lifted and tilted back. (From a 16 mm film taken by the author.)

(a)   (b)   (c)   (d)

2.2.2 *Laughing*

All deaf-and-blind-born children laugh (Fig. 5). During laughter the head is often thrown back and the mouth opened. The rhythmical pattern of sound production characteristic of normal laughter is always recognizable; the sounds produced do, however, vary. Mostly chuckling sounds, reminiscent of the giggling of normal persons, are heard. Sometimes, however, almost no sound is produced except for the rhythmical breathing movements characteristic of laughing. Laughing occurs during rougher social play (wrestling) and when the deaf-blind children are tickled. In the latter case initial smiling often turns into laughing.

Fig. 5. Sabine laughing. (Photograph by the author.)

Beatrice often laughed when she ate a chocolate. Harald laughs during tugging games, and in particular when he wins. He laughs in anticipation of pleasant events (e.g. when about to be taken for a walk), and he laughs when exploring an object new to him or after succeeding in performing a difficult task. He even shows a primitive sense of humour. Upon request, he may offer a person a piece of chocolate which he is eating. Sometimes, however, he just holds the titbit for a moment, as if offering it to the other person, but then hastily puts it in his own mouth and laughs.

2.2.3 *Crying*

In situations of distress or despair the deaf-and-blind cry (Fig. 6 and Fig. 7(a–c)). Typical distress crying occurred, for example, when they had hurt themselves by banging against an obstacle, or when left alone in an unfamiliar environment. The corners of the mouth are then drawn downwards and often opened, the eyelids are pressed tightly together and tears are shed. In strong distress the eyebrows are raised and the forehead is horizontally wrinkled. Less often, vertical folds

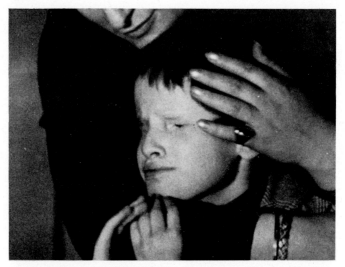

Fig. 6. Sabine crying and being soothed by her mother. (From a 16 mm film taken by the author.)

become visible. The shoulders sag and prolonged soft whining sounds are uttered. The pattern is reminiscent of the behaviour of normal people crying in despair. In such a situation the deaf-and-blind seek bodily contact, snuggling and huddling against another person's body. When Sabine was in despair, and nobody was in reach, she made embracing movements in the air, as if seeking somebody to hold on to. Self-clasping in a huddled position often followed. Once, when sitting on the floor, she took hold of her leg and clasped this while sobbing. Embracing movements in the air were also observed in healthy babies of 6 months of age when they were lying on their back and crying. They reached out with open hands and brought them together above the chest, finally performing self-clasping. They did it also when in a

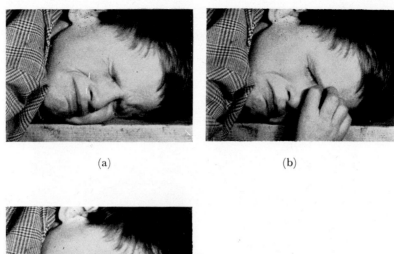

(a)   (b)

(c)

Fig. 7. (a-c) Sabine crying. (From a 16 mm film taken by the author.)

"happy mood", while smiling and laughing as the mother bent over the crib, in clear attempts to grasp her.

In the deaf-blind another type of crying was observed, which I would interpret as angry crying. It occurred in Sabine when she was upset by someone persistently offering her a disliked object. In such cases Sabine refused contact by pushing the person away, or by turning away herself, shaking her head, stamping her feet, and waving and pushing with her hands. The crying occurred in loud bursts and vertical folds were prominently displayed on her forehead.

2.2.4 *Expression of anger*

As has been mentioned, Sabine could be made angry either by repeatedly offering her a disliked object or by persisting in social contact attempts when she was not willing. She would then turn away abruptly, shaking her head rapidly from side to side, finally jerking it backwards, closing her mouth firmly and sometimes biting against her lower lip

Fig. 8. Sabine biting herself after being angered. (From a 16 mm film taken by the author.)

or clenching her teeth. She stamped her feet alternately against the ground and occasionally clenched her fists. A clear frown (vertical folds on the forehead) was often visible and occasionally she bit at her hand (Fig. 8).[1] The whole syndrome occurs in very similar fashion in normal children, when they are angered but do not dare to retaliate. Such children will then turn away, lift their head in a gesture of refusal (related to the gesture of pride). They, too, bite themselves on the lip, but only seldom on the hand.

Florence Goodenough (1932) described the anger and temper tantrums of a deaf-and-blind girl in detail:

> Mild forms of resentment are shown by turning away the head, pouting the lips, or frowning; sometimes by crouching down into a little heap with the head on knees . . . More intense forms are shown by throwing back of the head and shaking it from side to side, during which the lips are retracted, exposing the teeth which are sometimes clenched. This is accompanied by whimpering or whining noises, rising at intervals to short high-pitched *staccato* yelps. In her most violent outbursts the entire body is thrown back and forth; the feet are twisted around each other or beat violently upon the floor; the vocalizations are intensified and as a rule become shriller in pitch; and the head and chest are beaten with sharp flail-like movements of the arms. These blows are usually struck with the open hand, but at times the clenched fist is used.   p. 331

[1] This hand-biting or biting the lower lip can be interpreted as a form of aggression directed against oneself.

2.2.5 *Surprise*

When we offered Heiko a piece of salted apple, he stopped chewing and raised his eyebrows for some seconds, while otherwise showing a motionless face. In Sabine raising of the eyebrows often occurred when sniffing at an object. Goodenough also gave a very detailed description of the startle reaction of the 10-year-old blind-born girl. Goodenough dropped a doll inside the neck of the child's dress and filmed her reaction. At first, she reported, the child's body was tensed, with mouth half opened, eyes opened to their fullest extent, and eyebrows raised. She emphasized that both posture and facial expression "are suggestive of what we should ordinarily interpret as startled attention" (Goodenough, 1932, p. 329).

Charlesworth (1970), in a study of surprise reactions in 14 congenitally blind (but otherwise normal) children and 11 sighted children, found no significant differences between the groups in 20–30 different facial and bodily reactions to three surprising situations. Blind and sighted individuals showed the same kind of facial expressions as well as the same overall amounts of different surprise behaviours.

2.2.6 *Gestures of refusal*

Shaking of the head was a usual response when Sabine refused an object or a person. When pushing the objects away with one hand she sometimes held her arm outstretched with the palm open for a while in a gesture of refusal, the palm continuing to face the direction in which she had pushed the object (Fig. 9(a–f)). When relaxing a hand gesture, the three last fingers were the first to bend, the index finger remaining upheld in a pointing gesture for a while. After shaking the head, she would tilt this backwards. Heiko was seen to exhale strongly after sniffing at an unfamiliar person with whom he had refused contact.

A "warding-off" with the open palm, similar to the motor pattern just described for Sabine, was observed in Harald when he approached the hot spotlight used for filming him. He turned his face slightly to the side while approaching further. With his right hand he covered his face, the palm of the open hand facing the lights. The other hand was stretched out and swayed sideways as if searching for the lights. Since it is easier to hold the hand before ones face with the palm facing it, one wonders why the hand was turned around in this particular instance. In normal people both patterns can be observed, but with different "meanings". The palm faces outwards when people ward

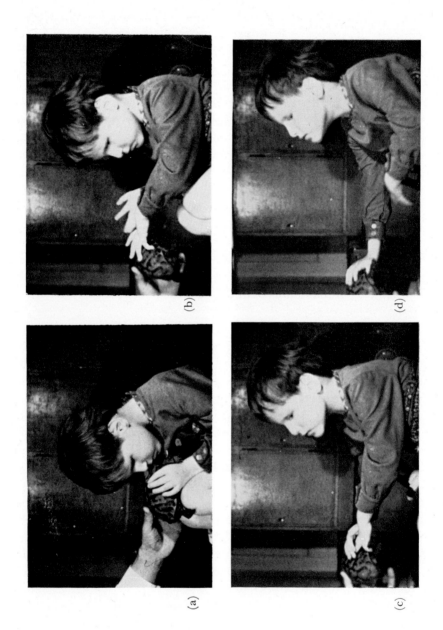

(a)

(b)

(c)

(d)

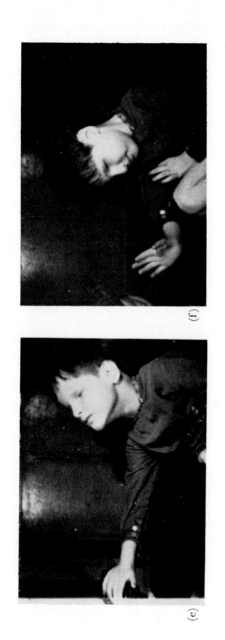

(e)   (f)

Fig. 9. (a–f) Sabine refuses an offer of a tortoise. She sniffs at the object and then pushes it back, at the same time lifting her head in an intention movement of withdrawal. She finally stretches her hand in a gesture of warding off. (From a 16 mm film taken by the author.)

something off, and it faces the face when people hide themselves behind the hand, e.g. when slightly ashamed. "Flicking-off" hand movements could also be released in the deaf and blind when touched on the back of the hand with bristly objects.

2.2.7   *Approval*
Clear approval has not been released so far. I should mention, however, that Sabine, when in high spirits, moves her head back and forth in a fashion resembling nodding, e.g. when scratched behind her ear.

2.2.8   *Embracing*
The deaf-and-blind-born embrace other people, or parts of them, with their arms on various occasions (Fig. 10(a–f)). When in distress they try to embrace the reference person, often hiding the face against the chest or lap. Embracing is also observed in greeting situations. It is shown finally in situations of sexual affection. In the summer of 1971 Sabine reached puberty and a special form of sexual behaviour became manifest. Sabine likes to climb on the leg of another person and ride on it in a clearly sexually motivated fashion (Fig. 11). She is only interested in legs and even likes to smell the feet. This pattern may have derived from early childhood experiences: when still a very small girl, she used to sit on her mother's foot. The mother used to enjoy playing with her by swinging her up and down in this fashion. If a person now sits besides Sabine on a bench Sabine will try to ride the feet or she will embrace and caress the feet as shown in the illustrations (Fig. 10(a–f)).

2.2.9   *Caressing*
In the above-mentioned situation Sabine strokes the leg that she holds in embrace, in a way which one is inclined to interpret as a sign of affection. Exploratory stroking is used by the deaf-blind to acquire information about a person or object.

2.2.10   *Nibbling*
Harald nibbles the skin of his lady teacher, biting tenderly with his incisors. It is an expression of affection. The pattern reminds one of the grooming activity of many mammals.

2.2.11 *Kissing*
When we offered a teddy-bear doll to Beatrice she tried to press the doll against her chest, assisted by the caretaker. She approached the doll with her face, evidently seeking contact and following the movements of the doll. During this phase her lips were protruded in the same way as people intending to kiss. Once lip contact was established she smiled widely, moving her head back again. This pattern was filmed only once, but it deserves attention. Harald kisses his sister only, and this as a sign of particularly strong affection.

2.2.12 *Rubbing the forehead against another person*
Harald rubs his forehead against another person's forehead as a sign of affection.

2.2.13 *Pouting*
When approached after an anger fit, or after crying, Sabine used to pout her lips and frown.

2.2.14 *Greeting*
When coming into contact with a person she likes, Sabine often smiles and tries to embrace the person. Heiko frequently laughs on such occasions, probably in anticipation of play or other activities to follow. Once while greeting a man not known to him, he embraced him and performed one strong pelvic thrust. In normal schoolboys such pelvic thrusts can readily be seen after aggressive mounting during playful wrestling. Shaking hands needs to be taught to the deaf-and-blind-born. I never saw nodding during greeting.

2.2.15 *Behaviour during conflict and slight frustration*
In slightly frustrating situations, like those of conflict and when puzzled, Sabine and Harald regularly scratched their heads.[1] Sabine did this, for example, when she was searching for her cart without finding it, or when trying in vain to open a locked door, or after turning away from somebody. Harald reacted in a similar way. Sucking of the fingers

---

[1] The pattern of self-grooming occurred in all the deaf-and-blind-born in perfect co-ordination. They all rubbed their eyes with the back of their hand (e.g. when crying), and this differed in no way from the pattern of normal children. They also wiped their nose with the back of the hand, and they scratched themselves with their fingers or just the index finger alone.

(b)

(d)

(a)

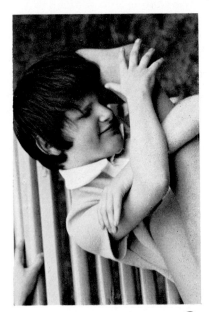

(c)

(e)   (f)

Fig. 10. (a–f) Sabine holding the legs of a woman on her lap: (a) relaxed; (b) after an attempt to withdraw the legs she holds one leg firmly; (c–f) embracing, caressing and sniffing at the feet. (Photographs by the author.)

was another form of response to such situations. Another response to slight frustration was biting the lips. When Sabine searched in vain for something she drew in her lower lip and bit upon it. A similar behaviour was observed in Beatrice: when a teddy-bear doll slipped from her stumpy hands she bit her lower lip and made efforts to lift the doll up to her. During the process of lifting she closed her mouth and when she had succeeded she opened her mouth and smiled.

Fig. 11. Sexually motivated riding on the leg. (Photograph by the author.)

2.2.16 *Infantile behaviours*
Crouching, hiding the face against another person's body, and sucking the fingers were regular responses of the deaf-and-blind-born to fearful events and to a wide range of puzzling and frustrating happenings.

2.2.17 *Distance communication*
Harald and Sabine often seek contact by stretching out one or both hands. We have already mentioned that Sabine tries to embrace others, particularly when distressed. When Harald seeks contact he often holds his palm open inviting communication. Of particular interest is the way he proceeds when he wants to address a distant person by means of his touch alphabet. He then telegraphs in his hand, but with the palm facing outwards, as if he knew that only then could the person perceive his message. This is the more interesting since mute children, when signalling in a similar way into their own hand, do this often with their palms inwards.

2.2.18   *Vocalizations*

Crying and laughing were easily recognized as such, although the deaf and blind were less loud in their performance than normal children.[1] According to her parents, Sabine did not babble. When I observed her during playing she uttered in rhythmic repetition, "hm hm hm hm", and less often, "da da da da" and "nam nam nam". Beatrice at 9 years old uttered a greater variety of sounds. When she was patted by her teacher she uttered a series of high-pitched sounds ("dee dee dee dee dee") starting at low pitch and gradually working up the scale. When climbing a staircase she uttered, "ja ja ja ja ja ja" and during eating she uttered, "hm hm hm hm". Dorothea McCarthy (1929) presented a whole list of mono- and bi-syllablic sounds uttered by the same deaf-and-blind-born girl that Goodenough (1932) studied. She described one two-syllable combination of particular interest, since it was uttered only in a very particular situation. The girl was unfamiliar with stairways and was highly excited when first led up and down one:

> On the third occasion on which she was taken down the stairs, she made a two-syllable sound "ah veuv" as soon as she felt the edge of the top step. Three trials were given on the stairway, and on each of them the same sound was uttered at the first step. The following day the sound was used again for two trials on the stairs and four days later it was used in the same way on four out of five trials. After an interval of about two weeks, with no experience on the stairs, the same sound was again uttered in the same situation. In all, this sound has been heard during about 18 out of 20 trips on the stairway.   McCarthy, 1929, p. 483

These observations on the vocalizations of the deaf-and-blind-born favour the assumption that an inner urge to form syllables, and the capacity to link them to certain situations, exists without the need for auditory feedback.

2.3   LIST OF OBSERVED ACTIVITIES

Summing up, we find that the behaviour of the highly deprived deaf-and-blind-born deviates less from the behaviour of healthy normals than one would expect. Uncontrolled, uncoordinated muscle movements (e.g. grimacing) are rarely observed. Movement stereotypies are numerous, but they are coordinated patterns. The following apparently

[1] Goodenough (1932) describes the laughter of the deaf-and-blind-born girl she had studied as "clear and musical, in no way distinguishable from that of a normal child" (p. 331).

non-functional and non-expressive behaviours were observed in the deaf-and-blind-born:

   a. Rhythmical eyebrow-raising.
   b. Kicking fits (in perfect quadrupedal running coordination).
   c. Synchronous waving of hands with head-nodding.
   d. Hitting the mouth with the palm.
   e. Pressing rhythmically both the index and middle finger against a particular spot on the chestbone.
   f. Nodding.
   g. Head-shaking.

Functional patterns of a non-expressive character which were observed were:

   a. Locomotion (walking) with outstretched arms.
   b. Huddling.
   c. Sitting.
   d. Touching and exploring with the hands.
   e. Rubbing eyes.
   f. Sweeping eye or nose with the back of the hand.
   g. Scratching with the fingers (often as displacement activity).
   h. Touching with the mouth (lips).
   i. Sniffing.
   j. Pushing away.
   k. Flicking movements directed at the other hand.
   l. Warding-off with outstretched arm and upheld palm.
   m. Handing back objects.
   n. Manipulating objects.
   o. Embracing.
   p. Pelvic thrusting.
   q. Sucking and thumbsucking.
   r. Drinking.
   s. Eating.
   t. Biting and hitting as aggressive display.

Expressive behaviour patterns which were observed were:

   a. Smiling.
   b. Laughing.
   c. Crying in distress and anger.

d. Frowning.
e. Pouting.
f. Surprise reactions.
g. Headshaking as a gesture of refusal.
h. Turning around and walking away.
i. Clenching teeth.
j. Clenching fists.
k. Stamping feet.
l. Biting of own hands and lips.
m. Jerking back of the head.
n. Strong exhaling.
o. Contact seeking by embracing movements.
p. Contact seeking by reaching out.
q. Signalling on the hand with the palm facing out.
r. Caressing.
s. Nibbling.
t. Rubbing the forehead against a person.

3 Discussion

Basic similarities between the expressive behaviour patterns of the
deaf-and-blind and the expressions of non-deprived persons are evident.
Whole syndromes of behaviour such as tne anger pattern are alike in
detail, and this likeness needs to be explained. Similarities occurring
by chance can certainly be excluded, since even the simple smile involves the concerted well-coordinated action of several facial muscles.

If we try to explain the similarities by learning hypotheses, we have
to deal with a number of difficulties. Theoretically the child could
learn about his mother's facial expression by touching her face. But to
adapt one's own behaviour appropriately from such information one
must at least be highly gifted in such respects, i.e. "biased" for a specific
type of learning by phylogenetic adaptations. This may well be the case
for some learning; however, we can exclude such a possibility here since
thalidomide children, who have no arms to reach out for their mother's
face, none the less show the adequate facial expressions. One could
alternatively think of the occurrence of learning by shaping, i.e. step-
by-step reinforcement could build up a behaviour pattern. A smile
could be rewarded by the mother from the slightest signs of its appearance, and thus the habit of smiling might be acquired. We know, in fact,
that children who get social reward smile more than neglected ones do.

However, smiling already occurs as a complete pattern at a very early stage of development and, furthermore, it can be observed even in highly retarded deaf-and-blind-born children who have to be taught even how to guide a spoon to their mouth, so poor is their learning ability. It would also be extremely difficult to imagine how the pattern of anger behaviour could possibly be acquired in such a way since this type of behaviour is considered as undesirable and never rewarded at all.

We have to assume then that patterns like laughing, crying, the anger syndrome, etc. are based on action patterns which mature during ontogeny through a process of self-differentiation. In this sense they are inborn and can be considered as "fixed action patterns". Possible exceptions are a few simple patterns like pushing away of an object that could easily be imagined as being acquired by trial-and-error learning. The derived gesture of warding off with the outstretched hand, as was filmed in Sabine (Fig. 9 (f)) is, however, not so easily explained this way.

There are certainly differences in the expressive behaviour of the deaf-and-blind in comparison to normals. The deaf-and-blind often lack the minute gradations of an expression. An expression suddenly appears, and equally suddenly wanes without warning leaving a completely blank face. Superposition of various expressions also occurs in the deaf-and-blind (e.g. angry crying), but many of the composite expressions of normal persons have not yet been observed. This might be the case for the simple reason that the channels by which such activities are released (eye and ear) are closed. This suggestion is to a certain extent backed up by the observation of very complicated reactions in those blind-born whose hearing is intact. When I once complimented a 10-year-old girl on her piano playing she looked in my direction, flushed, turned away and at the same time lowered her head, a pattern which can be observed in healthy girls of the most diverse cultures as an expression of coyness and coquetry.

The study of the deaf-and-blind-born provides only limited information concerning the extent to which motor patterns are inborn in Man. Nevertheless, their study is of great theoretical interest, since they provide the proof of the principle that ethological concepts, as developed by the study of animals, hold true for man as well.

Note: Since this chapter was written a further film (HF56) has been made documenting the behaviour of a chinese deaf-and-blind-born child. His repertoire is basically identical to that of Europeans. Cross-cultural studies have also confirmed the generality of stranger-rejection (cf. p. 173).

References

Birdwhistell, R. L. (1963). The Kinesic level in the investigation of the emotions. *In* "Expression of Emotions in Man" (Ed. P. H. Knapp), pp. 123–139. International Universities Press, New York.

Birdwhistell, R. L. (1968). Communication without words. *In* "L'Aventure Humaine" (Ed. P. Alexandre), pp. 157–166. Kister, Geneva.

Bowlby, J. (1969). "Attachment and Loss. Vol. I. Attachment". Hogarth Press, London.

Charlesworth, W. R. (1970). Surprise reactions in congenitally blind and sighted children. NIMH Progress Report.

Darwin, C. (1872). "The Expression of Emotions in Man and Animals". Murray, London.

Eibl-Eibesfeldt, I. (1970). "Liebe und Hass, Zur Naturgeschichte elementarer Verhaltensweisen". Piper, Münich.

Freedman, D. G. (1964). Smiling in blind infants and the issue of innate versus acquired. *J. Child Psychol. Psychiat.* **5**, 171–184.

Freedman, D. G. (1965). Hereditary control of early social behaviour. *In* "Determinants of Infant Behaviour" (Ed. B. M. Foss), Vol. 3, pp. 149–155. Methuen, London.

Fulcher, J. S. (1942). "Voluntary" facial expressions in blind and seeing children. *Arch. Psychol. N.Y.* No. 272.

Goodenough, Florence L. (1932). Expressions of the emotions in a blind-deaf child. *J. Abnorm. Soc. Psychol.* **27**, 328–333.

Holst, E, von and Saint-Paul, V. von. (1960). Vom Wirkungsgefüge der Triebe. *Die Naturwissenschaften*, **18**, 409–422.

Hooff, J. A. R. A. M. van (1971). Aspects of the social behaviour and communication in human and higher non-human primates. Bronder Offset, Rotterdam.

Jensen, D. D. (1961). Operationism and the question "Is this behaviour learned or innate". *Behaviour*, **17**, 1–8.

LaBarre, W. (1947). The cultural basis of emotions and gestures. *J. Pers.* **16**, 49–68.

Lawick-Goodall, Jane van (1968). The behavior of freeliving chimpanzees in the Gombe Stream Reserve. *Anim. Behav. Monogr.* **1**, 161–311.

Lorenz, K. (1965). "Evolution and Modification of Behaviour". Chicago University Press, Chicago.

McCarthy, Dorothea (1929). Note on the vocal sounds of a blind-deaf girl. *J. Genet. Psychol.* **6**, 482–484.

Montagu, M. F. A. (1968). "Man and Aggression". Oxford University Press, New York.

Myklebust, H. R. (1956). "The Deaf-Blind Child". Perkins School for the Blind, Watertown, Mass.

Prechtl, H. F. R. (1950). Zur Entstehung von Wackeltics. *Osterr. Z. Kinderheilkunde und Kinderfürsorge*, **4**, 362–364.

Sackett, G. P. (1966). Monkeys reared in isolation with pictures as visual input: evidence for an innate releasing mechanism. *Science*, **154**, 1468–1473.

Salmon, P. J. (1950). The deaf blind. *In* "Blindness" (Ed. P. A. Zahl), pp. 224–232.

Thompson, Jane (1941). Development of facial expression of emotion in blind and seeing children. *Arch. Psychol. N.Y.*, No. 264.
Tinbergen, N. (1951). "The Study of Instinct". Oxford University Press, London.
Wade, W. (1904). "The Blind-Deaf, A Monograph". Hocker Bros., Indianapolis.

5

The Role of Facial-Visual Signalling in Early Social Development[1]

Ian Vine

1 The ontogeny of facial-visual signalling

1.1 INTRODUCTION

The current interest in description and explanation of non-verbal aspects of our behaviour in face-to-face social encounters has, as yet, involved little attention to developmental issues. This is to be regretted in view of the probable significance of early social behaviour, and its relevance to the construction of any general theory of communication. Multi-channel social signalling has already been shown to be highly complex, and studies of its ontogeny would be of value in elucidating the structural and functional relationships within the face-to-face communication system. The necessary priority of non-verbal cues in our

[1] Based on a paper presented to a European Association of Experimental Social Psychology working group on Non-verbal Communication, Amsterdam, 31 March to 3 April 1969. The research was undertaken partly while the author held an SSRC Research Studentship, and partly while receiving a stipendium from the Max-Planck Society. Dr Nick Blurton-Jones kindly provided critical comments on a draft manuscript. The literature review for the current chapter was completed during 1971; although many relevant papers have subsequently appeared they do not materially affect the overall conclusions of this discussion.

infant–adult and infant–infant communication facilitates valid investigation of this more "primitive" signalling system and how its elements become integrated. Furthermore, the study of how older infants begin to adapt their signalling behaviours as they learn new ones, especially language, should provide insights into the important interrelations between verbal and non-verbal behaviours in adult communication.

Developmental psychologists have good reason to be vitally concerned with communication themselves. Non-verbal behaviour must at first transmit all meaning communicated from infant to mother and vice versa: not only affective meaning, but also volition, intention, indication, instruction, and so on. This is a substantial area for research, but traditionally almost the only segment studied in any detail has been that concerned with the expression and recognition of affect, mostly by facial signals. In young infants, only two behaviours of significance in communication, namely smiling and looking, have been studied at all extensively, providing us with sufficient data on developmental trends in the evoking situation and the response for a theoretical analysis. Even here, most studies have focused only on the infant, so that any sequential dependence of the mother's behaviour on the infant's signals is little understood.

The bias of research to date can be seen as a reflection of a true predominance of affective expression in early infancy. Looking and smiling can be regarded as the first truly social responses of the infant, remaining important for the development of mother–infant interaction. Nevertheless, we have very little detailed knowledge of the role of other behaviours in early communication; and viewing the smile as simply an emotional expression may lead us to ignore other important aspects of development. These gaps need to be filled before the full significance and complexity of the genesis of communicative systems can be appreciated. This chapter, which deals almost exclusively with the behaviours of social smiling and social gazing, cannot possibly give a complete picture, but hopefully it shows the probable significance of these behaviours in early social interaction, and may stimulate further detailed investigations into these and other behaviours and the links between communication and social attachment.

From the literature on visual communication involving facial signals it appears that what I have called the "facial-visual communication channel" plays an important role in human and animal social encounters (Vine, 1970). Both the receptive and the signalling aspects of visual behaviour are of importance in adults, and, although much more data is needed on infant gazing, it has been suggested that this may play a major role in normal mother–infant interaction. It seems likely that, in association with smiling, gazing between mother and infant may be rather critical for the emergence and characteristic development of social attachment.

The developmental issues raised in the earlier paper will be treated here more fully. General questions concerning the nature of communication processes will not be considered, having previously been discussed at length. The brief review of studies on infant facial-visual signalling included in this earlier work will be extended with emphasis on the most recent studies. Two main bodies of research will be discussed in some detail: the first concerns the early perceptual abilities of infants, with special reference to attention to facial stimuli; the second concerns social smiling. The relation of these behaviours to the development of communication and of social attachment will be investigated, refining and extending the proposals made earlier (Vine, 1970).

1.2.1   Studies of facial expressions

As with adults, the first investigations of non-verbal communication behaviours used by infants and children emphasized gross facial configurations in which a number of movements of facial elements combine to produce a "facial expression". The assumptions of this approach seem to have been that gross expressions were the only significant type of signal arising from the face, and that their semantic content was exclusively affective—reducible in fact to some discrete and fundamental "emotional state", expressed by a genetically programmed response. Accordingly, the early studies followed a simple paradigm of naming the emotions shown in an infant's expressions and charting their development, or of asking the child for names of the expressions of others who were portraying emotions.

Watson argued that three basic emotions of rage, fear, and love were found in young infants as innate responses to specific types of stimulation. Subsequently, they showed development of more differentiated affective responses as a result of conditioning processes (J. B. Watson, 1924). Research failed to show that facial expressions could be reliably differentiated in terms of emotions or situations for newborn infants (Sherman, 1927; Bridges, 1932); but Bridges found that in the second month it was possible to distinguish between expressions of apparently pleasurable or unpleasurable states, and during the first year further differentiation took place. Goodenough (1931) found that the average success of adult judges matching photographs of the expressions of a 10-month infant to the actual evoking situations was well above chance. She concluded that facial expressions of affect were innately programmed: despite the fact that some of the 10 expressions were matched rather poorly, suggesting limited differentiation even by 10 months. The common belief of mothers that they can accurately judge their infants' expressions is probably largely explained by Sherman's (1927) finding that showing judges the situation in which an expression is evoked greatly improves "recognition".

Less equivocal evidence on the development of expression comes from studies of infants blind from birth (Goodenough, 1932; Thompson, 1941; Fulcher, 1942). Their course of expressive development was found to be similar to that for sighted infants, suggesting that factors such as learning by imitation can play no more than a minor role in comparison with maturational processes. Freedman (1964), who reported in detail on the development of smiling in blind infants, reached a similar conclusion (see also Eibl-Eibesfeldt, Chapter 4). On the basis of the still rather scanty evidence on expressive development, it appears that while at birth there is no clear repertoire of expressions linked to discrete emotions, differentiation progresses thereafter, so that by the end of the second year the repertoire of expressions is fairly similar to that of adults, at least for the more "simple" emotions. If indeed visual experience is fairly unimportant for expression, it seems that development of the responses depends more on the maturation and differentiation of the infant's central affective processes than on the refinement of the motor processes which are involved in the production of the actual expressions.

Studies of development of the ability to recognize expressions also reveal age-related changes, but with much slower differentiation. Ahrens (1954) found that infants of 5 months could evidently discriminate between what we may call "positive" and "negative" affective expressions of adults, but studies of older infants' possible discrimination on a finer level are lacking. However, studies of children's recognition ability have covered the range 3–14 years, and found it remains below the adult level even at the latter age (Gates, 1923; Dashiell, 1927; Kellogg and Eagleson, 1931). Posed photographs of six "simple" emotions were used, but at age 3 years correct identification by a majority of children was only achieved with the joy-amusement picture. In view of the poor recognition ability of the first few years, it may well be that the effective judgements which are made of others' expressions are in fact based only on particular local features (principally the mouth and the eyes) rather than the total configuration. Learning to attend to the more subtle aspects of expressions may be a limiting factor in identification, although other writers have again emphasized maturation. Honkavaara (1961) investigated development of affect recognition and found it proceeded through four sequential stages: "dynamic-affective", "matter-of-fact", "physiognomic" and "intersensory". She saw the regularity of this process as evidence for maturation. Forrai-Bànlaki's (1965) comparison of 7- and 9-year-old children's ability to recognize photographed expressions showed that intelligence was of more importance than age in governing success, but this no more than Honkavaara's study rules out the role of learning.

1.2.2 *Methodological issues and alternative approaches*

It appears from the previous section that there is little reason to expect sophisticated communication of affect in infancy through facial-visual signalling. However, caution is demanded in evaluating these studies. The basic assumptions of the research tradition may be questioned on various grounds. First, the emphasis on classic "emotional states" may by-pass other important aspects of communication. Second, gross facial configurations may not be the effective cues during infancy. Even within its own terms of reference the research can be questioned, since the older studies used small samples and only elementary statistical analyses, and also highly artificial experimental paradigms. The use which is actually made of facial expressions during natural social situations is still barely studied for the first few years of life. More general problems associated with judgement experiments have been discussed elsewhere (Vine, 1970).

The meaning of an expression involves at least three components: situational reference, anticipation of action, and affective experience (Frijda, 1969, see also Chapter 7). The naming of emotions from expressions is a complex process (even more so when photographic or other representations are used), involving not only perceptual skills but also sophisticated linguistic ability and cognitive skills. Thus for young children, even where semi-non-verbal techniques are used to test

H

recognition (Dashiell, 1927), the data must be difficult to interpret. Even the data from expression in blind infants are somewhat equivocal. Despite their general similarity to normal expressions, the facial configurations of the blind do differ from normal in details, and the range of individual variation is larger. They also appear rather later: prolonged social smiling appears at 5–6 months rather than 2–3 months (Freedman, 1964). Smiling also tends to be more infrequent and fragmentary than is the case for normal infants during later childhood, but it is of course possible that maternal behaviour towards blind infants differs from that towards normals. Nevertheless, the role of visual experience of faces, even for the production of expressions, may well be significant.

In effect, the data on expression and recognition of affect involving gross facial expressions have contributed rather little to our understanding of the importance of the facial-visual channel in early social relations. While the body of research on social smiling in infancy is in a different tradition, having shown how smiling develops not only in relation to age but also in relation to various aspects of stimulus conditions, even this has yielded little ethological data on natural social interactions. The need for an ethological approach to infant behaviour, especially to communication, is strong, but this need is only now being realized (e.g. Richards and Bernal, 1972). Recording methods and check-lists of behaviours have been developed for detailed investigation of natural social interactions (Haas and Harms, 1963; Blurton-Jones, 1968; Grant, 1969; Brannigan and Humphries, 1972); and data is beginning to accumulate which suggests the importance of specific facial-visual signals in child–child interaction. Early results from Blurton-Jones (1967) suggest that pre-school or nursery school children (3–5 years) make relatively sophisticated use of certain facial-visual cues. He found, for example, that intention movements preceding serious versus play fighting differ in several ways, the former including a direct-gaze-plus-lowered-eyebrows complex. Since recipients of these signals tended to respond differently in the two situations, it is possible that the facial cues were utilized communicatively.

While the ethological studies of young children initiated by Blurton-Jones, by Brannigan, and by McGrew (1969, 1972) are likely to contribute considerably to our understanding of child–child interaction, and of the role of facial-visual signals in this process, data is still urgently needed on mother–infant interaction during the first two years of life. The major ethological investigations initiated by Richards and Bernal

(1972) should partly meet this need. The need for quantitative data on natural behaviour sequences cannot be over-emphasized, although such investigation must of course go hand in hand with experimental investigations (White, 1969a). It is unfortunate that some recent studies using sophisticated methods have recorded only interpretative data (e.g. Hatfield *et al.*, 1967), while in other cases only non-human primates have been studied (e.g. the use of complex sequence analyses with data on mother–infant interaction in monkeys by Bobbitt *et al.*, 1969).

Blurton-Jones (personal communication, 1969) reports that most facial cues in the check-lists devised by himself (1968) and by Grant (1969) have been observed in neonates, confirming the general observation of Gesell *et al.* (1949) that facial mobility is well developed at birth. It is thus possible that detailed analysis, perhaps from ciné-films, would reveal more facial-visual communication between mothers and infants than is usually noticed. Infant–infant encounters might also prove of interest. These have hitherto been neglected, perhaps largely due to the finding of Maudry and Nekula (1939) that interaction between infants of less than two years was minimal. But although they found little evidence of cooperative interaction, social encounters did take place in essentially "impersonal" disputes over toys and so on. In fact there have been reports of infants looking and smiling at each other as early as 5–8 months (Bridges, 1932; Bühler, 1935), while Vincze (1971), who reported on infants reared together, found they would engage in considerable tactile contact as well, and judged that their encounters were predominantly pleasurable until the infants were able to walk.

In view of the preliminary status of studies on older infants' and young children's use of facial-visual signalling, we will deal here almost exclusively with early infancy, and with communication between infants and adults, principally the mother. Since the genesis of social attachment is most likely to involve the mother, and since looking and smiling are the most predominant and well-studied aspects of facial-visual signalling between mothers and infants, it will be necessary to concentrate on these. Future studies may well show that other signals are important, and may demand revision of the present approach.

1.3 PERCEPTION OF THE FACE

1.3.1. *Basic visual abilities and attention to visual stimuli*
The visual capacities of young infants, and the course of development of

these, must be carefully assessed before any analysis of social signalling involving the facial-visual channel is possible, as clearly they will set inescapable limits on its role. The sensory and perceptual abilities of neonates are relatively limited, but change rapidly with age during the normal course of development. It may be helpful to consider this development in terms of a number of stages which occur in sequence. In preference to the familiar subdivisions proposed by Piaget (1952) for his "sensory-motor period", the first 18 months will be subdivided on the basis of more descriptive perceptual steps. The sequence shown in Table 1 is adapted with slight modification from that of Mussen *et al.*

TABLE 1

Stages of early perceptual development: principal features

Stage	Approximate ages	Principal features
1	0–1 week	Basic visual behaviours present in crude form, but with minimal visual alertness.
2	1–8 weeks	Attentiveness and visual capacities increase steadily; first social smiles and then social vocalization are exhibited.
3	2–3 months	Differentiation between familiar and novel visual stimuli; social stimuli more easily elicit smiling and vocalization.
4	3–7 months	Most visual behaviours approaching adult characteristics; attention and smiling to faces reach a peak, but habituation becomes more rapid, except to mother; first hand–eye coordinations; beginnings of the mother concept.
5	7–12 months	Finer discrimination of visual detail such as facial expression; first anxious reactions to strangers; mother and object concepts are elaborated.
6	12–18 months	Perceptual development mainly linked to motor coordinations; emphasis on perambulation and on language.

(1969). No theoretical approach is implied by the sequence of stages, beyond that the order of development is relatively invariant. It is simply convenient as a heuristic scheme, avoiding the problem of specifying age variability in describing development. Rather stable individual differences in attentiveness are evident from early in life (Thomas *et al.*,

1960; Lewis et al., 1967a; Korner, 1970), and sex differences can be appreciable (e.g. Kagan and Lewis, 1965; Kagan et al., 1966), so more precise specifications of age levels in perceptual development are difficult to generalize.

Considering first the neonatal period of stage 1, a substantial body of data deals with visual abilities at or just after birth. Brain and visual system electrical activity is inadequately developed, though maturing rapidly in the first months (Ellingson, 1967), while foveal differentiation and myelination of the optic nerve fibres are minimal (Spears and Hohle, 1967). On the other hand recent studies recording electro-retinograms and evoked visual potentials suggest that retinal and central photopic activity is sufficient at birth to permit some response to patterning and to colour (Lodge et al., 1969). Behaviourally, the pupillary reflex is operative and there is evidence of some ability to discriminate brightness differences (Doris et al., 1967), and Miranda (1970) has recently demonstrated differential fixation times between black-and-white striped patterns and uniform grey patches. Visual pursuit attempts to moving stimuli have been recorded within hours or even minutes of birth (Greenman, 1963; Wolff and White, 1965; Richards, 1972), but continuous conjugate tracking cannot generally be elicited at first, and most evidence suggests that reliable binocular convergence is possible, if at all, only with stationary stimuli (Hershenson, 1964; Wickelgren, 1967, 1969). Optokinetic nystagmus to moving stripes can be elicited soon after birth (Gorman et al., 1957).

Several problems must be mentioned in assessing neonatal visual abilities. One is that neonates spend very little time visually alert, and their visual activity depends very much on their immediate arousal state. These state-dependent effects may be substantial (Wolff, 1965; Hutt et al., 1969; Korner, 1970), and inadequate control for this factor makes a number of studies suspect. A related problem is that maternal sedation by drugs during labour depresses the neonate's attentiveness for some days (Stechler, 1964; Richards and Bernal, 1972), presumably through effects on general arousal. It is possible that visual stimulation can in turn affect arousal state, introducing a further complication. Finally, at birth the eyes very commonly exhibit refractive errors (e.g. Ruskell, 1967; Spears and Hohle, 1967), so individual abilities can vary considerably in the first months.

Just what the infant can see depends critically on his visual acuity and power of accommodation. Haynes et al. (1965) used dynamic retinoscopy to investigate accommodation development, and found that during the first month focusing is limited to some set distance, the median for their subjects being 19 cm. This result casts doubt on studies of various kinds where the precise distance of stimulus presentation has been chosen unsystematically. Hershenson (1967) suggests the result may have been an artefact of poor acuity, and Fantz *et al*. (1962) found no evidence of accommodation effects when testing acuity with targets at 5–20 in. Further investigation is needed here, but since Haynes *et al*. used a target which moved towards or away from the infant's eyes it may be that the primary difficulty is in the *speed* with which infants can accommodate to targets displaced from some optimum distance. Combined with poor convergence and conjugate following this could well be enough to seriously impair perception of certain stimuli in certain situations.

Recent reviews of the development of visual acuity reveal some variability between different assessments of the infant's resolving ability at any given age, especially with neonates (Weymouth, 1963; Ruskell, 1967). As in studies of adult acuity, much of the variation can be explained in terms of different methodologies, different illumination conditions, and similar factors. However, acuity at birth is probably adequate for the resolution of simple, bold patterns, since results using optokinetic nystagmus and differential fixation time measures are in fair agreement, showing that stripes subtending one degree of arc, or even less in some conditions, can be resolved (e.g. Fantz *et al*., 1962).

The elementary neonatal abilities begin to show signs of improvement during stage 2 (1–8 weeks). According to Haynes *et al*. (1965) the first signs of flexibility in accommodation are shown by the start of the second month. Ling (1942) reported binocular fixation was evident by the end of the stage, although initially convergence of the eyes was somewhat jerky. Ling also found that visual pursuit and compensatory eye movements during head rotation became efficient early in the second month, and at the same time attention to the test stimulus reached a peak. However, other investigators have found that general attentiveness to visual objects is still increasing at 4 months (White and Held, 1966), so stimulus characteristics appear to be crucial in this respect. By the end of the stage motion and binocular parallax cues to depth seem to be discriminated, and there is some evidence that perceptual constancies begin to develop (Bower, 1966, and see Gibson, 1969). During stage 3 (2–3 months) acuity and accommodation improve rather rapidly, convergence becomes smoother, and brightness and colour discrimination also improve. The blink response to a looming object is first seen clearly (White and Held, 1966), although Bower *et al.* (1970c) reported that head retraction, bringing the hands up to the face, and opening the eyes wide were elicited by optical expansion of a disc from the first weeks of stage 2.

Another, and very significant, sensory–motor adaptation which can be seen in stage 3 is crude but visually directed reaching towards objects (White *et al.*, 1964), although Bower *et al.* (1970a, 1970b) claim to have shown that these first crude swipes may even be made by neonates. Bower *et al.* also claim that their experiments reveal depth perception during stage 1 and a distal "intention" in early reaching behaviour. However, their method depends on the doubtful assumption that neonates have efficient stereoscopic vision (see Hershenson, 1967), and there are other grounds for doubt concerning the process mediating the response. Other studies have not shown responsiveness to the cues associated with solidity of objects until stage 3 (e.g. Fantz, 1966).

During stage 4 (3–7 months) the infant's visual perceptual abilities become progressively more refined. Before it ends accommodation has approximated to adult performance, and acuity is of the same order, being as low as 3 to 5 minutes of arc. The visual system is now physiologically capable of complex functioning (Ellingson, 1967). Visually directed reaching and grasping is also basically efficient. Experiments showing that mobile infants will not crawl over a visual cliff (Gibson, 1969) give unequivocal evidence of depth perception before the end of this period, although differential cardiac responses from infants placed alternately on the shallow and deep sides indicate that some of the relevant cues are discriminated as early as 2 months (Campos *et al.*, 1970).

Stages 5 and 6 (7–12 and 12–18 months) are relatively unimportant with regard to basic visual abilities, although particularly during the first of these there are important developments in social perception. These are best left for discussion in later sections, while other features of perception in later infancy have been well reviewed elsewhere (Rivoire and Kidd, 1966; Gibson, 1969; Mussen *et al.*, 1969).

The final question which remains, before we can discuss responsiveness to specifically facial stimuli, is the problem of when the infant becomes able to perceive visual form *per se*. While Fantz (1963), Miranda (1970) and others have reported preferential fixation of patterned stimuli such as stripes rather than uniform patches even in the neonate stage, these findings are difficult to interpret. In the first months visual attention seems to have a distinctive character, and sustained fixations, when they occur, often appear to be quite involuntary and "stimulus-bound" (Ames and Silfen, 1965; Stechler and Latz, 1966; Bruner, 1969a), with general motor quietening (Stechler et al., 1966). It is difficult to ascertain whether all or just a part of a target is being perceived by the infant in such circumstances; and the picture is further complicated by demonstrable position preferences in the paired-comparisons stimulus situation (J. S. Watson, 1968). Since it is so difficult to control simultaneously the "organismic" variables and all the external variables of brightness, colour, contrast, complexity, novelty, etc., great caution is required in asserting that a true "form" preference has been demonstrated in any given study (Hershenson, 1967; Gibson, 1969; Bronson, 1969a).

Equally problematic is the interpretation of negative results, since discrimination between stimuli need not inevitably be manifested in differential attention. Alternatively, differences may show up only after repeated viewings. Two recent studies by Friedman et al. (1970a, 1970b) on newborn infants showed that after only 8 one-minute trials of exposure to checkerboard stimuli, with 5–10 s intertrial intervals, neonates tended to show reduced fixation times. In particular, males shown 2 × 2 checks showed larger decrements than those shown 12 × 12 checks, and the reverse was true for females. This suggests that had infants been presented with both check sizes, individuals would have manifested differential decrements, i.e. it might have been found that although initial fixation times did not differ, discrimination was manifested after repeated viewings.

We can thus have little confidence in the supposed perception of form per se (in the sense of a spatial gestalt) during stage 1 or the first weeks of stage 2. Fantz and Nevis (1967a, 1967b) controlled contour, number and size of elements, brightness and contrast of visual shapes, and were unable to show form discrimination in infants below one month of age. However, the precise specification of these confounding factors is itself of interest, and various interpretations of fixation time differences have been offered. Salatapek and Kessen (1966) and Salatapek (1968) found that neonates' scanning patterns tended to follow the contours of the figures presented to them, but with some predominance of horizontal scanning and attention to the vertices of triangles. Salatapek did not see this as evidence of discrimination between particular patterns; for example, areas of brightness contrast may attract attention to contours. Nevertheless, as he suggested, characteristic patterns of scanning elicited by different shapes on such a basis may well contribute to the later development of form discriminations.

Aspects of the "complexity" variable have often been invoked in explaining data showing developmental trends in fixation-time differences between targets. Hershenson (1964) presented checkerboard patterns of varying fineness and found that neonates fixated the "simpler" check most; but he pointed out that a brightness preference interacting with only partial scanning of targets could account for the result. Hershenson et al. (1967) found that neonates fixated random shapes with an intermediate number of contour turns for longer than those with few turns; but they argue that to show involvement of such a variable it is necessary to demonstrate a monotonic transitive relation involving at least three values of that variable, and this they could not do. Number of turns was, however, shown to determine preference according to these criteria in another study with older infants of 9 months or more (Munsinger and Weir, 1967). McCall and Kagan (1967a) found that mean length of contour rather than number of turns governed numbers of fixations given to targets by 4-month infants, but durations of these were more closely related to perimeter or area, in a non-linear fashion. Similar results were found in older infants by Karmel (1969).

The finding of non-linear relationships, whereby stimuli of intermediate "complexity" receive most attention, has not been uncommon. Cohen (1969) used as stimuli lights which moved randomly between either 4, 8, or 16 positions. With 2–6-month infants preference was for the intermediate number. Similarly, Haith et al. (1969) varied predictability of the motion of a light for infants of 2–4 months, and found the preference for intermediate values. These results seem to contrast with those using checkerboard targets: Moffett (1969) used irregular checkerboards and found that fixation in 9–19-week infants increased with the number of white rectangles, while Caron and Caron (1969) found that finer checks received most attention at $3\frac{1}{2}$ months. An earlier study by Brennan et al. (1966) had in fact shown that age was a crucial factor in these attention relationships: at 3 weeks the least complex checks were preferred, at 2 months the more intermediate, and at $3\frac{1}{2}$ months the most complex. A possible resolution of the relationships

between attention, fixation and "complexity" has been provided by
Karmel (1969), who uses a measure of amount of contour: the total
length of black–white transitions in a target pattern. This measure is
applicable to most types of black-and-white target forms, and his re-
analysis of the results of several earlier studies suggests a general trend.
He finds that fixation time follows an inverted-U function with respect
to the square root of the amount of contour, and that the function
spreads out along the contour axis as age increases (Fig. 1).

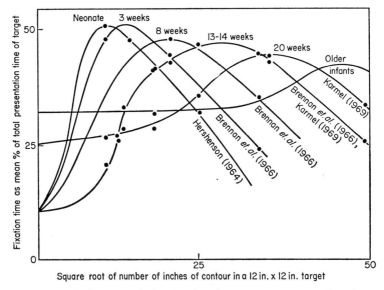

Fig. 1. Hypothetical curves relating fixation time, as a percentage of total presentation time, to the square root of the amounts of contour in visual targets presented to
infants of various ages. Curves are fitted to data points of the studies indicated, after
correction for variations in absolute size of stimuli, and averaged across trials and
subjects. Adapted from Karmel (1969).

Karmel's curves indicate an optimum "complexity" for gaining
attention, which increases with age, and they can be seen as reflecting
the development of the infant's capacity for processing visual data.
Measures other than fixation time support this view, since Harter and
Suitt (1970) have shown that visually evoked cortical potentials, studied
from 3 weeks to 5 months in an infant presented with various sizes of
checkerboard pattern, were first greatest to the largest check, but
ultimately the finest check evoked the greatest response. There was
indirect evidence that development of visual acuity as well as processing

ability was involved. It seems that a basically similar approach to Karmel's could be used where the stimuli (e.g. flashing lights) cannot easily be interpreted in terms of contour; however, it must be doubted whether any single unidimensional variable can account exclusively for the complex stimulus-fixation relationships revealed by the various studies. But if one may tentatively use a single term such as "complexity" in a generic sense to embrace all the stimulus characteristics which may be relevant, a broad summary statement may be attempted. While there is no clear evidence that anything more than brightness and contrast functions lead to apparent preferences for particular visual forms before about 3 weeks of age, from birth onwards the patterns of fixation are related to the contours of forms, and very soon fixation durations become thus related. Thereafter, fixation appears to be linked to a developing optimum value of the complexity of contour.

While the above generalization may be true for novel geometric forms and other targets not met with normally in the typical infant's environment, it will not suffice where one is considering objects to which an infant is repeatedly exposed, such as human faces. From about 2–3 months onwards, repeated presentation of non-human stimuli within a testing session leads to a response decrement manifested as visual preference for a novel stimulus (e.g. Saayman et al., 1964; Fantz, 1964; Lewis et al., 1966a; Fagan, 1970). Hunt (1970) has pointed out that some caution is needed in interpreting such results in that the decrement may be due to "perceptual satiation" and may not imply that the infant actually recognizes the repeated stimulus. Recognition is more safely inferred when there has been a period of long-term familiarization and a fairly substantial delay before the novel and familiar stimuli are presented in a test situation. Studies by Greenberg et al. (1970) and by Uzgiris and Hunt (1970) found that while this method revealed a preference for novel stimuli by about $2\frac{1}{2}$ months, the familiar stimulus was presented at the earlier age of 2 months. Weizmann et al. (1971) found attentional preference for a familiar stabile at 6 weeks, while by 8 weeks a novel one was preferred. Other investigators have found similar evidence for a novelty preference by about 3 months (McCall and Kagan, 1967b), and it appears that by this age only a few minutes' experience with a pattern is required for it to be recognized as familiar 2 hours later (Fagan, 1970). The finding that familiar stimuli can receive more attention than novel ones at a certain age has led Hunt (1970) to suggest that the preference is found only while the stimulus is *becoming* familiar, and thus needs close examination in order to be recognized. Once an internal model of the object is well established recognition is rapid, and little attention is demanded. McCall, Kagan, and others have argued that when such a schema is established visual interest centres on discrepancies from the schema. This approach will prove particularly useful in interpreting the data on attention to faces, and will be discussed later at greater length.

First this data, together with that on other responses to facial stimuli, must be presented in some detail. The early studies of attention to faces arose out of the discovery by Fantz that schematic drawings of faces seemed to be of intrinsically greater visual interest to infants than were geometric stimuli (summarized in Fantz, 1965, 1966, 1967). This suggested the possibility of "innate" responsiveness to faces (cf. Sackett, 1966, on lower primates), and led to a substantial research effort in the area.

1.3.2   *Attention to faces and facial representations*

Despite the obviousness of the interest which infants show in the face of the mother or caretaker, it was not until the 1960's that attention to facial stimuli was first studied in detail. Fantz (see above) presented various visual stimuli, including schematic representations of faces, in paired or sequential comparison tests and recorded relative times spent on different targets. Studies of infants of various ages up to 2 years suggested preference for faces as a general finding, while from 1 month preference was for correct rather than "scrambled" facial features; from 2 months a three-dimensional head model was preferred to a flat representation.

Differential attention is, as was indicated above, an ambiguous measure, but where differential fixation favours faces rather than other forms we would expect to be able to identify dimensions responsible for such differences, as in the case of geometric targets. A number of studies have followed on from Fantz's early work, attempting to delineate critical facial cues eliciting attention, and age-related changes in that attention during the first year. Other response measures have sometimes been used, but the fixation measure remains the most direct and popular. The principal studies on attention reactions to facial stimuli are summarized briefly in Table 2, excluding those using smiling and other affective indices, which will be discussed in the next section of this paper. From these results it is possible to summarize the relevant developmental

TABLE 2

Summary of principal studies of infants' attention responses to facial stimuli

Author	Stimuli used	Response measure etc.	Principal findings	Age of infant
Ahrens (1954)	Drawing of face and face-masks: complete or upper or lower half only, various expressions	Observational notes on institutional infants (semi-longitudinal)	Gaze averted from half-face or "angry" face-masks	5 months onwards
			Attention to face drawings brief or intermittent with gaze at experimenter	5–6 months
Wolff (1963)	Face of experimenter	Observational notes (longitudinal)	Infant's eyes focus on those of other in true mutual gaze	3–4 weeks onwards
Fantz (1963)	Bull's-eye target and circular forms of schematic face, newsprint, uniform coloured disc	Paired-comparison fixation time	Schematic representation of face obtains fixation "preference"	Neonate
	Facial oval forms with correct, partial or "scrambled" features	As above	The faces with all features present are preferred over incomplete ones	Neonate
Stechler (1964)	Blank area, random dots, or schematic face	Fixation time	Schematic face obtains more attention	Neonate
Caldwell (1965, see Schaffer, 1971)	Seven situations involving mother and/or stranger, mobile or immobile, silent or talking and smiling	Fixation times	No differential attention in infants below—	
			Greater attention to stranger after this time	3 months

TABLE 2—*contd*

Author	Stimuli used	Response measure etc.	Principal findings	Age of infant
Fantz (1965, 1966)	Realistic drawn face. Solid head model	Paired-comparison fixation time	Solid head preferred	2 months onwards
	Schematic faces in ovals, complete or with eye-spots only in correct or scrambled arrangement	As above	Preference for correct position of eye-spots	1 month onwards
			Preference for correct arrangement of complete face	2–3 months onwards
Kagan and Lewis (1965)	Mother's face and colour photographs of male or female faces. Black and white bull's-eye target, checkerboard, photographs of nursing bottle and panda bear	Fixation time, cardiac deceleration, body mobility etc. (longitudinal)	Fixation and motor quietening greater to face representations	6 months
			More sustained fixations by girls, but both sexes habituate rapidly across trials	6 months
	Achromatic stimuli as above, but schematic face replacing panda	As above	Less attention to targets than at 6 months, but most still to faces, especially schematic face	13 months
Thomas (1965)	Checkerboard, stripes, drawing of person and schematic face	Paired-comparison fixation time	Facial representation not preferred	2–14 weeks
			Facial presentation preferred	15–26 weeks

Author (Year)	Stimuli	Measures	Results	Age
Kagan et al. (1966)	Coloured solid models of realistic, eyeless, scrambled, and blank faces	Fixation times, cardiac deceleration	Longer first and total fixations by boys, more to faces with eyes, but longer first fixations to eyeless than to blank faces	4 months
			Cardiac response greatest overall to either complete face, but greatest to correct one for girls	4 months
			First fixations shorter, no fixation preference between faces, but more cardiac response to scrambled	8 months
Lewis, et al. (1966c)	Photographs of male and female faces, schematic face, checkerboard, bull's-eye target, nursing bottle, three patterns of flashing lights	Fixation time (five measures)	Different measures showed different preferences, but first and total fixation times showed faces preferred by girls only	6 months
			Boys showed differential first fixations between light patterns	6 months
Stechler and Latz (1966)	Schematic faces, geometric forms, real faces either still or moving and speaking	Fixation time, skin potential, body mobility etc. (longitudinal)	Two of three infants showed "obligatory attention" terminated by fussing and crying, sharply peaking at—	1–2 weeks
			Two of three infants preferred real faces, while one avoided these	2 weeks onwards

TABLE 2—contd

Author	Stimuli used	Response measure etc.	Principal findings	Age of infant
J. S. Watson (1966, 1968)	Circular schematic face, circles containing either a dot, or a "T": all upright or inverted	Paired-comparison fixation time	With face stimulus, fixation greatest when upright	7–26 weeks
			Result due only to infants of— and contaminated by position preference bias	13–14 weeks
Carpenter and Stechler (1967)	Mother's face, model head, solid form with protruding coloured knobs: all nodding or still	Fixation time, body mobility etc. (longitudinal)	Overall attention increase with age from 30 per cent of trial at birth to 50 per cent at—	8 weeks
			Peak of attention to non-human stimuli	2 weeks
			"Deliberate" target avoidance between fixations	3 weeks onwards
			Attention greater to nodding objects, head and mouth motion greatest to mother's face	1 week to 1 month
Haaf and Bell (1967)	Schematic face: complete, two scrambled forms, and nose and ears only	Paired-comparison fixation time of male subjects	Ordering of fixations fitted a paradigm of greater "faceness" rather than greater complexity	4 months

Hershenson (1965, see 1967)	Photograph of face: complete or scrambled with or without contour intact	Paired-comparison fixation time	No differential fixation independent of brightness and complexity	Neonate
Fantz and Nevis (1967a, 1967b)	Photograph of face, schematic face: correct or scrambled, solid face model. Various geometric and other stimuli (cf. earlier Fantz studies)	Paired-comparison fixation times of both home and institution-reared infants (longitudinal)	Most consistent overall preference was for bull's-eye target from birth to—	24 months
			Schematic face preferred over photograph	Neonate to 4 months
			Photograph preferred over schematic face representations	4 months onwards
			Correct rather than scrambled schematic face preferred	4–5 months
			Solid model face preferred to two-dimensional representations	2 months onwards
			Slight preference for correct orientation of eye-spots in face oval, from 2 months in institutional infants, but in home-reareds from—	Neonate onwards
			No preferences independent of contour, number of elements and size, brightness, and contrast	Neonate to 1 month

TABLE 2—contd

Author	Stimuli used	Response measure etc.	Principal findings	Age of infant
Lu (1967)	Schematic face, correct or scrambled. Bull's-eye target, newsprint, stripes, coloured circles	Paired-comparison fixation time of normals and of retardates (same M.A.)	Face representations preferred by both samples	3–7 months
McCall and Kagan (1967a)	Photographs and schematic faces: correct or scrambled. Random shapes	Fixation time, cardiac deceleration	First fixation and cardiac response greater to facial forms, somewhat more so when correct	4 months
Moss (1967)	Mother's face	Fixation time (longitudinal)	Attention increases between 3 weeks and—	3 months
Fitzgerald (1968)	Face of mother or stranger, checkerboards, triangle	Pupillary dilation following fixation	Dilation greatest to faces (but not at 2 months)	1 month and 4 months
			Differential response between mother and stranger	4 months
Gough (1968)	Mother gazing at infant	Observational notes and film (longitudinal)	Staring at mother's face during feeding at the breast or bottle	1–2 weeks onwards
Koopman and Ames (1968)	Schematic faces: correct, symmetrically or asymmetrically scrambled	Fixation time, paired-comparison fixation time	No differential responses	10 weeks

Study	Stimulus	Measure	Results	Age
Moss and Robson (1968, 1970)	Mother's face	Naturalistic observation of mutual gazing (longitudinal)	Mutual gazing doubled from 1 month to—	3 months
	Photographs of face, schematic faces: correct and symmetrically scrambled. Three checkerboards	Fixation time	Attention to facial and non-facial stimuli correlated, with preference for facial stimuli	13 weeks
			Females' facial fixation amounts correlated with mutual gazing with mothers, but males' fixation correlated with arousal states	13 weeks
Wilcox and Clayton (1968)	Colour ciné film of female face moving or still. Light stimulus (control)	Fixation time	More fixation to the film, especially when face moving, but no differential response to expression	5 months
Kagan (1969a, 1969b)	Schematic faces and photographs of faces: realistic or scrambled. Models of correct, scrambled, eyeless, eyes only, and blank heads: still or mobile	Fixation times (longitudinal)	Fixation times (first fixation and total) decreased, and stability of inter-subject differences was low, from 4 months through 8 months to— Fixations increased again	13 months 27 months
		Fixation times, cardiac deceleration	Amount of contour or motion was main determinant of fixation	3 months
			Facial model elicits least attention and cardiac response is decreased, but less so for higher social class infants	8 months

TABLE 2—*contd*

Author	Stimuli used	Response measure etc.	Principal findings	Age of infant
Lewis (1969)	Schematic faces: correct and scrambled. Face photographs: correct and one-eyed "Cyclops"	Time of first fixation only	Fixation times decreased with age from 3 months to—	13 months
			Overall decrease in interest of correct faces in relation to distorted ones with age, but overall ranking as follows: correct photograph, schematic, "Cyclops", scrambled	3–13 months
			Photographs preferred to schematics	3 months
			Correct preferred to distorted	6 months
			Longer fixations by males	3–9 months
Wilcox (1969)	Photograph of face, realistic drawn face and schematic faces: correct, eyes only, mouth and nose only, or outline only	Fixation times (four measures)	Total fixation only increasing with age from 1 month through $2\frac{1}{2}$ months to—	4 months
			No difference between eyes only and mouth and nose only faces	1–4 months
			Overall fixation greatest to photograph of face, or to schematic face with photograph best by—	4 months

Author	Stimuli	Method	Results	Age
Carpenter et al. (1970)	Face of mother or experimenter, model head, round form with coloured protruding knobs: all still or nodding	Fixation and avoidance times of female negro infants (longitudinal)	More attention to model or abstract form than to mother	1–7 weeks
			Attention to all forms increased with age from 1 week to—	8 weeks
			Non-significant trend for greater attention to stranger than to mother	2 weeks onwards
McGurk (1970)	Schematic face, funnel shape: both upright or inverted	Paired-comparison fixation time	More attention to face, but no effect of orientation	6–26 weeks
		Response recovery to stimulus change after habituation, paired-comparison fixation time after stimulus change	Response recovery to orientation change	6–26 weeks
			Paired-comparison discrimination of facial orientation	20–26 weeks
Miranda (1970)	Stripes, squares, grey area, large and small schematic faces, face photograph etc.	Paired-comparison fixation time in full-term or premature infants	Patterned stimuli preferred. Schematic face preferred to photograph, large face preferred to small	Neonate

trends in terms of the stage sequence proposed earlier. Since many of the studies suffer from the methodological problems already mentioned, details must remain somewhat tentative.

In stage 1 (0–1 week) the more carefully controlled studies of Hershenson (1965, see 1967) and of Fantz and Nevis (1967a, 1967b) have failed to replicate earlier findings of preferential attention to facial patterns. Fantz and Nevis did find that when schematic faces and more realistic photographs of faces were compared the former gained more attention (up to 90 per cent), but they attributed this to the greater complexity and fewer black–white contrasts of the photographs. While Miranda (1970) found similar results, some doubt remains, and the situation highlights the need for standardization of stimuli if findings from different studies are to be comparable.

Data on stage 2 (1–8 weeks) are especially ambiguous. Stechler and Latz (1966) reported the "obligatory attention" phenomenon (cf. p. 206), with a sudden peak at about 10 days, which was shown by three of their infants. In one case a target was fixated for 54 min with no breaks greater than 10 s. Following this age, attention seemed to be different in character, the aversions having a "deliberate, volitional appearance"; and attention would now typically lead to motor excitement 20–30 s after the onset of fixation. With two infants the behaviour appeared to be pleasurable (with smiles, rhythmic limb movements and cooing vocalizations), and was more easily elicited by a real face than by other stimuli. Another infant appeared to show neutral excitation, but specifically *avoided* real faces. Carpenter and Stechler (1967) reported an attention peak at 2 weeks to all stimuli *other* than a real face, but found for the first month a general trend favouring the real face (of the mother) in frequency of head and mouth movements following presentation. From 3 weeks, attention to all stimuli rose steadily, with nodding objects eliciting more fixation than did still ones. Carpenter and Stechler suggest that their first finding shows that the infant already recognizes the mother's face by 2 weeks, but since this study, like that of Stechler and Latz (1966), used few infants and did not control the dimensions of brightness, contrast, etc., the conclusion is not compelling. Similar problems apply to the group's most recent study (Carpenter *et al.*, 1970) on female Negro infants. Here, attention was greatest to non-human objects until 7 weeks, and the experimenter's face gained more attention than the mother's from 2 weeks. However, it does seem clear that some rather important changes in attentive behaviour occur at about 2 weeks, and that some sort of discrimination between forms is present.

Greater pupillary dilation to faces than to other stimuli is found at 1 month (and at 4 months), but is absent at 2 months (Fitzgerald, 1968). Attention to the mother's face is strongly conspicuous during stage 2 (Gough, 1968), which is also important for the onset of genuine mutual gazing between mothers and their infants (Wolff, 1963). A slight preference is indicated for correct rather than incorrect arrangement of eye-spots within the facial oval, appearing earlier in home-reared infants than in institutional infants (Fantz and Nevis, 1967a, 1967b). This difference might be due to a symmetry preference. In general, the evidence suggests that the discriminations and visual preferences cited are as likely to be due to the various basic dimensions of visual stimuli as to any special qualities of faces for infants of 2 months or less. None of the data indicates any innate reaction to the facial *gestalt*. The various conflicts of data emphasize the need for further extensive longitudinal studies of early attention to faces, including naturalistic data, in which precise specification or control of stimulus characteristics and infant perceptual abilities is achieved.

Evidence from several studies indicates that in stage 3 (2–3 months) the three-dimensional character of faces comes to be discriminated and can elicit more attention than can two-dimensional representations. By the end of the stage there is clear evidence for preference of facial representations over other forms in some circumstances (Lu, 1967; Moss and Robson, 1968; McGurk, 1970). There appears to be discrimination between various types of facial stimuli, with some evidence that complete and correct forms are preferred (Lewis, 1969; Wilcox, 1969), although some negative evidence casts doubt on this finding (Fantz and Nevis, 1967a, 1967b; Koopman and Ames, 1968). Again it is not clear that, except in respect of the orientation of eye-spots, differences are independent of brightness, contrast, and "complexity". The combined face and voice of a stranger are more effective than the mother's in reinforcing head-turning at 2–3 months (Koch, 1967), which suggests a preference for novel faces after repeated stimulation; but in the absence of confirming evidence it is safer to regard this discrimination as based more on vocal recognition than facial recognition.

In stage 4 (3–7 months) the preference for facial stimuli is maintained, and the study by Haaf and Bell (1967) suggests that at 4 months correct arrangement of features itself, rather than complexity, is now the factor eliciting the preferential attention. The longitudinal study by Fantz and Nevis (1967a, 1967b) found that from this age realistic photographs began to receive more attention than the schematic drawings. Correct orientation, as well as solidity, is preferred, and Ahrens (1954) noted differential reactions to expressions from 5 months, indicating discrimination of facial cues to be well advanced, as one would expect in view of the maturation of acuity, accommodative power, etc. However, this discrimination need not lead to differential fixation at this age (Wilcox and Clayton, 1968). Although the time for which an infant will maintain fixation on a visual target decreases during this stage, mother–infant mutual gazing is maintained at high levels. Discrimination between the mother's face and strange faces is established by 4 months, on the evidence of differential pupil dilation (Fitzgerald, 1968).

Little can safely be said about subsequent stages, as relatively little work has been done on older infants' attention responses, but it is evident from Table 1 that the interest of normal and familiar facial stimuli has fallen by the end of the first year, and more novel and incongruous variations on the facial schema are preferred (Kagan and Lewis, 1965; Kagan et al., 1966; Lewis, 1969; Kagan, 1969a).

In general, the data on attention to faces give a far from unequivocal picture of developmental transitions. It is clear that different measures can give differing results at a given age, and that individual and sex differences can be appreciable. Evidently the determinants of attention to faces are complex and many sided. A major source of variability in results is probably that of familiarity and within-sessions habituation effects (cf. p. 209) from repeated presentation of the same stimulus, and more consideration of memory and related cognitive functions of the infant will be needed before a more unified picture can be given. These factors may be more important than has hitherto been realized, since it has now been shown that habituation to repeated visual stimuli can even be demonstrated in neonates (Friedman et al., 1970a, 1970b). Since earlier investigators failed to find such effects (e.g. Haith, 1966), it seems probable that factors such as stimulus duration and inter-trial interval are critical, and may remain so for perhaps several months.

Before returning to these questions the other main body of data on early facial-visual signalling must be presented, namely that dealing with apparently "affective" responses to faces, including smiling and protest reactions.

1.4 INFANT RESPONSES TO THE FACE

1.4.1 *The ontogeny of social smiling*

The smile is an important component of adult facial-visual signalling, and is commonly regarded as the main indicator of "positive" affects such as happiness, delight, tender feeling, and so on. This bias is clearly indicated in the literature on expression and recognition of affective expressions (cf. section 1.2, and Vine, 1970). However, ethologists have shown more interest in the actual behavioural contexts in which smiling occurs, and from such knowledge have been able to hypothesize on its functions in social behaviour. van Hooff (1967; see also Chapter 3) has discussed the possible homology between the human smile and the "silent bared-teeth face" of many other primate species, which appears to serve "appeasing" or "reassuring" functions in primate communication. Probably such functions are at times served by the adult human smile, but they seem less appropriate to that of the young infant. van Hooff now finds that there are at least three sub-categories of the primate expression, at least in the chimpanzee, and analysis of their contexts of occurrence shows that the "open-mouth bared-teeth face" variant appears to invite approach by another animal, as well as being behaviourally most similar to the human smile.

Cross-cultural investigations of adult smiling have found it to occur in the most diverse human cultures (Eibl-Eibesfeldt and Hass, 1967; Eibl-Eibesfeldt, 1968; Ekman *et al.*, 1969), and its appearance in even blind infants suggests that it is definitely a species-specific behaviour (see Chapter 4). While these authors have inclined towards seeing the smile as an innately programmed expression of positive emotion, there is equal reason for interpreting it as an invitation to approach, especially as one of its commonest contexts of occurrence is in greeting behaviour. The approach interpretation seems readily applicable to the infant's smile, since it clearly does elicit approach and attention from adults from the age at which it first appears in the infant's repertoire. Such a function would suggest strongly that reciprocal smiling between mother and infant might be of significance in the emergence of mother–infant social attachment during the first year of life. Other functions of smiling might well derive from the basic biological function of permitting and sustaining social proximity.

Functional aspects of smiling are clearly of importance but should not lead us to neglect other facets of the behaviour, including of course its experiential correlates in infancy and beyond. Functional investigations may indicate its biological survival value, but the question of interest in the present context is its motivational basis and meaning for the infant. Before this question can be considered adequately it will be necessary to present and evaluate the data on the ontogeny of smiling, relating eliciting conditions to age-related trends in the frequency of its appearance. Interest in infant smiling goes back at least to Darwin (1872), and a number of major investigations took place during the 1920's and 1930's.

The early studies differed as to the reported age at which social smiling was first observed (from 2 weeks to 2 months), this variability doubtless reflecting discrepancies in stimulus situations used, criteria for scoring responses, and the environmental backgrounds of the infants. Individual differences were found to be considerable, for example Jones (1926) found that an adult smiling or talking back to an infant could reinforce smiling from as early as 5 weeks in some infants, while in the slowest this was difficult before 3 months. The early studies also indicated that a variety of stimuli could elicit smiling. Faces and voices were particularly potent, although expression or tone of voice were not important during the first half-year. Bühler and her associates showed that even later a scolding adult might still evoke smiling, although only after some delay (Bühler, 1931). According to Kaila (1932) the *gestalt* composed of eyes, forehead, and the bridge of the nose, presented in normal frontal orientation, was alone responsible for eliciting smiles until after the age of 5 months.

The precise configuration of the smile also received some attention. It was observed that the "social" smile differed in its appearance from the very early smiles which J. B. Watson had observed in infants after a feed or as a result of touching, rocking, etc. (Bühler, 1935). Washburn (1929) performed a semi-longitudinal study specifying changes in the form of the smile with age, and noted that the superficially related behaviour of laughing emerged later than smiling—and as a distinctly more stereotyped response. In fact there is reason to regard smiling as motivationally and functionally distinct from laughing, the latter perhaps being homologous with the "relaxed open-mouth face" of other primates (van Hooff, 1967, and Chapter 3).

Post-war interest in the smiling response began with the classic investigation by Spitz and Wolf (1946), involving some 250 infants. Many subsequent reports have yielded further information, though results have often been complex, and findings are still somewhat divergent. The main features of the post-war studies are summarized in Table 3. More detailed treatment of some of these studies, and of the older investigations, can be found in a number of reviews of the smiling response (Freedman, 1964; Gewirtz, 1965; Walters and Parke, 1965; Freedman *et al.*, 1967). A number of representative studies dealing with other reactions to facial stimuli, which will be discussed in the next section, are also included in Table 3.

The principal conclusions from the smiling studies may best be presented in terms of the stage sequence introduced earlier. For the neonatal stage 1 there is substantial observational evidence that smiling can be observed, but most authors agree that this behaviour appears to be due to spontaneous discharge of the facial musculature, and not specific to any stimulus situation. Korner (1969) raised the interesting question of whether those infants who show the earliest or most frequent spontaneous smiling might also be precocious in social smiling, but the isolated evidence from Freedman (1964) shows no such relationship, since infants who failed to show spontaneous smiling showed elicited social smiling at the normal age. Studies by Söderling (1959) and by Dittrichovà (Robinson, 1969) suggest that age from conception governs emergence of the social smile; so although the basic response is normally present at birth, maturation of neural connections is presumably needed at some point in the system before social smiling is possible.

It is often stated that while the neonate's smiles show the distinctive retraction and partial elevation of the mouth corners, stage 2 (1–8 weeks) brings a broader smile, with partial opening of the mouth and with wrinkling at the corners of the eyes, reflecting involvement of more of the facial musculature (e.g. Wolff, 1963). Since this fuller smile shows some stimulus dependence, notably on socially emitted signals, a special form and function has been assumed for social smiling. While the term "social smile" is useful enough to be retained, it is important to guard against elevating it to any special status. In a recent symposium (Robinson, 1969) a number of experts emphasized the dangers of such an assumption, and Hanada reported data showing that both eliciting stimuli and muscular involvement in smiling continue to show progressive changes up until the twelfth year. With these reservations, we can state that the data show clearly that smiling to social stimuli emerges

TABLE 3
Summary of principal studies of smiling and other affective responses to facial stimuli

Author	Stimuli used	Response measure etc.	Principal findings	Age of infant
Spitz and Wolf (1946)	Real faces, masks, all varying in expression, detail, motion or stillness etc. Non-social stimuli	Smiling rates and durations in institutional infants	Frontally oriented face or mask, especially when nodding, elicits smile, with configuration of two eyes, nose, and forehead as necessary and sufficient stimulus	2–3 months onwards
			Decline in responsiveness to all faces except those of regular caretakers	6–7 months onwards
			Crying and other protest reactions to strange faces	8 months
			1 per cent of sample failed to smile socially during study period	
	None	Observational notes	Spontaneous mild smiles	Neonates
Piaget (1952)	Real faces, toys, etc.	Observational notes (longitudinal)	First smiles of experimenter's son were to persons	6 weeks
			Most smiles recorded were to toys etc., moving or still	2–4 months

Study	Stimulus	Measure	Findings	Age
Ahrens (1954)	Oval face cut-out with bar, dots, or angles. Round cut-out with dots. Realistic drawn face, complete or eye or mouth region only	Smiling rate etc. in institutional infants	Dots best elicit first smiles, face contour etc. unimportant	6 weeks
			Facial configuration becomes important as infant comes to scan face before smiling, which is greatest to realistic face, but still mainly due to eyes	3 months
	Real, realistic drawn, and schematic faces: neutral, smiling, or crying expressions. Mask cut-outs with or without mouth removed by cutting at nose	As above	All faces effective but most smiling to real face, no effect of expression	3–4 months
			No smiling to cut-off face, so mouth or contour is attended to	5 months
			Smiling limited to real face with full expression	8 months onwards
			Strong smiling to moving mouth, especially when widened into smile	5 months onwards
	Model and drawn faces of child, laughing or crying, moving or still. Real face of smiling 4-month infant	As above	Some smiles to child faces, best when moving or real, but less than to adult face	5–7 months onwards
Brackbill (1958)	Female experimenter's face, motionless and neutral or smiling with vocalization and touching of infant	Conditioning and extinction of smiling rate	Conditioning effective, with slower and more distressful extinction in infants on partial reinforcement. Negative relation between smiling and protest. Rapid habituation of baseline smiles to unsmiling face	14–19 weeks

TABLE 3—contd

Author	Stimuli used	Response measure etc.	Principal findings	Age of infant
Rheingold et al. (1959)	Female experimenter's face, motionless and neutral or smiling with vocalization and touching of infant	Conditioning of vocalization rate in institutional infants	Smiling etc. face effective in conditioning	3 months
Söderling (1959)	Real face	Observational notes on Swedish infants	Fixation on faces common by second week and may be followed by a smile. The eyes "light up" and there is head and trunk motion and sometimes vocalizations. First smiles to faces appear anywhere from 2 weeks to— Distribution of first smiles (11 per cent at 2–3 weeks, 60 per cent by 3–4 weeks, 100 per cent by 6 weeks) depends on gestational factors rather than age from birth	6 weeks
Géber (1960)	Face, voice, touch etc. of mother	Observational notes on African Ganda infants	Social smiling typically seen	1 month

Study	Stimuli	Measure	Findings	Age
Ambrose (1961, 1963)	Still, neutral face of experimenter presented after a feed	Smile durations of institutional and home-reared infants during successive presentations	Some smiling typically by 6–10 weeks in home-reared infants, but in institutional infants not until—	9–14 weeks
			Peak amounts of smiling by home-reared infants	11–14 weeks
			Peak for institutionals	16–20 weeks
			Following peak periods there is reduced smiling, and habituation to repeated presentation of unsmiling face with virtually no smiling by—	8 months
Freedman (1961)	Real faces	Observational notes	Before 2 months infrequent smiles to various stimuli or spontaneously, then first fixation of face is followed by smiling	2 months onwards
			Reduced smiling to strange faces	5 months onwards
			First fearful responses to faces	7–10 months
L'Allier (1961, see Freedman, 1964)	Sixteen combinations involving still or moving face, voice, caress, picking up, and non-social stimuli	Smiling rate etc.	Peak smiling was shown	3–4 months
			The face alone was four times as effective as voice alone. Voice with moving face was best, but adding caress, picking up etc. reduced smiling	

TABLE 3—*contd*

Author	Stimuli used	Response measure etc.	Principal findings	Age of infant
Rheingold (1961)	Seventeen stimulus situations, social and non-social	Smiling, crying, vocalizations, and movement in home- or institution-reared infants	Institutionals smiled more quickly and often, vocalized and reached out more, gave fewer negative responses to the experimenter. Both groups smiled to non-social as well as social stimulation	3–4 months
Laroche and Tcheng (1963)	Combinations with static or moving faces, voice, etc.	Smiling rate etc. (longitudinal)	Smiling showed a peak responsiveness in infants at—	4–6 months
			The voice was superior to a static face in eliciting smiles but no better than a moving or smiling face; the voice-plus-face was the most effective at least until—	6 months
Salzen (1963)	Brightness or contrast changes in facial and other objects, moving or still	Observational notes (longitudinal)	First smiles to brightness changes	7 weeks
			Vocalization increased response to faces, but all stimuli still effective at—	11 weeks
Weisberg (1963)	Contingent or non-contingent smiling, touching etc., or sound of bell: with or without neutral face of experimenter visible	Conditioning and extinction of vocalization in institutional infants	Unresponsive face did not increase vocalization, nor did non-social stimulus, but smiling etc. yielded weak conditioning	3 months

Study	Stimulus	Method	Observation	Age
Wolff (1963)	Face of experimenter or mother, voices etc., face-masks	Observational notes. Smiling rate etc. (longitudinal)	Non-specific, spontaneous smiles	Neonates
			High-pitched vocalization would elicit broader "social" smile in periods of alertness	2–3 weeks
			Silent nodding face becomes effective and rapidly takes precedence	4–5 weeks onwards
			While mother's voice is still best elicitor, vocal reply becomes normal response	4–5 weeks onwards
			Static face will elicit smile once mutual gazing becomes necessary condition of smiling to faces	5–6 weeks
			Habituation to repeated presentation of face, but motion etc. lead to recovery of response	2 months onwards
	Tactile "pat-a-cake" game		From introduction at 4 weeks the most potent elicitor of smiles, repetition increasing intensity, until—	6 weeks
Freedman (1964)	Sequential presentation of experimenter's neutral face, then adding speech, smile, nodding, and touch	Observational notes on congenitally blind infants (semi-longitudinal)	Earliest smiles very reflexive and fleeting, with vocalization and touch effective elicitors	2–4 months
			Full smiles shown	4–6 months onwards

TABLE 3—*contd*

Author	Stimuli used	Response measure etc.	Principal findings	Age of infant
Polak *et al.* (1964a, 1964b)	Nodding face of experimenter	Latency, intensity, and duration of smile	Peak smiling with smallest latency	15 weeks to 5 months
			Rapid waning of response to zero	6–8 months
			Habituation to repetition begins to be seen	2–3 months onwards
	Real face, colour photograph of face: both either nodding, approaching, or receding	Smiling and vocalization measures	Real face more effective for smiling and for vocalization	10 weeks to 3 months onwards
			Temporary aversion more frequent to real face, peak amount	3–4 months
			Approaching face elicits most smiles	3 months
Schaffer and Emerson (1964b)	Mothers, strangers, etc.	Interview data from mothers	Fear responses shown to strangers and to visual loss of mother	8–9 months
Gewirtz (1965)	Experimenter's neutral face	Smiling time during 2 min. of infants in four different Israeli environments	Some smiling seen in only 20 per cent of institutional but in 80 per cent of kibbutz infants	1 month
			Peak smiling responsiveness of all infants	4–6 months

Study	Stimuli	Measure	Findings	Age
			Slow and slight decline of response in all infants	6 months onwards
			Some smiling still shown to strange faces	18 months
Kagan and Lewis (1965)	Mother's face, colour photographs of male and female faces, bull's-eye target, checkerboard, nursing bottle, panda bear photographs	Vocalization rate	Female faces elicited most vocal response, but repetition led to habituation	6 months
	Human speech including that of mother, music, tone	As above	Vocalization greatest to voices, especially female voices and for female infants	6 months
Kagan et al. (1966)	Coloured models of realistic, scrambled, eyeless, and blank faces	Smiling rate etc.	Smiling most to regular face, more to eyeless than blank, and all smiling consistently higher by males	4 months
Schaffer (1966)	Graded degrees of approach by experimenter in the mother's presence. Still and neutral face, moving with vocalization, touch etc.	Crying, smiling, grimacing, gaze aversion etc. (longitudinal)	Irregular and brief signs of fear shown in most infants	6–9 months
			Lag in smiling to stranger only	13–19 weeks
			Fear shown typically only to closest approaches involving touch, only rarely to face or voice alone. Slightly earlier fear onset in first-borns and in girls	

TABLE 3—contd

Author	Stimuli used	Response measure etc.	Principal findings	Age of infant
J. S. Watson (1966)	Face of experimenter or mother, complex multi-coloured mask: all at 0°, 90° or 180° orientation	Rate, latency, and intensity of smiles	Strongest smiling to faces in 0° orientation	13–14 weeks
			Smiling peak greatest to mother's face and subsequent decline to strange faces (all orientations)	5–6 months
Carpenter and Stechler (1967)	Mother's face, model head, solid form with coloured protruding knobs: all nodding or still	Smiling and vocalization rates (longitudinal)	More smiling and vocalization to mother's face	6–7 weeks
Etzel and Gewirtz (1967)	Experimenter's face, neutral and still or nodding and vocalizing	Conditioning and extinction of mutual gazing leading to smile rather than crying in institutional infants	One infant was reinforced for mutual gazing without crying, and for smiling, from 6 weeks, using a shaping procedure with toys etc. Successful conditioning was achieved by—	8 weeks
			A 20-week infant who frowned and then cried following mutual gazing (91 per cent of occasions) was con-ditioned rapidly not to cry but to smile back at a smiling face in mutual gaze with it	

Study	Stimulus	Topic	Findings	Age
Moss (1967)	Mother's face	Smiling duration etc. (longitudinal)	Mother's smiling at infant and infant's returning smile both increased markedly (in association with more gazing at mother by infant) from 3 weeks to—	3 months
Wahler (1967)	Face of mother or female stranger, either still and neutral or smiling, or touching, with vocalization	Conditioning and extinction of smiling rate	Stranger scarcely effective as reinforcer, mother much more so	15 weeks
J. S. Watson (1967a)	Mother engaging in caretaking activities and looking at eyes and mouth	Facial orientation of mother in relation to infant's face	Face-to-face (0°) orientation used only in 21 per cent of feeding time, 18 per cent of changing infant, but in 70 per cent of looking at eyes and 79 per cent of looking at smile, i.e. face-to-face used mainly in social interaction rather than caretaking	9–10 weeks
Brossard and Décarie (1968)	Eight contingent reinforcement situations involving experimenter's face plus auditory and/or tactile and/or kinesthetic stimuli	Conditioning of smiling consequent on mutual gazing in institutional infants	Time to criterion of 20th smile was less for face plus picking up than face plus touch. Face alone was second most effective stimulus	4–5 months
Todd and Palmer (1968)	Vocal reinforcement, with or without face of experimenter visible	Conditioning of vocalization	Conditioning more effective with experimenter visible	11–14 weeks

TABLE 3—*contd*

Author	Stimuli used	Response measure etc.	Principal findings	Age of infant
Dittrichová (Robinson, 1969, p. 165)	Voice and face	Observational notes on premature and full-term infants	Social smiles typically appear Age of smiling depends on conceptional age of infant	6 weeks
Kagan (1969a, 1969b)	Face photograph or schematic face, correct or scrambled. Solid face-masks	Vocalization rate	Vocalization to facial stimuli shows peak	10–12 weeks
	Model head	Smiling rate etc.	Only 60 per cent of infants would smile at face stimulus, decreasing subsequently, from—	4 months
Korner (1969)	None	Smiling rate, startle rate etc.	Spontaneous smiles and startles Smiling more common in females, startling in males, with consistent individual differences across arousal states	Neonates
Lewis (1969)	Face photographs: correct or one-eyed "Cyclops". Schematic face, correct or scrambled	Smiling duration, vocalization and fretting or crying rates	Vocalization rate was low, greatest to photographs and in girls, increasing with age from 3 months to—	13 months

		Girls showed more smiling to realistic faces	3–13 months
		Smiling to all stimuli was lowest at 6 months, and lower at 3–6 months than at—	9–13 months
		Fretting and crying frequencies were low to all stimuli, decreasing with age from 3 months to—	13 months
Morgan and Ricciuti (1969)	Face of male or female experimenter, with or without voice, approach, touch, and all with mother either holding infant or 4 ft away from it. Face-mask, correct or distorted	Overall positive–negative rating based on smiles, frowns, aversions	
		Positive responses decreased with age from 20 weeks to—	54 weeks
		Responses were predominantly positive for infants held by mothers, and became negative only for separated infants at—	54 weeks
		Reactions were always positive to masks, especially to distorted mask at—	19 weeks
		Positive mask reactions increased slightly with age, being greater than those to strangers from—	35 weeks onwards
		No indication of fear peak during 19–54 week study range. More positive reactions to male experimenter	

TABLE 3—*contd*

Author	Stimuli used	Response measure etc.	Principal findings	Age of infant
Wolff (1969)	Face-masks, face of experimenter or mother, both silent and nodding, Tactile "pat-a-cake" game etc.	Observational notes (longitudinal)	Cries of "anger", pain, hunger etc. differentiable and in first weeks numerous causes are evident. Crying stopped by pacifier, monotonous stimuli, complete swaddling etc. Same stimuli that elicit smiles can elicit crying in fussy infant by—	3 weeks
			Face can stop infant crying, but disappearance can elicit it	5 weeks onwards
			Strange faces and distorted masks elicit no crying before 6 months, but mother's distorted face causes crying	3–6 months
Scarr and Salatapek (1970)	Female experimenter with graded approach (cf. Schaffer, 1966). "Horror" and teddy-bear face-masks; also tests on visual cliff and with various surprising objects, and a loud noise	Fear rating on 3-point scale	Fear of strangers not shown until—	7 months
			Intensity and percentage of infants showing some fear increased with age up to—	2 years
			Fear of masks more constant with age and shown from before 7 months by 40 per cent of infants, though increasing later	

Fear of visual cliff, strangers, and sudden events only moderately related, with fear of masks as well correlated with fears of sudden events as of strangers (about 0.35)

Infants' scores were fairly stable over a 2-month period, but were not related to scores on a test of the object-permanence concept during stage 2. The age of onset is variously reported (as in the pre-war studies) as between 2 weeks and 2 months.

A variety of reasons can be proposed to account for the variations in the onset of social smiling. While the reliability of smile judgements by observers can be high (Simpson and Capetanopoulos, 1968), research reports have often failed to specify just how much mouth movement etc. was required before recording a smile, and criteria have probably varied. The same doubts apply to factors such as the latency following stimulus presentation, or whether mutual gazing between mother and infant is considered a necessary condition of a contingent response (e.g. see Brossard and Décarie, 1968). Differences between measures such as frequency or duration of smiling might also affect results obtained, but differences in stimulation conditions would be expected to be even more significant. From the conclusions of the previous section we may expect that for young infants the presentation duration or repetition, the distance away, the size, and the mobility of stimuli are of importance, while colouration, contrast, contour and so on may be critical, especially where masks are used. Stimulus orientation and solidity also appear to be important. Apart from the variance due to the above factors, it seems clear that individual differences in age of onset of social smiling can be substantial (Söderling, 1959; Ambrose, 1961), and that infants in highly stimulating environments smile earliest (Géber, 1960; Gewirtz, 1965). Further aspects of methodological and other discrepancies of detail between results on social smiling are discussed in Gewirtz (1965) and in Gibson (1969), and it is clear that further research remains to be done before precise determinants of the various age-related changes in infant's social smiling can be specified.

Returning to the data on stage 2 infants, there is some conflict evident from the studies in Table 3 as to which social stimuli first elicit smiling and remain most effective. While most studies have found or assumed the face to be the first stimulus, Salzen (1963) cites brightness contrast; and Wolff (1963) cites vocalization. He also found kinesthetic stimulation to be more effective than facial stimuli from its introduction at 4 weeks until about 6 weeks. Since Salzen used only a single infant, and Wolff used only 8, there is reason to doubt the generality of their findings. However, since Wolff was careful to control for state changes in the infants, which some studies have not, and since results were very consistent within his sample, it may be the case that the voice rather than the face of the mother is actually the first stimulus eliciting social smiling, at least in his particular mother–infant population. It is of note that his intensive longitudinal data collection may have permitted familiarization which could favour early emergence of smiling to particular stimuli, as well as giving data more representative of events in the normal social environment of the home. The question may not be of great consequence since Wolff agrees that the face quite rapidly becomes the best elicitor of smiles. Smiling to voices declined after 4–5 weeks to the point where "the preferred response to vocalization is now vocal reply" (Wolff, 1963, p. 130). While Wolff found kinesthetic stimulation to be a potent elicitor of smiling, the response declined after 6 weeks; although Brossard and Décarie (1968) found it was still effective at 4–5 months, it is significant that it was so only when combined with facial presentation.

In general, as the earlier studies found, it appears that the combination of a nodding face and vocalization by the stimulus person can best elicit early social smiling (e.g. Kistyakovskaya, cited in Freedman et al., 1967). Other stimuli, including non-social stimuli, can elicit smiles during stage 2, but typically they are less effective. It appears that during this stage the critical stimuli associated with the face are the eyes, or at least the eye-region *gestalt*. Ahrens (1954) found that a pattern of six dots was as or more effective than just a two-dot pattern at first, but the former may be seen as a "supernormal" variant of the latter. It may be that in the first few weeks, when the infant's visual abilities are still very limited, the presence of more than two dots simply increases the probability that the infant will fixate some one pair of dots before his attention wanders elsewhere. The simplified nature of the critical stimulus for stage 2 social smiling is further suggested by the effectiveness of face-masks during this period. If these are in motion there is little evidence that they are substantially inferior to faces.

In stage 3 (2–3 months) smiling can be much more readily elicited and sustained, and many infants are virtually at their peak of responsiveness by the end of the stage. With facial stimuli the influence of the eye region remains dominant. There is evidence of habituation of response to repeated invariant presentations, but introduction of variations by motion, smiling back, etc. reinstate smiling. Because real faces are clearly more effective than masks by the end of the stage, Polak et al. (1964b) argue that depth or solidity is discriminated. While other factors might account for their result, it is reasonable to suppose that improving visual capacities do lead to an elaboration of the necessary facial stimulus attributes from this time.

By the first or second month of stage 4 (3–7 months) all normal infants have reached a peak of smiling responsiveness to facial stimuli, though apparently facial expression is not differentially responded to. Smiling back at the infant, and other additional stimulation, can still prevent the otherwise now rapid habituation to an unsmiling face, but motion and stimulus variability *per se* are probably the critical factors here. The peak in temporary aversions of gaze from a real face which is found at 3–4 months (Polak *et al.*, 1964b) may indicate that the infant is now taking active steps to increase stimulus variation. In infant and mother interactions the timing of their behaviours has been shown by film analysis to be important in maintaining smiling, and too much continuous stimulation can lead to aversion with crying (cf. White and Held, 1966; Richards, 1972). Faces which are tilted in relation to that of the infant are now smiled at less than those at a 0° orientation (J. S. Watson, 1966). Peak smiling is maintained for at least the first month of stage 4, after which there is a decline in responsiveness to strange faces, indicating individual recognition of the mother. The decline in smiling comes rather later in institution-reared infants, following a later peak, so that at 3–4 months institutional infants may actually smile more to strangers than do home-reared infants (Rheingold, 1961). A further development of this stage is the enlargement of the facial *gestalt* eliciting smiling, since from 5 months the presence of a mouth is necessary, and wide smiles on the stimulus face are maximally effective.

By stage 5 (7–12 months) smiles may be hard to elicit in response to faces, with even the mother's face needing to be dynamically expressive to elicit a smile. However, in some cases it has been found that the decline in responsiveness, even to still and silent faces, is rather small (Gewirtz, 1965). Cultural differences in the typical extent and variety of the infant's previous exposure to faces may account for such effects by this age. It is of particular interest that reactions to schematic face pictures and to photographs increased during this stage according to Lewis (1969), and that masks were preferred to strange faces (Morgan and Ricciuti, 1969), though Kagan (1969b) reported a decrease in response to a model head from 4 months onwards. It may well be that degree of realism is a critical factor here, interacting with experience of faces. Attempts to explain these and other smiling phenomena in more detail will be made in a later section.

1.4.2   *Other affective responses to facial stimuli*

Developmental changes in responses other than smiling have been investigated much less extensively and will only be presented here in brief, since most of the data concerns signals outside the facial-visual channel.[1] "Positive" affective vocalizations to facial stimuli increase during the first half-year, and can be reinforced by a responsive face from 3 months onwards. Real faces elicit the most vocalization, and it appears that female faces are more effective than male ones, perhaps even before the end of stage 2 (Carpenter and Stechler, 1967). The "negative" vocal response of crying, associated with facial grimacing, aversion of the eyes and head, etc., is negatively correlated with the appearance of smiles (Spitz and Wolf, 1946; Brackbill, 1958), but it can be elicited by the same facial stimuli in some circumstances (from 3 weeks in "fussy" infants, Wolff, 1969; and from stage 4 onwards by strange faces). However, it is of interest that the presentation of a face can often inhibit crying from the second month onwards (Brackbill, 1958; Robson, 1967; Wolff, 1969), and the disappearance of a face already present can elicit crying (Spitz, 1963; Schaffer and Emerson, 1964b; Wolff, 1969). It seems possible that stimulus change rather than any factor specific to faces may be responsible for these effects in the first few months, since crying is also effectively inhibited (and visual attentiveness is increased) by simply picking up the infant and putting it to one's shoulder (Korner and Grobstein, 1966).

Distortion of the familiar face of the other can lead to crying between 3 and 6 months of age, while there appears to be no evidence that very unfamiliar schematic or scrambled faces can have this effect at any age. Data on the development of "fear of strangers", a topic which has been considered in detail by Bronson (1968a, 1968b), Freedman *et al.* (1967), Morgan and Ricciuti (1969) and Scarr and Salatapek (1970), suggests overall that the supposed suddenness and universality of onset of the response has been overestimated. The relevant studies listed in Table 3 indicate that this fearfulness develops rather later than the ability to discriminate one face from another, as indicated either by differential smiling or by differential perceptual measures (see Table 2). Its appearance is critically dependent on the exact degree of approach and interaction initiated by the stranger (Schaffer, 1966; Morgan and Ricciuti, 1969). The actual amount of fearfulness shown probably depends on the extent and variety of a particular infant's prior

[1] Data on vocalization was reviewed by Walters and Parke (1965).

experience of faces (as does the extent of an infant's reduced smiling responsiveness to faces other than the mother's once hers can be recognized). Bronson (1969b) found individual and sex differences in the age at which fear of the visual unfamiliar could first be evoked, and argued that sex-linked constitutional factors could be involved here. However, caution is evidently required in considering factors related to fear responses, since Scarr and Salatapek (1970) have recently shown that the patterns of development of fear of a visual cliff, of strangers, and of sudden events are far from perfectly correlated, and may be considered to develop somewhat independently.

Scarr and Salatapek also reported a finding which is of particular interest in relation to fearful responses to faces. They *were* able to elicit fear responses to masks in a substantial proportion of infants of 7 months or younger; but in this case the masks were worn by the already familiar experimenter, while the studies which failed to record fear had presented the masks in isolation. This suggests that in this study the masks were seen as distortions of a familiar face, and the similar developmental trend for fear of the masks and the fear of sudden events suggests that violation of expectancy was responsible for the evocation of fear responses.

From our consideration of "affective" responses to facial stimuli it is clear that both smiling and negative responses follow a complex developmental path, and that particularly close attention to the precise characteristics of stimuli presented to the infant is essential. It also appears that individual and sex differences are of importance in terms of general responsiveness, but generalization is again hazardous. Differences in responses to faces by male and female infants have been reported, but results are inconsistent (Kagan *et al.*, 1966; Lewis, 1969). Differential response to the sex of a stimulus person's face has also been noted, usually showing more positive response to a female face, but Morgan and Ricciuti (1969) found a male face was favoured. Systematic studies of these variables are clearly required for both attentional and affective responses.

As yet this chapter has done little more than review data on developmental aspects of attention and subsequent response to facial stimuli. No systematic attempt has been made to integrate the findings on these two developments, nor to consider them in relation to socialization of the infant. These tasks will occupy the remainder of this chapter, with particular attention being given to the role of experience in the infant's behaviour. In many cases it will be necessary to reconsider the studies already referred to or listed in Tables 2 and 3, but with emphasis on aspects so far left implicit or mentioned only in passing. In particular, it will be argued that the cognitive aspects of attention and smiling, seen in relation to a variety of variables concerned with experience of stimulation, are of more importance than has usually been recognized for understanding the course of facial-visual signalling. We shall begin with a detailed consideration of the role of the eyes of a stimulus face in eliciting responses from the infant.

2 Facial-visual signalling and schema development

2.1 THE SMILE AS A RECOGNITION RESPONSE

2.1.1 *Eyes as elicitors of smiles*
It is clear that faces are particularly potent elicitors of smiles during the first year of life, although certain configurations can lead instead to negative responses, especially with infants of stage 5 (7–12 months) or older who are shown unfamiliar real faces. The stability of the form of smiling development, across individuals and variations of the social stimulation in their environment, is suggestive of a maturational basis for the infant's reactions to the human face. While other stimuli can elicit smiles, especially when presented by a visible person, in isolation they typically lead to other reactions. Further very careful study is necessary to ascertain whether other stimuli are initially effective because their presentation usually leads to face-to-face confrontation between the infant and the adult.

Even if this is the case, it is of doubtful value to regard smiling as a simple "innate" response to faces, with a course of development based just on maturation of the physiological systems of the infant. A naïve learning theory viewpoint is equally unhelpful, as this must suppose that smiling is just a response in the infant's early repertoire, ready to be conditioned to facial presentations associated with the provision of primary reinforcement. Despite assertions to the contrary, evidence for the latter viewpoint is not impressive. Dennis (1935) was unable to obtain appreciable amounts of smiling to feeding bottles, despite his claim that smiling at persons was on account of their relief-giving properties. More sophisticated interpretations of smiling as a learned response have been suggested more recently (Gewirtz, 1961, 1965), and these may well account for differential rates of development of smiling in terms of the reinforcement contingencies of different infant environments. Likewise, the characteristic form of smiling development might reflect stimulation patterns which are in fact common to most environments. Nevertheless, the basic question of why infants smile at all awaits a satisfactory answer, although we can go some way towards specifying the critical cues and stimulation contingencies which seem to evoke early smiles.

Apart from Ahrens (1954) and Kaila (1932), a number of more recent investigators have emphasized the role of mutual gazing between infant and adult in eliciting social smiles (Rheingold et al., 1959; Wolff, 1963; Freedman, 1965; Etzel and Gewirtz, 1967). The eye region appears to have important cue functions, especially in the first few months, in governing the appearance of smiles. Wolff found that the latency of smiling following presentation of a face was determined by the time the infant spent scanning it before fixating the eyes. Freedman's study is of interest in that identical twins were used, and he found that not only did smiling to faces appear at the same ages, but that this followed about 10 days after the first sustained fixations of faces. While fraternal twins began to fixate faces at different ages, the delay before smiling emerged was similar. This data suggests that maturational factors are involved in governing the onset of social smiling, but that perceptual development may be the critical factor. If perceptual development does govern this onset, it seems mandatory to adopt an interactionist view of early social smiling rather than to attempt any simple isolation of learning from the maturation of pre-programmed systems.

A group of studies by Moss and his co-workers have shown a number of relationships between mother–infant mutual gazing and other variables. Like social smiling (Moss, 1967), this behaviour increases substantially between 1 month and 3 months of age (Moss and Robson, 1968), principally because the infant looks more at the eyes of the mother; but the mother herself contributes to mutual gazing with the infant, as this correlates with her positive feelings for it as assessed during pregnancy. However, the relation between mutual gazing and maternal attitudes did not hold for gazing by males at 3 months, nor could Moss and Robson find a relation between gazing at the mother and at pictures of faces in 3-month males (see Table 2), and they suggest that this may reflect slower perceptual development in male infants. Robson *et al.* (1969) found that mother–infant mutual gazing at 1 month for males was also negatively related to fear of strangers, and positively to mutual gazing with strangers, at around 9 months. The latter measure was also related to positive maternal attitudes during pregnancy. Gaze aversion and other fear indices have also been shown to be less in infants receiving more early stimulation by the mother (Moss *et al.*, 1969). This rather complex set of findings indicates the interaction between the mother's behaviour and the extent of development of the individual infant in governing social responsiveness.

It appears then that the mother's eyes become increasingly fascinating to the infant during the first few months. A number of the studies listed in Tables 2 and 3 presented stimuli from which the eyes were omitted, or in which they were present in abnormal configuration in relation to facial features. Despite the complexity of findings in some of these studies, it can be seen that during the first months there was little or no smiling to eyeless faces, and more smiling to faces with eyes. Attention measures tended to yield a similar advantage to faces with eyes, though rather less clearly. Both measures tended to show at least a slight advantage for the correct orientation of eyes within the face with infants older than 1 month. It is not clear that the eyes are the only important feature as regards attention measures, as their enclosure by a facial contour may be important. But the evidence of Ahrens (1954) suggests that contour is relatively unimportant at first in the elicitation of smiles. This might indicate that the finding by Spitz and Wolf (1946), that a facial profile would not elicit a smile before 6 months, was due mainly to the absence of the regular two-eyes pattern in the configuration.

The suggestion has already been advanced (p. 241) that the effectiveness of Ahrens' six-dot patterns in eliciting the earliest smiles may have been due to their functioning as a supernormal two-eyes stimulus. A study of adults by Coss (1970, see also Chapter 6) showed that pupillary dilation was greater to a two-spots stimulus, especially when oriented horizontally, than to either one or three spots; but this result may depend on adult symbolism rather than any more fundamental response mechanism. If the eyes are, however, an important elicitor of early smiles, the mother's attention to the infant can be an important influence on its facial-visual behaviour. If fixating her eyes causes the infant to smile, this is likely in turn to cause her to smile back (Gewirtz and Gewirtz, 1969), providing additional stimulation which reinforces the infant's behaviour sequence. (In this connection it is interesting that, although other species do not engage in mutual smiling, Bobbitt *et al.*, 1969, found that mothers of macaque monkeys do tend to assume a characteristic facial expression when engaged in mutual gazing with their infants.) The potency of the mutual gazing phenomenon is indicated by the fact that its occurrence can actively disrupt suckling during a feed (Robson, 1967). Other studies have also reported mutual gazing as occurring during feeding (Koehler, 1954; Wolff, 1963; Gough, 1968), but this does not give clear support to secondary reinforcement interpretations, as Watson (1967a) reported that its incidence was much lower than in interactions with an exclusively social orientation.

Robson (1967) has reviewed at some length studies where mother–infant gazing has been investigated, and concludes that mutual gazing is an innate "releaser" of maternal caretaking. While the evidence that the infant's fixating her own eyes rewards the mother is fairly compelling, it may well be that the infant's smile which typically follows this mutual gaze is equally rewarding to her. However, in the case of the infant there is better reason for suggesting that perception of the eyes themselves is directly rewarding from the beginning, and Robson makes the important point that "the eye *gestalt* is a highly discriminable stimulus configuration that can focus and hold the infant's attention more successfully than many competing internal and external perceptual events" (p. 17). Wolff (1963) concluded, despite the fact that non-facial stimuli could also evoke smiles during the first months, that "eye-to-eye contact is as important in the development of social interchange between parent and offspring, as it seems to be for all adult communication" (p. 122). Robson also sees mutual gazing as the perceptual cornerstone of early communication and attachment, but neither author has proposed clearly how the effective tie grows out of the behaviour, and the task of attempting such a formulation remains.

2.1.2 *Smiling and recognition of the two-eyes* gestalt
The association of the smile with positive affect in the infant is based on necessarily indirect but plausible inference from its similarity to the adult smile. Further evidence comes from the negative association between the appearance of smiles and of protest or distress behaviours (Spitz and Wolf, 1946; Spitz, 1963). Spitz sees smiling as evidence of a rudimentary "ego" in the infant, as an affectively positive response to

stimuli associated with the gratification of bodily needs (particularly for food and warm contact), but capable of becoming conditioned to other related stimuli. Difficulties with this orientation which arise in connection with attachment will be discussed later, but the question of the "meaning" of the smile must be dealt with here.

It is clear that whether or not its appearance is associated with the subjective experience of positive affect, smiling can also be regarded as a functional behaviour. Ethological comparisons suggest alternative candidates for its possible function, including appeasement, reassurance, greeting, and even ritualized aggression according to Lorenz (1966). As was suggested earlier (p. 223), its first function in infancy appears to be the elicitation of social approach by adults. But neither the subjective nor the functional interpretations of the smile suggest compelling reasons why the particular stimulus of the two-eyes configuration should predominate as an early eliciting cue. Another level of analysis is needed if this is to be explained.

The approach which we shall adopt is to regard early smiling as a *recognition response* elicited by successful matching of a perceptual input to an internal model of a familiar object. Variants of this approach have been proposed by several authors, and it will be argued that this interpretation of smiling has the advantage of being able to explain findings which would not be readily encompassed by other theories. The view that the eye-pattern elicits the smile through the operation of an appropriate "innate releasing mechanism" (e.g. Ploog, 1964) presents difficulties in accounting for smiling at other, especially non-social, stimulus configurations.

Tomkins (1962) suggests the smile is an unlearned expression of positive effect, but one which is triggered by recognition of a familiar object. Recognition leads to a reduction of neural activity within the cortex, and the "relatively steep reduction of the density of stimulation and neural firing" is rewarding, and in turn elicits "the smile of joy" (Tomkins, 1962, p. 371). Smiling is thus explained in terms of satisfactory information processing, a view which was also implicit in Goldstein's assertion that smiling expresses "adequacy between the demands of the stimulus and the capacity of the organism" (Goldstein, 1957, p. 178). Goldstein suggested that smiling thus marked the first stage in the genesis of the infant's object relationships, and also that a mismatch between the stimulus demands and the infant's capacity would lead to anxiety in the infant. Most recently, McCall (1970) has argued for a view very similar to that expressed in this chapter, namely that smiling may be elicited either by a stimulus for which a memory engram is immature and still developing, or by a stimulus which is moderately discrepant from a more established engram, i.e. by "effortful recognitory assimilation".

The attraction of such an approach lies in its admission of perceptual and cognitive factors into the ontogeny and causation of smiling. Since these *must* be taken into account in any consideration of social attachment, their introduction provides a convenient means of explaining how smiling may contribute to the ontogeny of attachment. While it may be difficult to confirm the relevant physiological hypotheses, such as that proposed by Tomkins (1962), the heuristic value of an approach which permits early social behaviour to be seen in terms consistent with general frameworks of child development, such as those of Piaget or Bruner, may be considerable. By invoking recognition, it also becomes possible to link together the data on both attention and smiling to facial stimuli, each of which has been seen to follow a rather similar developmental course. The attention preference for visual patterns achieving "recognitive familiarity" (Hunt, 1970) suggests that attention and smiling are very closely linked. Kagan *et al.* (1966), in attempting to interpret their fixation-time data, first introduced the concept of a *facial schema* in referring to the infant's acquisition through experience of some internal representation of the facial *gestalt*. According to Mussen *et al.* (1969) the facial schema is crucial to smiling in that "an overt sign that the young infant displays when he has acquired a schema of a face is a smile in response to it" (p. 221). The present approach attempts to begin one step further back, and we propose that the smile to faces emerges during stage 2 (1–8 weeks) as a consequence of the infant's internalization of an *eyes schema*.

In general terms, the information processing approach proposes that when confronted with new perceptual inputs we attempt to classify these according to existing cognitive categories, i.e. to assimilate them to some part of an exisiting model of the environment. Where this is not immediately possible further attention is demanded, and surprise or orienting responses which facilitate this closer attention may be evoked, depending on the degree of mismatch (Sokolov, 1963; Charlesworth, 1969). Closer inspection may permit matching, although some modification of the existing model may be necessary before the inputs can be accommodated. This formulation clearly has close parallels with that of Piaget (e.g. 1952), who did in fact suggest that smiling might be linked to recognitory assimilation.

The present argument assumes that the motivation to process information, i.e. to reduce the perceptual uncertainty of inputs, and to actively seek out stimulation when this is not already forthcoming, is a basic characteristic of active organisms, including young infants. Hunt (1965) introduced the term "intrinsic motivation" to separate this from "primary" drives and from motivations which derive from these. Furthermore, we propose that the successful reduction of uncertainty by recognition, or achieving a match between input and internal model, is rewarding and reinforces behaviours which facilitate such inputs. General evidence for such a position was collected by Hunt (1965) and Walters and Parke (1965), while Berlyne (1960) considered exploratory motivation at length. Furthermore, the evidence of Table 3 shows that smiling by the infant tends to elicit continued or varied stimulation from the mother, and in this respect is functionally equivalent to search behaviours such as visual attention in eliciting new inputs. If these can be successfully processed both searching and smiling will be reinforced.

The final link in the present argument involves a further proposition, namely that the two-eyes pattern is the first aspect of the face which the infant successfully incorporates into an internal schema. It is thus the first aspect to be recognizable, and this recognition following on attention will thus lead to an uncertainty reduction signified by the appearance of a smile. It may be noted that other behaviours, such as cooing vocalizations, which also tend to elicit further stimulation from the mother should, like this smiling, be reinforced. Also, it must be emphasized that learning to smile or to coo in order to elicit further stimulation is not regarded as the fundamental basis of these behaviours, which must be presumed to be a fairly simple neurophysiological linkage activated by recognitory assimilation. We may also propose that this successful processing has experiential correlates of positive affect which is expressed by the smile, but this is not central to the basic theory.

It can be claimed with some conviction that there is no problem in accounting for the two-eyes *gestalt* becoming the infant's first social schema in the visual modality, without invoking specially programmed releasing functions for the eyes. The infant's visual resolving powers are initially rather poor (p. 203ff), and while it is difficult to envisage accurately the infant's perception of the visual world, it seems clear that only the most salient stimulus characteristics will be resolved during the first stages. It is likely that only the most strongly patterned environmental stimuli will elicit attention at first, and that these must be presented frequently under optimal temporal conditions in order to be assimilated into an internal model which can form a template against which subsequent inputs can be matched, yielding recognition.

There are good reasons why the face should provide the most probable configuration for the infant's first visual schema. Firstly, it is typically presented by the mother both frequently and for fairly long periods, probably more during the first weeks and months than is any other visual stimulus. This occurs not only during feeding and caretaking, but also during the periods where she is just watching or playing with the infant (cf. Robson, 1967). This is probably particularly important for assimilation purposes, since there is evidence that early infant learning is very dependent on provision of suitable stimulus–response contingencies. Immediate memory for objects temporarily displaced from view can be of the order of only a few seconds in young infants (Bower, 1967). Watson (1967b) found that reinforcement of a selective fixation response was only effective if the next response occurred between about 3 and 8 seconds after the first. He suggested that the rapid forgetting between trials is a feature of early infancy which makes the presence of cues which elicit attention, or of stimuli which elicit responses reflexively, imperative for learning to occur in conditions of infrequent stimulus presentation. Whatever are the precise requirements for perceptual learning during the first months, no configurations are more likely to be presented in accord with these than is the mother's face.

Apart from the fact of its extensive exposure to the infant, the face has characteristics of mobility, brightness contrast, colouration etc. which make it an attractive and salient object of attention for the very young infant. Vocalization by the mother will add to the probability of attention to the face, since the reflexive movements made in order to optimize sound reception at each ear bring the infant into the face-to-face orientation with the mother (Turkewitz et al., 1966; Diebold, 1968). What appear to be attempts to "fixate" faces by blind infants in response to sounds (Freedman, 1964) can probably be explained this way. Of course the infant's own vocalizations tend to elicit a similar orientation from the mother also. A further factor is that when attending to young infants mothers do typically position themselves so that their faces are close to the infant's. A distance of about 9–15 inches separation corresponds fairly well to the distance of easiest clear focusing of the infant visual system (Haynes *et al.*, 1965). Relatively few other stimuli would normally be presented within this rather critical range with regularity during the first weeks and months.

Thus the face of the mother or regular caretaker is in several ways facilitated as the source of the infant's first visual schema. Within the facial configuration, the eyes stand out on the basis of the marked brightness contrasts between the pupils and the whites of the eyes, and an overall contrast between the eyespots and the remainder of the face. As a form, the two separated spots constitute one of the simplest possible spatial patterns, and should thus be most readily assimilated. On this basis it can be hypothesized that the two-spots *gestalt* formed by the eyes is the first pattern incorporated by the infant into an internal recognitive model or schema. The active attempt to assimilate a perceived eye-spots stimulus to the developing schema can be regarded as the first type of effortful processing to elicit social smiles. The eyes are thus the perceptual cornerstone of the infant's attention to faces and ultimate internalization of a sophisticated model, which not only permits discrimination between faces, and between their expressions, but also links up with other models as part of an overall mother-as-object concept. It is when this concept is achieved that we can talk of true "attachment" to the mother; and attachment thus depends on the achievement of suitable developments of the facial schema.

2.2 DEVELOPMENT OF THE FACIAL SCHEMA

Initially, recognition of the two-eyes pattern as being familiar will involve effortful searching by the infant, in the attempt to match such an input with what must be a weak internal representation of the pattern. It appears from Freedman's (1965) study that it normally requires about 10 days of regularly fixating the mother's eyes before these fixations culminate in a smile, and if smiling does indicate successful recognition it would appear that by this time a rudimentary two-eyes schema is internalized, permitting the recognition. On subsequent encounters progressively less attention will be required before the infant recognizes the configuration, until ultimately this becomes automatic and instantaneous. From this point onwards one might expect smiling to become difficult to elicit in response to the two-eyes configuration, since no effortful processing would be required.

However, according to the model, attending to the face has so far been rewarding, and so further attention to the same general area may be expected even though the eyes themselves have limited continuing interest. In other words, the infant's motivation for acquiring new inputs is likely to result in attention to the next most easily resolved aspects of the face, which in turn become capable of being recognized after being attended to sufficiently often. In effect this further experience will lead to the elaboration of the simple two-eyes schema, maintaining the assimilation opportunities provided by the face, and thus also its interest and reward value. The assumption that smiling is a recognition response, emitted when some optimal amount of information processing is demanded to match an input to a developing schema, thus permits us to account for the fact that faces readily elicit smiles during the first few months of life. Providing that such confrontations are active ones, in that the mother smiles back, vocalizes, and otherwise maintains stimulation, it is clear that the attraction of these confrontations for the infant may be maintained even longer. These active behaviours will also have an important role while the facial schema is in its earliest stage of development, in ensuring that the infant's attention is initially attracted to the mother's face.

The above account of early schema development is not only tentative but oversimplified, avoiding the details of reinforcement contingencies presumed to be operative, and the other organismic variables which will affect behaviour in any particular mother–infant encounter. Any approach which invokes optimum stimulation concepts must clearly allow that such an optimum is itself flexible and dependent on temporary arousal states and adaptation levels of the infant (Helson, 1964), as well as changing with age and experience. (cf. p. 208). Whether a mother–infant encounter actually provides rewarding stimulation will depend on whether the precise behaviour of the mother permits information to be processed at the presently desired level. Richards (1972) found from film analysis that maintenance of smiling depended critically on the phasing of the mother's behaviours in relation to those of the infant. Appropriate pauses were necessary in order to avoid the situation where the infant would become fussy and exhibit crying and persistent avoidance of the mother's face thereafter. Further research is required before any precise quantification of the various factors involved becomes possible.

At this point it will be useful to elaborate further on the "schema" concept which has been adopted here. Kagan *et al.* (1966) introduced it in their discussion of data on visual attention, proposing that long fixations on a stimulus pattern could be elicited either when the pattern was consistent with a recently acquired or "emergent" schema, or when it represented a moderate violation of a fairly well-established schema. Their study showed that although both regular and scrambled faces elicited the same amounts of attention in 4-month infants, other measures showed discrimination. Smiles were given most to the regular face, and in girls cardiac decelerations were also greater to this than to the scrambled face. Further measures taken at 8 months revealed that by now the scrambled face gave the largest decelerations for both sexes. Kagan *et al.* suggested that both smiling and cardiac deceleration were best indices of an emergent schema, while fixation measures were more ambiguous.

Other studies by Kagan, Lewis, and others have further investigated the interrelations of fixation times, cardiac deceleration, smiling and also vocalizations in relation to facial and other schemata. The cardiac measures are of particular interest in that they are closely associated with the orienting response. When neonates are exposed to moderately intense sounds there is an initial acceleration prior to deceleration (Graham *et al.*, 1968), but there is little or no indication of this prior acceleration in 6-month infants shown flashing lights (Lewis *et al.*, 1966b). The predominance of deceleration has been interpreted as showing that the older infants block new inputs while processing already present information (Bruner, 1969a), and the absence of an acceleration component may indicate that the input is being matched against an existing schema, i.e. is not perceived as entirely novel. This view is consistent with the finding by Graham *et al.* (1970) that deceleration increases in extent between 6 and 16 weeks of age. Kagan (1969b) tested infants' reactions to face-masks at 4 months and again at later ages, and found that the extent of deceleration to the stimuli decreased with age, probably indicating that assimilation of the masks to an existing facial schema was easier at the later ages.

While fixation times and amounts of smiling to face-masks also decrease with age during the first year, fixation begins to increase again towards the end of this year (Kagan, 1969b, 1969c). Kagan suggests that there are in fact three different age-related meanings of long fixations: first these are elicited simply by contrast and motion cues; then from around 2 months when visual schemata are first becoming established they occur when an assimilative effort is required to match an input to a schema; finally towards the end of the first year long fixations can arise when quickly recognized discrepancies between an input and a schema lead the infant to consider a variety of "cognitive hypotheses" in relation to the wider associations that the schema now has (Kagan, 1969c).

The details of this third process remain to be explored, but it may help to account for the continuing ability of novel stimuli to evoke attention and related responses in later infancy. For example, Lewis *et al.* (1967b) and Lewis and Goldberg (1969), using geometric stimuli, found that fixation, cardiac deceleration, smiling etc. showed decrements to repeated presentations, but that introduction of a novel stimulus led to reinstatement of the behaviours in infants aged 3–4 years. The second process to which Kagan refers, involving response to stimulus-schema discrepancies during the middle months of the first year, has received rather more attention. McCall (1969, 1970), has argued that during this period attentional responses depend critically on the *amount* of the discrepancy between an input and the infant's schema, proposing that an inverted-U function is applicable whereby either very familiar or very novel stimuli elicit little interest. Long fixations or smiling can thus be obtained either when the schema or engram of an object seen is rudimentary, or when the schema is more developed and particular examples of the stimulus configuration are attended to because of detailed discrepancies from the general schema.[1] The process probably is not applicable to infants of stage 1 or 2, since violation of expectancy in 2-month infants can lead to "obligatory aversion" from the new stimulus—such as when a picture goes out of focus (Bruner, 1969b).

Unfortunately the considerable body of research which has now investigated variables like fixation times, cardiac deceleration, smiling, and vocalization in relation to stimulus familiarity and stimulus-schema variations, has revealed a far from simple picture of the interrelations between these measures. There are sex differences in trends for the different measures: Kagan (1969a, 1969c) found that fixation was a sensitive index for boys but more equivocal for girls. He found that the amount of vocalization to a stimulus, seen as an index of the arousal associated with information-processing, was a better index of stimulus-schema relations for girls, and has shown how the sex differences may

[1] Zelazo and Komer (1971) have recently reported more evidence showing that smiling to non-social stimuli may reflect recognitory assimilation.

depend on more rapid cognitive development and different maternal practices in their case. McCall (1969, 1970) has also shown individual differences over and above age effects, which suggest not only that differential memory limitations may lead to variability of results, but also that the best measure of schema development may differ between individuals. Thus in relation to smiling, which interests us particularly here, generalization is still difficult, although McCall clearly favours seeing it as a recognition response associated with schema acquisition and elaboration. Despite the amount of research effort, the complexity of findings where multiple indices have been used has permitted rather little progress towards precise formulation of the schema model.

Despite these problems, the data on development of smiling to faces during the first years, as presented in Table 3, is consistent with the present approach although open to other interpretations. The data on responses to schematic faces is of particular interest in that Morgan and Ricciuti (1969) found that after 6 months more positive responses were given to masks than to real faces. Kagan and Lewis (1965) found that by 13 months attention to schematic faces, but not to realistic facial photographs, remained relatively high. Lewis (1969) also compared pictorial stimuli, and while attention was greatest to the realistic facial pictures in the first half-year, by 13 months unrealistic ones received equivalent attention. However, Lewis found that realistic faces received rather more smiles throughout the whole period, which led him to suggest that "innate releasing functions" of the normal face might govern smiling responses. This interpretation is not compelling since it may be that the older infants were not able to assimilate the unrealistic face to their existing facial schema rapidly enough. The infants were shown only 3 exposures of 12 s each for each picture, so the more realistic stimulus could still have provided the optimal discrepancy from their existing schema. The small number of infants who actually smiled to the stimuli at all, and the small amounts of smiling time, together with significant sex differences again, make it difficult to draw clear conclusions given that all stimuli would have been relatively novel at all the ages tested.

The main problem for theories which see smiling simply as a response elicited by innate mechanisms adapted to facial stimuli *per se* is to account for smiling to other objects in early infancy. The recognition model linked to schema development is more general in that smiling to any stimulus with certain attributes of familiarity can be accounted for by a single principle, and in this chapter it has been argued that the particular salience of faces as elicitors of smiles can be explained in terms of contingent factors of earlier experience. A recent study by Watson and Ramey (1969) has provided supporting evidence for this general view. Watson and Ramey placed special cribs in the homes of 2-month infants, from which geometric mobiles could be hung to provide visual stimulation. The infants lay on a pressure-sensitive pillow linked so that a slight head movement would cause a 1 s rotation of the mobile. The infants spent 10 min per day in the situation for 14 days consecutively. Head movements were recorded automatically during each session. Infants rapidly learned to operate the mobile, and comparison with control groups showed that this movement-rotation contingency was responsible for the high rate of responding by the infants. But the most significant finding was in no way predicted, and was discovered from the comments of the mothers themselves. Smiling and vocalizing at the mobile emerged rapidly, despite their ineffectiveness as operant behaviours, and were much more frequent in the experimental infants than in those controls provided with randomly operating mobiles or with equivalent stabiles. Thus the opportunity to control the source of stimulation was apparently more rewarding than being merely provided with the stimulation itself.

J. S. Watson (1970) suggests this result is particularly important in that the Watson and Ramey situation is one of the few in which infants have the opportunity at such an early age to control stimulation by a non-elicited truly operant response. Furthermore, they are enabled to repeat this operation within the limits of their initially very brief span of immediate memory. These conditions thus permit them to overcome the "natural deprivation" (J. S. Watson, 1967b) of opportunities for active information processing which he believes characterize the first 3 months of the infant's experience. There is actually one notable case where these conditions are otherwise fulfilled, and this is where by his own attention, smiling etc. to the mother's face he can elicit similarly contingent stimulation from her.

It appears from Watson and Ramey's (1969) discovery that the contingency aspect of situations evoking smiling is critical, and the result is strongly supportive of the view of infancy which emphasizes the active nature of the infant's early interactions with his environment. Smiling evidently occurs when the infant is himself in control of stimulation inputs, and where information input can thus be regulated to keep in step with his rate of processing. The "contingency analysis", whereby the infant is able to register his own potency in controlling rewarding inputs, is seen by Watson as an alternative candidate for the explanation of smiling, but there is no major obstacle to the reconciliation of Watson's approach with schema development approaches. McCall (1970) suggests that contingency analysis may be a special case of the concept of recognitory assimilation, perhaps having more responsibility for early smiling than does the development of special visual schemata such as that for the face. If we regard the smile as a behaviour emitted, when some optimal amount of information processing is demanded and successfully achieved, there is no conflict. The expectation with which the input must be matched can either derive from a residual engram, dependent on extended previous experience of inputs which had salient characteristics shared with those of the present input, or from the immediate memory trace in which both the previous response and stimulus input are represented. In both cases recognition of familiarity is involved.

We may now propose that smiling has essentially the same basis whether it occurs in social or non-social situations. We can also account for situations where socially provided stimuli elicit smiling through modalities other than vision. The kinesthetic and tactile stimulation which Wolff (1963) found evoked smiles so readily is a classic example of a contingency game fitting the Watson and Ramey paradigm. It seems probable that contingency opportunities provided by most mothers are such that the first smiles will be evoked by her face in the manner already suggested, and that lack of extensive alternative opportunities will guarantee that faces remain the most potent elicitors of smiling through at least most of the first year. But this is not inevitable, and in fact Watson and Ramey (1969) report that some infants had not begun to smile at the mother's face by the time that smiling to the mobile began.

In admitting that contingency analysis can be a powerful elicitor of early smiles, we are in no way forced to devalue the significance of normal facial-visual interaction and development of the facial schema in the socialization of the infant. While Watson sees contingency analysis as a possible basis of social attachment, the more general recognitive familiarity approach is able to provide a clearer and more detailed formulation of how attachment may develop, and in this the role of facial schema development remains paramount. This is not to deny that during the first months perceptual stimulation *per se* is apparently quite adequate for development. Brossard and Décarie (1971) have recently shown that institutional infants given extra stimulation each day for 10 weeks from age 2 months gave a normal developmental profile when tested at 5–6 months, whereas control infants in the institution were relatively retarded. However, it made no difference whether the stimulation was asocial or was provided by a single person. Thus during the first half-year frequent social interaction is not itself essential. But the question remains whether the longitudinal follow-up will reveal a similar picture at later ages when, in the home-reared infant, differential attachment to the mother emerges as a result of his structuring of specifically social experiences.

3   The face schema and social attachment

3.1   EARLY SOCIAL ATTACHMENT PROCESSES

3.1.1   *Perceptual integration and the mother concept*
It has been argued that conditions typically favour the gradual emergence of an increasingly elaborated facial schema during the infant's first few months. While a schema associated with the mother's voice may precede this as the first social schema, the relative independence of the perceptual systems in early infancy probably militates against its extension much beyond the point at which the characteristics such as pitch permit discrimination of the mother's voice from other voices. The face schema, on the other hand, can be extended by a process of assimilation and accommodation so that recognition develops from the initial two-eyes *gestalt* to include the whole face, and finally differences between faces as well as expression differences. While faces are highly complex configurations, their *effective* complexity for an infant will depend on his perceptual abilities at a given age. At first he is unlikely to be able to resolve more than the simplest characteristics of a face, which may well be fortunate, as otherwise its presentation might provide more complex stimulation than could successfully be processed, in which case avoidance habits might be acquired. The fact that attentional and smiling responses continue to increase during the first few months suggests that increasing perception of its complexity proceeds in step with developing processing abilities.

If the facial schema has reached a fairly advanced developmental stage by 3–4 months, the question arises as to whether faces can be expected to retain their interest beyond this age, by which the infant's perceptual abilities have improved considerably, and the competition of other stimuli for his interest has increased. For a fairly short period this will be likely, in that differential expressions and the unfamiliarity of strangers' faces will provide the required stimulus-schema discrepancies to maintain interest and permit further schema elaboration. After this we would expect a diminution of interest and smiling elicitation, since faces will be rapidly assimilated and thus provide little opportunity for effortful assimilation to the schema. The smiling data do in fact show that typically by the end of stage 4 (3–7 months) faces are much less rewarding to the infant than hitherto, but the face of the mother is evidently at least a partial exception to this rule.

Caretaking or individual familiarity is clearly implicated in the maintenance of both general responsiveness and the special place of the mother. Rheingold (1956) found that even during the first week of her experimental regular caretaking of 6-month old institutional infants they began to show more positive responses to her than they did to strangers. At this point it is tempting to associate the caretaker's face with the satisfaction of basic bodily needs and argue for a secondary reinforcement process which would maintain the infant's interest in the face through this association. In claiming that this explanation is not satisfactory, and that the effects can be explained within the framework of a schema approach, it becomes necessary to take account of further aspects of the infant's perceptual-motor as well as cognitive development.

Before the end of the second month the infant shows signs of linking perceptual and motor activity together in ways which are no longer exclusively reflexive. Not only does he respond with head movements in the direction of sounds or touches on the cheek, and with visual pursuit of bright objects, but he begins to show more active and spontaneous behaviours. Piaget (1952) termed these first repetitions of motor acts which have sensory consequences "primary circular reactions", and emphasized the importance of visually guided manual activity in permitting a transition from these to intentional interactions with the environment in subsequent months. Initially the infant makes crude reaching and swiping movements towards seen objects, brings his hand to his mouth and sucks it, or just watches his hand; but gradually these activities become coordinated (Piaget, 1952; White *et al.*, 1964; Bruner, 1969a, 1969b; White, 1969b; Bower *et al.*, 1970a, 1970b). Thus by 4–6 months the infant is engaging in relatively sophisticated visually directed reaching for and grasping of objects, and will bring an object to his mouth to suck it. He will also repeatedly shake or hit or scratch and pull at objects when such activities lead to a variety of simultaneous sensory consequences.

It is clear then that by the middle of the first year he is in a position to take a variety of active steps to control his environment and elicit stimulation from it. His "secondary circular reactions" are effectively an elaboration of the "contingency analysis" described by J. S. Watson (1967b), and provide many more opportunities for the construction of new cognitive schemata, with an emphasis on cross-modal linking of previously isolated schemata. This new dimension of integration applies not only to the sensory-motor schemata but also to perceptual-cognitive integration of object qualities. In understanding these developments, which in our case are of particular interest in relation to the emergence of an overall schema of the mother as a unique person, it is necessary to look rather more closely at the contributions of particular sensory channels.

While previously it was often held that touch "teaches" vision in perceptual development, it now seems that vision dominates touch in conflict situations (Pick *et al.*, 1967). A study by Bower *et al.* (1970b) has been interpreted as showing that the infant has cross-modal expectations from birth, with visual information again dominating, but their inferences are not convincing. Their results do show, however, that tactile feedback has little effect on reaching and grasping during the first few months, and Schaffer and Parry (1969, 1970) have provided further demonstrations of poor tactile discrimination by infants younger than 8 months. Nevertheless, any temptation to conclude simply that vision teaches touch must be resisted. To the adult, a particular object property such as distance away or solidity may be cued by a variety of feature analysers linked to a variety of sensory modalities. Yet particular aspects of the property will be modality-specific, and the adult's percept of it depends on a sophisticated unification of the signals available. Our possession of an appropriate multi-feature schema may allow us to identify the property by perceiving only a limited sub-set of cues, but one cannot expect this of the young infant. Thus while it seems likely that the separate visual cues which inform us of depth or distance or solidity are discriminable quite early in infancy, this does not mean that the infant's perception of the property is equivalent to our own.

Mero significantly, proprioceptive and tactile information is associated with reaching for and touching objects, and must contribute to our overall perception of their properties. Discriminations of these kinds are implied in our adult concepts of distance or solidity and form. Achievement of such integrated schemata is a major task for the infant, and must depend on experience of making a variety of discriminations in several modalities. Even if the young infant can integrate the visual cues of distance, his experience must be qualitatively different from our own until he has learned to discriminate the sensations of reaching for near and far objects and succeeding or failing in making contact with them. Therefore a variety of spatially and temporally contiguous experiences of objects must be undergone before the infant can form fully elaborated schemata appropriate to them. In fact touch cannot be exclusively taught by vision. Where vision is able to fulfil a vital role, however, is in integrating the modality-specific schemata. In both ontogeny and adult experience vision permits us to perceive that tactile, auditory and other sensations arise simultaneously or in close sequence from a source which has stability or continuity in space. The continuity of visual experience, and the presence of visual concomitants of most other stimuli, gives vision a powerful role in infancy, greatly facilitating the acquisition of multi-channel schemata.

The foregoing analysis should help to show that it is possible to account for the infant's continued interest in the mother or familiar caretaker after the point at which her face can be readily recognized, and that his continued responsiveness can be explained in terms of information processing rather than secondary reinforcement. While the typical infant will have acquired a discriminative schema of the mother's face by about 3–4 months, she is probably not yet individually discriminated from other persons in any respect other than by her voice (which according to Banks and Wolfson, cited in Schaffer, 1971, is recognized at about 6 weeks). Nor is there evidence that the infant associates her face with her voice or with other particular inputs. But once the face schema is well established, so that her face itself makes only slight processing demands on the infant when presented, he may begin to search for other stimulation. However, even if she is not a particularly affectionate and stimulating mother, most of the attention-eliciting

K

stimuli available when she is present are likely to emanate from her. Typically, she will often speak while her face is presented to the infant, thus providing simultaneous visual and auditory stimulation which should facilitate the linking of his facial and vocal schemata. In response to the smile, arising from his brief recognitory effort when she first presents her face, the mother is likely to smile back, vocalize, and perhaps touch the infant, thus providing contingent stimulation which rewards his continuing attention, and facilitates his expansion of her face schema to include additional characteristics. By actively reaching out and touching her face he can obtain still more varied stimulation from her.

It is thus not difficult to see how a normally responsive mother can retain her infant's interest in such a way that repeated interactions between them lead to the continued elaboration of the original face schema into a more and more complete concept of her as a person. She provides stimuli which yield continual variations on the existing schema, maintaining his attention and providing him with opportunities for rewarding processing of new information. When ultimately the infant can readily relate the whole variety of inputs which emanate from the mother, linking them to his own means of eliciting and responding to these, and when he can retain a basic image of her in her absence, he can be said to have a rudimentary concept of her as a *person*. For this the ability to *recall*, as well as recognize her, is, as Schaffer (1971) points out, an essential feature.

By the time the general *mother schema* has emerged and become consolidated, the infant's behaviour towards her will have taken on many of the characteristics which we regard as indices of attachment. On the present argument these behaviours will be specifically directed towards her rather than other persons in proportion to her relative predominance as a source of stimulation for her infant, especially stimulation contingent on his own responses. Other persons who interact with the infant infrequently or inappropriately will not elicit the same intensity of approach responses, and may even elicit avoidance if the unfamiliar stimulation they provide is too intense.

It must be pointed out here that prior to the emergence of the general mother schema, stimuli rewarding to the infant, whether arising from provision of food, relief of bodily distress other than hunger, or from simple provision of opportunities for effortful information processing, will not have been perceived as coming from a *single* source. It is hard to see how specific attachments could be built up on any simple second-ary reinforcement view unless a general mother schema, or at least an integrated person schema, was *already* possessed by the infant. Once the attachment behaviours are already part of his repertoire, and focused towards a particular person or persons as a result of the schema ac-quisition itself, it of course becomes meaningful to suggest that the care-taker's provision of food and so on leads to her acquiring secondary reward value for the infant.

According to the present hypothesis, the genesis of attachment de-pends on the interaction between mother and infant, but not just during caretaking activities. Because of the particular attributes of the visual modality and of the eyes and face, an important foundation for the mother schema can be built up, through facial-visual interaction between mother and infant, before the latter is able to form associations between cross-modal inputs. When these *do* first arise, they are more likely to involve auditory, tactile, and related experiences of a positively stimulating type than are those connected just with the relief of distress.

This view has the further advantage that it can account for the significant proportion of cases in which the infant does not show most attachment responses to the principal caretaker. It is consistent with Schaffer and Emerson's (1964a) finding that in most families in their Scottish sample the mother was the first principal attachment object, when specific attachments began to emerge at around 8 months, but that quite commonly attachments to the father or occasionally to several persons emerged at about the same time. At 18 months a further study showed a positive relationship between intensity of attachment to the mother and her responsiveness to the infant's demands for attention. There was no evidence of a relation between alleviation of physical needs and attachment for a substantial 39 per cent of the sample.

3.1.2 *Alternative accounts of early attachment*

No attempt will be made here to evaluate in detail the various alterna-tive theories of attachment. The main viewpoints and their difficulties and advantages have recently been evaluated by Ainsworth (1969), Bowlby (1969) and Schaffer (1971), and there are signs that in recent years differences between them have begun to diminish as each has been gradually modified to take account of new data. Present disputes are largely those of terminology and emphasis. Our attention here will be confined to their accounts of how attachment begins to emerge during the first year, since it is in this respect that the present approach can claim certain advantages.

Psychoanalytic and social learning theorists have both, for the most part, relied on the mother's role in gratifying the infant's so-called "primary" needs in their accounts of the emergence of attachment to her. Proximity seeking, contact and attention seeking, smiling and other behaviours apparently expressing positive affect, protest at disappearance, and in later infancy the seeking of help and approval and the use of the mother as a refuge: all these are held to derive from the mother's association with need-gratification.

Positive evidence which would clearly relate the attractiveness of social stimuli to their association with need-gratification has not been found. On such a view one would equally expect attachment to develop to objects such as nursing bottles, but neither smiling (Dennis, 1935), vocalization (Kagan and Lewis, 1965), nor attentional responses (Fantz and Nevis, 1967a, 1967b) are found to be elicited as often by these as they are by human faces. It is established that the principal caretaker need not be the person towards whom the first or strongest attachments are formed (Schaffer and Emerson, 1964a), which also goes against the theory. In macaque monkeys the well-known work by Harlow (e.g. 1961, 1963) indicated clearly that "contact comfort" rather than provision of food determined infants' preferences for the mother-surrogates which he provided. Since in human infants tactile stimulation does not appear to be a critical factor (Schaffer and Emerson, 1964b), even this source of "primary" gratification is a poor candidate as a basis for dependency associations. In general the distance receptors seem most clearly implicated in social attachment, and social learning which depends on drive-reduction concepts is most difficult to invoke in their case (Walters and Parke, 1964, 1965).

More recent learning theorists regard "attachment" or "dependency" merely as a label covering various behaviours, and emphasize the active role of the infant in interaction with the mother (e.g. Gewirtz, 1961, 1969). In providing reinforcing stimuli of whatever kind the mother becomes discriminated as a source of reward, since her behaviours are contingent on those of her infant. Mother–infant interaction is seen as a chain of mutual influence and reinforcement (cf. Bell, 1968), with the infant's behaviours in turn providing reinforcement for the mother. Thus any mother–infant dyad will build up a pattern of characteristic interactions dependent on the ways in which mother and infant reward each other, and these interaction behaviours can be seen as defining the types and intensities of the attachments of each to the other. While there is nothing in such an approach which conflicts with the present view, it has certain omissions which Ainsworth (1969) has pointed out. Social learning theorists have tended to ignore organismic determinants of behaviour, and are unable to give satisfactory accounts of any aspects of "inner structure" which may affect or be affected by the infant's socialization. In fact the approach is able to offer almost no explanation of why the behavioural contingencies which do in fact reinforce mother–infant interaction should first come to do so.

The ethological view of attachment, advanced by Ainsworth (1969), Bowlby (1969), Freedman et al. (1967), and several others is concerned more directly with this question. The common ground of the various formulations is that attachment originates from the operation of a number of species-characteristic behavioural systems which emerge in the infant at various ages and which maintain mother–infant proximity and interaction. Towards the end of the first year these begin to be integrated together in complex fashion, until eventually a relationship of reciprocal attachment between infant and mother can be said to exist. Bowlby (1969), through his concern for evolutionary questions and for common aspects of different species' behaviour, feels that it is necessary to suppose that the component systems which promote attachment have become fixed as part of the infant's genotypically determined behaviour because they are essential to survival during the extended period of infantile vulnerability and dependence on the mother for satisfaction of bodily needs. In adopting this view Bowlby is not committed to explaining attachment as actually resulting from the satisfaction of these needs by the mother. The function and predictable effect of behaviours which may be taken as indices of attachment may be the satisfaction of these needs, but each behavioural system is initially autonomous and internally motivated. As cognitive development proceeds each system begins to take on features of goal-correctedness, and the common "set-goal" of attachment behaviours becomes the maintenance of a general proximity to certain discriminated persons, especially the mother if their history of interaction has been normal.

The above summary has not begun to do justice to Bowlby's ethological approach, with its subtle appreciation of the interaction of "innate" predispositions, experience, and the infant's cognitive development.

In most respects it is compatible with the view presented here. However, some doubt must remain regarding Bowlby's specification of the distinct behaviour systems which initially bring about mother–infant proximity. These are claimed to be sucking, clinging, crying, smiling, and following—although for most of the first year the latter must clearly be limited to visual tracking of the mother. There is relatively little precise data on the actual effectiveness of these behaviours in governing the mother's proximity to the infant. Richards (in press) notes that almost any infant behaviours may elicit maternal attention and pattern her behaviour, and he is led to doubt whether the interdependence of mother–infant behaviour in humans is really comparable to its control by fixed-action patterns in other species. The present approach, by emphasizing the information-processing opportunities which are provided by the "proximity seeking" behavioural systems, and thus by invoking cognitive factors in the very earliest developmental stages, makes a clearer distinction between animal fixed-action patterns and the human behaviours involved in attachment, without denying that particular stimulation contingencies can be important in the socialization of the infant.

An ethological orientation towards human behaviour must be adopted with caution, for it is too easy to be impressed by similarities between human maternal–infant behaviour and that of other species. The temptation to regard attachment to the mother as a result of "imprinting" comparable to the rather rigid determination of following and associated behaviours in nidifugous birds has sometimes been strong (Gray, 1958; Ambrose, 1963; Morris, 1967). Linked with this is the postulate of a "critical period" for the development of attachment, whereby unless a suitable attachment object is found within a limited time period fully satisfactory attachments can never be formed. Bowlby (1952, 1958) was inclined towards such a view, but the "imprinting" and "critical period" concepts have since undergone considerable modification, and the evidence is clearly for more complex processes, especially in human development (Caldwell, 1962; Hinde, 1962; Sluckin, 1970).

However, the extreme difficulty of establishing normal social relationships following sustained deprivation during the first year of life is not in doubt, and any theory of attachment must account for this fact. Development of fearful responses to stimuli which are novel is commonly invoked, and the role of the mother in keeping this fear within controllable limits is often emphasized (Bronson, 1968a). The schema-development orientation adopted here is consistent with such an account, through its emphasis on the importance of the mother in providing stimulation contingencies which permit the infant to develop means of resolving information inputs. The mother's role in stimulating the infant, and its effects on attachment and fearfulness, must now be considered in more detail.

3.1.3 *Maternal influences on schema development and attachment*

If the precise quality of the stimulation available to the young infant, especially from the mother, is as important in governing his rate of perceptual and social development as we have implied, then maternal practices should exert an important influence on his attention habits and on the quality of his reactions to persons. The extent to which variations in these practices affect the infant's opportunities for obtaining rewarding stimulation will determine their effects on his rate of development of social schemata; and on the present view the state of schema development is an important determinant of the infant's reactions to others.

The role of maternal stimulation of the infant in influencing his readiness for social gazing has already been referred to (p. 247), and it is noteworthy that the amount of early social gazing with the mother is correlated with responses to strangers at around 9 months. Infants whose mothers' attitudes to them during pregnancy were strongly positive showed high levels of gazing at the mother at 1 and 3 months, but also high levels of gazing at strangers, and low incidence of fear, much later in the first year (Robson *et al.*, 1969). Other investigators have found that maternal practices affect attachment, for example maternal behaviour in the feeding situation is related to the infant's response to brief separations at 12 months. Infants whose mothers were most responsive and sensitive to the infant's own initiatives in feeding during the first 3 months showed most efforts to regain and maintain contact after the separations (Ainsworth and Bell, 1969). In fact a fairly substantial literature indicates that both quantity and quality of mother–infant interaction during the first year influences the strength of attachment behaviours of the infant (Bowlby, 1969). There is also evidence of maternal influences on visual alertness, which in the neonatal stage 1 is enhanced by vestibular stimulation (Korner and Thoman, 1970), and on preference for novel stimuli at 6 months, which is greater for infants of more attentive mothers (Rubenstein, 1967). The effectiveness of maternal stimulation in these cases does, however, appear to be greater for males than for females, with males' attention being more dependent on arousal state (Moss and Robson, 1968,1970).

The data at present available does not permit us to state conclusively that the links between maternal practices and attachment depend exclusively on the influence of the former on the infant's rate of schema development, nor to propose in further detail just how this influence is exerted. Nevertheless, the fact that perceptual behaviour is affected by the mother and is implicated in schema development is consistent with the general view that schema development is closely related to attachment. Bell (1970) has recently shown that acquisition of the concept of the mother as a person with an identity separate from the infant's tends to precede concepts of other inanimate objects, and to relate to attachment behaviours. This priority of the mother concept was shown by 70 per cent of infants, while 27 per cent showed a more developed concept for inanimate objects, both concepts being assessed using an object-hiding test administered several times between 8 and $11\frac{1}{2}$ months of age. The infants with the weaker mother concept failed to show normal seeking for proximity with the mother following the brief separations used to assess attachment. The infants with the stronger mother concept did show this proximity seeking, and in fact showed a stronger object concept in absolute terms than did the other infants. Bell's results thus essentially confirm the view that in optimum development the person schema is the first object concept to be acquired, and that its early acquisition is associated with strong attachment behaviour. Bell's interviews with the infants' mothers also confirmed earlier findings of more accepting attitudes and greater responsiveness in interaction on the part of mothers of the more advanced infants.

The question of what level of stimulation does in fact promote the fastest rate of schema development and the strongest attachment to the stimulus source must now be investigated. Schneirla (1959, 1965) proposed the simple and general hypothesis that young organisms tend to approach sources of "mild" stimulation and to avoid more "intense" stimuli. During most of his first year the human infant cannot make active approach or avoidance locomotions, but his attentional responses to visual stimuli are functionally approach behaviours, and other forms of stimulation such as a light touch on the cheek will evoke orientation towards their source, even in neonates (Blauvelt and McKenna, 1961).

On the other hand, intense stimulation may elicit startle, protest, or distress reactions, with aversion of the head and eye-closure (e.g. Bridges, 1932; Spitz, 1963; White and Held, 1966; Bridger and Birns, 1968). Looming objects may also elicit head retraction and bringing of the hands in front of the face even during stage 1, according to Bower *et al.* (1970c). Too continuous stimulation may have similar aversive effects (Richards, 1972). While Schneirla's hypothesis may hold, it is too general to be of much use in the present context. Related formulations have suggested that organisms attempt to maintain certain optimum levels of either stimulation or "arousal" (e.g. Hebb, 1955; Fiske and Maddi, 1961) through balancing their approach and avoidance behaviours; but any such theory must also take account of fluctuations of the optimum (cf. the "adaptation level" of Helson 1964), and allow that the optimum may also shift with age and long-term experience. The present approach embodies this view inasmuch as acquisition of a schema which enables some input to be easily recognized as familiar can be seen as reducing the effective intensity of the stimulation itself.

We have already suggested that a high stimulus-schema discrepancy may put processing demands on the infant which are too great for his capacity, which would then lead to attempts to avoid the stimulation, and to negative affect. This approach makes the necessary allowance for quality as well as quantity of stimulation recognized in the more recent optimum stimulation models (McReynolds, 1962). If the infant does attempt to maintain an optimum information-processing rate, we would expect the understimulated infant initially to seek out more stimulation, although the long-term effects of understimulation might be otherwise if adaptation of the optimum occurs. It has been claimed that the "excitement" behaviours which infants often show can be interpreted as attempts to make contact with stimulation sources: Morris (1967) sees smiling as an approach behaviour, and mentions that it may be associated with kicking, arm-waving, chin-protrusion, attempts to lean forward, vocalization, and even tongue-protrusion. While these activities can be seen as attempts at approach by the immobile infant, it is also the case that they virtually exhaust the infant's repertoire of behaviours which provide self-stimulation or increase the probability of receiving stimulation from some external source. However, the situation is probably more complex than this, since Stechler and Latz (1966) report that the excitement bouts of 2-week infants can be affectively negative in some cases, with crying, fussing etc. Where there is actual smiling its concomitants can also vary. Several authors find motor relaxation and cardiac deceleration associated with attention and the smile (e.g. Kagan and Lewis, 1965; Kagan *et al.*, 1966), while Gewirtz (1965) and Wolff (1963) indicate that either relaxation or excitement accompany smiling.

It seems probable that behaviours associated with the smile depend on the state of development of the infant's schema for the object smiled at. If the infant has only a partial schema excitement reactions aimed at gaining further stimulation would be less likely, since as soon as the salient features are recognized (and smiled at) attention should be turned rapidly to the other features not as yet fully assimilated into the schema and therefore demanding more attention. It is, however, possible that excitement behaviours may sometimes result simply from a general motor discharge elicited by the affective component of recognition (smiling being the most easily evoked component of such a discharge). Where excitement behaviour is of a negative kind—as when evoked by a stimulus-schema discrepancy which is too large—it may perhaps be interpreted as an attempt to cut out the source of stimulation, but it is significant that the behaviour itself in fact increases stimulation. This may be functional if it elicits attention from the mother, as she may remove the disturbing source or provide soothing stimulation of a different type, but in her absence a positive feedback loop may be set up in which the infant's own actions continue to exacerbate his discomfort. We can go little beyond this in the absence of further empirical data, since specification of precise optimum processing rates and the effects of discrepancies from these must depend not only on the state of schema development, but also on background arousal and short-term adaptation.

The above formulation should not be taken to imply that information-overload or unsuccessful attempts to redress understimulation are the only causes of negative reactions in early infancy. Internal conditions of body tissues etc. may lead to painful stimulation of specific kinds which can only be relieved by food, warmth or what ever is appropriate. It is very doubtful whether the motivation for processing of information can be operative when specific needs are unsatisfied. Nevertheless, too much or too little stimulation of the distance receptors will not normally have direct effects on tissue conditions, and so if visual auditory stimulation leads to affective responses it will normally be necessary to invoke perceptual and cognitive processes in accounting for these. Where this stimulation is social in origin it is appropriate to consider how the various components of the schema for the mother or for persons are involved.

Although crying can have other causes, and can be used operantly by understimulated infants to elicit attention, it has been noted that for some infants mutual gazing with a caretaker leads to crying, which may in fact follow an initial smile (Etzel and Gewirtz, 1967). Although crying is principally a vocal behaviour, it is commonly accompanied by head-shaking, eye-closure, and a strong frown (Blurton-Jones, 1968). Its components are characteristic responses of rejection, cutting down the inputs of all external sensory channels (cf. Andrew, 1963). Wolff (1969) also noted that facial and other stimuli which later elicit smiles can elicit crying at 3 weeks of age, long before they can reasonably be expected to have conditioned associations with other noxious stimuli. This we might expect if an infant's perceptual abilities have matured, but there has been insufficient experience of a particular stimulus configuration for it to be incorporated in a perceptual schema permitting recognition, since the configuration may then provide a complex but unresolvable input. Such a mismatch between perceptual maturation and complexity of experienced stimulation was proposed by Sackett (1965) to account for the abnormal attentional and social responses of rhesus monkeys reared under stimulus deprivation conditions. The generalized harmful effects of extended visual deprivation in early life are now well established for a variety of species (e.g. Fantz, 1967; Bronson, 1968a, 1968b), and so the long-term consequences of inadequate visual experience for human infants could well be substantial. But it is unlikely that many infants do suffer such deprivation, and the eventual appearance of smiling, even in understimulated institution-reared infants, shows that initial problems in resolving social stimuli are normally overcome.

Since crying and protest are components of the "fear" reactions which infants may show to strangers from around stage 5 (7–12 months) onwards, we may consider whether this fear may arise because strangers effectively overstimulate the infant. Bronson (1968a, 1968b) points out that fear responses only develop to certain stimuli after they can be contrasted with the familiar and thus discriminated as novel. The data on infants' fear of strangers (p. 243) shows though that novelty alone is an insufficient explanation of the phenomenon. Morgan and Ricciuti (1969) found that with increasing age physical separation from the mother became more critical in determining the amount of fear shown, Schaffer (1966) found slight or transitory fear responses if infants were tested with the mother present. These findings, among others, show that fear of strangers is somehow linked to attachment to the mother. Furthermore, Scarr and Salatapek (1970) showed differential development of the fear for various types of event. Although they did not find a relationship between fear of strangers and performance on an object-permanence test, this does not rule out the possibility of a developed mother schema being a precondition for fear of strangers, since object-permanence and person-permanence concepts may develop differentially (Bell, 1970).

Assuming that an infant has, by the middle of the first year, developed a rudimentary mother schema with the face as its focus, so that the mother is readily recognized, and that their history of interaction has been such that the infant associates her appearance with affectively positive experiences, then the sudden appearance of a stranger who can be identified as not being the mother should evoke surprise as a consequence of the discrepancy. The more discrepant is the stranger's appearance from the mother's the more rapidly will this surprise be evoked, as the discrimination will be made more easily and with less need for extended attention to that person's face. Speed of discrimination will also increase with the age of the infant, as older infants will have more detailed mother schemata. Initially the infant will have no positive expectations associated with the stranger, as he has for the mother, and may simply turn his attention elsewhere in search of configurations which he knows can provide optimal amounts of stimulation. If, as will typically happen, the stranger takes further steps to attract the infant's attention, he will provide further stimulation. Most importantly, this stimulation will be outside the infant's control, whereas stimulation provided by the mother is normally expected and influenced predictably by his own behaviour. On this basis we would expect to find a point at which the increasing efforts of the stranger to engage the infant in interaction yield a level of stimulation of the infant which exceeds some currently critical value of effective input, whereupon the infant exhibits negative reactions. Thus on the present view, the mere presentation of an unfamiliar face is not likely to elicit fear in the first instance from younger infants, while active touching and picking up is very likely to do so. The data from the studies of fear of strangers do in fact support this position, although it may well be that further experience of strangers leads infants to learn that an unfamiliar face is linked with overstimulation, so that later they show fear to strange faces alone. An interesting parallel to this has been found with surrogate-reared macaques, as Harlow and Suomi (1970) report that drastically changing the form of the surrogate's model head for a 90-day infant led to extreme terror reactions.

The above interpretation of the fear of strangers is not intended as a complete account of this or other avoidance syndromes, which are not the main concern here, but as a demonstration that the schema approach is able to account for the main features of the data on negative responses to faces within a framework of the infant's normal development during the first year. It remains now to consider how abnormal social responsiveness may arise as a result of experiences which grossly distort development.

3.2 CONSEQUENCES OF ABNORMAL STIMULATION

According to the present theory, inappropriate contingencies of early facial-visual interaction between the infant and the mother or caretaker should delay schema acquisition, and thus also delay the growth of the infant's first social attachment. Unfortunately there appear to have been no longitudinal studies in which detailed patterns of facial-visual interactions have been monitored, and so direct empirical evidence on this point is lacking. There are, however, a number of scattered findings in the literature which reveal that unusual patterns of facial-visual interaction can be seen in young infants, and there are some clues as to the possible effects of these.

Stechler and Latz (1966) found that one infant strongly avoided faces from 3 weeks. Robson (1967) notes that some infants of less than 3 months old will persistently avoid their mothers' gazes, which can lead to anxiety or annoyance in the mother. Since Richards' (1972) film analysis revealed that failure by the mother to allow the infant time to respond during interaction led to crying and protest, it may be that avoidance habits are acquired by infants to avoid information overload in the first months. This would delay schema acquisition and smiling at facial presentations, and, if it tends to make the mother reject the child, might have more serious effects. While in general the provision of extra stimulation for young infants enhances attentiveness (and so presumably schema development) from birth onwards (e.g. White and

Held, 1966; Ottinger *et al.*, 1968; White, 1969a), very high sensory enrichment can depress attentiveness according to White's studies. However, the puzzling aspect of these studies was that at about 3 months the trend was reversed and highly enriched infants began to show higher attentiveness and performance on visually directed reaching tasks than did other infants. Clearly apparent overstimulation can have long term advantages, and early avoidance habits may not be maintained, though the mechanism here is obscure.

We have also argued that understimulation should impose difficulties and delays in schema development. This might be implicated in the case of the small percentage of infants who apparently do not smile socially during their first year (Spitz and Wolf, 1946), but in the absence of follow-up data we cannot be sure of the long-term stability and effect of this. The isolated reports of infants not fixating and not smiling at faces cannot be interpreted without such information, nor can abnormal stimulation histories necessarily be invoked in the absence of data on possible sensory or arousal system abnormalities.

There is one group of infants and young children showing abnormalities of facial-visual signalling about which much more is known, namely those suffering from the syndrome of "early infantile autism" (Kanner, 1944). An important feature of these children is their abnormal social behaviour, with poor attachment to parents, limited interest in interaction with others, poor communication skills (often including absence of language), together with markedly stereotypic behaviours (Rutter and Bartak, 1971). The most interesting aspect of this syndrome from our present viewpoint is that not only do these children show little facial expressiveness, but also they show considerable reluctance to meet the gaze of another person or just to look at his face (Hutt and Ounsted, 1966). From detailed examination of ciné-films they found that 3–6-year-old autists do in fact look at people, but with unusually brief gazes, and very rarely permit mutual gazing (cf. Castell, 1970). This regulation is evidently achieved by peripheral vision. Hutt and Ounsted found that social responsiveness to adults was actually much improved if they did not attempt to engage the children in mutual gazing. The extreme difficulty experienced by the nurses in following this rule is an indicator of how strong is the gazing habit in normal persons. Using a semi-experimental situation, Hutt and Ounsted found that autists spent a much lower proportion of their time in a play-room looking at face masks than at non-human stimuli, as compared with normals, and there was slight evidence that eyeless faces were preferred to mouthless faces.

Hutt and Ounsted were inclined to see the autists' habit of gaze-aversion as a major factor in their abnormality, but doubts have since been raised on this point. It has been found relatively easy to teach autists to show fairly normal gazing and social approach behaviours using operant techniques (e.g. McConnell, 1967; Means and Merrens, 1969; Mundas, 1969), and Currie and Brannigan (1970) found that once these had been conditioned other social behaviours such as the "upper" smile of social greeting emerged spontaneously. The relatively simple improvement of their social interaction behaviours does not, however, lead to much reduction of stereotyping or to improvement in linguistic facility, which casts doubt on the hypothesis that social withdrawal is the cause of other handicaps (cf. Rutter and Bartak, 1971).

A further and related suggestion has been that autists are characterized by chronic high cortical arousal, so that arousal increasing stimuli must be avoided if arousal is to be kept below some maximum tolerable level. This might account for avoidance of novel objects, their stereotyping (an arousal reducing mechanism—see Delius, 1970), and their social avoidance (e.g. Hutt et al., 1965; Hutt, 1969; Hutt and Hutt, 1970). Hutt and Ounsted (1966) suggested that visual avoidance of persons and novel objects acted as a "cut-off" posture (Chance, 1962), reducing arousal (and incidentally, making them less likely targets for aggression, even in crowded playrooms—Hutt and Vaizey, 1966). Unfortunately for this hypothesis, other investigators have found that arousal and novelty preference are not necessarily abnormal (O'Connor and Hermelin, 1967; Hermelin and O'Connor, 1968), although visual attentiveness in general is certainly low (Frith and Hermelin, 1969). Furthermore, O'Connor and Hermelin found that in paired-comparisons fixation tests "psychotic" children showed a preference for facial stimuli comparable to that found with normals.

The inconsistencies between results, and the complexity of findings in some of the studies, suggest various possibilities. One is that different investigators have been working with different sub-groups of disturbed children. Another is that some of the measures used have been unable to show up real differences. Autistic children have normally shown abnormalities from the first year of life (Rutter and Bartak, 1971), so it is possible that abnormal patterns of mother–infant interaction have led to slow or aberrant development of the facial and mother schemata, and thus attachment, without other cognitive developments being affected substantially. Two-dimensional static representations of facial stimuli might not elicit aversion simply because for such children they are only weakly associated with the schema for maternal or other faces. Language development could be impaired just because mother–infant interaction had been very infrequent or unrewarding to the infant. In the absence of detailed research data on the early mother–infant interaction histories of autistic children it is difficult to evaluate these possibilities, or the most popular alternative hypothesis that autists suffer from some as yet unspecified organic brain deficit. While it has been suggested that abnormal patterns of stimulation by the mother might lead to autism (Tomkins, 1962), and while some evidence has been put forward to suggest that autists' mothers have been unresponsive to their infants (Schopler, 1965), others have reported fairly normal family backgrounds, and explanations of this type seem unlikely to explain the high preponderance of male infants among autists (Rutter and Bartak, 1971).

Thus we cannot claim that there is clear evidence that the social behavioural abnormalities of the autism syndrome can be explained simply in terms of abnormal mother–infant interaction histories which affect social schema development. On the other hand this remains possible as at least a partial explanation, in terms of which avoidance of the mother's gaze is acquired as a habit early in infancy, perhaps to avoid inadvertently excessive maternal stimulation, setting up a positive feedback system which leads to progressive deterioration in the quality and frequency of their interaction, with a variety of unfortunate consequences. The fact that autists have sometimes been reported to have a normal history of social smiling (Shaffer, in Ambrose, 1969, p. 197) may indicate that the avoidance habit arises later after the facial or mother schema has developed; but if, as we have argued, the smile is a recognition response not necessarily elicited by faces, their early smiles may alternatively have focused on stimuli other than the mother's eyes and face. Certainly in later infancy and childhood their social smiling can be very low (e.g. Means and Merrens, 1969; Currie and Brannigan, 1970).

Finally, we may mention another group of infants who would be expected to develop atypical signalling if the present approach is valid. These are of course blind infants, or at least those blind from birth or an early age. We have already indicated that their expressive behaviour is delayed, but otherwise only slightly atypical (p. 200). But their obvious inability to develop a normal face schema, and thus the impossibility of their mother schema developing along the lines here suggested for normal infants, does not in any way imply that social schemata and attachment will be completely inhibited. If they are totally deprived of the most convenient channel these developments must take quite a different course, with other channels compensating for the lack of vision. The congenitally blind can discriminate the mother's voice from other voices by about 10 weeks (Freedman *et al.*, 1969), and so social schemata should be able to develop using the mother's voice as an initial focus, later incorporating inputs from other modalities such as touch and smell. In the case of the deaf-and-blind (see Chapter 4) the difficulty would be greater, but still recognition (and thus smiling), schema development, and ultimately attachment should occur.

In these cases, as seems to be found empirically, late development would be expected, due to the particular utility of the visual sense in integrating various types of stimulus inputs from the mother or other sources. The blind do tend to show some abnormalities of social behaviour and attachment (Scott, 1969), as one would expect if they are deprived of the richness of facial-visual stimulation, but it is likely that other aspects of the mother's own responsiveness are involved. If, as Robson (1967) reports, mothers of normal infants experience some irritation and dissatisfaction in the period before infants fixate and follow their eyes, then mothers of blind (or autistic) infants can be expected to be less accepting than mothers of normal infants. If the attachment of the mother herself is weak, she is unlikely to behave in such a way as to allow the infant to develop readily a strong attachment to her, thus both partners will derive less than the normal satisfaction from interaction.

While it has not been possible to show that the present theory provides a unique explanation of cases where young children show abnormalities of behaviour and attachment involving atypical facial-visual signalling as a component, it has been possible to indicate in fairly general terms how existing empirical data on these abnormalities might be accounted for within the schema development framework. In the absence of any substantial body of pertinent detailed descriptive data, any more precise hypotheses dealing with how under- or overstimulation during early infancy might lead to deviant development would be excessively speculative. Nevertheless, it is to be hoped that the above discussion has highlighted aspects of early mother–infant communication which would repay closer empirical study in view of their possible importance. Further data on several crucial points would permit the present approach to be refined into a more formal and testable theory; and longitudinal data on the subsequent social development of infants whose early interactions with the mother were abnormal would be a convenient means of testing the general approach.

4 Summary and conclusions

The present paper has been concerned with two main tasks. The first has been to indicate the scope of our present knowledge concerning developmental aspects of facial-visual signalling, with particular attention to the important and rapid changes during the infant's first year. The second has been to outline a theoretical framework within which the empirical data can be interpreted, a framework which accords to early mother–infant social interaction an important place in the infant's social development, and permits us to account for the beginnings of his attachment to the mother in a more satisfactory way than has been proposed hitherto.

It has been argued that investigations of the ontogeny of facial-visual signalling, especially between mother and infant during his first year, are particularly important for our understanding of the development of communication skills; yet studies of the production and recognition of global "facial expressions" have yielded little insight into the processes and significance of early facial-visual signalling, largely because of their almost exclusive concern with questions of emotional differentiation. In consequence we have concentrated on two areas in which there have been numerous studies, dealing with what, strictly, are only the precursors of communication skills, namely attention to faces and the infant's early responses to faces, principally the smiling response. By viewing side-by-side both the perceptual and expressive sequences of early infancy, it has been possible to relate these behaviours to recognition processes and the associated development of social schemata, or perceptual-cognitive "maps" of social objects. This approach permits us to argue that in normal development such processes provide a natural foundation for the growth of the infant's first social attachments.

Early facial-visual signal exchanges between infant and mother can be interpreted in terms of what can be seen as a basic characteristic of advanced organisms, namely the motivation to process information from the environment and incorporate this into memory schemata, which in turn structure further perceptual-cognitive operations. It has been claimed that the typical contingencies of normal mother–infant interaction, in conjunction with early sensory limitations on the infant's perception, will ensure that the two-eyes configuration is one of the first stimulus patterns provided by an external object which is incorporated into the infant's experience as a perceptual schema. Recognition of a stimulus presentation as familiar through successfully matching it to a schema is seen as rewarding, reinforcing the search for stimulus inputs and producing positive affect expressed by smiling. In this manner the potency of faces in eliciting attention is maintained, and, provided that presentation conditions permit processing to proceed at a rate which is optimal for the infant's stage of perceptual development and fluctuating arousal state, more and more features of the human face will become incorporated into the schema.

Interaction with the mother is thus intrinsically rewarding to the infant because of the opportunities for successful resolution and control of stimulation which this typically provides. Recognition can be re-garded as effectively reducing the complexity or amount of information in incoming stimuli, thereby permitting the infant to accept more varied inputs without exceeding some current maximum rate at which infor-mation can be dealt with. Eventually the infant will come to incorporate into his face schema unique features of the mother's appearance, after which she will be discriminated from strangers, and subsequently this schema will be extended to include other aspects of the stimulation she provides, until the infant can be said to have acquired the concept of the mother as a unique and independent social object.

Once strange faces can be discriminated from the mother's they may become less preferred, as typically they will be less likely to provide the infant with optimum stimulation. If in addition the infant associates the appearance of the mother with other sources of direct reward (satisfaction of bodily needs, alleviation of distressful conditions, etc.) his selective preference for her presence may be further increased. At this point he can be said to show "attachment" towards her, which can be interpreted simply in terms of proximity-seeking habits arising from her ability to provide rewarding stimulation, or in terms of the positive affect which her appearance and responsiveness may have come to elicit.

Thus mother–infant interaction is likely to follow a course which is adaptive for the infant, and in which the role of facial-visual signal exchange between mother and infant is most important, since it contributes directly to the infant's general perceptual-cognitive development, especially during the early months when other such opportunities to make active intellectual advances are severely limited by his perceptual and motor immaturity. The success of this sequence depends considerably on the mother herself, as unless she provides the necessary contingencies for the infant to succeed in developing schemata some retardation in social and other development should follow. Fortunately it appears that the infant's own behaviours can themselves help to pattern the behaviour of the mother, especially at first through his engaging her in mutual gazing and his smiling, but any factors which impair the frequency and quality of their interactions may establish positive feedbacks which hamper rather than facilitate the development process. It is difficult in our present state of relative ignorance to specify precisely how, and by which of the alternative possible routes, abnormal interaction patterns may account for later deficiencies in social behaviour or in mother–infant attachment, but a number of suggestions have been made as to how further investigation could permit precise hypotheses to be formulated and tested regarding specific issues.

It is necessary to re-emphasize the limited claims made for the approach presented here. It embodies no major concepts which have not been put forward elsewhere, although it may serve to link these in ways which have not previously been made fully explicit. Nor can it be claimed that this framework approaches a formal theory of social development in early infancy, since many details remain to be explicated, and a number of aspects remain speculative. Furthermore, I have concentrated almost exclusively on the facial-visual channel, partly because its importance has previously been underestimated or accepted without close analysis. By neglecting other channels I have sought to highlight facial signals and visual attention, but undoubtedly other channels are important. The vocal-aural channel in particular is likely to be important, partly in schema development but principally because early exchange of vocalizations between mother and infant must form the basis from which language development begins. In blind infants it must be one of the main channels, with touch, involved in development of the mother schema and of social attachment. A major task which has scarcely been approached in this paper is of course to specify in detail how signals received through the various channels are integrated to yield a total message, how the infant comes to perceive the complex meanings of multi-channel messages, and how he integrates his own signal emissions.

It may be objected that the framework proposed here provides little more than alternative language for describing a given set of phenomena, since the approach of regarding early development in information-processing and schema development terms generates no unique predictions, and depends on several constructs which are not directly observable. Gibson (1969) objects strongly to the schema approach, although her reasons are somewhat obscure. It is true that the framework does not as yet constitute a theory capable of disproof, but its constructs are hopefully more plausible or more capable of such refinement than those of other existing approaches which seek to encompass a similar range of phenomena. It may also serve a useful heuristic functioning in establishing new emphases or promoting new lines of research. The present lack of detailed knowledge on the development of communication is remarkable in view of its fundamental position as the basis for social skills and attachments which may be critical determinants of success and satisfaction in adult life.

The problems of obtaining this data are considerable (Yarrow, 1963; Lytton, 1969). Laboratory studies may fail to reveal subtle but important factors, particularly where young infants and social interaction processes are being studied, while the naturalistic data which might facilitate the achievement of realism in laboratory experiments are difficult to acquire in view of the measurement problems. The extensive use of videotapes and sound-films is becoming rapidly more feasible (Polunin, 1970), but this leaves measurement and analysis problems substantially unsolved. The particular constructs used in the present approach suggest the utility of deprivation studies in investigating hypotheses. But deliberate deprivation of specific kinds of stimulation for experimental purposes, or substantial overstimulation, is ethically unjustifiable, while accidental deprivation usually yields only retrospective and imprecise or uncontrolled data. A case can perhaps be made though for depriving other primates of social or visual experience when the likely human pay-offs may be substantial.

Animal deprivation studies have produced results which suggest that massive visual or social deprivation has very serious effects on development of communication skills and related activities, but these findings are not surprising, nor do they give much help in selecting from a variety of theories which would lead to such a prediction. More specific investigations have shown that some primate social responses are independent of social experience (Sackett, 1966; Harlow and Suomi, 1970), but undoubtedly others do depend on the provision of suitable stimulation. It is interesting to consider Harlow's early finding that infant monkeys reared on cloth-covered surrogate mothers providing tactile stimulation and warmth developed normally in most respects, but showed specific abnormalities in social behaviour. A major deficiency of the surrogates was their lack of mobility, one consequence being the restricted variation in visual stimulation which they could provide for the infant, especially stimulation contingent on his own behaviour. Mobile surrogates have since been shown to elicit more contact from young infant monkeys (Harlow and Suomi, 1970), so it would be of particular interest to investigate the role of surrogate facial mobility in further studies.

A number of other questions invite research. We would expect the incidence of early gazing and smiling to be indicators of social responsiveness in later childhood, while the individual's experience of behaviours accompanying gazes given him by others may modify these relationships. Older infants may well learn to associate an extended mutual gaze with threat if it commonly precedes punishment (cf. Darwin, 1872). This may contribute to the tendency towards reduced tolerance of long gazes as the child grows older, though the complexity of communicative and situational determinants of gazing may provide further reasons why this should be so.

Further questions arise concerning effects of maternal practices on the precise parameters of signalling behaviour. Cross-cultural variations in mother–infant interaction may well be related to differences in adult interaction styles, and class differences may also exist within cultures. Recent studies by Hore (1970) and Schmidt and Hore (1970) have provided interesting data on class differences in interaction patterns of mothers and 5-year-old children. In pairs of low socioeconomic status there was a tendency for more physical contact, while in high SES pairs mothers looked at their children more often and more of the child's gazes were reciprocated by the mother. Bugental et al. (1971) found that mothers of 8–12-year-old middle-class children were no less likely to smile at them when making negative evaluative statements than when making positive ones, but that working-class mothers scarcely smiled at all. Since Kagan (1969b) found some evidence that at

8 months high SES infants showed signs of greater social schema development, which suggests that these infants received more frequent or more contingent stimulation of the distance receptors before this time, it seems probable that early interaction patterns are maintained during childhood, and probably affect the child's expectancies in interpersonal encounters.

Another respect in which early interaction may affect later styles concerns sex differences. We have seen that a variety of studies have found early sex differences in a variety of variables associated with facial-visual signalling. While some of these are particularly perplexing, such as the predominance of males amongst autistic children, others can probably be explained by differences in the rate of early development, though why this should be so is not clear. If differential development of the face schema can be established with more certainty, it may be possible to relate this to sex differences in adult interaction, for example the tendency of females to give longer glances than males (cf. Vine, 1970).

In conclusion, the study of early patterns of mother–infant interaction poses a number of questions of considerable empirical and theoretical interest for our understanding of face-to-face communication and social affiliations. Investigation of the genesis of these processes must be recognized as an essential part of the attempt to further our knowledge of interpersonal behaviour.

References

Ahrens, R. (1954). Beitrage zür Entwicklung der Physiognomie und Mimikerkennens. *Z. Exp. Angew. Psychol.* **2**, 414–454; 599–633.

Ainsworth, Mary D. S. (1969). Object relations, dependency, and attachment: a theoretical review of the infant–mother relationship. *Child Dev.* **40**, 969–1025.

Ainsworth, Mary D. S. and Bell, Sylvia M. (1969). Mother–infant interaction in the feeding situation. *In* "Stimulation in Early Infancy" (Ed. J. A. Ambrose), pp. 133–170. Academic Press, London and New York.

Ambrose, J. A. (1961). The development of the smiling response in early infancy. *In* "Determinants of Infant Behaviour" (Ed. B. M. Foss), Vol. 1, pp. 179–196. Methuen, London.

Ambrose, J. A. (1963). The concept of a critical period for the development of social responsiveness in early human infancy. *In* "Determinants of Infant Behaviour" (Ed. B. M. Foss), Vol. 2, pp. 201–226. Methuen, London.

Ambrose, J. A. (Ed.) (1969). "Stimulation in Early Infancy". Academic Press, London and New York.

Ames, Elinor W. and Silfe ,C. K. (1965). Methodological issues in the study of age differences in infants' attention to stimuli varying in movement and complexity. Paper to Society for Research in Child Development, Minneapolis.

Andrew, R. J. (1963). The origin and evolution of the calls and facial expressions of the primates. *Behaviour*, **20**, 1–109.

Bell, R. Q. (1968). A reinterpretation of the direction of effect in studies of socialization. *Psychol. Rev.* **75**, 81–95.

Bell, Sylvia M. (1970). Development of the concept of object as related to mother–infant attachment. *Child Dev.* **41**, 291–311.

Berlyne, D. E. (1960). "Conflict, Arousal, and Curiosity". McGraw-Hill, New York.

Blauvelt, Helen and McKenna, J. (1961). Mother–neonate interaction: Capacity of the human newborn for orientation. *In* "Determinants of Infant Behaviour" (Ed. B. M. Foss), Vol. 1, pp. 3–29. Methuen, London.

Blurton-Jones, N. G. (1967). Some aspects of the social behaviour of children in a nursery school. *In* "Primate Ethology" (Ed. D. Morris), pp. 347–368. Weidenfeld & Nicolson, London.

Blurton-Jones, N. G. (1968). Description of components of facial expressions of children. Unpublished manuscript, Institute of Child Health, London.

Bobbitt, Ruth A., Gourevitch, V. P., Miller, L. E. and Jensen, G. D. (1969). Dynamics of social interactive behavior: a computerized procedure for analyzing trends, patterns, and sequences. *Psychol. Bull.* **71**, 110–121.

Bower, T. G. R. (1966). The visual world of infants. *Sci. American*, **215**, 80–92.

Bower, T. G. R. (1967). The development of object permanence: some studies of existence constancy. *Percept. Psychophys.* **2**, 411–418.

Bower, T. G. R., Broughton, J. M. and Moore, M. K. (1970a). Demonstration of intention in the reaching behaviour of neonate humans. *Nature (London)*, **228**, 679–681.

Bower, T. G. R., Broughton, J. M. and Moore, M. K. (1970b). The coordination of visual and tactual input in infants. *Percept. Psychophys.* **8**, 51–53.

Bower, T. G. R., Broughton, J. M. and Moore, M. K. (1970c). Infant responses to approaching objects: an indicator of response to distal variables. *Percept. Psychophys.* **9**, 193–196.

Bowlby, J. (1952). "Maternal Care and Mental Health". W.H.O., Geneva.

Bowlby, J. (1958). The nature of the child's tie to his mother. *Int. J. Psychoanal.* **39**, 350–373.

Bowlby, J. (1969)."Attachment and Loss: Vol. 1. Attachment". Hogarth Press, London.

Brackbill, Yvonne (1958). Extinction of smiling responses in infants as a function of reinforcement schedule. *Child Dev.* **29**, 115–124.

Brannigan, C. R. and Humphries, D. (1972). Human nonverbal behaviour, a means of communication. *In* "Ethological Studies of Infant Behaviour" (Ed. N. G. Blurton-Jones). Cambridge University Press, London.

Brennan, Wendy M., Ames, Elinor W. and Moore, R. W. (1966). Age differences in infants' attention to patterns of different complexities. *Science*, **150**, 354–356.

Bridger, W. H. and Birns, Beverly (1968). Experience and temperament in human neonates. *In* "Early Experience and Behaviour" (Eds G. Newton and S. Levine), pp. 83–101. Thomas, Springfield, Ill.

Bridges, Katherine M. B. (1932). Emotional development in infancy. *Child Dev.* **3**, 324–341.

Bronson, G. W. (1968a). The development of fear in man and other animals. *Child Dev.* **39**, 409–431.

Bronson, G. W. (1968b). The fear of novelty. *Psychol. Bull.* **69**, 350–358.

Bronson, G. W. (1969a). Vision in infancy: structure and function relationships. *In* "Brain and Early Behaviour—Development in the Foetus and Infant" (Ed. R. J. Robinson), pp. 207–210. Academic Press, London and New York.

Bronson, G. W. (1969b). Sex differences in the development of fearfulness: a replication. *Psychon. Sci.* **17**, 367–368.

Brossard, Louise M. and Décarie, Thérèse G. (1968). Comparative reinforcing effect of eight stimulations on the smiling response of infants. *J. Child Psychol. Psychiat.* **9**, 51–59.

Brossard, Louise M. and Décarie, Thérèse G. (1971). The effects of three kinds of perceptual-social stimulation on the development of institutionalized infants—preliminary report of a longitudinal study. *Early Child Dev. Care*, **1**, 111–130.

Bruner, J. S. (1969a). Eye, hand, and mind. *In* "Studies in Cognitive Development—Essays in Honour of Jean Piaget" (Eds D. Elkind and J. H. Flavell), pp. 223–235. Oxford University Press, New York.

Bruner, J. S. (1969b). Origins of problem solving strategies in skill acquisition. Paper to 19th International Congress of Psychology, London, July 1969.

Bugental, Daphne E., Love, Leonore R. and Gianetto, R. M. (1971). Perfidious feminine faces. *J. Person. Soc. Psychol.* **17**, 314–318.

Bühler, Charlotte (1931). The social behavior of children. *In* "Handbook of Child Psychology" (Ed. C. A. Murchison), pp. 392–431. Clark University Press, Worcester, Mass.

Bühler, Charlotte (1935). "From Birth to Maturity" (translated by Esther Menaker and W. Menaker). Routledge & Kegan Paul, London.

Caldwell, Bettye M. (1962). The usefulness of the critical period hypothesis in the study of filiative behavior. *Merrill-Palmer Q.* **8**, 229–242.

Campos, J. J., Langer, A. and Krowitz, Alice (1970). Cardiac responses on the visual cliff in prelocomotor human infants. *Science,* **170**, 196–197.

Caron, Rose F. and Caron, A. J. (1969). Degree of stimulus complexity and habituation of visual fixation in infants. *Psychon. Sci.* **14**, 78–79.

Carpenter, Genevieve C. and Stechler, G. (1967). Selective attention to the mother's face from week one through week eight. *Proc. 75th Ann. Conv. A.P.A.* 153–154.

Carpenter, Genevieve C., Tecce, J. J., Stechler, G. and Friedman, S. (1970). Differential visual behavior to human and humanoid faces in early infancy. *Merrill-Palmer Q.* **16**, 91–108.

Castell, R. (1970). Physical distance and visual attention as measures of social interaction between child and adult. *In* "Behaviour Studies in Psychiatry" (Eds S. J. Hutt and Corinne Hutt), pp. 91–102. Pergamon Press, Oxford.

Chance, M. R. A. (1962). An interpretation of some agonistic postures: the role of "cut-off" acts and postures. *Symp. Zool. Soc. Lond.* **8**, 71–79.

Charlesworth, W. R. (1969). The role of surprise in cognitive development. *In* "Studies in Cognitive Development—Essays in Honour of Jean Piaget" (Eds D. Elkind and J. H. Flavell), pp. 257–313. Oxford University Press, New York.

Cohen, Leslie B. (1969). Observing responses, visual preferences, and habituation to visual stimuli in infants. *J. Exp. Child Psychol.* **7**, 419–433.

Coss, R. G. (1970). The perceptual effect of eye-spot patterns and their relevance to gaze behaviour. *In* "Behaviour Studies in Psychiatry" (Eds S. J. Hutt and Corinne Hutt), pp. 121–147. Pergamon Press, Oxford.

Currie, Katherine H. and Brannigan, C. R. (1970). Behavioural analysis and modification with an autistic child. *In* "Behaviour Studies in Psychiatry" (Eds S. J. Hutt and Corinne Hutt). Pergamon Press, Oxford.

Darwin, C. (1872). "The Expression of the Emotions in Man and Animals". Murray, London.

Dashiell, J. F. (1927). A new method for measuring reaction to facial expression. *Psychol. Bull.* **24**, 174–175.

Delius, J. D. (1970). Irrelevant behaviour, information processing, and arousal homeostasis. *Psychol. Forsch.* **33**, 165–188.

Dennis, W. (1935). An experimental test of two theories of social smiling. *J. Soc. Psychol.* **6**, 214–223.

Diebold, A. R. (1968). Anthropology and the comparative psychology of communication behavior. *In* "Animal Communication—Techniques of Study and Results of Research" (Ed. T. A. Sebeok), pp. 525–571. Indiana University Press, Bloomington, Indiana.

Doris, J., Casper, Myra and Poresky, R. (1967). Differential brightness thresholds in infancy. *J. Exp. Child Psychol.* **5**, 522–525.

Eilb-Eibesfeldt, I. (1968). Zur Ethologie des menschlichen Grussverhaltens. 1. Beobachtungen an Balinesen, Papuas und Samoanern nebst vergleichenden Bemerkungen. *Z. Tierpsychol.* **25**, 727–744.

Eibl-Eibesfeldt, I. and Hass, H. (1967). Film studies in human ethology. *Curr. Anthrop.* **8**, 477–480.

Ekman, P., Sorenson, E. R. and Friesen, W. V. (1969). Pan-cultural elements in facial displays of emotion. *Science*, **164**, 86–88.

Ellingson, R. J. (1967). The study of brain electrical activity in infants. *In* "Advances in Child Development and Behavior" (Eds L. P. Lipsitt and C. C. Spiker), Vol. 3, pp. 53–97. Academic Press, New York and London.

Etzel, B. C. and Gewirtz, J. L. (1967). Experimental modification of caretaker-maintained high-rate operant crying in a 6- and 20-week-old infant (*Infans tyrannotearus*): extinction of crying with reinforcement of eye-contact and smiling. *J. Exp. Child Psychol.* **3**, 303–317.

Fagan, J. F., III (1970). Memory in the infant. *J. Exp. Child Psychol.* **9**, 217–226.

Fantz, R. L. (1963). Pattern vision in newborn infants. *Science*, **140**, 296–297.

Fantz, R. L. (1964). Visual experience in infants: decreased attention to familiar patterns relative to novel ones. *Science*, **146**, 668–670.

Fantz, R. L. (1965). Visual perception from birth as shown by pattern selectivity. *Ann. N.Y. Acad. Sci.* **118**, 793–814.

Fantz, R. L. (1966). Pattern discrimination and selective attention as determinants of perceptual development from birth. *In* "Perceptual Development in Children" (Eds Aline J. Kidd and Jeanne L. Rivoire), pp. 143–173. London University Press, London.

Fantz, R. L. (1967). Visual perception and experience in early infancy: a look at the hidden side of behavior development. *In* "Early Behavior—Comparative and Developmental Approaches" (Ed. H. W. Stevenson), pp. 181–224. John Wiley, New York.

Fantz, R. L. and Nevis, Sonia (1967a). Pattern preferences and perceptual-cognitive development in early infancy. *Merrill-Palmer Q.* **3**, 77–108.

Fantz, R. L. and Nevis, Sonia (1967b). The predictive value of changes in visual preferences in early infancy. *In* "The Exceptional Infant" (Ed. J. Hellmuth), Vol. 1. Special Child Publications, Seattle, Washington.

Fantz, R. L., Ordy, J. M. and Udelf, M. S. (1962). Maturation of pattern vision in infants during the first six months. *J. Comp. Physiol. Psychol.* **55**, 907–917.

Fiske, D. W. and Maddi, S. R. (1961). A conceptual framework. *In* "Functions of Varied Experience", pp. 11–56. Dorsey Press, Homewood, Ill.

Fitzgerald, H. E. (1968). Autonomic pupillary reflex activity during early infancy and its relation to social and nonsocial stimuli. *J. Exp. Child Psychol.* **6**, 470–482.

Forrai-Banláki, E. (1965). Érzelmi kifejezések felismerésének kapesolata az értelmi fejlettséggel 7–9 éves korban. *Pszichológai Tanulmányok*, **8**, 139–151.

Freedman, D. G. (1961). The infant's fear of strangers and the flight response. *J. Child Psychol. Psychiat.* **4**, 242–248.

Freedman, D. G. (1964). Smiling in blind infants and the issue of innate vs. acquired. *J. Child Psychol. Psychiat.* **5**, 171–184.

Freedman, D. G. (1965). Hereditary control of early social behaviour. *In* "Determinants of Infant Behaviour" (Ed. B. M. Foss), Vol. 1, pp. 149–159. Methuen, London.

Freedman, D. G., Loring, Charlotte and Martin, R. M. (1967). Emotional behaviour and personality development. *In* "Infancy and Early Childhood—A Handbook and Guide to Human Development" (Ed. Yvonne Brackbill), pp. 428–502. Free Press, New York.

Freedman, D. G., Fox-Kolenda, B. J., Margileth, D. A. and Miller, D. H. (1969). The development of the use of sound as a guide to affective and cognitive behaviour—a 2-phase process. *Child Dev.* **40**, 1099–1105.

Friedman, S., Nagy, Alice N. and Carpenter, Genevieve C. (1970a). Newborn attention: differential response decrement to visual stimuli. *J. Exp. Child Psychol.* **10**, 44–51.

Friedman, S., Carpenter, Genevieve C. and Nagy, Alice N. (1970b). Decrement and recovery of response to visual stimuli in the newborn human. *Proc. 78th Ann. Conv. A.P.A.* 273–274.

Frijda, N. H. (1969). Recognition of emotion. *In* "Advances in Experimental Social Psychology" (Ed. L. Berkowitz), Vol. 4, pp. 167–223. Academic Press, New York and London.

Frith, Uta and Hermelin, Beate (1969). The role of visual and motor cues for normal, subnormal and autistic children. *J. Child Psychol. Psychiat.* **10**, 153–163.

Fulcher, J. S. (1942). "Voluntary" facial expressions in blind and seeing children. *Archs. Psychol. N.Y.* **38**, No. 272.

Gates, Georgina S. (1923). An experimental study of the growth of social perception. *J. Educ. Psychol.* **14**, 449–461.

Géber, M. (1960). Problèmes posés par le dévelopment du jeune enfant Africain en fonction de son mileu social. *Travail Hum.* **23**, 97–111.

Gesell, A., Ilg, Frances L. and Bullis, Gleena E. (1949). "Vision—Its development in Infant and Child". Hamish Hamilton, London.

Gewirtz, J. L. (1961). A learning analysis of the effects of normal stimulation, privation, and deprivation on the acquisition of social motivation and attachment. *In* "Determinants of Infant Behaviour" (Ed. B. M. Foss), Vol. 1, pp. 213–299. Methuen, London.

Gewirtz, J. L. (1965). The course of infant smiling in four child-rearing environments in Israel. *In* "Determinants of Infant Behaviour" (Ed. B. M. Foss), Vol. 3, pp. 205–248. Methuen, London.

Gewirtz, J. L. (1969). Mechanisms of social learning: some roles of stimulation and behavior in early human development. *In* "Handbook of Socialization Theory and Research" (Ed. D. A. Goslin), pp. 57–212. Rand, McNally, Chicago.

Gewirtz, Hava and Gewirtz, J. L. (1969). Caretaking settings, background events, and behaviour differences in four Israeli child-rearing environments: some preliminary trends. *In* "Determinants of Infant Behaviour" (Ed. B. M. Foss), Vol. 4, pp. 229–252. Methuen, London.

Gibson, Eleanor J. (1969). "Principles of Perceptual Learning and Development". Appleton-Century-Crofts, New York.

Goldstein, K. (1957). The smiling of the infant and the problem of understanding the other. *J. Psychol.* **44**, 175–191.

Goodenough, Florence L. (1931). Expression of the emotions in infancy. *Child Dev.* **2**, 96–101.

Goodenough, Florence L. (1932). Expression of the emotions in a blind–deaf child. *J. Abnorm. Soc. Psychol.* **27**, 328–333.

Gorman, J. J., Cogan, D. C. and Gellis, S. S. (1957). An apparatus for grading the visual acuity of infants on the basis of opticokinetic nystagmus. *Pediatrics*, **19**, 1088–1092.

Gough, D. (1968). Early mother–baby relationships. Film to Medical Section, British Psychological Society. (Abstract in *Bull. Br. Psychol. Soc.* **21**, 192.)

Graham, Frances K., Clifton, Rachel K. and Hatton, Helen M. (1968). Habituation of heart rate to repeated auditory stimulation during the first five days of life. *Child Dev.* **39**, 35–52.

Graham, Frances K., Berg, Kathleen M., Berg, W. K., Jackson, J. C., Hatton, Helen M. and Kantowitz, Susan R. (1970). Cardiac orienting responses as a function of age. *Psychon. Sci.* **19**, 363–365.

Grant, E. C. (1969). Human facial expression. *Man*, **4**, 525–536.

Gray, P. H. (1958). Theory and evidence of imprinting in human infants. *J. Psychol.* **46**, 155–166.

Greenberg, D., Uzgiris, Ina C. and Hunt, J. McV. (1970). Attentional preference and experience: III. Visual familiarity and looking time. *J. Genet. Psychol.* **117**, 123–135.

Greenman, G. W. (1963). Visual behaviour of newborn infants. *In* "Modern Perspectives in Child Development" (Eds A. Solnit and S. Provence), pp. 71–79. International Universities Press, New York.

Haaf, R. A. and Bell, R. Q. (1967). A facial dimension in visual discrimination by human infants. *Child Dev.* **38**, 893–899.

Haas, Miriam B. and Harms, Irene E. (1963). Social interaction between infants. *Child Dev.* **34**, 79–97.

Haith, M. M. (1966). The response of the human newborn to visual movement. *J. Exp. Child Psychol.* **3**, 235–243.

Haith, M. M., Kessen, W. and Collins, Doris (1969). Response of the human infant to level of complexity of intermittent visual movement. *J. Exp. Child Psychol.* **7**, 52–69.

Harlow, H. F. (1961). The development of affectional patterns in infant monkeys. *In* "Determinants of Infant Behaviour" (Ed. B. M. Foss), Vol. 1, pp. 75–89. Methuen, London.

Harlow, H. F. (1963). The maternal affectional system. *In* "Determinants of Infant Behaviour" (Ed. B. M. Foss), Vol. 2, pp. 3–33. Methuen, London.

Harlow, H. F. and Suomi, S. J. (1970). Nature of love—simplified. *Amer. Psychol.* **25**, 161–168.

Harter, M. R. and Suitt, Constance D. (1970). Visually-evoked cortical responses and pattern vision in the infant: a longitudinal study. *Psychon. Sci.* **18**, 235–237.

Hatfield, J. S., Ferguson, Lucy R. and Alport, R. (1967). Mother–child interaction and the socializing process. *Child Dev.* **38**, 365–414.

Haynes, H. M., White, B. L. and Held, R. (1965). Visual accommodation in human infants. *Science*, **148**, 528–530.

Hebb, D. O. (1955). Drives and the C.N.S. (Conceptual Nervous System). *Psychol. Rev.* **53**, 88–106.

Helson, H. (1964). "Adaptation Level Theory—An Experimental and Systematic Approach to Behavior". Harper & Row, New York.

Hermelin, Beate and O'Connor, N. (1968). Measures of the occipital alpha rhythm in normal, subnormal, and autistic children. *Brit. J. Psychiat.* **114**, 603–610.

Hershenson, M. (1964). Visual discrimination in the human newborn. *J. Comp. Physiol. Psychol.* **58**, 270–276.

Hershenson, M. (1967). Development of the perception of form. *Psychol. Bull.* **67**, 326–336.

Hershenson, M., Kessen, W. and Munsinger, H. (1967). Pattern perception in the human newborn: a close look at some positive and negative results. *In* "Models for the Perception of Speech and Visual Form" (Ed. W. Wathen-Dunn), pp. 282–290. M.I.T. Press, Cambridge, Mass.

Hinde, R. A. (1962). Some aspects of the imprinting problem. *Sym. Zool. Soc. Lond.* **8**, 129–138.

Honkavaara, Sylvia (1961). The psychology of expression. *Brit. J. Psychol. Monogr.* No. 32.

Hooff, J. A. R. A. M. van (1967). The facial displays of the catarrhine monkeys and apes. *In* "Primate Ethology" (Ed. D. Morris), pp. 7–68. Weidenfeld & Nicolson, London.

Hore, T. (1970). Social class differences in some aspects of the nonverbal communication between mother and preschool child. *Aust. J. Psychol.* **22**, 21–27.

Hunt, J. McV. (1965). Intrinsic motivation and its role in psychological development. *Nebraska Symp. Motiv.* **13**, 189–282.

Hunt, J. McV. (1970). Attentional preference and experience: I. Introduction. *J. Genet. Psychol.* **117**, 99–107.

Hutt, Corinne (1969). Exploration, arousal, and autism. *Psychol. Forsch.* **33**, 1–8.

Hutt, Corinne and Hutt, S. J. (1970). "Direct Observation and the Measurement of Behaviour". Thomas, Springfield, Ill.

Hutt, Corinne and Ounsted, C. (1966). The biological significance of gaze aversion with particular reference to the syndrome of infantile autism. *Behavl. Sci.* **11**, 346–356.

Hutt, Corinne, and Vaizey, M. Jane (1966). Differential effects of group density on social behaviour. *Nature (London)*, **209**, 1371–1372.

Hutt, S. J., Hutt, Corinne, Lee, D. and Ounsted, C. (1965). A behavioural and electroencephalographic study of autistic children. *J. Psychiat. Res.* **3**, 181–198.

Hutt, S. J., Lenard, H. G. and Prechtl, H. F. R. (1969). Psychophysiological studies in newborn infants. *In* "Advances in Child Development" (Ed. L. P. Lipsitt and H. W. Reese), Vol. 4, pp. 127–172. Academic Press, New York and London.

Jones, Mary C. (1926). The development of early behavior patterns in young children. *Pedagog. Sem.* **33**, 537–585.

Kagan, J. (1969a). Continuity in cognitive development during the first year. *Merrill-Palmer Q.* **15**, 101–119.

Kagan, J. (1969b). Some response measures that show relations between social class and the course of cognitive development in infancy. *In* "Stimulation in Early Infancy" (Ed. J. A. Ambrose), pp. 253–267. Academic Press, London and New York.

Kagan, J. (1969c). On the meaning of behaviour: illustrations from the infant. *Child Dev.* **40**, 1121–1134.

Kagan, J., Henker, Barbara A., Hen-Tov, Amy, Levine, Janet and Lewis, M. (1966). Infants' differential reactions to familiar and distorted faces. *Child Dev.* **37**, 519–532.

Kagan, J. and Lewis, M. (1965). Studies of attention in the human infant. *Merrill-Palmer Q.* **11**, 95–127.

Kaila, E. (1932). Die Reaktionen des Säuglings auf das menschliche Gesicht. *Annales Universitatis Aboensis*, **17** (Ser. B), 1–114.

Kanner, L. (1944). Early infantile autism. *J. Pediat.* **25**, 211–217.

Karmel, B. Z. (1969). The effect of age, complexity, and amount of contour on pattern preferences in human infants. *J. Exp. Child Psychol.* **7**, 339–354.

Kellogg, W. N. and Eagleson, P. M. (1931). The growth of social perception in different racial groups. *J. Educ. Psychol.* **22**, 367–375.

Koch, J. (1967). Conditioned orienting reactions in two-month-old infants. *Brit. J. Psychol.* **58**, 105–110.

Koehler, O. (1954). Das Lächeln als angeborene Ausdrucksbewegung. *Z. Mensch. Vererb. Konstit Lehre.* **32**, 390–398.

Koopman, Peggy R. and Ames, Elinor W. (1968). Infants' preferences for facial arrangements: a failure to replicate. *Child Dev.* **39**, 481–487.

Korner, Anneliese F. (1969). Neonatal startles, smiles, erections, and reflex sucks as related to state, sex, and individuality. *Child Dev.* **40**, 1039–1053.

Korner, Anneliese F. (1970). Visual alertness in neonates: individual differences and their correlates. *Percept. Mot. Skills*, **31**, 499–509.

Korner, Anneliese F. and Grobstein, R. (1966). Visual alertness as related to soothing in neonates: implications for maternal stimulation and early deprivation. *Child Dev.* **37**, 867–876.

Korner, Anneliese F. and Thoman, Evelyn B. (1970). Visual alertness in neonates as evoked by maternal care. *J. Exp. Child Psychol.* **10**, 67–78.

Laroche, J. L. and Tcheng, F. (1965). Phases de sommeil et sourires spontanés. *Acta Psychol.* **24**, 1–28.

Lewis, M. (1969). Infants' responses to facial stimuli during the first year of life. *De. Psychol.* **1**, 75–86.

Lewis, M. and Goldberg, Susan (1969). Perceptual-cognitive development in infancy: a generalized expectancy model as a function of mother–infant interaction. *Merrill-Palmer Q.* **15**, 81–100.

Lewis, M., Bartels, Betty, Fadel, Diane and Campbell, Helen. (1966a). Infant attention: the effect of familiar and novel visual stimuli as a function of age. Paper to Eastern Psychological Association, 37th Annual Meeting, April 1966.

Lewis, M., Bartels, Betty, Campbell, Helen and Goldberg, Susan (1967a). Individual differences in attention: the relation between infants' condition at birth and attention distribution during the first year. *Amer. J. Dis. Child*, **113**, 461–465.

Lewis, M., Goldberg, Susan and Rausch, Marilyn (1967b). Attention distribution as a function of novelty and familiarity. *Psychon. Sci.* **7**, 227–228.

Lewis, M., Kagan, J., Campbell, Helen and Kalafat, J. (1966b). The cardiac response as a correlate of attention in infants. *Child Dev.* **37**, 63–71.

Lewis, M., Kagan, J. and Kalafat, J. (1966c). Patterns of fixation in the young infant. *Child Dev.* **37**, 331–341.

Ling, Bing-Chung (1942). A genetic study of sustained visual fixation and associated behavior in the human infant from birth to six months. *J. Genet. Psychol.* **61**, 227–277.

Lodge, Ann, Armington, J. C., Barnet, Ann B., Shanks, Betty L. and Newcomb, C. N. (1969). Newborn infants' electroretinograms and evoked electroencephalographic responses to orange and white light. *Child Dev.* **40**, 267–293,

Lorenz, K. (1966). "On Aggression" (translated by Margaret Wilson). Harcourt, Brace & World, New York.

Lu, Elsie G. (1967). Early conditioning of perceptual preference. *Child Dev.* **38**, 415–424.

Lytton, H. (1969). Parent-child interaction studies: an unresolved dilemma. Paper to British Psychological Society Annual Conference, Edinburgh, March 1969.

McCall, R. B. (1969). Magnitude of discrepancy and habituation rate as governors of the attentional response of infants to new stimuli. Paper to Society for Research in Child Development, Los Angeles.

McCall, R. B. (1970). Smiling and vocalization in infants as indices of perceptual-cognitive processes. Paper to American Psychological Association, Miami.

McCall, R. B. and Kagan, J. (1967a). Attention in the infant: effects of complexity, contour, perimeter, and familiarity. *Child Dev.* **38**, 939–952.

McCall, R. B. and Kagan, J. (1967b). Stimulus-schema discrepancy and attention in the infant. *J. Exp. Child Psychol.* **5**, 381–390.

McConnell, O. L. (1967). Control of eye-contact in an autistic child. *J. Child Psychol. Psychiat.* **8**, 249–255.

McGrew, W. C. (1969). An ethological study of agonistic behaviour in preschool children. *Proc. 2nd Int. Congr. Primat.* 149–159.

McGrew, W. C. (1972). Aspects of social development in nursery school children, with emphasis on introduction to the group. *In* "Ethological Studies of Infant Behaviour" (Ed. N. G. Blurton-Jones). Cambridge University Press, London.

McGurk, H. (1970). The role of object orientation in infant perception. *J. Exp. Child Psychol.* **9**, 363–373.

McReynolds, P. (1962). Exploratory behaviour: a theoretical interpretation. *Psychol. Rep.* **11**, 311–318.

Maudry, M. and Nekula, M. (1939). Social relations between children of the same age during the first two years of life. *J. Genet. Psychol.* **54**, 193–215.

Means, J. R. and Merrens, M. R. (1969). Interpersonal training for an autistic child *Percept. Mot. Skills*, **28**, 972–974.

Miranda, S. B. (1970). Visual abilities and pattern preferences of premature infant and full-term neonates. *J. Exp. Child Psychol.* **10**, 189–205.

Moffett, Adrienne (1969). Stimulus complexity as a determinant of visual attention in infants. *J. Exp. Child Psychol.* **8**, 173–179.

Morgan, G. A. and Ricciuti, H. N. (1969). Infant responses to strangers during the first year. *In* "Determinants of Infant Behaviour" (Ed. B. M. Foss), Vol. 4, pp. 253–272. Methuen, London.

Morris, D. (1967). "The Naked Ape". Cape, London.

Moss, H. A. (1967). Sex, age, and state as determinants of mother–infant interaction. *Merrill-Palmer Q.* **13**, 19–36.

Moss, H. A. and Robson, K. S. (1968). Maternal influences in early social visual behaviour. *Child Dev.* **39**, 401–408.

Moss, H. A. and Robson, K. S. (1970). The relation between the amount of time infants spend at various states and the development of visual behaviour. *Child Dev.* **41**, 509–517.

Moss, H. A., Robson, K. S. and Pedersen, F. A. (1969). Determinants of maternal stimulation of infants and consequences of treatment for later reactions to strangers. *Dev. Pyschol.* **1**, 239–246.

Mundas, Mollie (1969). Physical contact and the one-to-one relationship with autistic children. Paper to British Psychological Association Annual Conference, Edinburgh, March 1969.

Munsinger, H. and Weir, M. W. (1967). Developing perception and memory for stimulus redundancy. *J. Exp. Child Psychol.* **5**, 39–49.

Mussen, P. H., Conger, J. J. and Kagan, J. (1969). "Child Development and Personality" (3rd edition). Harper & Row, New York.

O'Connor, N. and Hermelin, Beate (1967). The selective visual attention of psychotic children. *J. Child Psychol. Psychiat.* **8**, 167–179.

Ottinger, D. R., Blatchley, Mary E. and Denenberg, V. (1968). Stimulation of human neonates and visual attentiveness. Paper to American Psychological Association.

Piaget, J. (1952). "The Origins of Intelligence in Children" (translated by Margaret Cook). International Universities Press, New York.

Pick, H. L., Pick, Anne D. and Klein, R. E. (1967). Perceptual integration in children. In "Advances in Child Development and Behavior" (Eds L. P. Lipsitt and C. C. Spiker), Vol. 3, pp. 192–223. Academic Press, New York and London.

Ploog, D. (1964). Verhaltensforschung und Psychiatrie. In "Psychiatrie der Gegenwart". Springer-Verlag, Berlin.

Polak, R. R., Emde, R. N. and Spitz, R. A. (1964a). The smiling response: II. Visual discrimination and the onset of depth perception. J. Nerv. Ment. Dis. 139, 407–415.

Polak, R. R., Emde, R. N. and Spitz, R. A. (1964b). The smiling response: I. Methodology, quantification, and natural history. J. Nerv. Ment. Dis. 139, 103–109.

Polunin, I. (1970). Visual and sound recording apparatus in ethnographic fieldwork. Curr. Anthrop. 11, 3–22.

Rheingold, Harriet L. (1956). The modification of social responsiveness in institutional infants. Monogr. Soc. Res. Child Dev. 21 No. 63.

Rheingold, Harriet L. (1961). The effect of environmental stimulation on social and exploratory behaviour in the human infant. In "Determinants of Infant Behaviour" (Ed. B. M. Foss), Vol. 1, pp. 143–171. Methuen, London.

Rheingold, Harriet L., Gewirtz, J. L. and Ross, Helen W. (1959). Social conditioning of vocalization in the infant. J. Comp. Physiol. Psychol. 52, 68–73.

Richards, M. P. M. (1972). Social interaction in the first weeks of human life. Psychiat. Neurol. Neurochir.

Richards, M. P. M. and Bernal, Judith, F. (1972). An observational study of mother–infant interaction. In "Ethological Studies of Infant Behaviour" (Ed. N. G. Blurton-Jones). Cambridge University Press, London.

Rivoire, Jeanne L. and Kidd, Aline H. (1966). Perception of colour, space, and movement in children. In "Perceptual Development in Children" (Eds Aline H. Kidd and Jeanne L. Rivoire), pp. 81–112. London University Press, London.

Robinson, R. J. (Ed.) (1969). "Brain and Early Behaviour: Development in the Foetus and Infant". Academic Press, New York and London.

Robson, K. S. (1967). The role of eye-to-eye contact in maternal–infant attachment. J. Child Psychol. Psychiat. 8, 13–26.

Robson, K. S., Pedersen, F. A. and Moss, H. A. (1969). Developmental observations of dyadic gazing in relation to the fear of strangers and social approach behavior. Child Dev. 40, 619–627.

Rubenstein, Judith (1967). Maternal attentiveness and subsequent exploratory behavior in the infant. Child Dev. 38, 1089–1100.

Ruskell, G. L. (1967). Some aspects of vision in infants. Brit. Orthop. J. 24, 25–31.

Rutter, M. and Bartak, L. (1971). Causes of infantile autism: some considerations from recent research. J. Autism Child Schizophrenia, 1, 20–32.

Saayman, G., Ames, Elinor W. and Moffett, Adrienne (1964). Response to novelty as an indicator of visual discrimination in the infant. J. Exp. Child Psychol. 1, 189–198.

Sackett, G. P. (1965). Effect of rearing conditions upon the behavior of rhesus monkeys (Macaca mulatta). Child Dev. 36, 855–868.

Sackett, G. P. (1966). Monkeys reared in isolation with pictures as visual input: evidence for an innate releasing mechanism. Science, 154, 1468–1473.

Salatapek, P. (1968). Visual scanning of geometric figures by the human newborn. J. Comp. Physiol. Psychol. 66, 247–258.

L

Salatapek, P. and Kessen, W. (1966). Visual scanning of triangles by the human newborn. *J. Exp. Child Psychol.* **3**, 155–167.

Salzen, E. A. (1963). Visual stimuli eliciting the smiling response in the human infant. *J. Genet. Psychol.* **102**, 51–54.

Scarr, Sandra and Salatapek, P. (1970). Patterns of fear development during infancy. *Merrill-Palmer Q.* **16**, 53–90.

Schaffer, H. R. (1966). The fear of strangers and the incongruity hypothesis. *J. Child Psychol. Psychiat.* **7**, 95–106.

Schaffer, H. R. (1971). "The Growth of Sociability". Penguin Books, Harmondsworth, Middx.

Schaffer, H. R. and Emerson, Peggy E. (1964a). The development of social attachments in infancy. *Monogr. Soc. Res. Child Dev.* **29**, No. 94.

Schaffer, H. R. and Emerson, Peggy E. (1964b). Patterns of response to physical contact in early human development. *J. Child Psychol. Psychiat.* **5**, 1–13.

Schaffer, H. R. and Parry, M. H. (1969). Perceptual-motor behaviour in infancy as a function of age and stimulus familiarity. *Brit. J. Psychol.* **60**, 1–9.

Schaffer, H. R. and Parry, M. H. (1970). Effects of short-term familiarization on infants' perceptual-motor coordination in a simultaneous discrimination situation. *Brit. J. Psychol.* **61**, 559–569.

Schneirla, T. C. (1959). An evolutionary and developmental theory of biphasic processes underlying approach and withdrawal. *Neb. Symp. Motiv.* **7**, 1–41.

Schneirla, T. C. (1965). Aspects of stimulation and organization in approach-withdrawal processes underlying vertebrate behavioral development. *In* "Advances in the Study of Behavior" (Eds D. S. Lehrman and R. A. Hinde), Vol. 1, pp. 1–74. Academic Press, New York and London.

Schmidt, W. H. O. and Hore, T. (1970). Some nonverbal aspects of communication between mother and preschool child. *Child Dev.* **41**, 889–896.

Schopler, E. (1965). Early infantile autism and receptor processes. *Archs. Gen. Psychiat.* **13**, 327–335.

Scott, R. A. (1969). The socialization of blind children. *In* "Handbook of Socialization Theory and Research" (Ed. D. A. Goslin), pp. 1025–1045. Rand, McNally, Chicago.

Sherman, M. C. (1927). The differentiation of emotional response in infants: I. Judgment of emotional response from motion picture views and from actual observation. *J. Comp. Psychol.* **7**, 265–284.

Simpson, W. R. and Capetanopoulos, Cynthia (1968). Reliability of smile judgments. *Psychon. Sci.* **12**, 57.

Sluckin, W. (1970). "Early Learning in Man and Animal". Allen & Unwin, London.

Söderling, B. (1959). The first smile: a developmental study. *Acta Pediat.* **48** Suppl. 117, 78–82.

Sokolov, Y. N. (1963). "Perception and the Conditioned Reflex" (translated by S. W. Waydenfeld). Macmillan, New York.

Spears, W. C. and Hohle, R. H. (1967). Sensory and perceptual processes in infancy. *In* "Infancy and Early Childhood—A Handbook and Guide to Human Development" (Ed. Yvonne Brackbill), pp. 52–85. Free Press, New York.

Spitz, R. A. (1963). Ontogenesis, the proleptic function of emotion. *In* "Expression of the Emotions in Man" (Ed. P. H. Knapp), pp. 43–59. International Universities Press, New York.

Spitz, R. A. and Wolf, Kathrine M. (1946). The smiling response: a contribution to the ontogenesis of social relations. *Genet. Psychol. Monogr.* **34**, 57–125.

Stechler, G. (1964). Newborn attention as affected by medication during labor. *Science*, **144**, 315–317.

Stechler, G., Bradford, Susan and Levy, H. (1966). Attention in the newborn: effect on motility and skin potential. *Science*, **151**, 1246–1248.

Stechler, G. and Latz, Elizabeth (1966). Some observations on attention and arousal in infants. *J. Amer. Acad. Child Psychiat.* **5**, 517–525.

Thomas, H. (1965). An experimental study of infant visual fixation response. *Child Dev.* **36**, 629–638.

Thomas, A., Chess, Stella, Birch, H. B. and Hertzig, Margaret E. (1960). A longitudinal study of primary reaction patterns in children. *Compr. Psychiat.* **1**, 103–112.

Thompson, Jane (1941). Development of facial expressions in blind and seeing children. *Archs. Psychol. N.Y.* **37**, No. 264.

Todd, G. A. and Palmer, B. (1968). Social reinforcement of infant babbling. *Child Dev.* **39**, 591–596.

Tomkins, S. S. (1962). "Affect, Imagery, and Consciousness, Vol. 1 The Positive Affects". Springer, New York.

Turkewitz, G., Birch, H. G., Moreau, Tina, Levy, Linda and Cornwell, Anne (1966). Effects of auditory stimulation or directional eye-movements in the human neonate. *Anim. Behav.* **14**, 93–101.

Uzgiris, Ina C. and Hunt, J. McV. (1970). Attentional preference and experience: II. An exploratory longitudinal study of the effect of visual familiarity and responsiveness. *J. Genet. Psychol.* **117**, 109–121.

Vincze, Maria (1971). The social contacts of young children reared together. *Early Child Dev. Care*, **1**, 99–109.

Vine, I. (1970). Communication by facial-visual signals. *In* "Social Behaviour in Birds and Mammals, Essays on the Social Ethology of Animals and Man" (Ed. J. H. Crook), pp. 279–354. Academic Press, London and New York.

Wahler, R. G. (1967). Infant social attachments: a reinforcement theory interpretation and investigation. *Child Dev.* **38**, 1079–1088.

Walters, R. H. and Parke, R. D. (1964). Social motivation, dependency, and susceptibility to social influence. *In* "Advances in Experimental Social Psychology" (Ed. L. Berkowitz), Vol. 1, pp. 231–276. Academic Press, New York and London.

Walters, R. H. and Parke, R. D. (1965). The role of the distance receptors in the development of social responsiveness. *In* "Advances in Child Development and Behavior" (Eds L. P. Lipsitt and C. C. Spiker), Vol. 2, pp. 59–96. Academic Press, New York and London.

Washburn, R. W. (1929). A study of the smiling and laughing of infants in the first year of life. *Genet. Psychol. Monogr.* **6**, 397–535.

Watson, J. B. (1924). "Behaviorism". Norton, New York.

Watson, J. S. (1966). Perception of object orientation in infants. *Merrill-Palmer Q.* **12**, 73–94.

Watson, J. S. (1967a). Why is a smile? *Trans-action*, May, 36–39.

Watson, J. S. (1967b). Memory and "contingency analysis" in infant learning. *Merrill-Palmer Q.* **13**, 55–76.

Watson, J. S. (1968). Operant fixation in visual preference behavior in infants. *Psychon. Sci.* **12**, 241–242.

Watson, J. S. (1970). Cognitive-perceptual development in infancy: setting for the seventies. Paper to Merrill-Palmer Conference, Detroit, February 1970.

Watson, J. S. and Ramey, C. T. (1969). Reactions to response-contingent stimulation in early infancy. Paper to Society for Research in Child Development, Santa Monica.

Weisberg, P. (1963). Social and nonsocial conditioning of infant vocalizations. *Child Dev.* **34**, 377–378.

Weizmann, F., Cohen, Leslie B. and Pratt, R. Janene (1971). Novelty, familiarity, and the development of infant attention. *Dev. Psychol.* **4**, 149–154.

Weymouth, F. W. (1963). Visual acuity of children. *In* "Vision of Children" (Eds M. J. Hirsch and R. E. Wick), pp. 119–144. Chilton, Philadelphia.

White, B. L. (1969a). Child development research: an edifice without a foundation. *Merrill-Palmer Q.* **15**, 49–79.

White, B. L. (1969b). The initial coordination of sensorimotor schemas in human infants: Piaget's ideas and the role of experience. *In* "Studies in Cognitive Development—Essays in Honor of Jean Piaget" (Eds D. Elkind and J. H. Flavell), pp. 327–256. Oxford University Press, New York.

White, B. L. and Held, R. (1966). Plasticity of sensori-motor development in the human infant. *In* "The Causes of Behavior—Readings in Child Development and Educational Psychology" (2nd edition) (Eds. J. F. Rosenblith and W. Allinsmith), pp. 60–70. Bacon, Boston.

White, B. L., Castle, P. and Held, R. (1964). Observations on the development of visually-directed reaching. *Child Dev.* **35**, 349–364.

Wickelgren, Lyn W. (1967). Convergence in the human newborn. *J. Exp. Child Psychol.* **5**, 74–85.

Wickelgren, Lyn W. (1969). The ocular response of human newborns to intermittent visual movement. *J. Exp. Child Psychol.* **8**, 469–482.

Wilcox, Barbara M. (1969). Visual preferences of human infants for representations of the human face. *J. Exp. Child Psychol.* **7**, 10–20.

Wilcox, Barbara M. and Clayton, Frances L. (1968). Visual fixation on motion pictures of the human face. *J. Exp. Child Psychol.* **6**, 22–32.

Wolff, P. H. (1963). Observations on the early development of smiling. *In* "Determinants of Infant Behaviour" (Ed. B. M. Foss), Vol. 1, pp. 113–138. Methuen, London.

Wolff, P. H. (1965). The development of attention in young infants. *Ann. N.Y. Acad. Sci.* **118**, 815–830.

Wolff, P. H. (1969). The natural history of crying and other vocalizations in early infancy. *In* "Determinants of Infant Behaviour" (Ed. B. M. Foss), Vol. 4, pp. 81–109. Methuen, London.

Wolff, P. H. and White, B. L. (1965). Visual pursuit and attention in young infants. *J. Amer. Acad. Child Psychiat.* **4**, 473–484.

Yarrow, M. R. (1963). Problems of methods in parent–child research. *Child Dev.* **34**, 215-226.

Zelazo, P. R. and Komer, M. Joan (1971). Infant smiling to non social stimuli and the recognition hypothesis. *Child Dev.* **42**, 1327–1339.

6

Eyes, Eye-spots and Pupil Dilation in Non-verbal Communication

Ian Hindmarch

1 Eyes and eye-spots

This chapter aims to investigate the function played by the eyes and their representation as eye-like displays, or "eye-spots", in the non-verbal communication of both invertebrates and vertebrates, including primates and humans. An important parameter in studies on eye-spots has been found to be the relative size of the pupil. A consideration of pupillographic studies on humans will be presented with particular reference to the importance of pupil size both as an index of autonomic nervous system activity and as a cue of behavioural arousal in facial-visual signalling situations.

1.1 THE ETHOLOGICAL RELEVANCE OF EYE-SPOTS

Evolution is a temporal process of adaptation by a species to environmental contingencies. Selection pressures or selective forces in the environment direct, via a feedback process, the trans-generational changes. A measure of how effectively a species has adapted is in the mean survival value of particular genes or genetic attributes.

Coss (1970) has suggested that selection pressure in some animal species has caused evolutionary changes in their use of visual stimuli to satisfy the basic needs of intra-species communication and inter-species recognition, particularly of predators and other aggressors. Certain of these visual cues act as releaser stimuli to produce stereotyped behaviour patterns in some animal species. This is particularly noticeable in many of the courtship rituals of gannets and gulls, where "posturing" and "show" behaviours elicit reciprocal responses. Often the visual display is an integral part of the patterning of the animals' skin and needs no particular stimulus situation for it to be exhibited. The characteristic "V" pattern on the viper, and the particular colourings of birds occupying ground, bush or tree habitats are typical examples. The foregoing examples of visual display naturally preclude any patterning of skin pigments conducive to camouflage, although camouflage could be regarded as a case of negative visual communication in that the organism does not indicate his presence.

The eye-spot usually takes the form of two concentric circles with the smaller one filled in solid colour while the surrounding annulus is of a contrasting or lighter colour. The general effect is of a rudimentary "eye" with a distinct "pupil". Usually these eye-spots appear in pairs along a lateral axis. The display or possession of eye-spots can either act to enhance intra-specific communication, deter possible aggressors, or encourage aggressors to attack the eye-spots themselves, which are in such cases situated in the least important part of the animal well away from the main body and vital centres.

1.1.1 *Eye-spot configurations in invertebrates*

A number of butterflies and moths display eye-spot patterns on their wings either to deter aerial attack by birds, or to encourage the predator to peck the wing tips displaying the eye-spots, so preserving the life of the butterfly. The eyed hawk moth (*Smerinthus ocellatus*) and the emperor moth (*Saturnia pavonia*) both display two pairs of ocelli. Blest (1957) has shown the effectiveness of the display of eye-spots in the peacock butterfly in reducing the aggressive responses of the insect's natural enemies. Chaffinches, yellow-buntings and great tits all showed the greatest avoidance response to eye-patterns containing multiple concentric rings, when drawn on butterfly shapes. Certain other insects have parasitized the eye-spots via Batesian mimicry, for example the caterpillar *Leucorhampha ornatus* displays a vivid pair of eyes on his posterior segment which serve as a "false head" to deceive, if not deter, potential predators.

Lethbridge (1969) goes so far as to state that the eye-spots on the wings of the peacock butterfly could not possibly have been produced by the trial and error process of chance mutation. He further suggests that these designs could only have been produced by a mind similar to that of man himself. However, it is generally accepted that Darwinian evolution proceeds upon random mutations within the genetic structure of an animal. Only those mutations that have a species-survival value will be retained. The mutational changes can affect the anatomical and physiological structure as well as the behavioural responses of the animal. Selective adaptation, e.g. the development of anatomical and nervous structures increasing the escape potential of a preyed-upon species, can result in corresponding changes in the behavioural response of the predator.

It is suggested that eye-spots have evolved through selection pressures connected with predation. In experimental situations, where predator–prey relationships are examined using models, the elimination of the characteristic eye-spot, whether its presence on a prey animal functions for the defence of the prey or whether the predator's own eyes serve to facilitate the prey's recognition of the predator, results in a gross change of the inter-species behavioural patterns.

1.1.2   *Eye-spots in vertebrates*

Protective eye-spots are not confined to insects. They are also found on fish such as the John Dorey (*Zeus faber*), and Wickler (1968) suggests that the eye-spots on the tail of the archer fish (*Chaetodon capistratus*) serve to deceive natural predators. Tinbergen (1958) hypothesized that the pronounced eye-patterns of some predators, e.g. stoats, owls and cats, could be innately recognized as avoidance configurations in species habitually preyed upon by these animals. Support for this hypothesis has been shown by Hinde (1954) who produced mobbing behaviour in chaffinches to dummy owls with characteristic eye-patterns. More recently Curio and Blaich (cited in Coss, 1970) have reported a decrease in the mobbing behaviour of flycatchers on a dummy owl if one eye was removed from the dummy.

Coss (1968a) suggests that the mimicry of eyes and a crude facial pattern on the hood of the King Cobra has evolved because of its proved effectiveness in agitating the Indian mongoose, the snake's natural predator. Snakes also use their own ocellus to produce threat or startle responses. Darwin (1831) comments upon the *Trigonocephalus*:

> The expression of this snake's face was hideous and fierce; the pupil consisted of a vertical slit in a mottled and coppery iris . . . I do not think I ever saw anything more ugly . . . I imagine this repulsive aspect originates from features placed in positions, with respect to each other, somewhat proportional to those of the human face.
>
> p. 99

1.1.3 *Eye-spots in primates*

Many species of apes and monkeys use a combination of stare and the display of large eye-spots to enhance postural threat behaviours. van Hooff (1967) reports such behaviour in the mangabey monkey (*Cercocebus torquatus*), while baboons often use coloured eye lids pulled over their eyes in contrast with the surrounding eye socket, to produce a supernormal eye-spot. The primates are most sensitive to eye-spot displays, and Köhler (1921) reports the response of his chimpanzee, Sultan, to a pair of black buttons sewn onto a cloth dummy in an eye-spot pattern: ". . . he went into paroxysms of terror and threatened recklessly to bite my fingers." Köhler (1925) notes that the particular eye-spot pattern of a horizontally placed pair of black buttons produced the immediate impression in his apes of something frightful, surpassed only by their fearful reaction to snakes. In 1921 Köhler wrote that only stimulus objects which represent elements of an animal's experience and with which he is familiar will produce behavioural reactions, save of curiosity, which are meaningful. Probably the reaction Köhler noticed in Sultan to a rudimentary eye-spot pattern was produced by a much more innate biological mechanism than mere familiarity.

Exline (1969) produced violent displays of aggression in macaque monkeys following prolonged eye-contact with humans. Wada (1961) found the cortically induced brain-stem potentials of the monkey in such a situation were temporarily reduced, suggesting an increased attentiveness by the monkey during visual contact with the eye-spot. Eye-spots are of course relevant to gaze behaviour, and Hubel and Wiesel (1962) have indicated that, for monkeys, circular symmetrical patterns are the most effective shapes for triggering responses in the lateral geniculate body and the retinal ganglion cells. Both these neural systems are part of the human pupillary reflex system and we will examine the implications of Hubel and Wiesel's work later. In man it is probable that the patterns produced in these cell bodies would be further analysed by memory systems, and that non-physiognomic eye-patterns would not trigger anything other than pattern receptors. However, as we will see below, the autonomic nervous system may function even in response to representational eye-spot configurations. Fantz and Nevis (1967) have shown infants to be more attentive to representational facial patterns when the two "eyes" have their correct displacement about an horizontal axis (see Vine, Chapter 5).

1.2 THE SIGNIFICANCE OF EYE-SPOTS FOR MAN

There can be little doubt that eyes and their symbolic representation as eye-spots have a rich significance in human culture. Coss (1968b) believes that facial expressions, including eye-spots, are physiological artefacts from pre-human ancestry with the prime function of communicating social dominance. The symbolic and metaphoric properties of eyes and eye-spots are rooted deep in human history, from the potency of the "evil eye" to the all-seeing "eye of God". Significantly Tolkien (1968) in his modern mythology "The Lord of the Rings" attributes the powerful evil force of Saumeron to the hypnotic all-seeing eye. Heaton (1968) claims the eye-spot configuration to be a prototype mandala, one of the oldest and most universal religious symbols. Jung (1958) found evidence from his analytic studies that the mandala of the "eye of God" symbolized universal awareness and a primal order of the total psyche. When individuals draw mandalas of eye-spot like configurations they are attempting to bring a transformation of their lives from chaos to order. Jacobi (1962), in her analysis of Jungian mandalas, comments upon the significance of the eye as a symbol of the ever changing qualities of the psyche and of the process of self-realization.

The ancient Egyptians used the representation of the eye as a symbol of majesty and power, as can be seen from the accentuated eye and eyebrow configurations on Egyptian mummies and funerary ornaments. Desroches-Noblecourt (1965) illustrates the importance of the pectoral incorporating the "sacred eye" and found about the neck of the mummy of Tutankhamen. Fishermen in Portugal and the Mediterranean still decorate the prows of their fishing craft with a pair of eye-spots to ward off evil spirits. The symbolism of eye-spots has been treated extensively by Koenig (1970), who provides still more examples.

The belief that an individual's personality, temperament, or psychological state may be judged from the look of his eyes has historical origins reaching back at least to the activity of early Chinese jade dealers in bargaining situations. Hess (1965) reports that the gaze of the two dealers would be directed at each other in the hopes of obtaining some indication of how the transaction was progressing since "words might lie but the pupillary size indicated the truth". Present day Customs and Excise Officers use much the same index of autonomic activity, i.e. pupil size, in detecting import tax evaders. Ernesto Guevara (1967), the Bolivian revolutionary, noticed another aspect of human functioning displayed by human eyes. He writes of Bolivian peasants: "you talk to them, and in the depths of their eyes it can be seen that they don't believe or understand".

The importance of eye-spots in inter-personal communication could be attributed to the early visual experiences of the child. The cult of the Eye Goddess originated some 5000 years B.C. in Syria and was represented by a figurine with enlarged eyes and large breasts, the areolae and nipples of which formed concentric rings similar to a second pair of eye-spots. It could be argued that the motif of this ancient Goddess may be described in terms of the attributes within a child's cognitive experience. The breasts and nipples of the mother provide the child with nourishment and oral gratification; her eyes are also frequently directed towards him and so these stimuli are an essential part of the first few months of most infants' lives. The changes in the colouration of the areolae in lactating females has not yet been fully explained and it could be argued that such changes enhance the eye-spot configuration provided by the mother's breast. Significant also is the greater pupillary dilation found in female subjects viewing transparencies of newly born babies (Hindmarch, 1970). So while the mother's pupil dilates to the sight of her child, the child could also be aware of the dilation of his mother's pupil and the resulting eye-spot configuration could possibly be an important communicator in this earliest dyadic interaction. Darwin (1872), too, recognized the importance of the early mother–child communication via the eyes, when he wrote:

> . . . they [the expressions of the eyes] serve as the first means of communication between the mother and her infant; she smiles approval, and this encourages her child on the right path; or frowns disapproval . . . they reveal her thoughts and intentions . . . more truly than do words which may be falsified.
>
> p. 16

The outlining and enhancing of the human eye by the use of paints, dyes and cosmetics is an ancient ritual, the origin of which is lost in antiquity. Cosmetics and colourings for eyes have been found in the ruins of the earliest civilizations. By using artificial colourings the human is able to accentuate his eye pattern and produce a super eye-spot, the nature of the highlighting of the eye being dependent upon its proposed function. Cotlow (1966) reports the accentuation of the eyes with rings and rays of white pigment in the Gahuku-Gama natives of the Wahgi Valley in New Guinea when preparing for ritual dancing at a "sing-sing". The deadly nightshade allegedly owes its Linnean name, *Atropa belladonna*, to its characteristic property of dilating the pupils of the eyes and producing the "belladonna", or beautiful woman, of the Italian Renaissance. More recently, Virtue (1927), claimed a preparation of belladonna and lard was useful as "a local application for dilating the pupil of the eye".

Morris (1967) suggests that the wearing of spectacles or sunglasses enhances the eye-spot pattern, particularly in a fixed stare situation. He says: "If we are looked at by someone wearing glasses, we are being given a super stare." No doubt Morris would claim that the discomfort felt by individuals in such situations is due to the super-eye-spots seeming more aggressive. However, Argyle *et al.* (1968) would account for the discomfort in terms of a reduced visibility of interactional cues such as direction of looking, pupil size, eyebrow patterns, etc. Sommer (1969) reports that staring at an individual in order to dislodge him from a queue or seat is as effective, in many instances, as a "spatial invasion", i.e. entering into close physical proximity. Eye contact, gaze and directional looking behaviours are examined elsewhere in this book (cf. Argyle, 1969; Vine, 1970; von Cranach, 1971), and undoubtedly it is the interaction of the eye-pattern, the duration of the looking behaviour, and the relationship of the participants in the situation which produces the arousal or aggressive components noticed by many researchers. As we have noted, the signalling potential of the eye is often enhanced by local colouration, and Coss (1970) suggests that the white sclera surrounding the human iris, and the arcs of the eyebrows have evolved to strengthen the eye-spot pattern in gaze signalling behaviours. Blurton-Jones (1967), in his analysis of the social behaviour of children from three to five years old, reported that aggressive behaviour was normally accompanied by a fixed stare. Argyle and Dean (1965) postulate an affiliative-conflict theory of eye-contact which maintains an equilibrium of intimacy for any dyadic interaction. Intimacy is defined as a joint function of several non-verbal communicative factors, e.g. proximity, eye-contact, smiling. No doubt pupil dilation or constriction could play its part in maintaining this equilibrium, especially if the dyadic interaction takes place at close quarters. Coss (1967) maintains that eye-spots have arousing properties in humans which in some way parallel the flight or aversive reaction to eye-spots found in primates and some lower vertebrates. The phenomenological impact of eye-spots would thus seem to owe its origin to ethological factors.

2 The pupil

2.1 THE PUPILLARY REFLEX

Darwin (1872) was probably the first supporter of the theory that certain measurable variables can act as a general index of autonomic or emotional arousal. In "The Expression of the Emotions in Man and Animals" he states: "There is an intimate relationship which exists between almost all the emotions and their outward manifestations."

Before considering pupil size as an index of autonomic nervous system arousal, and its role in non-verbal communication processes, we must examine its prime function in controlling the amount of light entering the eye.

The neural pathways of the pupillary light reflex have been extensively investigated and are fairly well known (e.g. Trolestra, 1968). Incident light is detected by the retina and from there signals are transmitted via the pupillomotor fibres of the optic nerve to the pretectal region. This sends signals to the Edinger-Westphal nucleus, from which messages are transmitted via the 3rd cranial nerve, the ciliary ganglion and the short ciliary nerve to neuromuscular junctions in the iris muscles. Normally, that is under changing conditions of environmental lighting, a feedback loop operates from the pupil area output to light input, since the iris acts as a variable diaphragm for controlling the light incident upon the retina. The iris muscles which dilate the pupil in the light reflex are controlled by the sympathetic branch of the autonomic nervous system, but the postganglionic fibres of the ciliary nerve emanating from the ciliary ganglion are a branch of the parasympathetic nervous system. These two systems function in a complementary manner to constrict or dilate the pupil dependent upon the light entering the eye. The optic nerve (2nd cranial nerve) arises from the retina of the eye and proceeds via the optic tract, lateral geniculate body, and superior brachium to end near the superior colliculi. Light incident upon the retina will operate the pupillary reflex as well as stimulating the retinal-cortical system of visual perception.

Gardner (1969) regards the retina as part of the central nervous system, and we can thus now see the relevance of Hubel and Wiesel's (1962) work on the lateral geniculate body. Concentric and symmetrical circular patterns were found to be most effective in producing responses both in the lateral geniculate body and in the retinal ganglion cells. Since the lateral geniculate body is a crucial part of our visual system, and is linked to the pupillary reflex via the pupillomotor fibres of the 2nd cranial nerve, we could assume that pupillary change under conditions of constantly stable lighting would be indicative of changes in the nervous activity between retina and cortex, and of the variation in autonomic nervous activity. In fact under conditions of fixed background lighting the pupillary dilations occurring concomitant with emotional arousal are controlled via the parasympathetic branch of the autonomic nervous system. It is the ability of the pupil to indicate parasympathetic activity that makes it a useful tool in the investigations of emotional reactions.

2.2   PUPILLARY DILATION AND CONSTRICTION

As well as displaying concomitant variation with the level of autonomic activity, the pupil responds (in constant lighting conditions) by constricting or dilating in a variety of situations from cognitive processing tasks to affective response situations. These specific situations we will consider later, but first a consideration of pupil dilation as an index of general arousal is required.

2.2.1   *Pupillary response and other indices of autonomic arousal*

If the size of the pupil of the eye indicates our emotional condition or state of general arousal then it could function in an interpersonal communication network in much the same way as smiling, sweating, directional looking behaviour and other micro-cues such as the raising and lowering of the eyebrows. Indeed Coss (personal communication, 1970) has shown consistent correlations between verbal expression in a paired preference choice situation and the raising and lowering of the eyebrows, while Brunswik (1939) showed the importance of such micro-cues in establishing the characteristic features of the human expressions of intellect, sorrow and joy.

Autonomic activity has commonly been measured using several parameters. Heart rate, blood pressure, galvanic skin response and respiration rate have all been utilized to produce indices of arousal. However, few of these measures have any significant external correlates, so their ability to act as cues in communication processes is limited. Sweating on the palm of the hand is an index of autonomic arousal but is only of limited use in transmitting information or cues about a person's inner state, since a receptor has to touch the stimulus in order to sense the sweating. Apart from Coss' work on aspects of eyebrow positions, we may, however, mention that von Cranach et al. (1969) have explored the rate of eyeblink as an index of autonomic arousal. Both the positions of the eyebrows and the rate of eyeblink could act as cues in any interaction situation, and so, potentially, the receipt of information from the eyes of another can be an ongoing process en-abling a continuous monitoring of autonomic state independent of actual physical contact; although naturally it is dependent upon the physical proximity being close enough to allow discrimination of cues such as these or of pupil size to take place.

Multidimensional polygraphic studies have been made of heart rate, palmar conductance and blood pressure. However, intercorrela-tions between these measures, which might yield a general index of arousal, are typically poor and mostly of limited utility.

Lazarus (1965) admits that intercorrelations from these multidi-mensional studies are, at best, only modest. Even under the most favourable conditions there are spasmodic changes within the auto-nomic nervous system which produce unreliable data for intercorrela-tive studies. Emphasis has, therefore, been placed upon the unique, idiosyncratic variations of a single autonomic index, such as pupil dilation. There is still a variation in autonomic activity on a random basis, but it is possible to identify three specific sources producing the greater part of this variance (Ax, 1953). The individual's response specificity is one source of variance, so using one subject under a variety of stimulus conditions would be most fruitful in studies of the relation-ship between autonomic measures and subjects' responses. The indi-vidual's interpretation or perceptual "set" of the stimulus object is naturally another important variable, as is the nature of the stimulus object itself. Wikler (1952) lays great emphasis upon the importance of the stimulus object characteristics, and he further asserts the necessity of specifying the precise conditions under which the behavioural phen-omena of arousal, e.g. aversive reactions, potential aggression, pleasure and "fight" or "flight" responses are concomitant with or dissociated from our observations of autonomic activity. Different stimulus con-figurations no doubt produce patterning among the autonomic indica-tors of arousal; further variance is added from situational or contextual variables, viewing conditions and the personality characteristics of the observer. In short, one of the most important determining variables of autonomic activity is the particular overall stimulus situation under consideration. In the subsequent consideration of experiments on pupil dilation it will be seen that a number of aspects of the varying conclusions of different researchers are directly attributable to differ-ences in the stimulus objects.

There still exists, however, a relationship between electro-cortical arousal, autonomic arousal and behavioural arousal, which may be considered different forms of "arousal", each complex in itself (Lacey, 1956). Any study using autonomic activity as an index of arousal must beware of making false assumptions, based on the spasmodic variation of the autonomic measure, regarding behavioural responses to stimulus situations. As an illustrative case (Cohen *et al.*, 1962) consider the slight decrease in heart rate when viewing a "pretty girl" and the slight increase in heart rate when viewing an "obnoxious" stimulus, e.g. a post-mortem dissection. In these two situations the autonomic activity (heart rate) is as much determined by the subject's cognitive appraisal of the "pretty" and the "obnoxious" elements of the stimulus charac-teristics as it is by the actual physical stimulus.

Although pupil size may not be an effective general index of auto-nomic activity, it has proved useful in monitoring the course of specific functions during the course of various psychological investigations. Kahneman *et al.* (1969), report that of the various indices of autonomic activity—electrodermal, heart rate, blood pressure, peripheral vaso-constriction and pupil dilation—employed in their study of problem-solving performance, the most consistent index of arousal was obtained from readings of pupil size.

2.2.2 *Pupillary response as a specific index of autonomic activity*

We have mentioned the importance of considering the characteristics of the stimulus object, experimental and situational conditions and the attitudinal "frame of mind" of the subject when trying to establish relationships between pupillary response and autonomic activity. Nunnally *et al.* (1967) monitored subjects' pupil size during five different tasks: (1) while lifting weights; (2) during loud tone stimuli; (3) while viewing novel stimulus pictures; (4) while viewing pictures with unpleasant or pleasant characteristics; (5) during the threat of a gunshot. They found a covariant relationship only between the size of the pupil and the presence or absence of the threat of a gunshot. Enough has been said about the inter- and intra-subject variation in autonomic activity which could explain why the unpleasant–pleasant stimuli did not produce consistent variations across subject groups. Webster *et al.* (1968) suggest that just as there is great inter-subject difference in the magnitude of the pupillary response to light, and since the motor system controlling the pupil diameter must be the same for dilations under stable lighting, then there must be inter-individual variations of pupil size under stable lighting conditions which are not related to the stimulus objects. The suggestion is that the variations in pupil size reported by observers in subjects under different stimulus conditions could be due to differences in their pupillomotor systems and not to variations in attitudinal, cognitive or affectual arousal.

a. *Psychophysical investigations and pupil size* Using the psychophysical method of constant stimuli, Kahneman and Beatty (1967) found that as the discrimination between a standard stimulus and a comparison stimulus became more difficult, so the pupil increased in size, i.e. dilated commensurate with the increasing difficulty of discriminating between the two stimuli. The authors concluded that pupil dilation is a valid indicator of processing load.

Although various authors have supported the theory that an increased cortical arousal produces an increase in the size of the pupil, the constriction of the pupil due to non-light-reflex acitivity is not explained so easily.

In perceptual defence experiments utilizing the recognition threshold for "taboo" words, Hutt and Anderson (1967) found an inverse correlation between pupil diameter and recognition threshold. The recognition threshold is raised, when the perceptual stimulus is "taboo", due to the constriction of the pupil and a resulting drop in the amount of perceptual information entering the eye. The reduction in information content increases the time needed to process it to a conclusion and so the recognition threshold is raised.

Bradshaw (1968a) used a reaction time task in which, by changing the sensory modality, masking the stimuli, or making the pre-stimulus period variable, the level of stimulus uncertainty was manipulated. The pupil of the eye reduced in size, and the response peaks tended to be flattened, with increasing stimulus uncertainty. However, the anticipation of a stimulus sequence produced a characteristic dilation of the pupil. Under these conditions the pupil seems to reflect quite closely the activity of the autonomic nervous system in showing the alerting responses or "preparedness" of the subject anticipating a stimulus. A more recent experiment (Bradshaw, 1969) showed that a motor response, such as button pressing or lever pulling, was not a necessary condition for producing a dilation of the pupil. However, the presence of motor activity is necessary to obtain peak dilations (Simpson and Paivio, 1968). If background illumination determines the baseline for pupil size, and providing this illumination is held constant, then any other variation from the baseline is a response dilation or constriction.

As the processing load increases in continuous tasks requiring a motor response so does the pupillary dilation. Bradshaw (1968b) found that numbers were relatively easy to process (in terms of producing a smaller pupil dilation) when compared with letters. The greatest variations in pupil size are associated with the most difficult tasks (Kahneman *et al.*, 1968b), since there is a valid correlation between perceptual-cognitive load, or mental activity, and pupil size. One of the major advantages of measures of pupillary response in psychophysical experimentation, over recording verbal reports, is that the nature of motivated perception is considered. Bokander (1967) utilized pupillography to determine which of the subjects' eyes was inhibited in a binocular conflict situation. Normal oral reports of subjects in perceptual or interpersonal conflict situations can be most unreliable since arousing stimuli may produce responses which are "censored" as regards verbal transmission, but their true nature is registered via pupillary response. The author's research (Hindmarch, 1971), on the monitoring of pupil size during conflict resolution in a dyad, found that the pupil size varied in accordance with the individual's decision-making process, and not with what was expressed verbally.

Polt and Hess (1968) found no significant differences in pupillary response to words of different length. They did find sex differences in pupillary response to words such as "hostile", "squirm", "flay" and "nude", but these differences were not statistically significant. The pupil response is a highly individualistic mechanism, and so of course inter-subject variability in the nature of the response can lead to difficulties as to what constitutes a "stimulus" in this and other situations.

b. *Memory and pupil size* We have seen how an increase in processing load is covariant with an increase in pupil dilation. Beatty and Kahneman (1966) have shown that the pupil is especially sensitive to the momentary load on a subject in short-term memory tasks. Recalling from long-term memory stores also increases the size of the pupil. Kahneman *et al.* (1968a) found that the pupil dilations decreased if words in a short-term memory task were grouped into threes. Grouping is thought to impose a rehearsal structure improving recall, i.e. imposing less effort, and so reducing the pupil dilation. Elshtain and Schaefer (1968) found an increase in pupil size during memorization of word lists, and Kahneman and Beatty (1966) postulate that "task difficulty" relates to the rate of change of the pupil size. The act of verbalizing experiences produces an increase in pupil size, while under conditions of continuous internal reference, i.e. thinking about a problem situation, the pupil constricts (Bernick and Oberlander, 1968).

c. *Pupil dilation and cognitive functioning* Detection failures in vigilance tasks cannot be explained by way of changes in pupil size (Kahneman *et al.*, 1967). The probability of detecting a visual signal is dependent upon the duration of presentation and other environmental factors. However, Hess and Polt (1964) found that pupil size related to the difficulty of mental multiplication problems, in that pupil size increased commensurate with an increase in task difficulty. The work of Shachnowich and Smirnow (see Hess and Polt, 1964) shows that stimulation of the occipital cortex, under constant illumination, reduces pupil size while frontal or temporal lobe stimulation increases the pupil size. This Russian work is consistent with Hess and Polt's findings, since mental activity and problem solving would be expected to create activity in the association areas of the brain. Schaefer *et al.* (1968) found that novel or unexpected stimuli produced the greatest pupil dilation, and Bradshaw (1968) concluded that pupil dilation was a sensitive measure of the varying levels of attention and arousal associated with information processing.

Kahneman and Peavler (1969), using monetary incentives in association learning tasks, found that pupillary dilation occurred when the rewarded digit was presented and an "incentive" dilation followed the correct response. They conclude that pupillary responses are related to effort but not to emotionality or state of arousal. Simpson and Hale (1969) concur with Kahneman and Peavler that pupillary dilation is an index of cognitive load. Paivio and Simpson (1966) found a pupillary dilation in subjects asked to create images of either abstract or concrete concepts; the pupillary dilation was found to be greater for the more abstract words. However, Paivio and Simpson (1968) could find no relationship between imagery ability and pupil size, and the authors suggest that the latency as opposed to the magnitude of the pupillary response is a more accurate indicator of cognitive difficulty. Paradoxically Colman and Paivio (1970) support the notion that pupillary dilation is an index of mental "effort", "load" or "arousal" during cognitive tasks and further state that the major variable in determining pupil size in all types of cognitive activity is the response requirement.

d. *Methodological considerations* Dooley and Lehr (1967), have made specific criticisms of Hess and Polt's work for its faulty experimental design, failure to utilize control groups, and for the use of non-parametric tests for significance when the data from the dependent variable (pupil size) was on a ratio scale. Woodmansee (1966) indicates many of the methodological problems inherent in pupillographic experiments. The interference from the light reflex is not easy to control when visual stimulus material is presented. Variations in pupil size of 1–2 per cent have been found when viewing grey, black and white areas of a photograph even when the overall brightness was constant. The establishing of a base line is most difficult since sympathetic, parasympathetic and supra-nuclear mechanisms are all activated and interrelated. The accommodation of the eye is closely linked to pupil size, and changes in pupil size are necessary under difficult viewing conditions and low illumination levels to ensure an optimal depth of field. Spasmodic variation, as in most autonomic indices of arousal, of 1 per cent of the pupil size occurs without any apparent reason, and test-retest reliability is often low. Vacchiano *et al.* (1968) account for the lack of significant relationships between pupil size and value-linked words in terms of the general "experimental research problems associated with pupillometrics".

2.2.3   *Emotions, attitudes and pupil dilation*

We have considered the possible conditions, both cognitive and perceptual, that can seemingly produce changes in pupil size, and can now examine the pupil as an indicator of emotion. Hess (1965) holds that pupillary response is "an accurate measure of interest, emotion, thought processes and attitudes". Barlow (1969) found a "perfect" agreement between pupillary responses and verbal preferences, expressed by subjects of known political allegiance viewing transparencies of their candidates. We would expect, then, that the pupillary response would indicate subjective attitudes and preferences; and Collins, Ellsworth and Helmreich (1967) did find positive correlations between the potency and activity dimensions of stimulus assessments according to Osgood's semantic differential, and pupil size. However, no correlation was found between pupil size and the evaluative dimension of the semantic differential. Hess's (1965) now classic experiment, in which male college students choosing between identical photographs of a girl preferred the girl whose pupils had been enlarged (by retouching the photographic negative), is supported by Stass and Willis (1967). They found that when subjects were asked to choose a partner for an experiment, there was a significant relationship between the frequency of choice and the size of the partner's pupils.

Hess *et al.* (1965) found that the pupils of heterosexual males had a greater dilation when looking at pictures of semi-nude and "pin-up" females than when looking at "similar" pictures of men. Homosexual males responded oppositely, and Hess *et al.* conclude that these changes in pupil size "permitted a clear-cut discrimination between the two groups", i.e. between homosexual and heterosexual men. Scott *et al.* (1967) express surprise at the results of Hess *et al.*, since most autonomic responses show a spontaneous variability which makes the assessment of interest patterns for small groups impossible. Furthermore, Scott *et al.* found a no greater than chance difference between the pupil dilation of male and female college students to pictures of semi-nude males and females, and the link between preference and pupil size was not conclusively demonstrated. In fact there is similarity, though no covariance, between measures of pupil dilation and indices such as palmar skin responses, showing that both are acting as an index of general autonomic activity, and so are prone to the spontaneous, spasmodic, variability of such measures.

Perhaps we *are* able to judge, as did Hess's (1965) jade dealers, when someone is impressed or shows preference simply from looking at the state of their pupils; but judgements about personality or psychological state are much more difficult. Although McCawley *et al.* (1966) found a general increase in pupillary activity with age they failed to find any significant difference between the dilations produced by "normal" and "psychiatric" patients. However, an intimate relationship between personality and the general level of pupillary activity can be found by reasoning from the neurochemical basis of pupillary change. Acetylcholine accounts for the level of pupillary constriction through its action as synaptic transmitter in the parasympathetic nervous system, while norepinephrine stimulates the sympathetic nervous system and so produces pupil dilation. Holmes (1967) showed that an increase in acetylcholine level was related to an increased awareness of environmental contingencies, as measured by performance in verbal conditioning tasks. Pupil dilation, on the other hand, was not related to the level of norepinephrine. These results can be explained in terms of the greater efficacy of neural transmission when acetylcholine is the synaptic transmitter. The relationship between personality, conditioning and synaptic transmission has already been established (Rozhdestvenskaya, 1955; Eysenck, 1957; Gray, 1964; Luria, 1966) and it could be that pupil dilation acts as an index of cortical as well as sub-cortical activity.

The early perceptual environment of the infant has been previously held to account for the importance of eye-spots in human culture (see also Chapter 5). Fitzgerald (1968) has shown that social stimuli, i.e. the mother's and other female faces elicit an increase in pupil size in 1-month-old babies. By the time the baby is 4 months old he shows a differential response, i.e. a greater pupil dilation to his mother's face compared with his reaction to other female faces. There were no significant differences in pupillary changes when the child viewed non-social stimuli, i.e. chequered and triangular shapes, during these first four months of life.

Generalizing from the data reported in this section is difficult since so many researchers have provided evidence for effects and relationships which are then repudiated by other investigators. Some authors even change their minds, several times within the space of a year, depending upon the co-authorship. However, we are able to say that the pupil does respond in non-light-reflex situations to stimuli or tasks which impose mental effort or require a cognitive or affective appraisal of a situation. The small disparities or even gross differences which occur between the data of different observers is probably due once again to the characteristic stimulus conditions of the different experiments. Few observers of the effects of cognitive tasks on pupil size have taken account of the importance of the stimulus situation as a determinant of the autonomic response pattern, even though attention has been drawn (Wikler, 1952; Lacey, 1969) to the essential nature of such considerations. Different stimulus situations, whether they be looking at pictures, requiring motor responses, anxiety producing, or painful, produce a characteristic patterning of autonomic indicators of arousal. Even if the objective stimulus situation is the same, the subject's attitude, "set", expectancy and personality can influence his perception of a situation and also the pattern of excitatory measures. In short, one of the most important determinants of autonomic activity is the context and situation in which a particular stimulus is presented.

3 Summary and conclusions

We have presented information from a variety of sources to emphasize the importance of eyes and their parameters, such as pupil size, eyebrow patterns, and gaze, in animal and human communication processes. Coss (1967) using schematic representations of eye-spots found that two circles containing concentric annuli placed about an horizontal axis were more effective in producing arousal, as measured by pupil dilation, than any other configuration in vertical or diagonal arrangement. Humans do pay attention to eyes during communication processes, especially when the interaction is at close quarters. It would be fruitless, however, to build a theory of signalling based solely on eye patterns, for there are so many variables, e.g. posture, gaze, personal space, sex, race and social class, which interrelate in non-verbal communication.

Hindmarch (1970) found that both male and female subjects averted their gaze from photographs showing male and female faces with artificially constricted pupils, more quickly than they did from the same photographs with enlarged pupils. Males viewing female faces with enlarged pupils, and to a lesser extent males viewing schematic eye-spots with enlarged "pupils", showed pupillary dilation. On the other hand there was pupillary dilation in females viewing facial photographs of males with constricted pupils. Although general trends as mentioned above were observed, no significant correlations were established. The author hypothesizes that the different stimuli producing the same response, i.e. pupil dilation, are in some way related to the biological mechanisms of communication via the eyes. Hess (1965) has demonstrated preference in males for females with dilated pupils, and we have already noted the use of belladonna by females to increase their attractiveness. It could be, then, that the dilation of the male's pupils is in some way a recognition sign or response to dilation by the female's pupils acting as a sexual display. Conversely the dilation in the female pupil, when viewing the constricted male pupil, may be some form of appeasement gesture. The small constricted pupil was regarded by many subjects in the author's experiments as "uncanny", "staring", "uncomfortable" or "aggressive". Exline (1969) and van Lawick-Goodall (1969) have both illustrated the importance of appeasement gestures in monkeys and apes who inadvertently stare or indulge in eye contact with higher status members of their group. Perhaps the human female dilates her pupils in response to "staring" or "aggressive" male eyes so producing an attractive or sexual display likely to lessen the probability of aggression by appeasement. Naturally these hypotheses are tentative and await confirmation or refutation from further experiments.

Investigations in the relationships between eyes, eye-spots, pupils and human communication are in their infancy; but over the past few years an increasing interest has been shown in the general problem area of pupillary response and interpersonal communication. Perhaps for the moment we should move cautiously and concur with Vine (1970): "Even for the eyes we have not yet isolated the crucial cues which are responsible for our ascription of particular expressive looks." (p. 336.)

References

Argyle, M. (1969). "Social Interaction". Methuen, London.

Argyle, M. and Dean, Janet (1965). Eye contact, distance and affiliation. *Sociometry*, **28**, 289–304.

Argyle, M., Lalljee, M. and Cook, M. (1968). The effects of visibility on interaction in a dyad. *Hum. Relat.* **21**, 3–18.

Ax, A. F. (1953). The physiological differentiation between fear and anger in humans. *Psychosom. Med.* **15**, 435–442.

Barlow, J. D. (1969). Pupillary size as an idex of preference in political candidates. *Percept. Mot. Skills*, **28**, 587–590.

Beatty, J. and Kahneman, D. (1966). Pupillary changes in two memory tasks. *Psychon. Sci.* **5**, 371–372.

Bernick, N. and Oberlander, M. (1968). Effect of verbalisation and two different modes of experience on pupil size. *Percept. Psychophys.* **3**, 327–328.

Blest, A. D. (1957). The function of eye-spot patterns in the lepidoptera. *Behaviour*, **11**, 209–255.

Blurton-Jones, N. G. (1967). An ethological study of some aspects of social behaviour of children in nursery schools. *In* "Primate Ethology" (Ed. D. Morris), pp. 347–368. Weidenfeld & Nicolson, London.

Bokander, I. (1967). Pupillographic recording in stereoscopically induced perceptual conflict. *Percept. Mot. Skills*, **24**, 1031–1037.

Bradshaw, J. L. (1968a). Pupillary changes and reaction time with varied stimulus uncertainty. *Psychon. Sci.* **13**, 69–70.

Bradshaw, J. L. (1968b). Load and pupillary changes in continuous processing tasks. *Brit. J. Psychol.* **59**, 265–271.

Bradshaw, J. L. (1968c). Pupil size and problem solving. *Quart. J. Exp. Psychol.* **20**, 116–122.

Bradshaw, J. L. (1969). Background light intensity and the pupillary response in a reaction time task. *Psychon. Sci.* **14**, 271–272.

Brunswik, E. (1939). Perceptual characteristics of schematised human figures. *Psychol. Bull.* **36**, 553.

Cohen, S. I., Silverman, A. J. and Shmavonian, B. M. (1962). Psychophysiological studies in altered sensory environments. *J. Psychosom. Res.* **6**, 259–281.

Collins, B. E., Ellsworth, Pheobe C. and Helmreich, R. L. (1967). Correlations between pupil size and the semantic differential: an experimental paradigm and pilot study. *Psychon. Sci.* **9**, 627–628.

Colman, F. and Paivio, A. (1970). Pupillary dilation and mediation processes during paired associate learning. *Can. J. Psychol.* **24**, 262–270.

Coss, R. G. (1967). New aesthetic concepts and consumer behaviour. Unpublished manuscript.

Coss, R. G. (1968a). Designing for social display. *J. School of Architecture, University of Virginia.* (Mimeograph).

Coss, R. G. (1968b). The ethological command in art. *Leonardo*, **1**, 274–287.

Coss, R. G. (1970). The perceptual aspects of eye-spot patterns and their relevance to gaze behaviour, *In* "Behaviour Studies in Psychiatry" (Eds S. J. Hutt and Corinne Hutt), pp. 121–147. Pergamon Press, Oxford.

Cotlow, L. (1966). "In Search of the Primitive". Little & Brown, Toronto.

Cranach, M. von (1971). The role of orienting behavior in human interaction. *In* "Environment and Behaviour, the Use of Space by Animals and Men" (Ed. A. H. Esser), pp. 217–237. Plenum Press, New York.

Cranach, M. von, Schmid, R. and Vogel, M. W. (1969). Über einige Bedingungen des Zusammen hanges von Lid schlag und Blickwendung. *Psychol. Forsch.* **33**, 68–78.

Darwin, C. (1831). "The Voyage of a Naturalist Around the World in H.M.S. Beagle". Routledge & Sons, London.

Darwin, C. (1872). "The Expression of the Emotions in Man and Animals". Murray, London.

Desroches-Noblecourt, C. (1965). "Life and Death of a Pharoah: Tutankhamen". Michael Joseph, London.

Dooley, R. P. and Lehr, D. J. (1967). Critique of a pupillary response experiment. *Percept. Mot. Skills*, **25**, 603–604.

Elshtain, E. L. and Schaefer, T. S. (1968). Effects of storage load and word frequency on pupillary responses during short-term memory. *Psychon. Sci.* **12**, 143–144.

Exline, R. (1969). Paper presented to XII International Congress of Psychology, London.

Eysenck, H. J. (1957). "The Dynamics of Anxiety and Hysteria". Routledge & Kegan Paul, London.

Fantz, R. L. and Nevis, Sonia (1967). Pattern preference and perceptual-cognitive development in early infancy. *Merrill-Palmer Quart.* **13**, 77–108.

Fitzgerald, H. E. (1968). Autonomic pupillary activity during early infancy and its relation to social and non-social visual stimuli. *J. Exp. Child Psychol.* **6**, 470–482.

Gardner, E. (1969). "Fundamentals of Neurology". Saunders, London.

Gray, J. A. (1964). "Pavlov's Typology". Pergamon Press, Oxford.

Guevara, E. (1967). Comment, *Time* 90 (Oct. 20th) 27.

Heaton, J. H. (1968). "The Eye". Tavistock, London.

Hess, E. H. (1965). Attitude and pupil size. *Sci. American*, **212**, 46–54.

Hess, E. H. and Polt, J. M. (1964). Pupil size in relation to mental activity during sample problem solving. *Science*, **143**, 1190–1192.

Hess, E. H., Seltzer, A. L. and Shlien, J. M. (1965). Pupil response of hetero- and homosexual males to pictures of men and women. *J. Abnorm. Psychol.* **70**, 165–168.

Hinde, R. A. (1954). Factors governing the changes in strength of a partially inborn response as shown by the mobbing behaviour of the chaffinch (*Fringilla coelebs*): I, II. *Proc. Roy. Soc. B*. **142**, 306–331, 331–358.

Hindmarch, I. (1970). Pupil size and non-verbal communication. *Proc. NATO Symp. Non-verbal Communication*, Oxford.

Hindmarch, I. (1971). The monitoring of pupil size during dyadic interaction (in preparation).

Holmes, D. S. (1967). Pupillary response, conditioning and personality. *J. Pers. Soc. Psychol.* **5**, 98–103.

Hoof, J. A. R. A. M. van (1967). The facial displays of the catarrhine monkeys and apes. *In* "Primate Ethology" (Ed. D. Morris), pp. 7–68. Weidenfeld & Nicolson, London.

Hubel, D. H. and Wiesel, T. N. (1962). Perceptive fields, binocular interaction and functional architecture in the visual cortex. *J. Psysiol.* **160**, 106–154.

Hutt, L. D. and Anderson, J. P. (1967). The relationship between pupil size and recognition threshold. *Psychon. Sci.* **9**, 477–478.

Jacobi, J. (1962). "The Psychology of C. G. Jung". Routledge & Kegan Paul, London.

Jung, C. G. (1958). "The Psychology of Eastern Meditation". (Collected Works, Vol. 11). Routledge & Kegan Paul, London.

Kahneman, D. and Beatty, J. (1966). Pupil diameter and load on memory. *Science*, **154**, 1583–1585.

Kahneman, D. and Beatty, J. (1967). Pupillary responses in a pitch discrimination task. *Percept. Psychophys.* **2**, 101–105.

Kahneman, D., Beatty, J. and Pollack, I. (1967). Perceptual deficit during a mental task. *Science*, **157**, 218–219.

Kahneman, D., Onuska, L. and Wolman, R. E. (1968a). Effects of grouping on the pupillary response in a short-term memory task. *Quart. J. Exp. Psychol.* **20**, 309–311.

Kahneman, D. and Peavler, W. S. (1969). Incentive effects and pupillary changes in association learning. *J. Exp. Psychol.* **79**, 312–318.

Kahneman, D., Peavler, W. S. and Onuska, L. (1968b). Effects of verbalization and incentive on the pupil response to mental activity. *Canad. J. Psychol.* **22**, 186–196.

Kahneman, D., Tursky, B., Shapiro, D. and Crider, A. (1969). Pupillary heart rate, and skin resistance changes during a mental task. *J. Exp. Psychol.* **79**, 164–167.

Koenig, O. (1970). "Kultur und Verhaltensforschung". Deutscher Taschenbuch, Munich.

Kohler, W. (1921). Some contributions to the psychology of chimpanzees. *Psychol. Forsch.* **1**.

Kohler, W. (1925). "The Mentality of Apes". Harcourt Brace, New York.

Lacey, J. I. (1956). An evaluation of autonomic responses: toward a general solution. *Ann. N.Y. Acad. Sci.* **67**, 123–164.

Lacey, J. I. (1969). Somatic response patterning and stress: some revisions of activation theory. *In* "Psychological Stress" (Eds M. H. Appley and R. Trumbull), pp. 14–42. Appleton-Century-Crofts, New York.

Lawick-Goodall, Jane van (1969). Some aspects of communication in a group of free living chimpanzees, *Pan satyrus schweinfurthi*, in the Gombe National Park, Tanzania, East Africa. Paper to NATO Symposium on non-verbal communication, Wadham College, Oxford.

Lazarus, R. S. (1965). "Psychological Stress and the Coping Process". McGraw-Hill, New York.

Lethbridge, T. (1969). "The Monkey's Tail: A Study in Evolution and Parapsychology". Routledge & Kegan Paul, London.

Luria, A. R. (1966). "Human Brain and Psychological Processes". Harper & Row, New York.

McCawley, A., Stroenel, C. F. and Clueck, B. C. (1966). Pupillary reactivity, psychologic disorder and age. *Arch. Gen. Psychiat.* **14**, 415–418.

Morris, D. (1967). "The Naked Ape". Cape, London.

Nunnally, J. C., Knott, P. D., Duchnowski, A. and Parker, R. (1967). Pupillary response as a general measure of activation. *Percept. Psychophys.* **2**, 149–155.

Paivio, A. and Simpson, H. M. (1966). The effect of word abstractness and pleasantness on pupil size during an imagery task. *Psychon. Sci.* **5**, 55–56.

Paivio, A. and Simpson, H. M. (1968). Magnitude and latency of the pupillary response during an imagery task as a function of stimulus abstractness and imagery ability. *Psychon. Sci.* **12**, 45–46.

Polt, J. M. and Hess, E. H. (1968). Changes in pupil size to visually presented words. *Psychon. Sci.* **12**, 389–390.

Rozhdestvenskaya, V. I. (1955). The role of the pupil in conditioned changes in the sensitivity of the eye. *Probl. Fiziol. Opt.* **11**, 25–29.

Schaefer, T., Ferguson, J. B., Klein, J. A. and Rawson, E. B. (1968). Pupillary responses during mental activities. *Psychon. Sci.* **12**, 137–138.

Scott, T. R., Wood, D. Z., Wells, W. H. and Morgan, D. I. (1967). Pupillary response and sexual interest re-examined. *J. Clin. Psychol.* 433–438.

Simpson, H. M. and Hale, S. M. (1969). Pupillary changes during a decision-making task. *Percept. Mot. Skills*, **29**, 495–498.

Simpson, H. M. and Paivio, A. (1968). Effects on pupil size on manual and verbal indicators of cognitive task fulfilment. *Percept. Psychophys.* **3**, 185–190.

Sommer, R. (1969). "Personal Space". Prentice-Hall, Englewood Cliffs, N.J.

Stass, J. W. and Willis, F. N., Jr. (1967). Eye-contact, pupil dilation and personal preference. *Psychon. Sci.* **7**, 375–376.

Tinbergen, N. (1958). "Curious Naturalists". Country Life, London.

Tolkien, J. R. R. (1968). "The Lord of the Rings". Allen & Unwin, London.

Trolestra, A. (1968). Detection of time-varying light signals as measured by the pupillary response. *J. Opt. Soc. Amer.* **58**, 685–690.

Vacchiano, R. B., Strauss, P. S., Ryan, S. and Hochman, L. (1968). Pupillary response to value-linked words. *Percept. Mot. Skills*, **27**, 207–210.

Vine, I. (1970). Communication by facial-visual signals. *In* "Social Behaviour in Birds and Mammals" (Ed. J. H. Crook), pp. 279–354. Academic Press, London.

Virtue, S. (1927). "A Twentieth Century Medica". Vol. IV. Virtue, London.

Wada, J. A. (1961). Modification of cortically induced responses in brain stem by shift of attention in monkeys. *Science*, **133**, 40–42.

Webster, J. G., Cohen, G. H. and Boynton, R. M. (1968). Optimising the use of the criterion response for the pupil light reflex. *J. Opt. Soc. Amer.* **58**, 419–424.

Wickler, W. (1968). "Mimicry in Plants and Animals". Weidenfeld & Nicolson, London.

Wikler, A. (1952). Pharmacologic dissociation of behaviour and EEG "sleep patterns" in dogs: morphine, N-allylnormorphine and atropine. *Proc. Soc. Exp. Biol. Med.* **79**, 261–265.

Woodmansee, J. J. (1966). Methodological problems in pupillographic experiments. *Proc. 74th Ann. Conv. Amer. Psychol. Ass.* pp. 133–134. A.P.A., Washington, D.C.

PART 2

Structural Analysis of Facial Expressions

7

The Relation Between Emotion and Expression

Nico H. Frijda

1   Components of emotion

1.1   AMBIGUITIES IN EXPRESSION AND PERCEPTION OF EMOTION

This chapter concerns the relationship between emotion and expression. This relationship is far from simple and straightforward. Students of emotion, interested in diagnosing emotional reactions under different circumstances, are usually baffled by the variability of manifestations, the unreliability of cues, the lack of solid correlations. There exists a painful paradox. On the one hand, expression seems to be the clue to emotion in others, and a rich one at that. On the other hand, the ambiguity of expressive patterns is striking.

Except for strong primary emotions such as startle, fear or joy, expressions presented in isolation are rarely identified with a large measure of success. The percentage of correct judgements is usually low (Féléky, 1914; Kanner, 1931; Woodworth, 1938); in one study using films of spontaneous expressions, a "percentage correct" of only 48 per cent was obtained (Frijda, 1953). The variety of interpretations offered for any one expression may be quite large. Also, judges generally show little agreement with each other. Interpretation of expression, moreover, is strongly and often drastically influenced by situational cues (Frijda, 1969), sometimes modifying even the pleasantness–unpleasantness distinction (Frijda, 1958).

Examination of the variety of expressions naturally accompanying a given emotion demonstrates additional ambiguity. Any emotion, as labelled by observers having full knowledge of the situation and of the subject's reaction, or as labelled by the subject himself, may manifest itself in a number of ways. There are many different ways to be angry, sad or afraid (Landis, 1924; Frijda, 1953). There exists little systematic information concerning the ecology of expression; that information which does exist, however, clearly indicates that no one-to-one relationship holds between emotions and expressions. It is true that one can find expression patterns which unambiguously represent several of the "primary" emotions (Tomkins and McCarter, 1964; Ekman and Friesen, 1971); this does not imply, however, that those emotions are always expressed in that particular and seemingly characteristic way. For emotions other than the "primary" ones the variability of expression is even more pronounced (Frijda, 1953).

On the basis of these data it has been suggested that emotion and expression are only loosely connected to each other by some learned and conventional bond (e.g. Landis, 1924). This does not seem the most appropriate hypothesis, however. Subjectively it does not feel that way. Moreover, the fact that certain expressions appear to occur in widely different cultures (Ekman and Friesen, 1971), and in blind-born subjects (see Eibl-Eibesfeldt, Chapter 4; Thompson, 1941), as manifestations of the same emotions, precludes such an interpretation. Obviously, socially conditioned control of expression and mutual interference of blending emotions are among the determinants of this ambiguity and lack of specificity. Yet, they do not seem to be the major determinants.

Expressions which are ambiguous and generally misunderstood when presented in isolation appear fully appropriate, natural and intelligible when viewed in the context of the entire situation. They do, for the observer, shed light upon the subjects' emotional reaction. They appear fully acceptable once one knows what they stand for or, rather, where they stand. For instance, there are well-known photographs of people on the point of being shot; several recent ones have come from Vietnam. There is no question that the people concerned are terrified; yet their faces show little beyond what might equally be some oppressed sullenness or general discomfort, containing at any rate no trace of the classical and recognizable expression of fear or terror. Another example:

collect one hundred music lovers, present them with the finest concert imaginable and photograph their faces. Hardly any of these will manifest clear expressions of the joy, or admiration, or appreciation they may later confess to have felt (during which conversation they may, in fact, manifest those expressions of joy and the like!). Yet, when one knows they are the faces of music-lovers listening to a fine concert, the expressions may well be quite transparent as expressions of concentration, immersion, joy, "emotion", etc.

1.2 EXPRESSION AS PART OF EMOTION

Understanding this variable relationship between expressions and emotions will depend in the first place upon an appropriate conception of emotion. An emotion may be defined as a complex psychological event composed of three components: (1) A situational "valence-for-the-subject"; (2) An immediate behavioural tendency, consisting of a strong or weak, increasing or decreasing interaction with that valence, and thus embodying a resultant "stance" towards that valence; (3) A change in the pattern of probabilities of subsequent behaviours—a changed "readiness" profile.

The concept of "valence" occurring in this definition refers to the situation's meaning and significance for the subject in terms of the positive or negative consequences it promises, the evaluations it evokes and the values it embodies. Subjectively, as an experience, emotion is, first of all, perception of a meaningful event. Grief is experience of an unaccepted loss, together with a passive and hopeless reaction. Fear is the perception of a threat which cannot at once be fully countered, together with some response which fits or complements this perception. The valence thus enters in the definition of emotion, and forms part and parcel of emotional experience. Objectively, in the context of observing emotional reaction in others, valence also forms part of emotion. When perceiving someone's emotional reaction one invariably looks for the fearful object, the angering stimulus, or one questions about the lost object of grief; one looks around with the expectation of seeing a potentially fearful object, etc.

Now let us consider the following hypothesis. If an emotion consists of the three components indicated, questions should be asked and answered concerning the relationships between those components. One of these questions is whether different kinds of valence are linked

M

one-to-one to different kinds of behavioural tendency. This obviously is an empirical question. The above-mentioned evidence on ambiguity of expression suggests that the relationship is certainly not one-to-one.

The valence, the situation's significance, may be coupled to various kinds of behavioural tendency, in addition to unspecific emotional arousal. A fearful stimulus may lead to fascination and incessant observation; or to cowering and all-out protective behaviour. That is, a fearful expression may consist of either wide-open eyes, with eyebrows contracted, or it may consist of nearly closed eyes and hunched shoulders. Other reactions are also possible. The expression of fear may also consist of complete immobilization, a deadness and emptiness and state of no-response as it occurred, presumably, in the terror-reactions mentioned before. Or again, if the fearful stimulus is not at that moment physically present, hardly any specific behavioural tendency makes sense with respect to the situational valence; therefore, no specific facial expression would be relevant and the only behavioural manifestation of fear may consist of general restlessness.

This distinction between valence and behavioural tendency, as components of emotion, may explain the variability of behaviour corresponding to "one" emotion. If "fear" is that group of emotions, characterized by a fearful valence (uncomfortable threat), this characteristic leaves the behavioural tendency undetermined, and, thus, variable. In the naïve definition of emotion, such characterizations are, presumably, dominant, possibly together with some gross, not very specific, indications of the general nature of the behavioural response: "fear" is that group of emotions characterized by a fearful valence and by some decrease in the adaptivity of its corresponding behaviour.

The distinction between valence and behavioural tendency may explain something else as well. If our definitions are appropriate, it follows that the behavioural manifestation of emotion is something less specific, and hence more general than emotion as such. It represents a more abstract aspect. This conclusion is supported from another angle, that of the diversity of interpretations given by judges to one and the same expression. Experiments which allow the judges sufficient freedom of choice yield, for most expressions, a large array of interpretations. Sometimes these interpretations are close relatives, such as amazement and surprise; but quite often they widely diverge, such as, for instance, distaste, protest, irritation, suppressed anger, indifference, sad recollection, given as interpretations of one and the same expression photograph. The interesting thing is that, even in cases like the latter, each of these interpretations seems quite appropriate, given the facial expression concerned.

It would therefore seem that the same expressive pattern can occur in quite different emotional states; that is, it may be connected to quite different valences. As far as overt motor behaviour is concerned, the terrorized expressions referred to before are indeed quite similar to those occurring in sullenness. Or as another example, shrugging off a disagreeable thought, reacting to a distasteful remark, suppressing a movement of anger, closing oneself off from irrelevant information—all may consist of the same behaviour of rapid sideways turning of the head.

To summarize the present point of view: emotional behaviour constitutes part of the complex phenomenon called emotion. One and the same pattern of behaviour may "belong" to an array of different emotions; one and the "same" emotion may manifest itself in several different ways.

1.3 THE MEANING OF EXPRESSION

The behaviourally manifest aspect of emotion can be characterized more precisely. In the definition of emotion given above the expression "stance towards [the emotional] valence" was used. This "stance" may be taken as the meaning of emotional expression. A better, more specific term may be "positionality" (Frijda, 1969), meaning the subject's mode of relating to the environment at a particular moment. Emotional expression represents the expressor's positionality. This idea is, of course, fairly common in the literature on expressive behaviour. Expressive activity consists of partial or complete, real or symbolic approach and avoidance tendencies, protective movements and movements of abandonment, sensory readiness patterns and the like. In addition to positionality as such, expression represents the person's state of activity; and it would seem to represent not only the degree of overt emotional activation, but also a number of other aspects: something of the degree and nature of a person's control over his emotional activation, the extent to which his activity is intentionally steered, and the degree to which this activity entirely involves relational activity *per se*, or is free and "superfluous", as in joyful movements.

Obviously, a given relational activity pattern may indeed participate in quite different emotions. Obviously, too, one and the same emotion, as defined by its valence and some gross traits of the corresponding expressive behaviour, can give rise to a variety of relational activity patterns—to fascinated or cowering fear, for instance. Of course, this changes the nature of the emotion; it constitutes different kinds of fear. It doubtless changes the probability profile of possible subsequent behaviours. Notwithstanding the lack of a one-to-one relationship between emotion and expression, emotional expressive activity intimately belongs to emotion. It is an integral part of emotion: emotion *is* expression (or, rather, is its impulse, the "intention" leading to it) *plus* something else, the valence. In another sense, there does exist a one-to-one relationship between expression and its meaning. Each expressive movement pattern can fruitfully be interpreted as representing one specific relational activity state.

To summarize our position so far: *emotion* is defined as an attitudinal or "positional" response to a specific valence carried by an outer or inner event. Expression is this positional response, to the extent that the response is externalized. The meaning of expression consists of the corresponding positionality, and the activation pattern in which this positionality is manifested.

1.4 EMOTIONS AND FEELINGS

The relationship between emotion and expression is complicated by the fact that emotions may vary as to the centrality, the importance, of the relational activity component. Some emotional states are characterized more by their cognitive and evaluative components than by their behavioural impulse; for other emotions this may be different. Startle, for instance, is a sudden reaction of the protective or orienting, or disoriented, kind to an unexpected stimulus. The nature of the reaction—mainly its interrupting suddenness—belongs to the stimuli which leads us to describe our own reaction as one of startle. Admiration, on the other hand, is the high evaluation of a quality which is not in the first place satisfying a vital need. The evaluation, and the nature of the "quality", belong to the cognitive side of the emotion; whether the activity of evaluating has any behavioural component or not is immaterial to the definition of "admiration" and, in fact, admiration of music usually manifests itself only negatively, that is by the visually disinterested, relaxed features of passive auditory interest.

Quite generally, it would seem that the more "subtle" emotions, such as shame, admiration, remorse, pity, grief, love, do not have expressions which are truly specific for them, and for the reason given; they are all characterized mainly by perceived qualities and by evaluations. We may phrase it as follows: emotional expressive behaviour manifests the relational activity component of the emotional state, to the extent that this component can be translated into action. If, for instance, the only aspect of auditory interest and admiration which is translatable into action is general passivity, then that and only that is the expression of admiration of music.

The unspecificity of expression in daily life goes further. Many or most of our emotional reactions are *feelings*, and not emotions. That is, the emotional impulse is somehow transformed into an inner representation, a mental image of the action-tendencies involved. The degree to which this transformation is performed may vary. It can even be such that motor activity represents, on occasion, nothing but the subjects' orientation towards this inner experience—a more or less tense attitude, a more or less staring face, with perhaps some manifestations of general arousal. It is not only control of expression, as transformation of emotion into feeling, which thus further disrupts the correlation of emotion and expression. In view of these complexities, it may be useful to introduce the concept of the "expressive radical" of an emotional state. The expressive radical is that aspect of an emotional state which is in principle capable of motor expression, and is, moreover, in fact expressed. The expressive radical, then, is not co-extensive with the emotion, and may even be relatively peripheral to it.

Emotional life, on this view, consists of a stream of relational activity, of attitudes taken and activation rising and falling, controlled and released, steered and influenced by a stream of perceptions and evaluations. These streams from time to time crystallize, "thicken" so to speak, into very distinct evaluations and very pronounced and unitary forms of relating: that is when one "has an emotion". And, of course, the stream of relational activity is constantly modified by suppression and play-acting, positive and negative control over the expressive activity as such, with intent to hinder or help communication, and which contributes to further complication of the picture.

2 The analysis of emotion and expression

2.1 THE DIFFERENTIATION OF EXPRESSION

If one expression, and thus one "positionality", may correspond to several emotions, then what is the differentiation of these positionalities? In other words, what various "positions" exist, or along which dimensions do they vary? To what extent is the differentiation of emotion reflected in behaviour? The answer to these questions may be derived from the analysis of the confusions of judgement of expressions. Confusions point to similarities, and similarities to classes or dimensions.

From the data obtained so far, the degree of differentiation of expressive behaviour appears to be fairly subtle, more so at least than was assumed in the more well-known dimensional studies (Schlosberg, 1954; Osgood, 1966), but not as fine as for emotion-as-distinguished-in-the-language. The data stem from some recent experiments, which will be briefly reviewed.

The experiments consisted of having a group of judges indicate on a checklist which terms referring to emotions or related states (doubt, attention, etc.) would apply to a given facial expression. The photographs showed expressions posed by professional actors. In two experiments, 62 photographs of an actress were used; in two others, 68 photographs of an actor. Both sets were selected from very large (220 and 385, respectively) series of expression photographs; selection was made so as to try to obtain as varied a collection of expressions as possible.

Photographs were projected onto a screen. Judges were requested to check as many terms per photograph as they thought appropriate. The first two experiments used a 98-item list; the two others, which served as replications, a list of 110 items. These terms were derived from the answers which 30 other subjects had previously given to 30 photographs, in response to the demand to supply three terms to characterize each photograph; these responses were grouped intuitively into 112 categories, and one term was selected from each. Rejection of ambiguous terms led to the final list, while some terms were added or changed in the replication.

Frequencies of usage of particular terms per photograph were correlated and, on the matrices of product-moment correlations, hierarchical cluster analyses (Elshout and Elshout, 1967) were executed. In the case of the first two experiments factor-analyses were also performed, with

Varimax rotation. The results are interesting in two ways. First, as just mentioned, the number of discriminable expression-patterns seems to be larger than that usually found in studies of this kind. About 18 factors with contributions to the variance larger than $1\frac{1}{2}$ per cent emerged in the two factor analyses, and an equal number of clusters at the level of average intra-cluster correlations of 0.60 appeared in the cluster analyses of all four experiments.

Second, the cluster analyses clearly yield a hierarchical structure. That is, terms cluster, and such clusters may themselves cluster at distinctly lower levels of inter-cluster correlations. These higher-order clusters may again correlate with other clusters with correlations of about 0.40–0.20. This hierarchical structure is not an artificial by-product of the method of cluster-analysis employed: only the clusters differing by at least 0.10 in average intra-cluster correlation were considered as different levels of clustering. Finally, highest-order clusters may correlate negatively with each other, manifesting bipolar dimensions of the kind found in the more traditional studies.

The contents of the various clusters are not precisely identical in the different analyses; they resemble each other fairly closely, however. The list of factors for the first two analyses is given in Table 1; the list of clusters at the level of inter-cluster correlations of about 0.60 is given in Table 2. The hierarchies found in one of the experiments are given in Fig. 1.

2.2 THE HIERARCHICAL MODEL OF EMOTION

The hierarchical structure found seems to be a very adequate representation of the system of emotions. It unites the dimensional point of view, as expressed by Wundt or Schlosberg, with the traditional classificatory viewpoint, which distinguishes a larger number of emotion classes. A small number of unipolar and bipolar dimensions forms an emotion space, the various regions of which are differentiated and sub-differentiated in ways specific to these regions.

It is plausible to assume that the hierarchical structure yielded by the experimental data reflects an analoguous structure of the expressive movements or traits themselves. It is likely that large groups of emotional states share some fairly general or gross behavioural manifestations. All moods recognizable as positive, in the studies described, manifest a smile or laughter. Different emotional states within such a

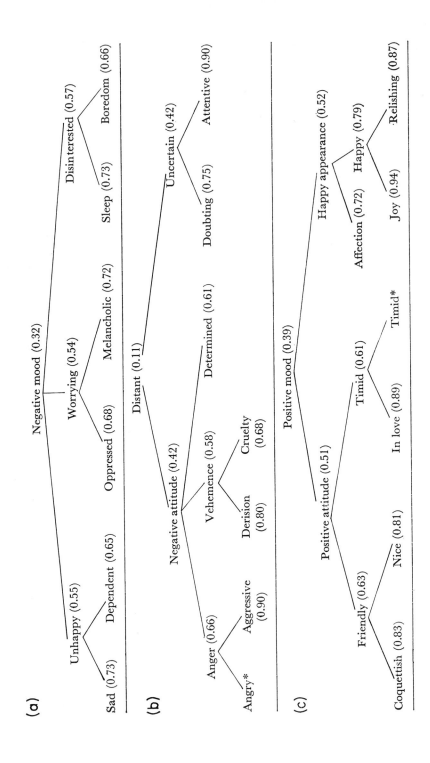

(a)

Negative mood (0.32)

Unhappy (0.55) — Worrying (0.54) — Disinterested (0.57)

Sad (0.73) — Dependent (0.65) — Oppressed (0.68) — Melancholic (0.72) — Sleep (0.73) — Boredom (0.66)

(b)

Distant (0.11)

Negative attitude (0.42) — Uncertain (0.42)

Anger (0.66) — Vehemence (0.58) — Determined (0.61) — Doubting (0.75) — Attentive (0.90)

Angry* — Aggressive (0.90) — Derision (0.80) — Cruelty (0.68)

(c)

Positive mood (0.39)

Positive attitude (0.51) — Happy appearance (0.52)

Friendly (0.63) — Timid (0.61) — Affection (0.72) — Happy (0.79)

Coquettish (0.83) — Nice (0.81) — In love (0.89) — Timid* — Joy (0.94) — Relishing (0.87)

(d)

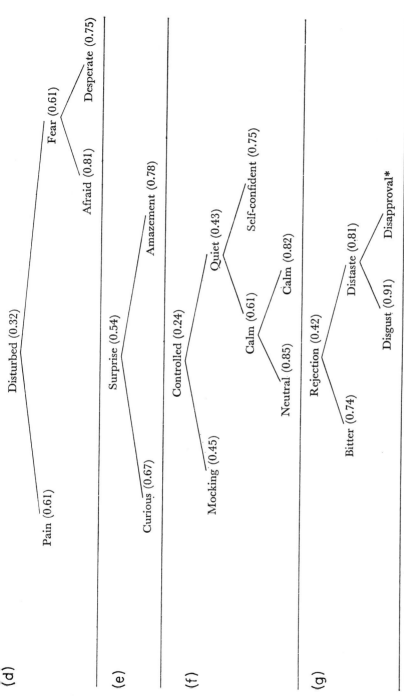

Disturbed (0.32)

Pain (0.61)

Fear (0.61)

Afraid (0.81)

Desperate (0.75)

(e)

Surprise (0.54)

Curious (0.67)

Amazement (0.78)

(f)

Controlled (0.24)

Mocking (0.45)

Quiet (0.43)

Calm (0.61)

Self-confident (0.75)

Neutral (0.85)

Calm (0.82)

(g)

Rejection (0.42)

Bitter (0.74)

Distaste (0.81)

Disgust (0.91)

Disapproval*

Figures in brackets are average intra-cluster correlations.
* Single terms (not clusters).

Fig. 1. (a-g) Cluster hierarchies: "Nelly" Photographs Study 2.

TABLE 1

Factors based upon frequencies of co-occurrence of terms assigned to
photographs (from Frijda, 1970)

		% Variance		
Factor-name*		"Nelly" Photographs Study I	"Jerôme" Photographs Study I	Congruence-coefficient
1	Happy	14.1	11.2	0.885
2	Sad	9.5	8.2	0.892
3	Calm	8.2	5.2	0.831
4	Disgust	6.8	6.3	0.864
5	Surprise	5.8	4.7	0.785
6	Bitter	5.7	—	(0.690)†
7	Attention	5.4	5.2	0.555
8	Fear	4.7	4.6	0.781
9	Pride	4.2	6.1	0.683
10	Irony	3.1	3.2	0.696
11	Anger	4.5	7.7	0.796
12	Insecure	4.2	3.2	0.396
13	Moved	2.1	—	
14	Aggrieved	1.9	—	
15	Gay	2.0	—	
16	Pain	1.9	—	
17	Guilty	1.7	—	
18	Scepticism	1.4	1.9	0.231
6+	Disinterested	—	4.9	
12+	Distrust	—	2.2	
13+	Childish	—	2.7	
14+	Amusement	—	5.1	
15+	Pondering	—	3.0	
16+	Curiosity	—	2.2	
17+	Reserve	—	2.2	
	Total	87.4	84.6	

* Terms with the highest loadings on each factor are used to indicate the factor.
† Congruence coefficient between "Nelly" Studies I, factor 6, and II, factor 11.

group on occasion manifest themselves by more specific variations on,
or additions to, those more general expressive manifestations: friendliness tends to be expressed by smiling, happiness by laughter, mockery
by laughter with lips closed, etc. And, again, this optional differen-

TABLE 2

Clusters of emotion-terms (at the level of inter-cluster correlations of about 0.60). Subdivisions represent higher-order clusters with inter-cluster correlations of 0.2–00.40)

"Nelly" Study I	"Nelly" Study II	"Jerôme" Study I	"Jerôme" Study II
unhappy sentimental	unhappy pain disinterested worrying	unhappy pain worrying	unhappy dependent disinterested
anger bitter happy friendly mocking	anger vehemence happy friendly timid affectation	anger vehemence happy friendly timid dependent	anger bitter happy friendly tender affectation*
fear surprise dumb insecure	fear surprise	fear surprise curious	fear surprise
calm attentive*	calm attentive doubting	calm attentive	calm attentive
self-confident*	self-confident* mocking	self-confident	self-confident mocking
distaste*	distaste bitter† distrust	distaste*	distaste

* Clusters occur in a different super-cluster from the one given in the Table.
† Clusters occur in other super-clusters in other experiments.

tiation may proceed further down the hierarchy, "joy" and "relishing" being distinguished by further details.

Analysis of correlations between cluster scores (or raw scores) and facial feature ratings seems to support this view. In our studies, ratings were obtained of expressive features such as "lips slightly parted" or "eyebrows raised" or "head tilted sideways". Some expressive features correlate with all, or nearly all, terms in a cluster, even at the highest level of clustering. Some other traits correlate only with the terms of one or several subordinate clusters, and some only with certain terms. Our facial feature ratings are fairly crude and the correlations therefore not always reliable, but we expect the indicated relationships to emerge more clearly when a more refined measurement technique, as developed by Ekman *et al.* (1972) is used in future studies.

The hierarchical model, then, embodies the system of "relational activity patterns". But recall that emotion is supposed to consist of this relational activity plus the situational or cognitive components. The system of emotions derived from similarities in expression does not represent the only relationships between emotions. When talking about the various forms of anger, fear, love, happiness, we talk about groupings based upon valences; and anger and fear are closely related because both may be founded in perceived threat. It is possible to develop a system of emotion based upon similarities between cognitive and evaluative aspects of emotion; but the basic dimensions or categories of emotional experience are yet to be described. It is then to be expected that the study of emotion may yield relationships which have nothing to do with such dimensional, or classificatory, systems as the one discussed, because they stem from other components of emotion.

References

Ekman, P. and Friesen, W. (1971). Constants across cultures in the face of emotion. *J. Pers. Soc. Psychol.* **17**, 124–129.

Ekman, P., Friesen, W. and Ellsworth, Phoebe (1972). "Emotion in the Human Face: Guidelines for Research and Integration of Findings". Pergamon Press, New York.

Elshout, J. J. and Elshout, M. (1967). Marimaxcor: methode van cluster-analyse van correlatiematrices. Technical Report, University of Amsterdam, Department of Psychology.

Féléky, Antoinette (1914). A study of the emotions. *Psychol. Rev.* **21**, 33–41.

Frijda, N. H. (1953). The understanding of facial expression of emotion. *Acta Psychol.* **9**, 294–362.

Frijda, N. H. (1958). Facial expression and situational cues. *J. Abnorm. Soc. Psychol.* **57**, 149–154.

Frijda, N. H. (1969). Recognition of emotion. *In* "Advances in Experimental Social Psychology". (Ed. L. Berkowitz), Vol. 4, pp. 167–223. Academic Press, New York and London.

Frijda, N. H. (1970). Emotion and recognition of emotion. *In* "Feelings and Emotions" (Ed. Magda B. Arnold), pp. 241–250. Academic Press, New York and London.

Kanner, L. (1931). Judging emotion from facial expressions. *Psychol. Monogr.* **41**, No. 186.

Landis, C. (1924). Studies of emotional reactions. II. General behavior and facial expression. *J. Comp. Psychol.* **4**, 447–509.

Osgood, C. E. (1966). Dimensionality of the semantic space for communication via facial expressions. *Scand. J. Psychol.* **7**, 1–30.

Schlosberg, H. (1954). Three dimensions of emotion. *Psychol. Rev.* **61**, 81–88.

Thompson, Jane (1941). Study of facial expression in blind and seeing children. *Archs. Psychol. N.Y.* **37**, No. 264.

Tomkins, S. S. and McCarter, R. (1964). What and where are the primary affects? Some evidence for a theory. *Percept. Mot. Skills*, **18**, 119–158.

Woodworth, H. S. (1938). "Experimental Psychology". Holt, New York.

8

Do Dimensions Have Face Validity?

Peter Stringer[1]

1 Introduction

Much of the early psychological research on facial expressions, particularly during the 1920's and 1930's, grew out of a basically philosophical question about the way in which we know about our own and other people's emotions. The emotions were thought of as invisible and objectively unknowable inner states. Nevertheless there are many occasions on which we are able to state what another person's feelings are and have him agree with us. Sometimes we ourselves are aware of trying intentionally to communicate our feelings to others, verbally or through other means, and meeting with varying degrees of success. The puzzle of what and how we know about emotional states has many facets. It

[1] This chapter is a development of papers given in a Symposium on Person Perception at the British Psychological Society Annual Conference, Sheffield, April 1968; and at a Symposium on Non-Verbal Communication, supported by the European Association of Experimental Social Psychology, held in Amsterdam, 31 March to 2 April 1969. While this chapter was written (1970) the author was supported in part by a grant from the Leverhulme Trust Fund.

involves questions of the self and others, of intention, and of different forms of language. Most of them have been forgotten by psychologists.

The original questions have become neglected and buried under lower-order questions generated by formalistic concerns internal to the pursuit of psychology. For example, although the basic philosophical questions that have to do with the emotions and their expression or communication would not separate verbal and non-verbal processes, psychologists have tended to do so. Under the influence of Behaviourism, and the earlier work of Darwin (1872), a large part of their efforts have been directed to attempting to elucidate the connection between inner emotional states and their behavioural, and particularly facial, expression. With historical hindsight we can see that their work was misdirected by three delusory preconceptions. First of all the emotions were singled out as inner states *sui generis*, worthy of isolated study. Secondly, their non-verbal behavioural concomitants were treated as more amenable to investigation. And third, the face was chosen as the most significant source of this behaviour—a preconception and delusion as powerful and unjustified as assuming the heart to be the seat of the emotions.

The purpose of this chapter is to persist with the delusions in order to trace some of their more recent outcomes. After briefly referring to the early recognition accuracy experiments, we shall trace the history of the dimensional approach to facial expressions. This has formed one of the main threads of psychological research on expressive behaviour and non-verbal communication over the past thirty years. The work of Schlosberg, Nummenmaa, and Osgood is described in some detail, not so much as being representative, but rather as, respectively, historically important, weighty, and theoretically suggestive. Their failure to give an adequate rationale for the dimensional model *is* representative, however, and this is discussed at length. An alternative clustering approach is introduced, and an attempt is made to explain the function of dimensions in tracking temporal arrays of facial expressions. It is argued that clusters and dimensions are different ways of explaining different types of judgement. Some of their characteristics are described, and a distinction is made between judgements of similarity and dissimilarity. A particular type of cluster-structure is the hierarchical one. This is illustrated with examples from both verbal and non-verbal (facial) forms of communication. It is concluded that, backed up by additional contributions, dimensional and clustering approaches do have much to offer.

2 Accuracy in recognizing facial expressions

The underlying theme of experiments on facial expressions until 1938 was the accuracy with which people read such expressions. Accuracy was variously defined. Could people judge the actual emotional state of another? Could they judge the intended emotional state behind a posed expression? Was there a reasonable consensus among subjects, and with the experimenter's own judgement, about an expression whose "real" content was irretrievable? Many of the experiments, particularly those using posed photographs or other static representations of the face, found that accuracy was low.

One extension of these accuracy studies considered the value of situational knowledge when judging expressions. Is it easier to make an accurate judgement when one knows something of the context of the expression? This question was necessary because facial expressions had been used as isolated stimuli, often in the form of static images, and because poor or negative results had emerged from the accuracy experiments. It was found that the addition of situational cues gave an increase in the accuracy or consensus of judgements. In one of the most recent theories of the recognition of emotion (Frijda, 1969) considerable importance is attached to the role of situational cues.

Another extension, conceptually if not historically, since Darwin had anticipated it, was to ask whether when accurate judgements did occur they were prompted by some parts of the face rather than others. Do the eyes contain more of the expression of an emotion than other parts of the face? Are certain emotions conveyed particularly by the mouth? Is there a firm correspondence between certain movements of a facial feature and the judgements of certain emotions? Some correlations have been found (e.g. Frijda and Philipszoon, 1963), but generally the tactic of narrowing down the effective stimulus in this way does not seem to be very helpful, at least when one is considering the accuracy of emotion recognition. In more ethological studies (e.g. Brannigan and Humphries, 1969), which aim to analyse the elements of facial expression in relation to particular ongoing situations, the role of specific features can take on a much greater significance.

Recent studies of recognition accuracy by clinicians (e.g. Ekman and Friesen, 1968) have the more valid goal of interpreting expressive behaviour in general, and not only facial expressions, for diagnostic and other purposes. The aim of the earlier studies, however, is unclear.

Although they conclusively demonstrate that accuracy depends upon experimental conditions such as the task subjects are asked to perform and the nature and sampling of stimuli, the importance of accurate recognition is unconvincingly argued. One may well be able to make deductions about a process by observing conditions under which it fails, but this method tends to assume that veridical judgements are crucial. In the case of facial expressions, or other isolated bits of expressive behaviour, they may well not be at all crucial. Judging the role of facial expressions in the communication of emotional states under the assumption that recognition accuracy is the key factor may be an experimental fantasy. In any case, studies such as these ignored questions of process.

3 Dimensions of emotion in facial expressions

The history of facial expression experiments saw a major change of direction in 1938, when Woodworth attempted to make sense of the errors made by subjects in recognition accuracy experiments. He showed that six categories of expression (love, mirth, happiness; surprise; fear, suffering; anger, determination; disgust; contempt) could be arranged in a linear order in such a way that responses to any particular facial expression generally fell within three adjacent categories; that is, erroneous recognition judgements tended to fall on either side of the correct category on a linear scale. Woodworth's contribution was to accept implicitly that accuracy of recognition itself may not be so important as the pattern within which *inaccurate* responses were distributed.

In the hands of Schlosberg the linear scale was developed into something approaching a model for facial expression judgements. He observed (1941) that errors occurred across the two ends of Woodworth's linear scale in such a way as to suggest that they be joined to form a circular scale. Since the surface described by a circular line can also be defined by two linear coordinates, he hypothesized that judgements might be made in terms of two dimensions. Schlosberg (1952) found that facial expressions could be reliably located at some point on this circular (or more nearly elliptical) surface when subjects made judgements of the expressions in terms of scales of "pleasantness–unpleasantness" and "attention–rejection". This was later (Schlosberg, 1954) expanded into a three-dimensional model, with the addition of a dimension of "sleep-tension". It was found that these scales could be used consistently and reliably by a variety of subjects and with several different sets of facial expression stimuli. Schlosberg not only advanced Woodworth's explanation of the errors made in recognition accuracy experiments by using a more sophisticated and inclusive model, he also showed how perceptions of an apparently very complex set of stimuli could be reduced to a two or three-dimensional scheme with little loss of information. The complexity of expressions was no longer seen as a source of error in human judgements; instead investigators turned their attention to specifying the number and nature of the dimensions necessary to account for the variance in their subjects' judgements of these complex stimuli.

3.1 MULTIDIMENSIONAL ANALYSIS

The extent to which two stimuli are confused, as in Woodworth's experiments, or their correlation when described by rating scales, or straightforward judgements of their similarity or dissimilarity, are widely used now in studies of perception and cognition as indicators of the way in which stimuli are perceived or encoded. Data of this kind are usually analysed on the basis of a geometric model. The stimuli are taken to be points in a multidimensional space. Their relative confusability, correlation or whatever, is taken as indicative of their positions with respect to one another in this space, i.e. of their metric distances apart. The goal of the analysis (for recent methods see Shepard, 1962; Kruskal, 1964; Lingoes, 1965; McGee, 1966; Young and Torgerson, 1967; Carroll and Chang, 1970) is to recover these distances, and the coordinates of the space, in such a way that the originally observed similarities or dissimilarities of stimuli are linearly or ordinally related to their distances in the metric space. An important practical aspect of the analysis is that the space can usually be of quite few dimensions without unduly diminishing this relationship.

If one assumes that the space is a representation of the psychological "map" of stimuli, parsimony in the number of dimensions by which the map is ordered is clearly desirable. The map is viewed as the psychological frame of reference for perception and cognition. Whenever a person comes upon a particular element, it is assumed that he refers it to the map which is appropriate to that type of element. To understand the dimensions of the map, according to this argument, is to understand the way in which a person organizes information about events he confronts.

Not all the dimensional studies of facial expressions use the same multi-dimensional methods of analysis, but in essence their aim is usually very similar (Schlosberg, 1941, 1952, 1954; Engen and Levy, 1956; Hof-statter, 1956; Engen et al., 1957, 1958; Nummenmaa and Kauranne, 1958; Triandis and Lambert, 1958; Royal and Hays, 1959; Levy and Schlosberg, 1960; Abelson and Sermat, 1962; Gladstones, 1962; Shepard, 1962; Frijda and Philipszoon, 1963; Harrison, 1964; Kauranne, 1964; Nummenmaa, 1964; Ekman, 1965; Williams and Sundene, 1965; Williams and Tolch, 1965, Hastorf et al., 1966; Osgood, 1966; Ekman and Friesen, 1967; Mordkoff, 1967; Cliff and Young, 1968; Sweeney et al., 1968; Frijda, 1969).

3.2   THE NUMBER AND NATURE OF DIMENSIONS

Schlosberg's dimensions, although reliable, were derived a priori rather than by analytic procedures like those just described. What dimensions can be found when they are allowed to emerge of themselves? A variety of methods have been used: similarity ratings, labelling, grouping, and rating scales; as well as different kinds of stimuli—posed or unposed photographs, actual faces, and drawings. Dimensions numbering anything from two to seven or eight have been found, and with the exception of Schlosberg's first and third dimensions there has been considerable disagreement about their nature. "Pleasantness–unpleasantness" and "level of activation" (Schlosberg's "sleep–tension") appear in practically all the dimensional studies. But while "attention–rejection" appears in some, it is renamed in others (e.g. as "attention–disinterest", or "expressionless–mobile"), or is found altogether redundant. Where more than three dimensions emerge, the additional ones tend to be unique to a particular study.

In view of the variety of experimental conditions, the fact that two dimensions appear consistently is noteworthy, and the additional disagreements are not surprising. The number of dimensions will clearly vary with the number and representativeness of the stimuli, and of rating scales where these are used. The nature of the dimensions depends again upon the representative sampling of stimuli and/or rating scales. This problem has not yet received much attention. Even if one were to sample from an exhaustive set of schematic stimuli as suggested by Brunswik (1956), there would be difficulties. Subjects might be predisposed to respond to these apparently highly simplified representations (see Brunswik, 1956, pp. 100ff.) according to the conventions that govern cartoon drawings rather than as natural faces. There are highly elaborated conventions whereby artists have contrived to render on the face expressions of emotions whose subtlety or extremity defies the power of normal musculature (cf. Gombrich and Kris, 1940). Historically much of the motivation for studies of the judgement of facial expressions may have come from a fascination with the power and conviction of graphic or theatrical conventions. One of the earliest investigators, Piderit (1859), was himself an actor, as well as being an anatomist. But psychologists have tended to overlook the possibility that different processes may underlie the different contexts, that drawings or photographs may be crucially different from everyday expressions, and that the study of "artificial" expressions that are surrounded by semi-formalized linguistic conventions may not be the best way to study naturally occurring expressions.

It may be that the recurrence of the dimensions of "pleasantness" and "activation" depend upon investigators having consistently put into their experiments the appropriate stimuli and terms of response. The relative ease with which these as opposed to other dimensions are named does not guarantee that they are fundamental entities. They may simply represent those areas of meaning that are readily accessible to the differing task-orientations of the experimenter and his subject, and that are also compatible. They may be rather trivial artefacts. The nature of any dimensions that are basic to the process of judging facial expressions may not be so readily nominated. The basic process is not necessarily isomorphic nor synonymous with our conscious representation of it.

But considerations such as these are otiose in the absence of any theory of emotional expression which makes it clear what role dimensions might serve. Why should one imagine that a dimensional treatment is likely to produce an adequate explanation of how judgements of expression are made? Schlosberg showed that it could account for the findings of earlier recognition accuracy studies; but it was never shown that these findings were in turn a necessary part of any explanation. Schlosberg and subsequent investigators who followed this scheme also showed that dimensions could be used consistently and reliably in a variety of experimental conditions, but their use was always internal to the experimental situation; there was no point of contact with any concept or entity external to the situation. The dimensions were discussed as a closed system. In one of the most sophisticated and elegant experiments in the facial expression literature, Abelson and Sermat (1962) produced results that were nevertheless characteristic of this approach. They showed that their own distance data, derived from a typical multidimensional scaling task, correlated highly and positively with Schlosberg's scale values for the same photographs; Schlosberg's *a priori* scales accounted for 75 per cent of the variance in the more undirected judgements of their own subjects. They showed how Schlosberg's dimensions could be calibrated with one another according to their contribution to the cognitive space. They were also able to demonstrate that for both sets of data a two-dimensional space was an adequate description. But like many psychological experiments this study was content simply to re-examine data and an experimental situation, even though an underlying theory was lacking.

4 The language of the face

Following the work of Schlosberg and his associates the next major study of facial expressions in point of time is the monograph by Nummenmaa (1964). Although he is interested in a number of questions relating to what he calls the "language of the face", the idea of a multidimensional representation of stimuli or responses is a dominant theme. In the monograph, it is introduced historically. An experiment by Nummenmaa and Kauranne (1958) is described which aimed to find "how many dimensions are needed to account for the main differences between different facial expressions, and what these dimensions are" (Nummenmaa, 1964, p. 3). The model of the experiment was a dimensional study by Ekman (1955) of verbal expressions of emotional states. Ekman (1954) had previously done a similar dimensional study of colour vision. It is an interesting aspect of studies of multidimensional scaling that, with nonsense shapes, colours and facial expressions are the most common stimuli chosen. Studies which are basically mathematical or methodological (e.g. Shepard, 1962; Rodwan and Hake, 1964; Sjöberg, 1968; Tversky and Krantz, 1969b; Isaac, 1970) sometimes use colours or facial expressions as convenient stimuli, in the same way as factor analysts use age-old correlation matrices. This often facilitates the comparison of scaling innovations with previous methods by which these stimuli have also been analysed.

The original use of colours as stimuli was not arbitrary, of course, and some investigators (e.g. Krantz, 1964) have rightly combined advances in scaling methodology with a fresh look at the substantive problems of colour vision. It is not at all unreasonable to assume that a dimensional analysis might point to physiologically identifiable entities that underlie colour vision. Existing knowledge about physical and psychological colour mixtures from the first made it plausible that a dimensional model might be appropriate. Dimensions, as Schlosberg (1952) indeed pointed out, enable one reliably to specify and interrelate complex stimuli in terms of their values on scales or quantifiable components. An impure colour as a mixture of two or three basic hues could readily take its place in a three-dimensional colour space, and scaling experiments have tended to confirm this *a priori* dimensionality. The physiological processes hypothetically underlying such dimensions might well rely on a similar number of independent receptors, responding in a continuous manner.

4.1   MULTIDIMENSIONAL SCALING

We have already seen how the dimensional approach to judgements of facial expressions arose out of the work of Woodworth and of Schlosberg. In Nummenmaa and Kauranne's work a new influence appears, in a rather devious way—the more sophisticated methods of multidimensional scaling, in particular of colour stimuli. Mathematically-oriented psychologists used facial expression stimuli as a convenient way of demonstrating the power of scaling techniques. Psychologists interested in facial communication then used the scaling techniques as a way of reducing and ordering large sets of complex data, and at the same time assumed that the dimensions arrived at were explanatory concepts. Thus: "The multidimensional scaling methods are one way of seeking 'explanatory concepts'." (Nummenmaa, 1964, p. 25.) In and of themselves, of course, the dimensions revealed by scaling analyses are not explanatory of anything. They are purely descriptive, a means of data reduction.

Properly used, however, any method of data analysis or data reduction in psychology should be concordant with hypothesized underlying processes. In this sense dimensions of facial expression *should* be explanatory; they should imply something about the process underlying judgements. But this is not so unless the appropriate process-model is made specific. Beals *et al.* (1968) have warned of the difficulties of arguing

that dimensional representations are merely a means of summarizing
data, rather than implicit models of psychological similarity:

> First, we note that unlike descriptive statistics, the calculation of dimensional
> or metric values requires minimisation of some criterion of error. If the underlying
> model is inappropriate, the procedure necessarily capitalizes on noise in the data to
> obtain the fit. This renders interpretation of the results difficult, and invariance
> across experiments unlikely. Furthermore, if the dimensions or the distances do not
> correspond to some underlying psychological processes, their theoretical value is
> severely restricted. Second, if multidimensional scaling models are regarded as use-
> ful data-reduction methods rather than as theoretical models one may ask what is
> the source of their usefulness. Any data reduction implies a certain loss of information
> to achieve greater clarity; some aspects of the data are suppressed so as to highlight
> the critical features. But if the model used to perform this reduction is logically in-
> compatible with the data-generating process, it may suppress the more interesting
> aspects of the data and give a misleading impression.

p. 141

Nummenmaa uses multidimensional scaling for three experimental
purposes, apart from simply establishing the number and nature of
dimensions necessary to account for the variance of facial expression
judgements. Firstly it is a convenient means to examine possible iso-
morphism between verbal and facial expressions of emotion; and it is
concluded that very similar dimensions of content of emotional communications may be found for differing means of communication.
Secondly it is used to "explain" simple and complex expressions: "In
a multidimensional model the expressions falling . . . on any of the axes
could be considered as simple or elementary expressions, and the
expressions not falling on any of the axes as complex or combined expressions". (Nummenmaa, 1964, p. 25.) In a two-dimensional system
of "pleasure–anger" and "surprise–fear–rejection" combinations of any
two of pleasure, surprise–fear, and anger produced possible complex
expressions that were identifiable. For meaningful complex expressions
it proved possible to predict their position in the multidimensional
system. Finally the dimensions are related to regions of the face, which
are assumed to define the cues that people use when interpreting
expressions (cf. Frijda and Philipszoon, 1963). One conclusion was:
"Certain simple expressions, especially perhaps anger and pleasure, can
be identified from the areas of the eyebrows, eyes, nose, and mouth.
But complex expressions can only be read in the eyes . . ." (Nummenmaa, 1964, p. 45.)

4.2 THE ADDITIVITY ASSUMPTION

For the most part these experiments show only that multidimensional scaling is a convenient method of data reduction which produces consistent, reliable results, on a par with the *a priori* dimensions of Schlosberg. In only one respect does Nummenmaa build on a distinctive feature of the multidimensional model. He points out that a recurring question in early studies of emotion is whether elementary feelings occurring simultaneously retain their separate identity or become fused into a new compound feeling. Analogously one may ask whether the meaning of a complex facial expression can be equated with a conjunction of the meanings of two or more simple expressions; and whether acceptable complex facial expressions result from the addition of cues in different regions of the face which separately denote individual simple expressions. In concluding that acceptable combinations are located at the intersection of lines connecting the relevant simple expressions in a multidimensional system, Nummenma is exploiting a peculiar property of the model, that of additivity.

The full significance of the property of additivity in multidimensional scaling has only recently been examined. Beals *et al.* (1968) show that for dissimilarity data to be represented in specific metric spaces certain conditions have to be fulfilled; otherwise the blind use of multidimensional scaling techniques is inappropriate. The rational and theoretical justification of dimensional representations rests on these conditions. Thus, in their additive difference model, properties both of additivity and subtractivity are assumed. In a later paper (Tversky and Krantz, 1969a) a more unified "decomposability" model is introduced which has three fundamental assumptions: (1) decomposability—the distance between points is a function of component-wise contributions; (2) intradimensional subtractivity—each component-wise contribution is the absolute value of the scale difference; (3) interdimensional additivity— the distance is a function of the sum of component-wise contributions.

The assumption of interdimensional additivity has been tested (Tversky and Krantz, 1969b) in a multidimensional scaling analysis of eight schematic faces each of which varied on three components. It was hypothesized that the perceived distances of faces along each of the components would contribute additively to the overall judged dissimilarity between faces. The results supported the idea that "a simple combination rule can describe mental processing of independent impressions, and it encourages attempts to use this simple rule as a criterion for isolating the dimensions on which subimpressions are formed." (Tversky and Krantz, 1969b, p. 127). At the same time, it should be stressed that a very small sample of faces was used as stimuli and that their attributes were independent of one another. It will be necessary to test the assumption also in a case where dimensions interact and there is clearer evidence of representative sampling from a continuous space. However, the main lesson for the present argument is that an unthinking application of sophisticated mathematical models to psychological data may involve flouting fundamental conditions and be theoretically nonsensical.

4.3   SOME FURTHER IMPLICATIONS OF FACIAL DIMENSIONS

There are several additional points made in Nummenmaa's (1964) monograph, which, although not apparently crucial to the theme and not a part of a developed theory, will become more significant at a later stage of this discussion. On the question of the number and nature of dimensions of facial expression, he notes that his two dimensions do not include Schlosberg's rather contentious "sleep–tension" dimension. "Quite obviously the dimensions of pleasure–anger and surprise–rejection are intensitive in themselves. What else could they be? What would the idea of a dimension refer to if not to intensity?" (Nummenmaa, 1964, p. 50.) The idea is not pursued. Also on the nature of dimensions:

> . . . the names one gives to dimensions of facial expressions also guide one's thinking about facial expressions. Names such as pleasant–unpleasant and sleep–tension (activation) have an association with the study of emotions, whereas names such as pleasure–anger and surprise and fear-rejection have more a social–psychological flavour.
>
> Nummenmaa, 1964, p. 50

The first sentence here may appear to be upside-down, but attention is drawn to the misleading assumption of early experiments, mentioned above, that it is emotional states that facial expressions are expressing. Nummenmaa expands this point only in a summary way in a short section concluding the monograph, on the "meaning" of facial expression:

> It remains to be seen whether this multidimensional model can be applied to anything. One possibility is in fact implied in Schlosberg's 1941 paper. If we consider

these axes from the social–psychological point of view, we could conceive of the pleasure–anger axis as relating to the kind of information that is wanted, i.e. this could be the rewarding–punishing axis. And again, an expression of surprise begs for more additional non-redundant information, the content of which remains otherwise unspecified; rejection again indicates that no information whatever is wanted.

Nummenmaa, 1964, p. 55

The argument throughout this chapter is that multidimensional or any other models *must* be applied to something external to themselves to do them justice. It is disappointing that this is not done in "The Language of the Face".

Finally, an additional interesting point is made in relation to the "expressions of emotion" misconception:

> . . . the position that interpretations are also made of probable courses of action is defendable, vague as inferences concerning these may be. Common usage makes a difference between two kinds of facial expressions, posed and natural ones. It is conceivable that for predictions concerning "emotional states" the "natural" ones might be better, and for predictions concerning "probable courses of action", the "acted" ones.
>
> p. 48

Nummenmaa follows up his idea by relating it to the problem of intent in facial expressions, and contends that expressions can be considered as deliberate signs in social communication. We shall return later to the notion of interpreting "probable courses of actions" from a rather different angle.

5 The structure of facial semantic space

Two years after Nummenmaa's monograph, Osgood (1966) published a paper in which he reported on an experiment done twenty-two years previously. The data had subsequently been analysed several times in different ways, but on this occasion the analysis was primarily multidimensional and was intended to determine the number and nature of dimensions necessary to account for judgements of facial expressions. It is of historical interest that the experiment was originally designed to test an implication of the James–Lange theory of the emotions and the hypothesis that accuracy in interpreting facial expressions is correlated with accuracy in expressing oneself facially. The recognition accuracy theme persists in the 1966 paper, as does the idea that facial expressions are primarily about emotional states. In 1950 the dimensional treatment was overlaid on the research when Osgood applied the type of distance analysis that he was developing for the semantic differential (Osgood and Suci, 1952). Five years later (Osgood, 1955) the concepts of information theory revived an interest in recognition accuracy. The facial-visual channel was treated formally as an information transmitting system, and previous findings were confirmed by concluding that the system was noisy and unreliable, but not random. But finally the 1966 paper seems to have been motivated by a desire to make sense of recent dimensional studies, to take account of Tomkins and McCarter's (1964) interesting return to a categorical as opposed to dimensional approach to the problem, and to introduce two important unpublished studies by de Rivera (1961) and Harrison and MacLean (1965).

5.1 THE SHAPE OF FACIAL EXPRESSION SPACE

Osgood found three dimensions to be involved in facial expressions, both in judgements of the expressions and also in acting the expressions. Two of these, "pleasantness" and "activation", corresponded satisfactorily with other findings in the literature. The third dimension, about which there had been more disagreement in other studies, he called "control". Perhaps because a number of studies had conveniently only found two or three dimensions, or on an analogy with the representation of the colour solid, there has been some interest in representing the actual shape of the facial expression dimensional space (cf. Nummenmaa, 1964, pp. 53–54). Osgood produced a representation of his three-dimensional space that is much more carefully drawn and inclusive than other attempts. His truncated pyramid not only accounts for his own findings, but also describes graphically the correlation found by previous studies between the contentious third dimension and the other two. The pyramid represents, for example, what may be an inevitable tendency for "active–unpleasant" expressions to be controlled. It also describes the relatively greater differentiation of expressions on one of the two poles of a dimension; "active" or "unpleasant" expressions seem to be more differentiated than "passive" or "pleasant" expressions.

Osgood makes a considerable, if speculative, addition to his dimensional system by suggesting a way in which it might develop in the individual human being. At first, he suggests, neonates' behaviour might vary along one dimension only, namely "pleasant–passive/unpleasant/active". This would be followed by differentiation of "active" expressions into "pleasant" or "unpleasant"; and subsequently of "unpleasant" expressions into a "control" dimension. Finally "passive" expressions become increasingly differentiated, although the process is never fully developed. These developmental suggestions add considerable significance to the notion of a dimensional system. They are much more apposite than attempts to correlate dimensions with regions of facial activity. But there is still no compelling reason offered as to why the system should be *dimensional*. The developmental pattern could as readily apply to a hierarchical, set-theoretical model.

5.2 DERIVED CLUSTERS OF EXPRESSIONS

In order to test the work of Tomkins and McCarter (1964), who had recently produced a list of nine "primary affects" ("enjoyment", "interest", "surprise", "fear", "anger", "disgust", "shame", "distress", "neutrality"), Osgood (1966) looked for clusters in the labels used to describe the facial expressions in his experiment. He used three different clustering methods; but all of them centred on looking for clusters in an already defined dimensional space. Although his approach seems to have been a matter of convenience, it points to an extremely important characteristic of these dimensional studies, the significance of which Osgood makes quite explicit. Facial expressions rarely seem to be evenly distributed through a dimensional space; there tend to be "holes" in the space defined by people's judgements which contain no stimuli. This sort of patchy distribution suggested to Osgood that there might be valid "types" of expression, similar to those assumed by Allport (1924), Woodworth (1938), and Tomkins and McCarter (1964). The clusters he found were generally quite similar to those named by the earlier investigators. He suggests:

> [they might be] *either* structurally determined (a species-specific organization of the neurophysiology of emotions) *or* psycho-linguistically determined (a culture-specific, and rather arbitrary, matter of the way continuous psychological variables are mapped into discrete linguistic categories—much in the way different languages differently carve up the color spectrum).
>
> Osgood, 1966, p. 26

This is expanded into a hypothesis that appropriate cross-language and cross-culture studies would show that, whereas dimensions of facial expressions are common to all humans, clusters within the space will vary noticeably with language or culture. Osgood does not initially argue any reasons for assuming a dimensional system; but by relating clusters, or types, and dimensions in this way he attempts to explain a recurrent characteristic of many dimensional systems derived from judgements of a wide range of stimuli (not facial expressions), and makes a significant addition to the dimensional approach.

5.3 DENOTATIVE AND CONNOTATIVE EXPRESSIVE MEANING

If the dimensions are primary and communicate affective, connotative meaning, Osgood argues, they should be related to his semantic differential factors. He equates "pleasantness" and "activation" with "evaluation" and "activity", and "control", less confidently, with "potency". The experiments of Ekman (1955) and Nummenmaa (1964) referred to above, as well as his own, are cited as evidence of the extension of these dimensions, in an isomorphic way, into the realm of labels of emotion, as well as of their facial expression. De Rivera (1961), in a study of denotative and connotative aspects of emotion labels, derived *a priori* six denotative features of emotion which he called "end-decisions": (1) subject–object (referring to the self or an external object, e.g. ashamed versus afraid); (2) attraction–repulsion (referring to associative or dissociative tendencies in the emotion, e.g. envious versus horrified); (3) extensor–contractor (a distinction between outward and inward orientation, e.g. pity versus shame); (4) presence–likeness meaning (a distinction between contacting, comparing, and empathizing, e.g. anger versus scorn versus rejection); (5) involved–detached (akin to intensity, e.g. loathing versus disapproving); (6) express–inhibit (a decision depending on the availability of actions, e.g. anger versus hatred). His thesis was that the denotative meaning was governed by end-decisions, whereas connotative meaning could be described by the three factors of the semantic differential. Nummenmaa, we recall, suggests that interpretations about "probable courses of action" might be made from facial expressions, presumably referring to judgements about action expected from the person expressing an emotion. The end-decisions of de Rivera also seem to be referred to from the viewpoint of the expressor's actions.

5.4 SEQUENCES AND SITUATIONAL CONSTRAINTS

Osgood takes the analogy with linguistics further:

> Temporal sequences of facial, gestural and postural movements seem analogous to *sentences*, momentary patterning of the whole (as might be caught in a still photograph) to *phrases*, the configuration of significant parts (e.g. the eye-brows, the mouth, the shoulders) to *words*, and the patterns of movement of the components of these significant parts (e.g., lips curled, mouth partly open) as the *phonemes*.
>
> 1966, p. 28

A number of studies of the structural significance of the movement patterns of facial features and other parts of the body have been made (e.g. Dittmann *et al.*, 1965; Ekman and Friesen, 1967; see also Chapter 2) but an unpublished study by Harrison and MacLean (1965) makes one particularly interesting suggestion about the possible structure of the facial code. In Osgood's paraphrase:

> ... sequentially, in shifting from a neutral face to any face in which all features are modified in some fashion, one may follow N "pathways" depending on the order of feature changes. In other words, just as we may use different sentences to convey different shades of meaning, so there may be six different ways to "get mad!"
>
> 1966, p. 29

Finally, Osgood interprets the findings of the earlier recognition accuracy studies and dimensional studies such as Schlosberg's:

> The low reliability of naming is due to confusability among labels. If such confusions were random, confusability would be identical with unreliability—but they are not. Rather, they are reasonably systematic, reflecting the loose mapping of names onto things, and the existence of conventionally determined quasi-synonyms.
>
> The difference between naming and scaling can be understood in terms of constraints: the greater the *constraints on the stimulus*, the more accurate the labelling. Situational context is one constraint, and it helps to differentiate denotatively among labels that are quasi-synonyms affectively.
>
> 1966, p. 29

6 The function of dimensions

6.1 DIRECT CLUSTERING OF FACIAL EXPRESSIONS

The clustering approach was taken further in an experiment performed in 1962 (Stringer, 1967). Osgood's clusters were composed of verbal labels derived from a dimensional analysis of labelling judgements of facial expression. I derived my clusters, however, directly from non-verbal clustering judgements without any dimensional intermediaries. In other words, clustering was assumed to be a process by which people judge facial expressions (and other stimuli), and a method of analysing such judgements was chosen which was congruent with the assumed judgemental process. The difficulty about dimensional analyses, as I have repeatedly implied, is that they are not accompanied by a full enough explanation of their congruence with the judgemental data.

I assumed that "a facial expression is generally perceived in the context of a series of preceding and succeeding expressions" and that "the primary response to one or more expressions would be to construe their contextual (or functional) similarity to other examples (past or present)" (Stringer, 1967, p. 72). The cluster analysis employed did precisely this: it identified clustered patterns of functionally similar variables. Subjects were asked simply to sort a set of thirty photographs of facial expressions into unordered groups, of any size or number, in such a way that each group was composed of similar expressions. The frequency, across subjects, with which each of all possible pairs of expressions occurred in the same group was used as a measure of similarity between expressions. Disjoint clusters, with maximum similarity between member elements, were then looked for. Five were found, representing "worry", "disgust–pain", "surprise", "thoughtfulness", and "happiness". The titles were derived from labels attached by subjects to their groups after they had formed them. It was shown that the internal and external structure of the clusters could be usefully described.

Since this was primarily a methodological study little emphasis was laid on the substantive results. In claiming that the results could not be used to strengthen or invalidate previous studies I pointed to the difference between cluster and dimensional analysis: "Cluster analysis identifies clustered patterns of functionally similar variables, rather than measuring component influences. A single cluster may contain several components, and a single component may be represented in several clusters." (Stringer, 1967, p. 78.) Given that congruence is assumed between the method of analysis and the mental processes being examined, what is the significance of this difference for our understanding of the processes themselves? The 1967 paper makes no suggestions. I shall return to the point below.

6.2 AN EXPERIMENT ON THE JUDGEMENT OF SEQUENCES OF FACIAL EXPRESSIONS

In referring to the assumption that a facial expression is generally perceived in the context of a series of expressions, I made a similar point, though for different reasons, to that of Harrison and MacLean (1965), who talk about sequential pathways of expression. Osgood drew an analogy between sentences and temporal sequences of facial and other forms of expression. In 1963 I followed up the clustering experiment with an investigation (Stringer, 1966) of sequential judgements of facial expressions.

Three sets of facial expressions were selected, based on the clusters identified in the previous experiment. These were the "thoughtfulness" and "happiness" clusters, and a composite group made up of the other three clusters. Subjects were asked to order the photographs in each of the three sets in a sequence that was personally meaningful. If the functional similarity that was assumed to pertain to the members of each of the clusters of expressions had any basis in the likelihood that they were contiguous expressions in a sequence, then there should have emerged a close relationship between the similarity of pairs of expressions in the clustering experiment and the frequency with which the same expressions were placed adjacent to one another in this sequential ordering task. Furthermore there should be much less agreement between subjects when ordering the composite group made up of three clusters. The relative lack of functional similarity between these clusters should lead to confusion about the ordering of their members in a joint group, if functional similarity is based on the probability of sequential contiguity.

The results of the experiment turned out in accordance with these expectations. There were highly significant positive relationships between the similarity measures derived from the clustering and ordering tasks; and there was much less concordance over ordering the composite group—although for all three groups of expressions the agreement between subjects was nevertheless highly significant. This is not, of course, an adequate test of whether inferred sequential contiguity is in fact the basis of clustering or similarity judgements. But the findings are consistent with the assumption.

N

6.3 THE INTEGRATION OF DIMENSIONAL AND CLUSTERING APPROACHES TO FACIAL EXPRESSION

It was argued that the grouping experiment required a cluster analysis for decomposing the judgements made. For comparative purposes, however, they were also analysed multidimensionally (following Kruskal, 1964). In addition to performing a multidimensional analysis of the total set of inferred similarity judgements, analyses were done for each of the three sets of elements used in the ordering experiment. The path of the mean sequences produced in the ordering experiment was then traced through the corresponding dimensional space. Two dimensions were sufficient to represent each of the groups, and it was possible to trace a simple path through the space for each sequence. When an attempt was made to describe the sequences, terms such as "control", "attention" or "intensity" seemed the most natural ones to use. These terms, of course, are ones that have commonly been used to describe dimensions of facial expression. One is reminded in particular of Nummenmaa's intensive concept of dimensions (cf. p. 352). For example, one sequence began by showing decreasing control and increasing attention; the degree of control continued to decrease, while attention began to shift towards rejection; finally the lack of control evened out and the sequence ended on a note of rejection. This rather serendipitous finding suggested a way in which one might integrate dimensional and clustering approaches to facial expression and provide a somewhat fuller model for facial communication than had been offered before.

One phenomenon which no previous investigators seem to have attempted to explain is how a continuously changing sequence of expressions can be followed—presumably because it was usually more convenient to work with static faces or still representations. One could imagine that fragments in a sequence might be sporadically sampled and their position in a multidimensional space worked out. With extra cues available from the context of the expression this would not be a complex operation, but if the fragments are considered in isolation the process of locating anew an expression on each of a number of dimensions seems excessively laboured. If a series of expressions is considered as a sequence which is tracked through a multidimensional space the amount of information in any fleeting sample of the sequence is greatly reduced, just as the amount of information in a single word is reduced when it is embedded in a sentence. The potential of a multidimensional system for mapping continuous change on several parameters simultaneously offers a very convenient model of how a wide variety of sequential phenomena might be processed.

The role of clusters of expressions can now be interpreted anew. A cluster can be considered as a set of points within a multidimensional space, which have particular expressive significance and have agglomerated a high density of connotative meaning. As Osgood suggests, where these clusters occur and what meaning they carry may vary individually and culturally; they will probably be dependent upon learning. They probably represent points in the individual's or culture's space which have particular implications for action or reaction (cf. Nummenmaa, 1964). They thus sound rather like de Rivera's (1961) "end-decisions". A sequence might be tracked through the space until it comes to a region with "action implications", where the observer makes a decision, and the sequence can be considered to end, if only temporarily. It is possible that within a cluster an independent dimensional system might operate for finer differentiation, as Rapoport and Fillenbaum (1969) suggest in the case of a verbal semantic structure.

I assume here that it is the dimensions which carry the denotative meaning of expressions. Connotations, or affective associations, accumulate in certain parts of the space very rapidly from birth. It is extremely difficult to appreciate how a dimension which we inevitably label "pleasantness" can have extensional significance.

The description of sequences of expressions as paths through a dimensional space is an alternative way of explaining Harrison and MacLean's (1965) six different ways to get angry. Instead of thinking of them as n different orders of feature-change, where n is limited by the number of features, they are multidimensional lines whose number is only limited by the fineness of discrimination of the dimensions.

I have accepted that the clustering of expressions into dense subspaces within a system is a "natural" phenomenon. It is plausible to think of the space being deformed because points that are in a region with strong connotations or action implications are seen subjectively as closer together than they might be if the system were purely physical and objective. However, it is possible to see this as an experimental artefact. I would conjecture that in all the facial expression experiments, even the dimensional ones, subjects were not responding in terms of dimensions, but in terms of clusters. All the various judgements required of them could have been satisfied by their making similarity judgements about which clusters the particular expression belonged to or about the probability of it belonging to one cluster rather than another. The clusters might be personal ones, or ones suggested, for example, by bipolar labels. Even in experimental tasks where two expressions have to be compared in terms of similarity or dissimilarity, although the subject may be giving an estimate of their relative distance apart within a multidimensional space, I prefer to assume that he is giving an estimate of the likelihood of their belonging to the same cluster. The two responses could, of course, contain very similar information.

In terms of the argument being developed at this point the assumptions behind the grouping experiment (Stringer, 1967) turn out to be somewhat misconceived; namely, that "a facial expression is generally perceived in the context of a series of preceding and succeeding expressions", and that "the primary response to one or more expressions would be to construe their contextual (or functional) similarity to other examples (past or present)" (Stringer, 1967, p. 72). The distinction between clustering and dimensional processing is confused in these statements. Judging the contextual similarity of any two expressions, which may be seen in isolation or be widely separated in time and space from one another, may be distinguished from responding to two temporally and spatially contiguous expressions in a series or sequence of expressions.

6.4   THE ROLE OF COGNITIVE CLUSTERING

Elements cluster cognitively because they have a certain number of attributes in common and because those attributes have a particular valency for the cognitive system. A particular everyday object or phenomenon involves a set of elements, members of which are frequently multi-attributive. Some differentiation between members of the total set is usually attempted by an individual. Unless the object or phenomenon is of crucial importance to the individual, the differentiation is limited to the formation of a number of subsets or clusters each of which contains more than one member. For any multitudinous, multi-attributive set the number of possible ways of clustering elements can be very large. Presumably what guarantees that a particular cluster be formed is that its members all produce a similar response or lead to a similar pattern of action which is of some importance to the organism. Where objects or phenomena can be treated as discrete, independent entities considered individually, a process of clustering is a quite adequate and economical method of ordering them. The process can be considered to include all the features of sets and subsets that are laid down in the mathematical theory of graphs.

Thus when a subject is faced with one or two expressions it could be a relatively simple process to allocate them to one of the small number of clusters, to whichever they seem most similar. Differentiation or discrimination from members of all other clusters is, of course, implied, but the process is primarily one of adducing similarities. There would be no need to locate the expression in a dimensional space by fixing its value on a number of coordinates. Such a procedure would mean, in computer terminology, that the judging individual would need access to a very large store indeed; the judgement would involve a great deal of "information".

It is perhaps only when objects or phenomena are no longer seen as discrete and independent, when they have to be considered as an ordered series, that clustering breaks down. Although a sequence of changing expressions could be conceived of as passing from one sub-cluster to another, through a succession of overlapping subsets, this would not specify any direction or amount or rate of change. Sets do not readily permit the necessary scalar nor coordinate features. For these purposes a fairly strict metric would appear to be required.

6.5 CLASSES AND DIMENSIONS DISTINGUISHED

The distinction between classes and dimensions has been discussed in general terms, in relation to judgement and choice, by Restle (1961). He makes the important point, which had previously been blurred in, for example, Bruner's (1957) discussion of categorizing processes, that the two viewpoints are not fully reconcilable:

> It would be possible to use set-theoretic methods for some problems and the classical dimensional analysis for others. This is not a fundamentally clean solution to the issue, for the set-theoretic and dimensional models are logically incompatible and lead to entirely different approaches to theoretical problems.
>
> Restle, 1961, p. 39

In the absence, however, of a unifying treatment, I am attempting to show here how the different approaches may be usefully applied to different aspects of non-verbal (and, later, of verbal) communication. Attneave (1962) also contrasts continuous, quantitative dimensional processes with discrete, qualitative classes. He compares them to Stevens' (1957) "prothetic" and "metathetic" variables. He shows how if one were to take either one as basic to judgement, there are various ways in which it could be reduced to the other. At the same time he recognizes that this poses an important, difficult, and unresolved question, and that the two processes may ultimately be irreducible. Different types of judgement may require different explanatory models.

Another way of conceiving the distinction that is being made here between clusters and dimensions as indicators of underlying perceptual-cognitive structure is in terms of learning. How might a person learn to discriminate facial expressions? Would the learning process lead to the formation primarily of clusters or of dimensions? Two major viewpoints of discrimination learning would tend to give rather different answers (cf. Tighe and Tighe, 1966). Mediation theories see such learning to be a matter of the supplementing or modifying of stimulus input by response processes occurring within the learner. Initially similar stimuli become distinctive by being associated with different responses. The distinctiveness is either elaborated by the addition of more and more differentiating attributes, or by selecting out irrelevant attributes from the total stimulation. These theories tend to assume that the crucial features of the stimuli can be perceived by the learner from the beginning. A set-theoretical or cluster model would be appropriate to these theories. Clusters are described in this chapter as having "action implications", and these are an obvious form of mediating response. Discussions which lay emphasis on situational cues as a necessary component in the reading of facial expressions (e.g. Frijda, 1969) basically rely on a mediation theory.

Differentiation theories, on the other hand, assume that permanent properties of the stimulus are in themselves the basis of discrimination, without recourse to mediating response processes. The learner cannot necessarily perceive these properties initially; perceptual learning is in fact a process of becoming sensitive to stimulus properties. Association learning is also held to occur, but only in relation to previously discriminated variables. Whereas a mediation process involves the enrichment or modification of stimuli, differentiation involves becoming more aware of the ways in which stimuli vary. Differentiation theory (e.g. Gibson and Gibson, 1955; Gibson, 1966) draws attention to the potential of objects as *arrays* of perceptual information, both spatial and temporal. Objects are typically perceived in a changing flux, and change conveys information both about their invariant properties and also about the way in which they change. From this viewpoint, perceptual learning can be seen as in part an increasing sensitivity to dimensions of change. Sequences of facial expression are both the means whereby dimensions of expression are learned and also the stimulation which subsequently is analysed dimensionally.

Both types of learning presumably occur in relation to facial expressions. Dimensional differentiation looks as though it should be primary. Distinctive responses would later become associated with stimuli in particular areas of the multidimensional space of expression. The responses would also become associated with a variety of situational cues not inherent in the facial stimuli themselves. Associational mediation and clustering differ crucially from differentiation in going beyond the facial stimuli. It is for this empirical reason, as well as for formal mathematical ones, that clusters will not be entirely accounted for in terms of dimensions, even if they can be given an approximate spatial location.

6.6 TYPES OF PSYCHOLOGICAL SIMILARITY

I am advocating that there are two sorts of psychological similarity underlying judgements of facial expressions. Two expressions may be subjectively similar because they have a number of important common attributes and very few important differences. They will have tended to occur in similar contexts, to have similar connotative meaning, and similar implications for action. Or they may be similar because they have occurred in close temporal contiguity as parts of a coherent, developing sequence of expressions. Wallach (1958) has discussed four ways of defining psychological similarity: in terms of common environmental properties, common responses, common primary stimulation gradients, and assignment to a common category. Contextual similarity of facial expressions probably belongs to the last type of similarity. Sequential similarity could be considered in the light of primary stimulation gradients. Torgerson (1965) distinguishes between similarity "as a basic, perhaps perceptual, relation between instances of a multidimensional attribute and similarity as a derivative, cognitive relation between stimuli varying on several attributes" (p. 389). The latter kind of similarity is that which I claim underlies most experimental judgements of facial expressions, where a variety of quite different classes of attributes are involved. Similarity judgements that are implicit in the tracking of sequences of expression are of a basic, perceptual kind, and are judgements in terms of a multidimensional attribute of expressiveness.

Torgerson also points out that perhaps most kinds of stimuli of interest to psychologists are multi-attributive and not inherently spatial or dimensional in nature, and that for this reason multidimensional scaling may be a technique of limited usefulness. Against this he puts the possibility that this kind of similarity data can nevertheless be embedded in a space, provided that we do not assume the appropriate metric properties nor expect a clear dimensional interpretation to emerge. The technique can be used as a heuristic device to find characteristic spatial configurations for essentially non-spatial structures. This is what I have done in the multidimensional analysis of the free grouping data. But in general it is far preferable to look for a configuration that one believes to be appropriate. I shall refer later to several examples of this in non-verbal and verbal communication.

6.7   CATEGORICAL, DIMENSIONAL AND HIERARCHICAL CONCEPTIONS OF
       EXPRESSION

In attempting to explain the meaning of dimensional studies of facial expression, Frijda (1969) distinguishes three conceptions for a system of emotional expression—the categorical, dimensional and hierarchical. Categories are thought to be distinct and unrelated, "or, what amounts to the same thing, unipolar emotional dimensions" (p. 188). No examples of such a strict categorical conception are offered, nor is its value argued for. The model of Schlosberg is taken as representative of dimensional systems. However its origin in accounting for categorical confusion data makes it different from the various multidimensional scaling treatments which are perhaps more satisfactory as dimensional models. The model is clumsy, Frijda claims, when dimensions increase in number and obtain a specific flavour, such as "surprise" or "anger". But according to the present argument, dimensions do not acquire this specificity. The hierarchical conception, Frijda continues, combines the other two, and is considered to give the best account of the various studies (see also Chapter 7). "It could be that at a given region of the n-dimensional space points are differentiated in terms of dimensions, meaningful only in that region." (Frijda, 1969, p. 189.) I suggest as a

result of the hierarchical cluster analysis described below that a hierarchy of categories may *reflect* a dimensional system; and that dimensions
might apply uniquely within particular categories. But this is not to say
that both categories and dimensions are necessary to explain any judgement process, or that either can be used to explain a judgement.

Frijda considers the question of whether a system of dimensions or
clusters defines emotion, and decides that emotion is constituted of a
behavioural element (dimensional) and a situational or cognitive
element (clusters). Dimensions are taken to represent a person's
"positionality" at a given moment. When emotions have important
situational aspects they cannot be correctly recognized from expressive
behaviour patterns alone. Numbers of emotions have very similar
behavioural manifestations and occur at the same region of a multidimensional space. This might explain why in recognition experiments
where situational cues are not provided performance has been so poor;
subjects are being asked to recognize an emotion when they can in fact
only hope to recognize an expression which might denote several quite
different emotions.

6·8 SEQUENTIAL TRACKING

Frijda (1969) points to the potential role of dimensions as sharply discriminating means of tracking sequences of expression:

> As a matter of fact, recognition of expression seems first and foremost to be recog-
> nition of this positional activity, and only secondarily recognition of emotion. If no
> need for categorizing or situational extrapolation exists, as in the theatre, all the
> observer does is to follow the play of varying opening and closure, approach and
> withdrawal, activity and relaxation patterns. In those terms, discrimination of ex-
> pression may well be quite acute . . .
>
> p. 192

But he does not elaborate the point. The recognition of emotion is
conceived of "as a two-stage process: assessment of the general positional
activity pattern, on the basis of expression, and subsequent specification
of this pattern on the basis of situational and other contextual cues"
(1969, p. 193). Considerable emphasis is laid on the latter stage; and it is
even thought that under real-life conditions the stage that relies on
dimensional judgements may be by-passed. I would agree with this in
the context of fragmented recognition tasks of the kind that occur in

laboratory experiments and in some everyday situations. But the more general task of following a dynamic flow of expressive movement is probably better catered for by a dimensional system. One may not choose to call this "*recognition* of emotion", but it is an important aspect of perceiving emotionally expressive behaviour.

The idea of tracking a sequence of contextually interrelated stimuli through a multidimensional space, and arriving at an area of strong connotative significance with implications for action, is forcefully exemplified in a study by Cliff and Young (1968). They describe three studies relating the uni-dimensional judgement of stimuli to their multidimensional scaling. Although one of the studies uses facial expressions as stimuli, and shows that judgement of their intensity seems to represent the distance of an expression in a two-dimensional space from a point representing the absence of any emotional expression, the most interesting results come from a study of judgements of simulated air-raids. Similarity judgements were made of twenty air-raids by naval officers undergoing training at the US Fleet Anti-Air Warfare Training Centre. It was found that the underlying dimensions could be clearly related to physical characteristics of the raids (principally to range, course and bearing) and that the first dimension correlated 0.97 with judgements of the raids' "threat" value. In addition, it was hypothesized that when subjects were asked to specify which of four alternative courses of action they would take to counteract the raids, their choice would depend on the location of the raid in the judgemental space. It was found that almost all raids with a common modal counteracting response were indeed clustered within a defined area of the multi-dimensional space.

Cliff and Young conclude that individuals use a multidimensional reference structure in different ways for making different sorts of judgement:

> While the judgement of the action taken in response to an air raid depends on the location of the air raid in the subject's structure, the judgement of the *threat* of the air raid depends on the projection of the air raid on a vector in the subject's structure. It is interesting that the multidimensional space provides a basis for both kinds of judgements, and the mapping of the judgements on the space is different in the two cases.
>
> 1968, p. 283

However, it might be preferable to say that it is possible to account for different kinds of judgement by referring to the multidimensional space, and not to assume that the space is actually used in making the judgements. Thus, on the basis of the sequential model outlined above, one might hypothesize that the judged threat of a developing air-raid might be tracked as it changed in range, course and bearing and that at various critical points of threat more or less drastic counteractive measures would be adopted. Provided that the sequence of information about stages in the air raid's development is non-saccadic, tracking it would involve highly redundant information and an economical processing.

6.9 ACTION-IMPLICATIONS AS SPATIAL REFERENCE POINTS

Some regions in the multidimensional space which are used for information processing have implications for action. The concentration of meaning in these areas of the space might lead to their being used as primary reference points. Thus at the first news of an air-raid it might be assigned tentatively to one of these points. Successive pieces of information would enable the raid's relative progress and potential threat to be monitored as finely as dimensional scales would allow. Quite small changes in range and course could be instantly interpreted as posing a greater or lesser threat. It is clearly more economical to suppose the raid to be capable of being tracked in this continuous way rather than for it to be re-assigned anew at each stage to a point in the judgemental space on the basis of all its relevant attributes.

The suggestion that there are primary reference points in areas saturated with action implications is borne out by Cliff and Young's (1968) data. Their two-dimensional representation of subjects' similarity judgements of air raids shows the raids clustered together into three groups, each of which corresponded to a specific course of action. It has been noted by Torgerson (1965) that judged stimuli are rarely spread evenly throughout a multidimensional space; and Osgood's "truncated pyramid" model of facial expressions was formulated in order to account for a similar observation, as were his "types" of facial expression. Everyday stimuli that have strong subjective implications for action responses are perhaps least likely to be evenly spread. Similarity or dissimilarity judgements of such stimuli seem to be made with reference to a limited number of points in the defining space rather than in a finely discriminating scalar fashion. If this is the case the rationale of multidimensional scaling as applied to subjects' judgements of certain

types of stimuli may be inappropriate, since it assumes that the judgements are made along underlying scalar dimensions, when in fact they
may be made in a set-theoretical clustering way. It is as an artefact of
this ill-founded assumption that any dimensions are found. Such dimensions should perhaps be treated in a highly tentative way, until they are
tested by reference to processes that might employ scalar judgements
within a multidimensional system.

The relatively greater ease with which people may make similarity
rather than dissimilarity judgements has been pointed out by Rapoport
and Fillenbaum (1968). When subjects are asked to rank order the
relative similarities of pairs of colour names, in the early part of the
ranking (which from other evidence appears to yield the most meaningful and reliable set of judgements), they must be sensitive to small
differences between stimuli when *all* the differences are small. When
they are in the early stages of ranking dissimilarities they have to discriminate small differences between stimuli which are all relatively
very different. The former is surely less exacting. In similarity judgements the crucial attributes impose themselves; in dissimilarity judgements they have to be sought after. This difference in the ease of the two
tasks might lead to subjects making similarity judgements even where
they were asked for dissimilarities. If they were rating dissimilarity on a
scale this switch could readily be achieved.

7 Hierarchical structures

The method of cluster analysis used for my free grouping experiment
(Stringer, 1967) simply partitions a matrix of distances or proximities
into subsets at varying levels of similarity between members (Constantinescu, 1967). The method reproduces the complete graph of associations in the form of a large number of overlapping clusters at different
levels of homogeneity. No further structural assumptions are built into
the analysis, although it would be perfectly possible to look for any
given type of structure among the clusters. For example, one might
assume that the clusters had a particular kind of hierarchical structure.
The data from the sorting experiment were accordingly examined in
terms of the hierarchical clustering schemes of Johnson (1967). Since
his methods look for particular hierarchical structures within graphs
they are more economical than a trial-and-error search for any hierarchies among the complete set of clusters.

Figure 1 shows the resulting hierarchical structure.[1] The thirty stimuli are listed according to their original index numbers and in terms of the labels most frequently given to them by subjects (Stringer, 1967, p. 76). The five principal clusters are separated and given summary labels. The first and highest-level partitioning of the complete set of expressions (on the right of the structure) produced three clusters, corresponding to the three used in the "sequences" experiment. The clusters can be described as (A) "worry", "surprise", "disgust–pain", (B) "thoughtfulness", and (C) "happiness". At the next level (A) divides, and the three separate clusters, (D) "worry", (E) "surprise", and (F) "disgust-pain", are found. "Happiness" (C) divides into two subsets of: (G) quiet, thoughtful pleasure, and (H) open, laughing happiness. The "thoughtfulness" cluster (B) divides into subsets of: (I) stubborn, disdainful expressions on the one hand, as distinct from (J) more calm, dreamy expressions. Below this level surprise produces two clusters corresponding to: (K) surprise proper, and expressions that carry (L) more connotations of fear, horror or even anger. The quieter aspect of pleased happiness produces two clusters: (M) a thoughtful happiness as opposed to (N) a more open pleasure. It is also apparent that (O) stubborn, and (P) disdainful aspects of thoughtfulness become distinguished in separate clusters.

This description parallels that given already (Stringer, 1967, pp. 76–77), but with the difference that a hierarchical structure is super-imposed. How acceptable does the description appear? The first primary partitioning seems to represent degrees of affect—positive ("happiness"), neutral ("thoughtfulness"), and negative ("worry", "suprise", "disgust–pain"). Subsequent partitions of these clusters might be interpreted in terms of "passivity" and "reactivity". (By "passivity" is meant "being acted upon by another" and by "reactivity", "acting upon another.") Thus, passivity may be represented by disgust–pain, by stubborn thoughtfulness and by laughing happiness. Reactive clusters may be worry and doubt (asking for information), disdainful thoughtfulness, and pleased happiness. Intermediate states are surprise and fear, where both passivity and reactivity may be present; or calm thoughtfulness and thoughtful happiness, where the expression seems to be withdrawn both from the influence of another and

---

[1] The published matrix of distances between elements (Stringer, 1967) has an error. The distance between elements 23 and 26 should be 16, not 26. The hierarchical analysis was performed on the original rather than the published matrix.

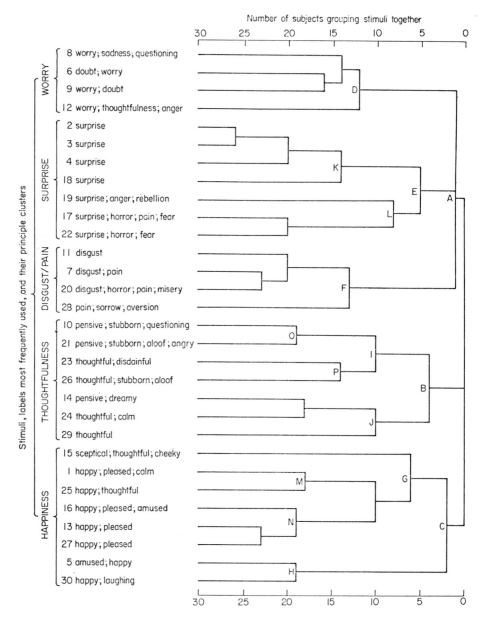

Fig. 1. Tree graph of hierarchical cluster analysis—results for 30 facial expression photographs grouped by 30 subjects

from wanting to affect another. Subsequent divisions of clusters perhaps represent levels of intensity. The passive–reactive clusters might alternatively be interpreted in terms of attention and rejection.

In order to see whether it is reasonable to assume that the data represent a hierarchical system, Johnson (1967) suggests that one should compare two methods of arriving at the clusters. In the method which gave the results above the clusters are determined in such a way that the elements in any cluster have their all-mutual distances below a certain level. The second method would form clusters such that each element in a cluster need be at or below the determining distance from only one other element in the same cluster. This is a much weaker definition of a cluster. If the two methods give approximately the same solution, one can conclude that a hierarchy is an appropriate representation of the data. In the present case there is approximately 65 per cent agreement between the two methods, which is much more than one would expect by chance.

7.1 THE SIGNIFICANCE OF HIERARCHICAL SYSTEMS

The ubiquity and power of hierarchies as descriptive and explanatory devices in a wide variety of fields has been fascinatingly outlined by Wilson (1968). Although a hierarchy is by no means the only structure to look for in cluster data, and one should, of course, beware of looking for the most obvious forms, nevertheless a hierarchical organization does seem to be a plausible structure for the interpretation of facial expressions. It is compatible with the main areas and distinctions of meaning in facial expressions which have been laid down in other studies (e.g. Chapter 7), and it does not do violence to the numerical data. But what is its theoretical relevance? Because of the dominance of the dimensional approach, little attention has been paid to hierarchical models, although the two are in no way incompatible. In fact it is noticeable that the description given above of a hierarchy of expressions uses terms very similar to those used to describe the main dimensions of expression in other studies. It would not be surprising if the main clusters had high loadings on two or more of the dimensions in the judgemental space, and were readily described in dimensional terms. The argument brought forward in this chapter is that clusters and dimensions are two different outcomes of analysing judgements of facial expressions. Because the judgements are different in the two cases and because the associated mathematical models are not reducible to one another, the relation of clusters to dimensions has been inferred rather than empirically demonstrated. But it *is* possible to infer a relationship.

The hierarchical arrangement of clusters might represent the relative readiness of the perceiving system to respond in various ways to minimal information. To distinguish clusters at a relatively low level of the hierarchy (e.g. worry from doubt, or surprise from fear) may require a good deal of contextual information. An appropriate and distinct response would not be so readily available. Or the hierarchy might correspond to developmental stages, along the lines of Osgood's exposition—although he does not use a strictly hierarchical scheme. The clusters might accumulate meaning at an early developmental stage as quite discrete and unrelated classes, strictly limited in number. Differentiation might proceed in two ways. Dimensional differentiation could arise as a result of observing sequences of expression, changing say from positive to negative affect or vice versa. The experience of continuous changes of expression from one state to the other, and to and from the neutral state, could allow the oppositional and exclusive nature of the two-dimensional poles, as well as their point of origin, to be appreciated. The progress of differentiation into several dimensions might be extended over a considerable period of time. Secondly, but contemporaneously, sub-clusters in the judgemental space could be formed, as a result of an increasing ability to differentiate the social situations in which the expressions are embedded and consequently their differing implications for response or action. This would, of course, be facilitated by some dimensional differentiation.

In practice the clusters would serve as reference points for judgement when one is initially confronted with an expression. Varying degrees of information about the situation in which the expression occurs would permit one to assign it to a progressively more finely differentiated sub-cluster, with its more finely differentiated implications for action. The dimensions would permit the fine processing of sequences of changing expressions without having recourse to an extensive partitioning of more and more sub-clusters.

There are a number of ways in which one could test whether clusters and dimensions do in fact serve different functions. One interesting hypothesis would be that in certain cases of schizophrenia patients would show bizarre sorting behaviour with facial expressions, but would be quite capable of ordering or rating the stimuli dimensionally. The assumption would be that their understanding of the action implications or situational background of expressions was disordered, leading to apparently random sets of subjectively similar stimuli. This might be due to arbitrary or inconsistent associations between the expressions and behaviour of another person, such as the mother, during early social learning. Experience of sequences of expression might have been quite regular and consistent. By contrast, some patients might show an opposite confusion, being able to sort stimuli into contextually similar groups in the same way as non-patients, but being unable to reproduce the same kind of sequential or dimensional judgements. Their social learning might have included perfectly consistent associations of expressions and context, but the significant actor may have modulated expressions in a very abrupt way, depriving them of the experience of the gradual transition of expressions on which we claim the formation of judgemental dimensions depends.

7.2 THE INCOMPATIBILITY OF DIMENSIONAL AND SET THEORETIC MODELS

The suggestion of a hierarchical system made earlier by Frijda (1969) has been followed up in two more recent contributions (1970 and Chapter 7):

> The hierarchical model can be described in two ways. The system of emotions can be seen as a set of discrete states, each of which has among its defining attributes some that represent values of more or less general variables: pleasantness, intensity, degree of attentional activity involved. Other attributes are specific for that group of emotions. Or else, it is possible to conceive of a n-dimensional system of emotional space with further differentiations in various regions which are specific for and relevant to each region. There is pleasantness and unpleasantness; and unpleasantness, for instance, may be divided into sorrow and disgust. Perhaps the hierarchical ordering reflects the process of recognising the emotional expression; placing it in a system of gross distinctions and subsequently making finer discriminations.
>
> Frijda, 1970, pp. 246–247

A hierarchy of categories and a hierarchy of dimensions are distinguished here. The recognition of emotion is conceived of as being served both by dimensions and clusters, the former being primary and general frames of reference, while the latter are more specific and situational.

Furthermore, he asserts:

> . . . the recognition of emotion consists of categorising the observed behavioral pattern in terms of a set of general dimensions, of further differentiating within the

framework of such general assessment, and of finally specifying, on the basis of situational cues or suppositions, which of the emotions compatible with the given behavioral tendency is actually present.

1970, p. 249

The peculiar strength of a hierarchical system as opposed to any other type of graph is not argued, although the general familiarity of hierarchies presumably makes it easy to appreciate how such a structure could help in any recognition task.

The logical incompatibility between dimensional and set theoretic models, which I have drawn attention to above, is at the root of Frijda's recourse to a dual system. He sees one of the major dilemmas in the recognition of emotion as being the fact that any one emotion may be represented by a variety of patterns of expressive behaviour, or points in a multidimensional space; and that any particular expression ("positional activity", or multidimensional point) may accompany several quite distinct emotional situations (or clusters). This dilemma is catered for, if not altogether explained, by positing the two systems. However, whether a dimensional system or a hierarchy of dimensions helps *recognition as such* is a point I have already doubted. Recognition could be efficiently achieved by a categorical or a hierarchical system which relied on situational cues and discrete bits of information about facial features. The importance of situational cues has repeatedly been stressed by Frijda (1958, 1961, 1969) and he demonstrates clearly the relation between clusters and facial features in his most recent papers (1970, Chapter 7). In an earlier experiment (Frijda and Van de Geer, 1961) the successful recognition of facial expressions was shown to bear a strong, positive correlation with their identifiability, in terms of verbal categories such as "surprised", "glad", "anxious", and so on. Categories such as these correspond more readily to clusters than to dimensions.

7.3   DIMENSIONS, SEQUENCES, AND HIERARCHIES IN VERBAL
      COMMUNICATION

The distinction between clusters and dimensions has also been brought out in the context of verbal communication by Miller (1969). A number of studies (e.g. Nummenmaa, 1964; Williams and Sundene, 1965; Osgood, 1966; Sweeney *et al.*, 1968) have drawn attention to similarities between the dimensions of visual (facial) and verbal expressions of emotion, and have suggested that they are important common features of different communication systems. Miller used a similar method of sorting to my own in order to study the way in which lexical information might be organized and stored in the memory. A hierarchical cluster analysis was performed on the matrix of inferred proximities. To justify this form of analysis, Miller distinguishes three different systems whereby lexical information might be organized: paradigmatic, linear and hierarchical systems. In a paradigmatic system all elements (e.g. kinship terms) have a value for each attribute that characterizes members of their set. In a linear system elements form a sequence (e.g. baby, child, adolescent, adult). In cases where elements are thought to be organized in either of these ways, a multidimensional scaling technique offers a more appropriate model than a form of cluster analysis. Sorting would appear to be appropriate where one may assume a hierarchical organization based on relations of class inclusion, in which not every element has a value for each attribute characterizing the set (e.g. some but not all living things can be classified as vertebrates). This type of organization was considered to be most frequent in subjective lexica.

The main characteristic of this kind of sorting behaviour, Miller claims, given that the elements being sorted are distinct to the subject, is that in order to group together elements the subject must ignore a number of attributes which distinguish them. He will search for a point of similarity between elements of a sufficiently high level of hierarchical superordinacy as to compensate for any observed differences. The present argument maintains that the focus of such cognitive processing is on similarity judgements; whereas in paradigmatic and linear systems, and in multidimensional scaling, it is on judgements of dissimilarity.

7.4 COGNITIVE SIMILARITY AND DISSIMILARITY

The distinction between similarity and dissimilarity in cognitive processing is most important. It can be a source of confusion when one is referring to the mathematical models. Both in multidimensional scaling and in cluster analysis it is necessary that similarity–proximity and dissimilarity–distance measures should be inversely equivalent. But this is a requirement of a theorem underlying the models, and says nothing about psychological processes. It does not mean that similarity and dissimilarity judgements are inversely equivalent psychologically. Thus although it is necessary that one should be able to use either proximities or distances in extracting the dimensions or clusters underlying stimulus interrelationships, it is not equally possible to assume that the associated judgemental process may be indiscriminate in terms of similarities or dissimilarities. The congruence of process with model is not at the level of measures derived or employed. It is a matter of the organizational structure responsible for the data or its analysis. It would be preferable to reserve the terms "similarity" and "dissimilarity" for references to judgemental processes, and to talk of derived measures in terms only of "proximity" and "distance".

In their structural analysis of the meaning of colour names Rapoport and Fillenbaum (1968) compared the results of two procedures in which subjects were variously asked to rank the relative similarity or dissimilarity of pairs of colour names. Approximately the same underlying multidimensional structure emerged from both procedures, with perhaps rather less spread of colour names in the "similarities" space. However, a graph-theoretical analysis of the earlier part of the two rankings showed noticeable differences. When subjects were focusing on similarities their early rankings tended to extract small clusters of three colour names, whereas when they were looking for dissimilarities significantly fewer of such clusters emerged. This reinforces our suggestion that similarity judgements are appropriate to a clustering model, and dissimilarity judgements to a dimensional model. The fact that one can retrieve a consistent and valid multidimensional representation by either procedure does not militate against the point.

7.5 FURTHER DISTINCTIONS BETWEEN CLUSTERS AND DIMENSIONS IN VERBAL BEHAVIOUR

Returning to Miller's (1969) study, we find that the attributes which his subjects were able to ignore, in order that they might group words together as having a similar meaning, were the "assertions" contained in the definition of a word; whereas the greater the number of "presuppositions" contained in the definition that had to be ignored in order to group together two more words, the fewer subjects in fact did so. The distinction between presuppositions and assertions is a somewhat different formulation of Katz and Fodor's (1963) distinction between "semantic markers" and "distinguishers". They proposed that a definition for some particular sense of a word should be given as a set of semantic markers followed by a distinguisher that summarizes attributes specific to the word's meaning. In the case of facial expressions we are not so much interested in definitions as in psychological meaning, but a similar discussion may be appropriate. In the facial vocabulary the semantic markers might be represented by the clusters that have been identified, while the distinguishers might be the dimensions. The distinguishing dimensions might be of two types: the general, applying to all clusters, and the more specific which might apply only to one or two areas of meaning. In the sequence "baby, child, adolescent, adult" one might take "person" as the semantic marker, and levels of maturity as the distinguishers. Similarly one might imagine a sequence of facial expressions carrying a general significance of anger, and being distinguished in a linear way by degrees of increasing or decreasing intensity, unpleasantness or rejection.

In an extension of their 1968 study of the meaning of colour names Rapoport and Fillenbaum (1969) take the discussion of clusters and dimensions a stage further. They compare several different methods of obtaining similarity judgements, which are each analysed both by hierarchic clustering and by multidimensional procedures. Similarity judgements were obtained by direct grouping (as in Stringer, 1967; Miller, 1969), by tree construction (a method in which subjects construct ordinary linear graphs—see Rapoport, 1967), and by complete undirected linear graphs (where the ordinal distances of all pairs of elements in a set are determined). An important aspect of their analyses was to supplement them with graph-theoretical analysis to ensure that the proximity matrices were not random and to see what biases operated at different stages of their construction. (One of these biases was referred to above—the differential emergence of clusters in the early stages of complete undirected linear graphs based on similarity and dissimilarity rankings.) One of the reasons for using multiple methods of analysis was the caution of Beals et al. (1968) against using multidimensional scaling techniques when their underlying assumptions cannot be satisfied. Rapoport and Fillenbaum remark quite reasonably upon the practical difficulties of satisfying these assumptions, and suggest that a multiple, supplementing approach can be adopted.

A more important reason in the context of this chapter for looking for both clusters and dimensions hinges on Rapoport and Fillenbaum's choice of stimuli. These were for one set of experiments colour names, and for another set verbs in the "have" family. The appropriateness of the two analytical techniques was to be examined, as ways of elucidating the structural organization of different semantic domains. Colour names were selected as a well-defined domain, whose physical counterparts have been subjected to repeated multidimensional studies, and whose dimensionality could therefore be compared with the known colour space. It was found that a dimensional representation was indeed the most appropriate for the colour names, which fell in a more or less circular array, corresponding to the circle of hues. It seems that both colour names and actual colours can be treated as homogeneous, unanalysable wholes of the same dimensionality. The dimensional representation of the "have" verbs, on the other hand, was uninterpretable and discontinuous; a taxonomic class-inclusion structure was required to account intelligibly for similarity data. This result ran counter to an earlier paradigmatic definition of some of the "have" verbs (Bendix, 1966), but it is pointed out that some subsets of the taxonomic structure may have different paradigmatic properties. This is analogous to my own suggestion above that a varying dimensional representation might be applied within different clusters of facial expressions. Rapoport and Fillenbaum conclude that "the general lesson of the present research is quite clear: the sort of hypothesis one holds regarding underlying structural organization governs the choice of technique for data analysis" (1969, p. 66). Just as they find different structures appropriate and meaningful for different domains of verbal semantics, so I am arguing that in non-verbal semantics also there may be different structures which correspond to different types of information processing.

8 Conclusion

Most of the experiments described here have used static stimuli, representations of expressions that are not intended to be seen as a slice from a moving and changing temporal array. I have argued that for this reason investigators have missed what might be a most important possible role for dimensions in explaining the process of interpreting facial expressions. The choice of this particular, restricted type of stimulus also prevented them from progressing beyond the study of the recognition and interpretation of expressions to considering the intended communication of emotion. Notable exceptions are the work of Thompson and Meltzer (1964), Williams and Tolch (1965), and Osgood (1966); and, of course, outside the dimensional approach there are many more exceptions. The verbal studies are cited as illustrating the value of considering alternative structures. I am not intending to suggest that the same verbal and non-verbal structure should be looked for within any particular domain, as has been found with colours, for example. But either area can probably inform the other in defining problems and looking for alternative explanations.

From a contemporary viewpoint it is sometimes hard to understand how the earlier discussions of facial expression could be apparently so blind to the dynamic and interactive nature of their subject-matter. The power of historical antecedents and methodological sacred cows in limiting the scope of these experiments is fascinating in itself. There is nothing in the dimensional approach which requires that it be involuted or exempts it from the need for justification. Yet there have been scarcely any attempts, for example, to build it into developmental, cross-cultural, or clinical investigations.

This discussion, however, has not simply been presented as a curiosity. Adequate accounts of non-verbal communication need to cater for three components; the interactive, the judgemental, and the temporal or mutative. The dimensional approach has been firmly committed to the second goal. The expanded treatment of both clusters and dimensions can define and cope with the second and third components, albeit in an as yet disaggregated way. It only remains for either or both of these models to be applied to the interactive communication of two or more individuals in a social setting. Such simple models are unlikely to seem satisfactory for very long, but until they are demonstrably superseded, they are worth exploiting to the full. Mathematical models have much to offer the study of topics contained in this book. It would be a pity if any shortcomings they may have had hitherto were to discourage investigators who are less mathematically inclined.

References

Abelson, R. P. and Sermat, V. (1962). Multidimensional scaling of facial expressions. *J. Exp. Psychol.* **63**, 546–554.

Allport, F. H. (1924). "Social Psychology". Houghton-Mifflin, Cambridge, Mass.

Attneave, F. (1962). Perception and related areas. *In* "Psychology: A Study of a Science" (Ed. S. Koch), Vol. 4, pp. 619–659. McGraw-Hill, New York.

Beals, R., Krantz, D. H. and Tversky, A. (1968). Foundations of multidimensional scaling. *Psychol. Rev.* **75**, 127–142.

Bendix, E. H. (1966). Componential analysis of general vocabulary: the semantic structure of a set of verbs in English, Hindi and Japanese. Part II. *Int. J. Amer. Ling.* **32**, No. 2.

Brannigan, C. and Humphries, D. (1969). I see what you mean . . . *New Scientist*, **49**, 406–408.

Bruner, J. S. (1957). On perceptual readiness. *Psychol. Rev.* **64**, 123–152.

Brunswik, E. (1956). "Perception and the Representative Design of Psychological Experiments". University of California Press, Berkeley.

Carroll, J. D. and Chang, J. J. (1970). Analysis of individual differences in multidimensional scaling via an *n*-way generalisation of "Eckart-Young" decomposition. *Psychometrika*, **35**, 283–319.

Cliff, N. and Young, F. W. (1968). On the relation between unidimensional judgments and multidimensional scaling. *Organisational Behaviour and Human Performance*, **3**, 269–285.

Constantinescu, P. (1967). A method of cluster analysis. *Brit. J. Math. Stat. Psychol.* **20**, 93–106.

Darwin, C. (1872). "Expression of the Emotions in Man and Animals". Murray, London.

Dittmann, A. T., Parloff, M. B. and Boomer, D. S. (1965). Facial and bodily expression: a study of receptivity of emotional cues. *Psychiatry*, **28**, 239–244.

Ekman, G. (1954). Dimensions of colour vision. *J. Psychol.* **38**, 467–474.

Ekman, G. (1955). Dimensions of emotion. *Acta Psychol.* **11**, 279–288.

Ekman. P. (1965). Differential communication of affect by head and body cues. *J. Pers. Soc. Psychol.* **2**, 726–735.

Ekman, P. and Friesen, W. V. (1967). Head and body cues in the judgement of emotion: a reformulation. *Percept. Mot. Skills*, **24**, 711–724.

Ekman, P. and Friesen, W. V. (1968). Non-verbal behaviour in psychotherapy research. *In* "Research in Psychotherapy" (Ed. J. Shlien), Vol. III, pp. 179–216. American Psychological Association, Washington, D.C.

Engen, T. and Levy, N. (1956). Constant sum judgments of facial expressions. *J. Exp. Psychol.* **55**, 454–458.

Engen, T., Levy, N. and Schlosberg, H. (1957). A new series of facial expressions. *Am. Psychol.* **12**, 264–266.

Engen, T., Levy, N. and Schlosberg, H. (1958). The dimensional analysis of a new series of facial expressions. *J. Exp. Psychol.* **55**, 454–458.

Frijda, N. H. (1958). Facial expression and situational cues. *J. Abnorm. Soc. Psychol.* **57**, 149–154.

Frijda, N. H. (1961). Facial expression and situational cues: a control. *Acta Psychol.* **18**, 239–244.

Frijda, N. H. (1969). Recognition of emotion. *In* "Advances in Experimental Social Psychology" (Ed. L. Berkowitz), Vol. IV, pp. 167–223. Academic Press, New York and London.

Frijda, N. H. (1970). Emotion and the recognition of emotion. *In* "Feelings and Emotions: The Loyola Symposium" (Ed. M. B. Arnold), pp. 241–250. Academic Press, New York and London.

Frijda, N. H. and Philipszoon, E. (1963). Dimensions of recognition of expression. *J. Abnorm. Soc. Psychol.* **66**, 45–51.

Frijda, N. H. and Van de Geer, J. P. (1961). Codability and recognition. *Acta Psychol.* **18**, 360–367.

Gibson, J. J. (1966). "The Senses Considered as Perceptual Systems". Houghton Mifflin, Boston.

Gibson, J. J. and Gibson, Eleanor J. (1955). Perceptual learning: differentiation or enrichment? *Psychol. Rev.* **62**, 32–41.

Gladstones, W. H. (1962). A multidimensional study of facial expression of emotion. *Aust. J. Psychol.* **14**, 95–99.

Gombrich, E. H. and Kris, E. (1940). "Caricature". Penguin Books, Harmondsworth, Middlesex.

Harrison, R. P. (1964). Pictic analysis: toward a vocabulary and syntax for the pictorial code; with research on facial communication. Unpublished doctoral dissertation. Michigan State University.

Harrison, R. P. and MacLean, M. S. (1965). Facets of facial communication. Unpublished report. Michigan State University.

Hastorf, A. H., Osgood, C. E. and Ono, H. (1966). The semantics of facial expressions and the prediction of the meanings of stereoscopically fused facial expressions. *Scand. J. Psychol.* **7**, 179–188.

Hofstätter, P. R. (1956). Dimensionen des minuschen Ausdruks. *Z. Exp. Angew. Psychol.* **3**, 505–529.

Isaac, P. D. (1970). Dissimilarities as indices of individual perceptual structure. *Percept. Psychophys.* **7**, 229–233.

Johnson, S. C. (1967). Hierarchical clustering schemes. *Psychometrika*, **32**, 241–254.

Katz, J. J. and Fodor, J. A. (1963). The structure of a semantic theory. *Language*, **39**, 170–210.

Kauranne, U. (1964). Qualitative factors of facial expression. *Scand. J. Psychol.* **5**, 136–142.

Krantz, D. H. (1964). The scaling of small and large colour differences. Unpublished doctoral dissertation. University of Pennsylvania.

Kruskal, J. B. (1964). Nonmetric multidimensional scaling: a numerical method. *Psychometrika*, **29**, 115–130.

Levy, N. and Schlosberg, H. (1960). Woodworth scale values of the Lightfoot pictures of facial expression. *J. Exp. Psychol.* **60**, 121–125.

Lingoes, J. C. (1965). An IBM-7090 program for Guttman-Lingoes smallest space analysis—I. *Behavl. Sci.* **10**, 183–184.

McGee, V. E. (1966). The multidimensional analysis of "elastic" distances. *Br. J. Math. Stat. Psychol.* **19**, 181–196.

Miller, G. A. (1969). A psychological method to investigate verbal concepts. *J. Math. Psychol.* **6**, 169–191.

Mordkoff, A. M. A. (1967). Factor analytic study of the judgment of emotion from facial expression. *J. Exp. Res. Pers.* **2**, 80–85.

Nummenmaa, T. (1964). "The Language of the Face". Studies in Education, Psychology and Social Research 9, University of Jyväskylä, Finland.

Nummenmaa, T. and Kauranne, U. (1958). Dimensions of facial expression. *Rep. Dept. Psychol.* 20. Institute of Pedagogics, Jyväskylä. Finland.

Osgood, C. E. (1955). Fidelity and reliability. *In* "Information Theory in Psychology: Problems and Methods" (Ed. H. Quastler), pp. 374–384. Free Press, Glencoe, Illinois.

Osgood, C. E. (1966). Dimensionality of the semantic space for communication via facial expressions. *Scand. J. Psychol.* **7**, 1–30.

Osgood, C. E. and Suci, G. J. (1952). A measure of relation determined by both mean difference and profile information. *Psychol. Bull.* **49**, 251–262.

Piderit, T. (1859). "Mimik und Phsysiognomik". Meyers, Detmold.

Rapoport, A. (1967). A comparison of two tree-construction methods for obtaining proximity measures among words. *J. Verb. Learn. Verb. Behav.* **6**, 884–890.

Rapoport, A. and Fillenbaum, S. (1968). A structural analysis of the semantic space of colour names. Report No. 60. Psychometric Laboratory, University of North Carolina.

Rapoport, A. and Fillenbaum, S. (1969). Experimental studies of semantic structures. Unpublished mimeographed report. Psychometric Laboratory, University of North Carolina.

Restle, F. (1961). "Psychology of Judgment and Choice". Wiley, New York.

Rivera, J. de (1961). A decision theory of the emotions. Unpublished doctoral dissertation. Stanford University.

Rodwan, A. S. and Hake, H. W. (1964). The linear discriminant function as a model for perception. *Am. J. Psychol.* **77**, 380–392.

Royal, D. C. and Hays, W. L. (1959). Empirical dimensions of emotional behaviour. *Proc. 15th Int. Cong. Psychol., Brussels*, 419.

Schlosberg, H. (1941). A scale for the judgment of facial expressions. *J. Exp. Psychol.* **29**, 497–510.

Schlosberg, H. (1952). The description of facial expressions in terms of two dimensions. *J. Exp. Psychol.* **44**, 229-237.

Schlosberg, H. (1954). Three dimensions of emotion. *Psychol. Rev.* **61**, 81–88.

Shepard, R. N. (1962). The analysis of proximities: multidimensional scaling with an unknown distance function, I and II. *Psychometrika*, **27**, 125–140, 219–246.

Sjöberg, L. (1968). Unidimensional scaling of multidimensional facial expressions. *J. Exp. Psychol.* **78**, 429–435.

Stevens, S. S. (1957). On the psychophysical law. *Psychol. Rev.* **64**, 153–179.

Stringer, P. (1966). Sequential proximity as the basis for similarity judgments of facial expressions. Unpublished report. University College London.

Stringer, P. (1967). Cluster analysis of non-verbal judgments of facial expressions. *Br. J. Math. Stat. Psychol.* **20**, 71–79.

Sweeney, D. R., Tinling, D. C., Eby, L. A. and Schmale, A. H., Jr. (1968). Factor analytic studies of four expressive modes of emotion. *Proceedings of the 76th Annual Convention, Am. Psychol. Assn.* 169–170.

Thompson, D. F. and Meltzer, L. (1964). Communication of emotional intent by facial expression. *J. Abnorm. Soc. Psychol.* **68**, 129–135.

Tighe, L. S. and Tighe, T. J. (1966). Discrimination learning: two views in historical perspective. *Psychol. Bull.* **66**, 353–370.

Tomkins, S. S. and McCarter, R. (1964). What and where are the primary affects? Some evidence for a theory. *Percept. Mot. Skills*, **18**, 119–158.

Torgerson, W. S. (1965). Multidimensional scaling of similarity. *Psychometrika*, **30**, 379–393.

Triandis, H. C. and Lambert, W. W. (1958). A restatement and test of Schlosberg's theory of emotion with two kinds of subjects from Greece. *J. Abnorm. Soc. Psychol.* **56**, 321–328.

Tversky, A. and Krantz, D. (1969a). The dimensional representation and the metric structure of similarity data. Technical Report MMPP 69–70. Michigan Mathematical Psychology Program, University of Michigan.

Tversky, A. and Krantz, D. (1969b). Similarity of faces: a test of interdimensional additivity. *Percept. Psychophys.* **5**, 124–128.

Wallach, M. A. (1958). On psychological similarity. *Psychol. Rev.* **65**, 103–116.

Williams, F. and Sundene, B. (1965). Dimensions of recognition: visual vs. vocal expression of emotion. *Audio-Visual Commun. Rev.* **13**, 44–52.

Williams, F. and Tolch, J. (1965). Communication by facial expression. *J. Commun.* **15**, 17–27.

Wilson, D. (1968). Forms of hierarchy: a selected bibliography. Unpublished mimeographed report. McDonnell Douglas Corporation, Huntington Beach, California.

Woodworth, R. S. (1938). "Experimental Psychology". Holt, New York.

Young, F. W. and Torgerson, W. S. (1967). TORSCA, a FORTRAN IV Program for Shepard-Kruskal multidimensional scaling analysis. *Behav. Sci.* **12**, 498.

PART 3

Concepts, Strategies and Methods

9

A Method for the Assessment of Body Movement Variability

Siegfried Frey and Mario von Cranach[1]

1 Introduction

1.1 THE TOPIC OF THIS INVESTIGATION

Empirical studies which investigate the role of body movement in interactive behaviour are often concerned with those elements of movement behaviour that are related to events which occur within communication processes. The units of analysis used in these studies are typically those behaviours whose *gestalt* character permits them to function as communicative signals. In order to assess behavioural differences as they occur with variations of communicative situations or partners, behavioural parameters that can characterize properties of the entire communication situation are clearly useful. In such investigations, behavioural properties which are frequently of a complex nature serve as the investigator's dependent variable. Differences that may occur in relation to experimental manipulations are typically

[1] The research underlying this chapter was undertaken during both authors' collaboration at the Max-Planck-Institut für Psychiatrie, Munich, Germany. We are indebted to Miss Christiane Mauderli for her help in the translation.

assessed in terms of quantitative differences in this complex variable. Here we shall be concerned with the assessment of certain features common to a variety of complex behaviours. First we shall present a method aiming at the quantitative assessment of that aspect of behaviour which we call "variability of movement", henceforth referred to as VaM.[1] The method consists of two component approaches: (1) a validated, operationalized classification method for the assessment of positional differences; (2) a formalized system which permits the quantification and subsequent analysis of nominally scaled data in terms of "variability". In the second part of this chapter we report on several empirical investigations in order to demonstrate the applicability of the method.

1.2 METHODOLOGICAL PROBLEMS IN THE DESCRIPTION OF MOVEMENT

Movement phenomena that are studied in the framework of communication research frequently show particularly distinctive patterns (*prägnante Gestalten*), and thus can be validly assessed without difficulty in most cases. Besides these "specific movement elements" (von Cranach and Frenz, 1969), a considerable number of complexly defined types of movement behaviour are considered important for the understanding of the processes of human communication (e.g. "dominant", "appeasing", "inhibited" or "threatening" movement behaviours). The complexity of such features mainly results from the quality, the number and the duration of the elements involved, and leads to considerably less distinctiveness (*Prägnanz*) of the behavioural phenomena in question, thus making it difficult for the observer to assess these phenomena validly.

The discussion of these methodological difficulties appears necessary, since complexely defined aspects of movement phenomena in fact assume the functions of response criteria in nearly all psychological disciplines and in the behavioural sciences in general. Thus in certain psychiatric contents it is regarded as relevant to establish whether an individual shows "agitated" (McReynolds, 1965), "bizarre" (Framo and Alderstein, 1961), "stereotyped" or "extravagant" (Spoerri, 1967), "nervous" or "alarmed" (Burdock *et al.*, 1964) movement behaviour. In deciding certain questions within the realm of personality

---

[1] A glossary of the abbreviations of certain features common to a variety of complex behaviours is given at the end of this chapter.

psychology, it is occasionally regarded as reasonable to examine empirically whether a person performs "angular", "desultory", "round", "retarded", "sweeping" or "inhibited movements" (Lersch, 1932). To analyse communication processes, it is sometimes important to know whether the communicating individuals show "threatening", "appeasing", or "dominating" movement behaviour (Lorenz, 1967).

Behaviours can only be classified on the basis of definitions of characteristics or of other behaviours that serve as a reference system. As long as no agreement is reached on the definition of concepts such as "agitatedness", "*Schablonenhaftigkeit*" (stereotypy), "nervousness" or "dominance", the observational criteria for agitated, stereotyped, nervous and dominant movement behaviours cannot meet methodological requirements of objectivity and validity. Whether they satisfy the postulate of reliability depends further on whether the item definition exactly specifies the coding operations. In reality, this is not typically the case for the great majority of complexly defined movement items. The assessment of complex movement phenomena mostly follows the methodological principle termed "reductive coding" by Campbell (1958). In these procedures the observer decides during actual observation whether and to what degree the behaviour of the object of observation presents the characteristic in question. Since the data thus result from the processing of an unknown number of indicators which have been computed using a non-objective weighting process, their validity and reliability is doubtful.

To eliminate the methodological shortcomings that are involved in descriptions of complex movement phenomena, it seems thus necessary to determine: (1) which single parameters ought to be assessed; (2) which computing process should be applied to them.

With regard to the objectivity and reliability of the process for transferring the expression of the complex variable to some quantitative equivalent, it can be recommended that, as a minimum, the method for the assessment of the basic movement data be kept separate from the computational method by which the basic data are transformed to a quantitative expression of the complex variable in question. By separating the procedural steps, we then have the opportunity to assess the objectivity and reliability of each step, and, if necessary, to improve the adequacy of a particular step by appropriate changes in the assessment procedure. In this manner we should be able to assure a high degree of objectivity and reliability not only for each operational step,

o

but, ultimately, for the quantitative statement about the complex phenomenon as a whole.

The question of validity of the operations which are used to assess the phenomenon in question remains to be considered. If we intend to assess empirically some phenomenon which has been clearly defined conceptually, we should be able to show that the operationally defined prescriptions refer strictly to the conceptual definitions used. But even if we fulfil this requirement, difficulties still can arise from disagreement between the investigators about the conceptual character of the phenomenon. As to the assessment of complex phenomena involving the registration of movement data, a time–space frame of reference will be accepted by most investigators as an appropriate criterion to assess the validity of the movement data themselves. On the other hand, we can expect considerable disagreement among investigators who are concerned with the validity of the inference procedures which lead to the subsequent statement about the complex phenomenon in question. Since, to a large extent, such disagreement will be systematically related to conceptual differences about the phenomenon, we can hardly hope to assess the validity of our computational prescriptions simply on theoretical grounds.

However, empirical examination of the validity and utility of the specifications used (which provides information about the appropriateness of competing conceptual definitions) is only feasible if the method itself is elaborated to an extent that allows an objective and reliable usage of the definitional prescriptions. This has rarely been the case in studies of complex movement phenomena.

2 The assessment of variability of body movement

2.1 PROCEDURE FOR THE RECORDING OF MOVEMENT BEHAVIOUR

The term "movement" will be used to indicate that during the observation time t_1 to t_n the object observed was seen at more than one spatial location in a certain spatial frame of reference. To describe movement behaviour according to this definition it is of course necessary to have an instrument that allows differentiation in the time dimension as well as in the spatial dimensions.

Since our "movement" definition allows us to understand "movement" as a continuous process, we could in principle demand that the instrument should be able to differentiate an infinite number of units in the time dimension as well as in the spatial dimensions. At least as a consequence of the limitations of accuracy of measurement, it is impossible to fulfil this demand in an empirical representation of actual movement, and therefore we start our analyses of continuous movement always on the basis of data that constitute a discrete scale. Thus the empirical assessment of continuous movement is always affected by an error of measurement which is determined by the insensibility of the method, and is therefore characteristic for the description system used.

The description system used in the present investigation has been explicitly reported by Frey and von Cranach (1971), and Frey (1971). Therefore it is only described here in its essentials. This system describes the movement behaviour of sitting subjects, by assessing the positions of the head, trunk, hands and feet at observation times $t_1, t_2, \ldots t_n$. The positions of the head and trunk are defined in relation to a three-dimensional, orthogonal system of reference based on the main spatial axes. Our system of reference permits the assessment of position differences on the basis of sagittal, rotational and lateral flexions. The "upright body position", which is considered the normal position, shows neither saggital, nor rotational, nor lateral flexion.[1] Deviations from the normal position in each dimension are distinguished according to the direction of deviation. Thus in each dimension three *locations* can be distinguished:

Location 1 The object of observation does not show a deviation from normal location in the dimension studied.
Location 2 The object of observation does show a deviation from the normal location in this dimension.
Location 3 The object of observation shows a deviation from the normal location in this dimension, but in the opposite sense to location 2.

In the *sagittal* dimension the classification scheme for head and trunk thus distinguishes the following *positions:* (1) normal position (the head–trunk is tilted neither forward nor backward); (2) deviation from the normal position (the head–trunk is tilted forward); (3) deviation from the normal position in the opposite sense to location 2 (the head–trunk is tilted backwards). The location in the *rotation* dimension (degree of

[1] This terminology has been chosen according to an anatomic language usage (Knese, 1949; von Lanz, 1963).

turning from the normal position) and in the *lateral* dimension (degree of sideways tilting from the normal position) are assessed likewise.

The positions for each of the body parts studied result from the combination of locations in the three dimensions, and they are considered as different if they differ at least in one dimension. Since according to this simple classification three locations can be distinguished in each of the three independent dimensions, the classification system for head and trunk thus allows one to distinguish $3 \times 3 \times 3 = 27$ positions in each case.

The positions of hands and feet are assessed differently, by means of their location in relation to different body or object areas. The features considered here apply to a person seated in proximity to some surface such as a desk. Hand positions are classified according to whether 11 spatial areas (hand, head, neck, trunk, upper arm, forearm, thigh, lower part of the leg, foot, chair and desk) are touched by the hand or not. To classify the position of the foot, four parts of the foot (heel, toes, inner and outer edge) are classified according to whether they touch one of five areas (floor, chair, thigh, lower part of the leg and foot). Thus the position of the hand is assessed by 11 and the position of the foot by 20 codings; on a simple touched/not-touched basis the positions are regarded as different if the combination of 11 symbols in the case of the hand (or 20 in the case of the foot) differs in at least one symbol of location.

2.2 A MODEL FOR THE CHARACTERIZATION OF THE VARIABILITY OF RECORDED MOVEMENT BEHAVIOUR

2.2.1 *Demands on the model*

Movement behaviour has been assessed by various classification systems, e.g. those of Ex and Kendon (1964), Frey and von Cranach (1971), Heimann and Lukacs (1966), Leventhal and Sharp (1966). It is represented typically in highly detailed and comprehensive protocols, which as a result of the amount of data and the number of coding aspects are hardly clearer than the processes on which the data are based. These protocols gain their scientific value only through the successive data analyses applied to the movement behaviour data according to the theoretical interests of the investigators.

The theoretical model for the quantification of the characteristic "variability of movement behaviour" (VaM), as described below, aims at the assessment of a behavioural aspect that assumes theoretical importance in various disciplines in the behavioural sciences. VaM serves, together with other characteristics, as an empirical criterion for the description of psychiatric syndromes, for example catatonic or excited schizophrenia, inhibited or agitated depression, or the manic or depressed phases of cyclotomia (Kloos, 1962; Yates, 1960). Modern personality psychology reports differences in the amount of motoric variability as depending on whether one is an intraverted or extraverted personality type (Brengelmann, 1960). Studies in cultural anthropology point to relations between differential VaM and ethnographic characteristics (Birdwhistell, 1970). In the study of communication, these characteristics perhaps could be used to specify the communicative behaviour of persons of different status. In spite of numerous hints at the systematic importance of the variability of human movement behaviour, no theoretical model exists to help in the systematization of the VaM characteristic. Descriptions of motor variability as given by studies in the disciplines already mentioned are mainly in the form of nominal findings. Thus motor variability is presented by means of a scale that assumes alternative qualities for a number of phenomena, while there exists no evidence for the assumption of categorical completeness of the items used in the description. This results in the restriction of the behaviour descriptions virtually just to the coding of extreme degrees of movement variability on the basis of a sign system, as well as greatly weakening the ordinal scaling of the recorded phenomena.

In contrast, the method here suggested is based on the quantitative scaling of VaM. In this model VaM designates a complex of three parameters indicating the differentiation of a series of ratings of positions. Those parameters are empirically assessed with reference to:

(1) definitional differences between observed positions (*nominal differentiation*, nD); (2) relative frequencies of observed positions (*frequential differentiation*, fD); (3) sequential order of observed positions (*sequential differentiation*, sD).

VaM is considered to be small if few positions with different definitions appear, if any positions can be allocated to one particular positional category, and if few positional changes occur during the time t_1 to t_n.

VaM is considered to be larger if more positions in different categories occur, if the positional categories are occupied more homogeneously, and if more positional changes occur in the observation time t_1-t_n.

2.2.2 Quantification of the aspect of "nominal differentiation of movement behaviour"

The term "nominal differentiation of movement behaviour", nD, is intended to designate the quotient of the number of empirically assessed positions of differing definition and the maximum number of possibly different positions. Maximal nD is achieved if as many positions as possible have been classified as nominally different. Minimal nD is obtained if as few positions as possible have different classifications.

For a sample of n assessments of positions the theoretical maximum number of nominally different positions can always be stated. In the case where the number of positions as defined by the system of reference is smaller than the number of observations, the possible maximum of different positions observed is fixed by the number of positions that can be differentiated by the classification system. In the case where the number of positions as distinguished by the system of reference exceeds that of the number of observations, the maximum number of different positions is fixed by the number of observations.

Since the frequency of occurrence of different positions thus shows a direct relation to the classification system applied and to the size of the sample, and can only be reasonably interpreted in the light of these, it seems appropriate to relate the number of observed different positions (k) to the maximum number (K) of distinguishable positions. So we get for the case of maximal differentiation of movement behaviour $(k=K)$ the value nD$=1$. If a category system is used, the minimum possible number of categories of position observed is $k=1$. If we define this minimal amount of nD as zero, the degree of nD is calculated according to the equation:

$$nD=(k-1)/(K-1), \qquad (1)$$

where nD stands for the amount of nominal differentiation of movement behaviour, k stands for the number of empirically observed categories of positions, and K stands for the maximum number of distinguishable categories of position (as defined either by the definition system or by the size of the sample).

2.2.3   Quantification of the aspect of "frequential differentiation of movement behaviour"

If a sample of n determinations of position is obtained, distributed over k positions, $n-k$ instances can be distributed in different ways between the k position definitions. The mode of distribution of these frequencies forms the basis for the judgement of the "frequential differentiation of movement behaviour" (fD).

In defining the term VaM we have determined that the amount of fD will be greater, the more categories show high frequencies of usage. The maximal usage of the k categories is achieved if the frequency in each of the k categories is $h_i = h = n/k$, i.e. where the n observations are equally distributed over k categories. In order to judge an observation protocol in respect of the distribution of n determinations of positions over k categories of positions, we assess the frequency h_i of the occurrence of each of the positions found, and analyse this distribution, making use of the measure of entropy given by information theory:

$$U = - \sum_{i=1}^{k} p_i \log_2 p_i, \qquad (2)$$

where U stands for the degree of entropy of a set of k equally or unequally probable alternatives, p_i stands in this formula for the probability of the alternative k_1, and k stands for the number of alternatives.

In this definition, the parameter p_i functions as a theoretical parameter. It cannot be assessed empirically, but can be estimated from empirical observations. This estimation is based on the relative frequency, such that $\hat{p}_i = h_1/n$ where h_1 designates the absolute frequency of instances recorded for the alternative k_1, and n the size of the sample of observations. If we now consider the empirical values necessary to assess the degree of entropy, we obtain the equation:

$$\hat{U} = - \sum_{i=1}^{k} \hat{p}_i \log_2 \hat{p}_i = - \sum_{i=1}^{k} (h_1/n) \log_2 (h_1/n) = - \frac{1}{n} \sum_{i=1}^{k} h_i \log_2 h_i + \log_2 n. \quad (3)$$

$\hat{U}$ stands here for the degree of entropy that was assessed over estimations of p_i from the relative frequencies $(\hat{p}_i)$. In this form, the measure of entropy characterizes the degree of equal distribution or regularity of a collection of symbols that can be ordered as alternatives with certain respective frequencies. (In information theory, the amount of equal distribution is interpreted with regard to the predictability or unpredictability of the symbols. The amount of predictability is considered maximal if all symbols of a series can be attributed to the same alternative, that is to say if the frequency of usage of one alternative equals the number of observations, and the frequency of all other possible alternatives is zero. The amount of predictability is assumed minimal if all alternatives show the same frequency of usage. In this case, the probability of occurrence of a certain alternative is as large as the probability of occurrence of every other alternative.)

In our case, we interpret the degree of equality of distribution in relation to the amount of fD. To assess the amount of regularity of a positional distribution over k alternative positions, the use of the measure of entropy in the form $\hat{U} = - \sum\limits_{i=1}^{k} \hat{p}_i \log_2 \hat{p}_i$ seems inappropriate. The size of the value gained by means of this measure depends on the number of alternatives occurring as well as on the degree of equal distribution of the observations (Attneave, 1959).

In order to judge the regularity of the positional distribution over a given number of alternatives (here k), it is therefore necessary to relate the value determined by equation (3) to the maximum value of regularity. The maximum regularity of a data distribution over k alternatives is given when all the frequencies of the single alternatives are given $h_i = n/k$. In this case, the value of maximum regularity is easy to determine. It corresponds to the logarithm to the base two of the number of alternatives (Attneave, 1959). In all cases, however, in which n cannot be divided by k without a remainder, the alternatives show different frequencies, even if the observations are distributed as regularly as possible. Thus, if we define h as the largest whole number $\leqslant n/k$, then $n - hk$ alternatives show—in the case of the most equal data distribution—the frequencies $h_i = h + 1$, while $k - (n - hk)$ alternatives have a frequency of $h_i = h$. In cases where n cannot be divided by k without a remainder the maximum entropy is therefore given (from equation 3) according to the following relation:

$$\hat{U}_{max} = - \frac{1}{n} [(n - hk)(h + 1) \log_2 (h + 1) + h(k - n + hk) \log_2 h] + \log_2 n. \qquad (4)$$

By relating the entropy value determined by equation 3 to the highest possible value of entropy obtainable with k alternatives, we then get the relation:

$$\frac{\hat{U}}{\hat{U}_{max}} = \frac{-\frac{1}{n} \sum\limits_{i=1}^{k} h_i \, \log_2 h_i + \log_2 n}{-\frac{1}{n}[(n-hk)(\bar{h}+1)\,\log_2(\bar{h}+1)+\bar{h}(k-n+\bar{h}k)\,\log_2\bar{h}]+\log_2 n.} \tag{5}$$

The minimum amount of equal distribution ($\hat{U}_{min}$) is reached when as many categories as possible show a minimal distribution. This case occurs if $k-1$ categories were observed only once. Then $k-1$ categories show the frequency of usage $h_i=1$, while one category has the frequency of usage $h_i=n-(k-1)$. Since the measure of entropy is based on the comparison of relative frequencies, for $n \to \infty$ the value for the minimum degree of regularity tends towards zero. If a finite sample is made, the value resulting from the relation $\hat{U}/\hat{U}_{max}$ is—for a minimal regularity of position distribution—always larger than zero. But the value of entropy for minimal regularity is actually determined by equation 3 according to the relation:

$$\hat{U}_{min} = -\frac{1}{n}(n-k+1)\,\log_2(n-k+1)+\log_2 n. \tag{6}$$

By defining the ideal case of minimal regularity as zero, the degree of fD can be determined according to the relation

$$fD = (\hat{U}-\hat{U}_{min})/(\hat{U}_{max}-\hat{U}_{min}). \tag{7}$$

From equations 3, 4 and 6 we thus obtain:

$$fD = \frac{-\frac{1}{n} \sum\limits_{i=1}^{k} h_i \, \log_2 h_i + \log_2 n -[-n^{-1}(n-k+1)\,\log_2(n-k+1)+\log_2 n]}{-\frac{1}{n}(n-hk)(\bar{h}+1)\,\log_2(\bar{h}+1)+\bar{h}(k-n+\bar{h}k)\,\log_2\bar{h}]}$$
$$+\log_2 n - [\frac{1}{n}(n-k+1)\,\log_2(n-k+1)+\log_2 n]$$

or:

$$fD = \frac{\sum\limits_{i=1}^{k} h_i \, \log_2 h_i - (n-k+1)\,\log_2(n-k+1)}{(n-hk)(\bar{h}+1)\,\log_2(\bar{h}+1)}$$
$$+\bar{h}(k-n+\bar{h}k)\,\log_2\bar{h}-(n-k+1)\,\log_2(n-k+1). \tag{8}$$

2.2.4 Quantification of the aspect of "sequential differentiation of movement behaviour"

If a sample of n assessments of position is made, representing the positions at the times t_1-t_n, successively occurring positions can belong to the same or different categories. The extent to which successive

positions fall into different categories forms the base for judging the
"sequential differentiation of movement behaviour" (sD).

In defining the characteristic VaM we stated that the degree of sD
is larger the more successive positions fall into different categories. To
find the degree to which the categories represented vary in temporal
sequence, we start with the position at the time t_1, and compare each
position with the following one, deciding whether the positions belong
to the same or to different categories. We will call it a change of position
(CP) if a position is followed by a position belonging to a different
category. Thus, in order to check how many CPs occur within a set of
n assessments of position, we have to make $n-1$ comparisons of successive positions.

Since at least $k-1$ CPs have to occur if there are k different categories,
the n positions should therefore yield a minimum (CP_{min}) when $k-1$
changes of position are present. The maximum sD is given when the
number of CPs actually determined is equal to the highest possible
number of CPs. The maximum number of CPs depends on the size of
the sample as well as on the value h_{max} of the most frequently occurring
category. If $h_{max} \leq n/2$, the maximum number of possible CPs is equal to
the number of comparisons. Thus if $h_{max} \leq n/2$, the highest possible
number of changes of position is $CP_{max} = n-1$. If $h_{max} > n/2$ the number
of possible CPs is limited by the number of positions not included in
h_{max}. Each position which does not fall into the category with the
maximal frequency yields at most two CPs (if it is preceded temporally
by a position of the h_{max} category and followed by a position of the
h_{max} category). The maximum number of CPs therefore equals double
the frequency of the number of positions which do not fall into the
category h_{max}. Because the number of the positions not belonging to
the category h_{max} is always equal to $n-h_{max}$, the highest possible
number of CPs for $h_{max} > n/2$ is given by $CP_{max} = 2(n-h_{max})$.

By defining the minimal sD as zero, the degree of sD is determined
according to the relation:

$$sD = (CP - CP_{min})/(CP_{max} - CP_{min}). \tag{9}$$

According to equation (9) the degree of sD for $h_{max} \leq n/2$ is thus determined by the relation:

$$sD\ (h_{max} \leqslant n/2) = \frac{CP - (k-1)}{(n-1) - (k-1)} = \frac{CP + 1 - k,}{n - k} \tag{10}$$

while for $h_{max} > n/2$ we have:

$$\text{sD}\ (h_{\max} > n/2) = \frac{\text{CP} - (k-1)}{2(n - h_{\max}) - (k-1)} = \frac{\text{CP} + 1 - k}{2(n - h_{\max}) + 1 - k,} \quad (11)$$

where CP stands for the observed number of changes of position, $\text{CP}_{\min}$ stands for the minimal number of changes of position, $\text{CP}_{\max}$ stands for the maximal number of changes of position, k stands for the number of different categories of position, n stands for the number of determinations of position, and $h_{\max}$ stands for value of usage of the most frequently encountered category of position.

2.2.5 Problems of weighting the individual parameters in determining a total value for "variability of movement behaviour" (VaM)

"Variability of movement behaviour" as defined above does not imply any predetermined rule about the relative weight of the three different aspects of variability. Depending upon the questions to be asked, the theoretical importance of the parameters may vary, and for this reason the experimenter may decide to make use of only one of the variability parameters or to weight the scores obtained differently (e.g. by multiplying the different scores by different constants). As no general weighting for each of the three parameters can be prescribed, any particular set of weightings must be determined and justified theoretically by the experimenter.

For the case in which the experimenter decides to combine all parameters with equal weight to form a total test-score, VaM, it is not advisable to use a simple summation of the test-scores nD, fD and sD. The structure of equation (7) shows that the value that we obtain for fD is calculated with reference to a maximal and minimal amount of fD which varies with variation of n and k. Since n specifies the number of observations and k the number of categories which have a frequency of at least one, the calculation of the regularity of the distribution of n observations over k categories is therefore actually based on the distribution properties of only $n - k$ data. The empirical basis of the assertions made about sD is, for any given n, also influenced by the value of k, since the number of positional categories determines a certain number of changes of position that are eliminated in the calculation of sD. In the case of $h_{\max} > n/2$, the number of data used for the calculation of sD is additionally reduced.

The smaller the number of observations on which the assertion is based, the less meaningful seems the information which is given by the VaM parameters, since if a numerical value is based on very few observations we can expect that it is strongly influenceable by random fluctuations. From this point of view, it seems desirable to limit, for equal weighting, the influence of a particular test-score on the composite test-score (VaM) according to the size of the sample actually analysed.

The number of observations to be used for determining the fD values depends on the size of the $n-k$ difference. With increasing n, the influence of k on this difference decreases and disappears if $n \to \infty$. If n is small, a correction to the obtained fD values seems justified, however. This correction should be made with regard to the number of observations on which the test-score is based. Since in the individual case, the fD test-score is not based on n but on $n-k$ observations, it is proposed to weight the obtained fD values with the factor

$$Wf_{\text{f D}} = (n-k)/n,$$

where $Wf_{\text{f D}}$ is a multiplying factor for the fD score obtained by equation (8). Through this weighting the numerical value of fD scores, in cases where $n-k$ does not differ very much from n, changes less than the numerical value of fD scores where $n-k$ does differ very much from n. With increasing n, the weighting factor grows less and less important.

As mentioned above, the evaluation of sD is based on $n-1$ comparisons of position. The calculations of sD, however, do not take into consideration $k-1$ of the CPs, the latter being already determined by the number of different categories of position. Since this reduces the empirical basis of the assessment sD by $k-1$ data, a weighting of the test values of sD is proposed using the factor

$$Wf_{\text{s D}} \ (h_{\max} \leqslant n/2) = (n-k)/(n-1),$$

where $Wf_{\text{s D}} \ (h_{\max} \leqslant n/2)$ is a multiplying factor for the sD score obtained by equation (10). In the case of sD $(h_{\max} > n/2)$, only 2 $(n-h_{\max})$ comparisons of position out of $n-1$ comparisons of position can lead to the registration of CPs. Additionally, the empirical basis for the assessment of sD test-scores is reduced by those $k-1$ CPs that are already determined by the number of occurring positional categories. We suggest that one should account for this by weighting sD with the factor

$$Wf_{\text{s D}} \ (h_{\max} > n/2) = [2(n-h_{\max}) - k + 1]/(n-1),$$

where $Wf_{\text{s D}} \ (h_{\max} > n/2)$ is a multiplying factor for the sD score obtained by equation (11). By this operation, the numerical test-scores of sD is reduced with an increasing k and with a decreasing $(n - h_{max})$.

With reference to the weighting procedures described here, it should be mentioned again, that along with an increasing influence of the weighting factors the test-scores for fD and sD decrease. Such a decrease also produces typically a decrease in the size of the differences between test-scores, thus making it difficult to answer the question about the influence of the experimental variables on fD and sD. Therefore, we in principle suggest a large sample of data in order to make the influence of the weighting factors as small as possible. But in those cases in which a large n cannot be achieved, a restriction of the analysis to nD or the use of a total score VaM that is composed by the weighted test-scores seems to be the statistically most reliable characterization of the variability of movement.

3 Empirical investigations

Individual movement behaviour may change with the variation of external circumstances as well as with different internal conditions of the subject. In order to find out to what extent the criteria nD, fD and sD show such variations, we conducted four studies registering the movement behaviour of subjects under the influence of several external and internal conditions, determining the test values of VaM in each case.

3.1 INDIVIDUAL DIFFERENCES IN BODY MOVEMENT VARIABILITY

Our first study dealt with the question of to what extent do VaM parameters show inter-individual differences? For this purpose we registered the movement behaviour of 8 subjects during 6 meals (on different days) and compared the variance of the test values between subjects with the variance of the test values within subjects.[1] The subjects were patients of a closed psychiatric ward. In each case movement behaviour was registered at 5-second intervals over $2\frac{1}{2}$ minutes, yielding 30 positions per subject per meal. Assessments of position were made from photographs taken through one-way windows of our observation station. The results of the analysis of variance are shown in Table 1.

According to these results, the variance of the nD values obtained for

---

[1] An evaluation of this experiment, according to an older procedure, is given by Frey and von Cranach (1971).

TABLE 1

The results of a Kruskal–Wallis analysis of variance (by ranks) for 8 subjects in 6 repeated observations, with respect to the "person" variable ($N=8$, $df=7$)

	nD		fD		sD	
	H	p	H	p	H	p
Head	31.47	<0.1%	10.03	ns	32.65	<0.1%
Trunk	31.46	<0.1%	12.47	ns	3.80	ns
Left hand	24.92	<0.1%	16.43	<5%	18.99	<1%
Right hand	21.68	<1%	19.57	<1%	22.31	<1%

the four parts of the body is, with a very small probability of error, attributable very largely to the variable "person". As to the fD values, their dependence on the variable "person" for head and trunk positions is less evident. For the test values of the right and left hand, relations to the variable "person" were found at a significant level. The sD values show a relation to the variable "person" for the head, left hand and right hand.

Altogether the variances of the test values seem, therefore, to show a stable, individually different determination of VaM. It is striking, however, to notice that the intra-individual stability is not the same for all the parts of the body examined; whereas the variance of the test values determined for the hands showed, in all three dimensions of variability, a close relation to the variable "person", the variance of the fD and sD test values of the upper part of the body, and the variance of the fD values of the head, are not explained by the variable "person". It seems, therefore, that extra-individual factors can modify relatively strongly the movement behaviour of the trunk in the fD and sD dimensions. As to the nD dimension, extra-individual factors seem to exert only a weak effect on all parts of the body.

3.2 THE INFLUENCE OF SITUATIONAL AND PHARMACOLOGICAL VARIABLES ON BODY MOVEMENT VARIABILITY[1]

In a further experiment, we studied to what extent individuals' behaviour differences remain stable while their physiological and situational conditions are changed. Three situational conditions were

[1] The study was conducted in collaboration with Dr D. Schwarz and Mrs Sedlmayr. We are indebted to the Deutsche Hoffman-La Roche A. G., Grenzach, Baden, for financial support.

defined as the situations: "waiting", "painting", and "interview". In the situation "waiting", the subject had to stay for five minutes in one place, unoccupied and alone in a room. In the situation "painting", the subjects were asked to paint as they wished on samples from a series of printed forms with regular designs. In the situation "interview", the subject was questioned by a physician about his present state of health and about his thoughts regarding his "painting".

The variation of physiological conditions was effected by intravenous injections of caffein benzoate (1.0 ml caffein benzoate $+1.0$ ml sodium chloride solution), Diazepam (valium) (1.0 ml valium $+1.0$ ml sodium chloride solution) and a placebo (2.0 ml sodium chloride solution). Caffein benzoate is considered in the literature (Eichholz, 1957; Møller, 1961) to have a stimulating effect, and Diazepam an inhibiting effect, on motor behaviour.

Each situation was tested under each of the following medication conditions: "no medication", "placebo", "drug (caffeine or valium)". Therefore in each experiment, the subject was tested in each situation three times; so providing nine behaviour protocols in each experimental session. While the sequence of the pharmacological conditions was always in the order "no medication", "placebo", "drug", the sequence of the situations, "waiting", "painting", "interview", was randomly assigned to each medicational condition.

In order to avoid contaminating effects of the drugs, we tested the drug variables on different days. Since all medication conditions were tested again in the second experimental session, we obtained from each subject a total of 18 behaviour protocols.

The subjects were doctors and nurses of the Max-Planck-Institute for Psychiatry $(N=10)$. They were unaware of the purpose of the investigation. Movement behaviour was registered under each condition by means of 30 snapshots, taken through one-way windows of our observation room, at intervals of 5 seconds, as in the previous study.

In a multifactorial rank analysis of variance according to Friedman's method (Lienert, 1962) the test values of nD, fD and sD from six parts of the body were examined, in order to check for dependence of the test values on the classification variables "person", "medication" and "situation".

3.2.1 *Individual differences*
Results on inter-individual differences in VaM are shown in Table 2.

TABLE 2

The results of Friedman's analysis of variance by ranks for 10 subjects in 9 different situations, with respect to the "person" variable ($N=10$, $df=9$)

	nD		fD		sD	
	χ^2	p	χ^2	p	χ^2	p
Head	22.15	<1%	8.25	ns	13.92	ns
Trunk	29.45	<0.1%	22.92	<1%	12.43	ns
Left hand	31.38	<0.1%	17.02	<5%	4.17	ns
Right hand	33.41	<0.1%	28.96	<0.1%	9.96	ns
Left foot	20.85	<5%	22.97	<1%	14.28	ns
Right foot	27.30	<1%	26.08	<1%	27.47	<1%

These results confirm the findings of the previous study, according to which individual factors constitute a major source of the variance of the nD test values. The effect of the variable "person" on nD test values remains despite the situational and medicational variations introduced here. Furthermore, it seems interesting that this result is also valid for the nD test values of the positions of the feet, whose VaM has not been determined in the first study. The analysis of the fD values again led to the conclusion that frequential differentiation of single parts of the body co-vary in different degrees with individual differences. As in the first study, we noticed once more that the degree of fD of the head is less determined by individual factors than for other parts of the body. Since the relations of the sD test values to the variable "person" are indistinct, we still have to check if their variance can be explained in the variables "situation" or "medication".

3.2.2 Situational effects

The analysis of variance resulted in the values indicated in Table 3. These results show a systematic effect of the variable "situation" on the nD values of parts of the body such as head, trunk and left hand. The test values fD, however, must be considered for almost all parts of the body to be independent from the situational variables examined here. The variance of the test values sD, which showed no appreciable relation to the variable "person", is explained to a great extent by the variable "situation". Only the sequential differentiation of movement behaviour of the feet did not show a significant relation to the variable "situation". It seems therefore interesting that the variance of the sD

TABLE 3

The results of Friedman's analysis of variance by ranks for 10 subjects in 3 situational conditions ("waiting", "painting" and "interview"). ($N=10$, $df=2$)

	nD		fD		sD	
	χ^2	p	χ^2	p	χ^2	p
Head	15.81	<0.1%	3.81	ns	13.42	<1%
Trunk	6.35	<5%	2.85	ns	6.35	<5%
Left hand	7.40	<5%	6.20	<5%	12.60	<1%
Right hand	1.83	ns	1.40	ns	15.00	<0.1%
Left foot	3.75	ns	3.05	ns	0.35	ns
Right foot	2.60	ns	1.85	ns	3.65	ns

test values of the feet revealed a clear relation to the variable "person" (see Table 2).

3.2.3 Effects of medication
The analysis of variance re-examination of the test values gave no hints whatsoever as to any systematic effect of the variable "medication" on the test values nD, fD and sD. This might be due partly to the low dosage of the drugs, partly to the fact that the weight of the other variables might have neutralized or covered the effect of the medication. Since the factor "person" explains a large part of the variance of the test values and since the pharmacological literature reports personality-specific effects of medication (Møller, 1961), it seemed indicated to consider these test values in such terms. For this purpose we made a paired comparison of test values of the medicational conditions of "caffeine" and "valium". In corresponding situations the scores nD, fD and sF of both medication conditions were compared. The relations show that under the condition "caffeine" some subjects achieved higher values for almost all parts of the body and all test values. Other subjects showed equally consistently higher test values under the "valium" condition.

3.2.4 Summary
The results of this study therefore permit the conclusion that the individual characteristics of VaM remain fairly stable under changing experimental conditions. The systematic effects due to situational variations of conditions and to medication variations interact with individual

characteristics of VaM. According to the results obtained here, such interactions are not always of a simple structure. In the case of varied situational conditions, the influence of the situational variations studied on the test values seems to lie in the same direction for the prevailing number of subjects. If the medication conditions vary, however, a more complicated interaction with personality characteristics seems to occur, which might lead to the effect that some subjects neutralize or perhaps even over-compensate for the physiological effects.

3.3   THE INFLUENCE OF COMMUNICATIVE CONDITIONS ON BODY MOVEMENT
      VARIABILITY

Situational effects in the study reported above hinted at the idea that VaM might be different in communicative and non-communicative situations. The two studies to be reported next give preliminary information on how far variations of communicative conditions do influence movement behaviour. This question differs from the traditional method of communication research, since we do not ask for the meaning of any specific movement units but employ a complex phenomenon of movement variability as the dependant variable, in order to assess the behavioural consequences of experimental manipulations of the communication situation.

3.3.1   *Body movement and communication content*
In the first experiment we checked whether different topics of conversation have systematic effects on VaM during communication.[1] For this purpose, 18 couples of conversation partners talked about the four topics: "Vietnam", "carnivals", "travelling", and "movies". Each topic was discussed for about 10 minutes. The subjects were school-girls from a secondary school. Their average age was 18 years. Movement behaviour of both persons was registered during conversation through one-way windows of our observation room, with intervals of 10 seconds between position recordings.

The analysis of the results confirmed once more the dependency of the test values of VaM on individual differences, but gave no indication of a systematic relation between the variable "subject of conversation" and the nD, fD and sD test values. Since the topics of this study did not

[1] This experiment was performed in collaboration with Ursula Stevens, M.A. Miss Stevens worked mainly on the linguistic aspect of the study, which is not referred to in this report.

vary very widely as far as the emotional involvement of our subjects was concerned, the generalization of this statement is limited.

3.3.2 *Body movement, emotional stress and group integration*

a. *Design of the study*

In order to study the effect of emotional stress on the movement behaviour of communicating people, one of our collaborators (Burkart, 1971) performed an experiment in which he systematically varied the degree of emotional stress. In this experiment, the topic "street-traffic" was discussed twice for 7 to 10 minutes; first from an aspect which stimulated an emotionally neutral state of the subject, then from a point of view which stressed the subject emotionally. In the emotionally neutral discussion (Neutral Interview, NI), the subject was asked to express his opinion on general street-traffic problems. His comments were listened to with great interest by the experimenter, who never opposed the subject's opinion. In the emotionally stressful conversation (Stress Interview, SI), the capacity of the subject to participate in street-traffic was discussed. In this talk, the experimenter doubted the subject's ability to drive competently. He stated that the subject constituted a risk to the safety of other traffic participants; the experimenter strongly opposed the subject's opinion that he was capable of driving competently.

In addition, the degree of stress in the (SI) situation was varied by varying an aspect of the social pattern, the mode of integration (MI) of subjects. The subjects were manipulated so as to be either integrated (MInt) or isolated (MIs) in their relations with the group of fellow subjects. This was achieved by inserting an Asch experiment (Asch, 1956)—purporting to be a perceptual achievement test relevant to traffic problems—between the neutral and the stressing interviews. Under the MInt condition the judgements of the subjects did not differ from the judgements made by three other group members that were, unknown to the subject, confederates of the experimenter. Under the MIs condition the judgements of the naïve subject were always different from the judgements that the confederate subjects made. In fact, in order to obtain from the subject the required (integrating or isolating) reactions we reversed the experimental set-up of Asch. In the classical experiments by Asch, the naïve subject receives information about the decisions of the instructed group members before giving his own opinion. In our experiment, the subject always gave his opinion first, thus feeding the other members of the group with information about his decision and thus enabling them to isolate the subject or to integrate him into the group.

According to the experimental conditions, the instructed subjects made estimates which were either equal (MInt) to those of the subject or different (MIs) from them. Under the MInt condition as well as under the MIs condition the experimenter explained (at the very beginning of the SI situation) that all judgements of the subject were wrong. Therefore in the MInt condition the naïve subject as well as all the confederate subjects were held to be unable to make appropriate assessments in the perception task, while in the MIs condition the naïve subject was the only member of the group held to be unable to make right assessments in the task. Therefore, in the SI situation under MInt conditions, the derogatory assertions of the experimenter as to the subject's capacity to drive concerned the other group members as well; in the SI situation under the MIs condition, the subject was made—through the discriminating assertions of the experimenter—an outsider in relation to the group.

The subjects were 18 students between 19 and 29 years. Nine of them were tested under the MInt and nine under the MIs condition. The subjects were assigned randomly to these conditions. Their behaviour was registered through one-way windows of our observation room by a video-recording system. Pictures of the subject were taken while he was sitting facing the camera. In the following analysis of the video records the positions of the different parts of the body were determined at intervals of 2.5 s—according to the usual system of classification—through direct judgement. The positional sample consists of 120 units each for the NU and for the SI and represents movement behaviour during the last five minutes before the end of the interview.

b. *Results*

i. *Emotional stress through conversational content*   The analysis of the differences of the paired test values from the conversational conditions NI, and SI summed over MInt and MIs, using the signed-rank-test by Wilcoxon (Lienert, 1962), gives information on how far test values of the VaM co-vary with the emotional stress caused by the conversational content (see Table 4). According to these results, the nD test values of the parts of the body—head, trunk and right foot—show a systematic

TABLE 4

Comparison of the differences between the test values summarized from the conversational conditions NI and SI (including both the "isolated" and the "integrated" conditions). (Wilcoxon signed-rank-test, T values and their significance levels.) $(N = 18.)$

	nD		fD		sD	
	T	p	T	p	T	p
Head	7[a]	<0.1%	61	ns	54	ns
Trunk	28	<1%	34	<2%	59[a]	ns
Right hand	49.5[a]	ns	78	ns	76	ns
Left hand	51.5[a]	ns	75	ns	80	ns
Right foot	17.5[c]	<2%	66[a]	ns	56[b]	ns
Left foot	38.5[b]	ns	35[b]	ns	35[a]	<5%

[a] two ties.
[b] three ties.
[c] four ties.

relation to emotional stress through conversational content. For the variance of the test values of fD, the test showed no such relation except for the trunk. This means that the comparison of the test values showed with some subjects a higher test value under the condition NI, with some other subjects a higher test value under the condition SI. Since the scores of the subjects in both social conditions MI are included in this sample, we still have to see whether these effects can be explained. This also holds for the sD test values of most parts of the body, since only the variance of the sD values for the left foot could be explained by the conversational content.

ii. *Emotional stress caused by social pattern*   In order to judge the influence of social isolation versus integration upon the behaviour during the SI situation, we compared both test value samples using the Mann–Whitney U test (Lienert, 1962). From our studies so far we know that the test values of VaM co-vary with individual differences. In order to eliminate these influences, we took the differences between the test values NI and SI as a basis for the analysis. The results are shown in Table 5. According to these results, the mode of integration exerts a distinct effect on nD. The variance of fD and sD scores, however, is not explained by our analysis; thus it can be assumed that these values are

TABLE 5

Results of Mann–Whitney U-test analysis for the differences between the situations
MInt and MIs based on SI–NI values. ($N=18$; $N_1=9$; $N_2=9$.)

	nD		fD		sD	
	U	p	U	p	U	p
Head	16.5	<5%	24	ns	31	ns
Trunk	9.5	<1%	21	ns	26	ns
Right hand	33.0	ns	22	ns	34	ns
Left hand	16.5	<5%	37	ns	35	ns
Right foot	9.5	<1%	26.5	ns	17	<5%
Left foot	36.5	ns	36	ns	38	ns

not influenced by the MI, at least not in a consistent direction. The problem of interaction effects between MI and other variables, especially individual differences in VaM, remains unresolved. Its investigation demands a larger sample.

iii. *Direction of variability changes*   Since the results above showed that some aspects of VaM are systematically changed by the communicative conditions, further analysis of the nature of these changes seemed desirable. For this purpose, we conducted paired comparisons between the scores of the NI and SI conditions for the subjects of both MInt and MIs stress conditions. In each case, we assessed which score was higher, which lower, or whether they were equal. The resulting Table is of considerable size and is not reproduced here; an overall comparison (over all parts of the body and all VaM parameters) showed that the test-scores of the subjects under MInt conditions generally decreased with the sI situation while the test-scores of the subjects under MIs conditions strongly increased with the sI situation. This difference between the MI conditions was shown to be significant ($p>5$ per cent) as tested by a two-tailed Mann–Whitney U-test. A more detailed analysis of the paired comparisons showed, however, that there was an important exception to this general trend. The variability scores for the head were found to be lower in the SI situation for both MInt and MIs subjects (Binomial test, $p>1$ per cent). It might be interesting to consider to what extent this result is to be interpreted in connection with the perceptive and orienting function of the head (see von Cranach, 1971).

4 Discussion

The construction of a method for behaviour description requires certain decisions as to the definition of its characteristics and the scale quality of its basic data. The decisions we made for the characteristic "variability of movement behaviour" (VaM) have been theoretically justified; starting from certain assumptions that have been mentioned in the literature, a system of formalized operational instructions meant for the ordinal description of this aspect of behaviour has been created. The extent to which these decisions can be considered as appropriate depends first of all on the answer to a question regarding the content validity of the method: Does the method lead to data that in fact characterize the aspect of behaviour that is claimed to be characterized?

In the method presented here, a number of positional states, which reflect movement behaviour, operate as the specific units which define the degree of variability of movement behaviour. Since movement behaviour is therefore not directly assessed, but indirectly inferred from the positional data of the moving object, the assertions made about its variability are true only to such a degree as the positional data can be accepted as a true representation of movement behaviour. If movement is defined as a continuously evolving process of spatial-temporal changes, we cannot perfectly illustrate movement behaviour by positional data since the latter always represent movement behaviour inaccurately (i.e. a positional datum does not define a non-extended spot, but marks a range within which different positions are attributed to the same positional category), and always incompletely (i.e. positional data for the time between the observation phases t_i are lacking).

While the empirical description of movement behaviour does not meet the requirements of the continuity postulate, the degree of approximation of the movement description to the requirements of the definition can be influenced by the choice of the descriptive method. Generally, we can say that the degree of approach of the discrete representation to a continuous representation of movement behaviour increases with increasing sensitivity of the frames of reference used for time and space description.

The question of how sensitive a certain system should be to establish an appropriate representation of movement behaviour can only be answered with reference to the theoretical context in which the data are used. If the theoretical concept operates on a specific level, thus assuming a specific psychological meaning of any specific movement unit, a very discriminating instrument seems appropriate, since errors in the assessment of the movement phenomena lead to errors about the psychological quality of the events. However, if the theoretical concept operates on a general (trait) level, the theoretical consequences of an erroneous statement seem to be less dramatic, since the inadequate assessment of position leads, at most, to an error about the degree to which the behavioural phenomenon was present.

The method proposed here operates on a trait level, assuming that variability of movement is not qualitatively related to a certain positional phenomenon but is quantitatively related to all positional events occurring during the observation time.

The question about the adequacy of the movement data that are recorded to be evaluated in terms of variability can now be specified as the question about the representativeness of the sample that is drawn from the population of positions. It can be expected that due to the relatively small number of assessments of positions along with relatively long time intervals between positional registrations, temporally stable positions have a greater detection chance than positions which last only for a short period of time. Therefore we can assume that mainly "end positions" of movement behaviour are included in the samples which have been used to constitute the basis for the assessment of variability. According to Ekman and Friesen (1967), as well as to our experiences from the studies done so far, such "end positions" last usually longer than two seconds. Therefore, we expect that a time interval of 2.5 s between the assessments of position will be most appropriate for the assessment of at least the end positions. Whether 2.5 s intervals will also be appropriate for the representation of short duration positions depends on how far these positions provide information on variability that is redundant in relation to the information obtained by the sampling procedure actually used. This aspect remains to be investigated by systematic variation of the time and space intervals.

Besides the question about content validity, the question of practical utility needs to be considered in a discussion about the appropriateness of the decisions that were made in defining the method. A basic requirement to meet the criterion of practical utility is, of course, that the method is able to assess behavioural differences which can provide an empirical datum for theoretical concepts. With reference to the trait level on which the method operates, we should expect that general rather than specific factors should be able to explain the variance of the data. Specific factors, represented by single movements, are not only neglected, but are intended to be eliminated by our sampling procedures. General factors, assumed to exert a modifying effect on all movement behaviour, should be adequately assessed by our method if the sample used for the quantitative evaluation of the whole of the movement behaviour that occurred during the observation time can be regarded as fairly representative. In order to examine this expectation empirically, we performed several studies in which we tested the influence of some general factors on VaM. The results allow a rather positive answer about the question of practical utility.

Since the likelihood of a factor's effectiveness should grow with the temporal extension of its influence, personality-specific factors should generally persist. Therefore it is to be expected that they have the strongest influence under all conditions, and, as we have seen, this expectation is confirmed. As to reliability, the assessment of these individual factors is certainly in no way inferior to the usual test procedures, since even the test values of subjects influenced by situational and medicational variables showed systematic individual differences. Which personal qualities are represented in movement variability (e.g. temperament, vitality, general degree of activation) we do not yet know. It would be interesting to check the constancy of development of the variability of body movement from early childhood.

Situation specific factors, linked by definition to the duration of the situation should lead to test values which remain constant in repetitions of the same situation, but discriminate between different situations. This expectation is also met by our results: the test criteria could identify clearly several experimental variations of situations, while the data we obtained were shown to be highly stable within at least the one situation of "eating". The differences we found between situational conditions may reflect in part the adaptation of instrumental motor activity to changes in situational conditions. They may also reflect relations between movement variability and emotional and motivational events.

In the second study reported, it was shown, for instance, that individual VaM is changed systematically when situational conditions vary. This result does not surprise us of course, since, especially for the situation of "painting", it is to be expected that functional qualities required by outside conditions call for an adjustment of individual VaM. Burkart's (1971) results, however (according to which the emotional stimulus of the topic of conversation co-determines the degree of VaM), reveal an influence of emotional factors on VaM. The relation between VaM and the degree of group integration needs further investigation because its suggests a possible importance of movement variability scores for socio-psychological questions. In this context it might be interesting to raise the question about a possible relation between VaM and EEG or PGR data, which often provide the dependent variable in such investigations. With regard to the level of analysis, such physiological approaches seem somewhat similar to the procedure presented here; but compared to these, the technique used to assess VaM has advantages: it can be used as a "non-reactive" measure (Campbell, 1957; Webb *et al.*, 1966) and is expected to be more reliable. The main methodological advantage lies in the fact that the components of the different indicators can be easily determined at any time subsequent to the experiment, thus providing an empirical basis for further improvement of both the methodological assessment and the conceptual understanding of body movement variability.

Glossary

VaM	Variability of Movement Behaviour
nD	Nominal Differentiation
fD	Frequential Differentiation
sD	Sequential Differentiation
CP	Change of Position
NI	Neutral Interview
SI	Stress Interview
MI	Mode of Integration
MInt	Integrated Mode
MIs	Isolated Mode

References

Asch, S. E. (1956). Studies of independence and conformity: a minority of one against a unanimous majority. *Psychol. Monogr.* **70**, No. 416.

Attneave, F. (1959). "Applications of Information Theory to Psychology". Henry Holt, New York.

Birdwhistell, R. L. (1970). Man and communications. *In* "Proceedings of the 11th Annual Conference Military Testing Association", pp. 410–417. Governor Islands, New York.

Brengelmann, J. C. (1960). Expressive movements and abnormal behavior. *In* "Handbook of Abnormal Psychology" (Ed. H. J. Eysenck), pp. 62–107. Pitman's Medical, London.

Burdock, E. I., Hakerem, G., Hardesty, A. S., Zubin, J. and Beck, Y. M. (1964). Verhaltensinventar für die Krankenstation. Biometrics Research Unit, Columbia University and New York State Department of Mental Hygiene.

Burkart, M. K. (1971). Motorisches Verhalten und Stress in einer kommunizierenden Gruppe. Unpublished thesis, University of München.

Campbell, D. T. (1957). Factors relevant to the validity of experiments in social settings. *Psychol. Bull.* **54**, 279–312.

Campbell, D. T. (1958). Systematic error on the part of human links in communication systems. *Information and Control*, **1**, 334–369.

Cranach, M. von (1971). Die nichtverbale Kommunikation im Kontext des kommunikativen Verhaltens. *Jahrbuch der Max-Planck-Gesellschaft*, 105–148.

Cranach, M. von and Frenz, H. G. (1969) Systematische Beobachtung. *In* "Handbuch der Psychologie" (Ed. C. F. Graumann), Vol. 7, pp. 279–331. Hogrefe, Göttingen.

Eichholtz, F. (1957). "Lehrbuch der Pharmakologie". Springer-Verlag, Berlin.

Ekman, P. and Friesen, W. V. (1967). Head and body cues in the judgment of emotion: a reformulation. *Percept. Mot. Skills*, **24**, 711–724.

Ex, J. and Kendon, A. (1964). A notation for facial postures and bodily positions. Institute for Experimental Psychology, University of Oxford. (Unpublished manuscript.)

Framo, J. L. and Adlerstein, A. M. (1961). A behavioral disturbance index for psychiatric patients and ward disturbance. *J. Clin. Psychol.* **17**, 260–264.

Frey, S. (1971). "Eine Methode zur quantitativen Bestimmung der variabilität des Bewegungsverhaltens". Unpublished Ph.D. thesis, University of Regensburg.

Frey, S. and Cranach, M. von (1971). Ein Verfahren zur Messung motorischer Aktivität. *Z. Exp. Angew. Psychol.* **18**, 392–410.

Heimann, H. and Lukacs, G. (1966). Eine Methode zur quantitativen Analyse der mimischen Bewegung. *Arch. Ges. Psychol.* **118**, 1–17.

Kloos, G. (1962). "Grundriss der Psychiatrie und Neurologie". Müller Steinicke, München.

Knese, K. H. (1949). Kopfgelenk, Kopfhaltung und Kopfbewegung des Menschen. *Z. Ant. Entw. Gesch.* **114**, 67–107.

Lanz, U. von (1963). Die Mechanik der Kopfgelenke. Unpublished paper.

Lersch, P. (1932). "Gesicht und Seele". Reinhardt, Munich.

Leventhal, H. and Sharp, E. (1966). Facial expressions as indicators of stress. *In* "Affect, Cognition and Personality" (Eds S. S. Tomkins and C. E. Izard). Tavistock, London.

Lienert, G. A. (1962). "Verteilungsfreie Methoden in der Biostatistik". Anton Hain, Meisenhain/Glan.

Lorenz, K. (1967). "Ueber tierisches und menschliches Verhalten. Aus dem Werdegang der Verhaltenslehre". Piper, Munich.

McReynolds, P. (1965). On the assessment of anxiety: I. By a behavioral checklist. *Psychol. Rep.* 805–808.

Møller, K. O. (1961). "Pharmakologie". Schwabe, Basle.

Spoerri, T. (1967). Motorische Schablonen und Stereotypien bei Schizophrenen Endzuständen. *Psychiat. Neurol.* **15**, 81–127.

Webb, E. J., Campbell, D. T., Schwartz, R. D. and Sechrest, L. (1966). "Unobtrusive Measures: Nonreactive Research in the Social Sciences". Rand, McNally, Chicago.

Yates, A. J. (1960). Abnormalities of psychomotor functions. *In* "Handbook of Abnormal Psychology" (Ed. H. J. Eysenck), pp. 32–61. Pitman's Medical, London.

10

Problems in the Recognition of Gaze Direction

Mario von Cranach and Johann H. Ellgring[1]

1   Introduction

1.1   PROBLEM

Gazing at the partner is an important element of non-verbal communication; eye-contact, gaze orientation towards the partner, and gaze aversion are behaviours which are frequently studied and cited in explanations of social behaviour. In this connection the question arises as to the function of the perception of gaze direction in the communication process.

Interaction may be defined as "mutual reference" in the behaviour of social partners, while *communication* is the "exchange of messages" in a communication system that consists of the partners and a common *code* (von Cranach, 1971b). The code defines the relationship between a repertoire of *signals* and their *meanings*. The communication partners are *sender* and *recipient* with respect to any single signal (cf. Introduction to

[1] The research underlying this chapter was undertaken during both the authors' collaboration at the Max-Planck-Institut für Psychiatrie, Munich, Germany. Parts of the paper were presented to the XIX International Congress of Psychology, London 1969, Symposium on Non-Verbal Communication, by the first author. We are indebted to Miss Christiane Mauderli and Mrs Anne Peters for their help in the translation.

this volume). According to our definition of interaction and communication, we may talk about interactive and communicative behaviour when we refer to the interactive and communicative acts of *one* of the partners.

It is generally agreed that looking behaviour functions as a means to monitor and observe the partner (information seeking) and serves as a communicative signal as well; it may thus be considered as both interactive *and* communicative behaviour. The communicative functions of looking behaviour are relatively well explored, and are summarized in several survey articles (Argyle and Kendon, 1967; Duncan, 1969; Vine, 1970; von Cranach, 1971). As far as this subject has been investigated so far, looking behaviour seems to signal the readiness or the reluctance to communicate by exchanging other signals, and to coordinate the communicative behaviour of both partners. In their particular characteristics both functions depend on the communicative and situational context. Another frequently studied aspect of looking behaviour is the role it plays in mother–child communication, especially as a releasing signal in infants (see Vine, Chapter 5). It can also exert arousing or threatening effects in a variety of species (Vine, 1970; and see Hindmarch, Chapter 6).

All assumptions concerning special signal functions of the gaze presume that it can be correctly assessed to a high degree. In this chapter we report on the design and results of studies in the recognition of gaze direction. Our interest is focused on the following questions: How good is the accuracy of gaze assessment by the recipient or by an observer unconcerned in the communication? Which factors affect it? How can it be improved? The answers we have obtained seem to show that the behaviours of the sender are coordinated to facilitate the recipient's impression of being looked at or looked away from.

1.2   TERMS, CONCEPTS AND OPERATIONS

The comparison of studies on looking behaviour is complicated by unclarity in the use of terms, concepts, and related operations. It can be noted that the same terms are used for different concepts, or different terms for the same concepts, and that the underlying concepts are inadequately represented by the observational operations chosen, as illustrated in Table 1. The finding that most of the concepts are operationally based on the recognition of gaze direction adds to the justification of our present methodological enquiries.

TABLE 1

Some terminology in research on looking behaviour

Term	Concept	Operation
1 "One-sided gaze" *or* "looking at the partner" *or* "visual orientation towards the partner", *or* "eye-gaze"	The sender looks at the face of the recipient, mainly at the eye region	Assessment of "gaze direction" ("line of regard", "focus") by judging pupil, *and/or* iris location, of one eye or both eyes by an observer or the recipient, *and/or* by inference from head position, *or* by self-report, *or* by previous instruction to the sender to fixate a specified target
2 "Mutual gaze"	Both partners look into each other's face, *or* eye region, thus acting simultaneously as sender and recipient	Gaze direction of both partners assessed by a combination of operations as described in (1)
3 "Eye-contact"	Both partners look into the other's eyes, *or* into one eye only, and both are aware of this mutual gaze; *or* the concept is identical with (2)	Assessed as in (2)
4 "Gaze movement" *or* "gaze shift"	Turning the gaze further towards or away from the partner	Assessment of movement of the eyeball in the socket as indicated by changes in the configuration of sclera, iris and pupil (as in (1)), *and/or* assessing head movement
5 "Gaze duration"	Duration of (1), (2) or (3)	Assessment of time period between a gaze movement towards the partner and a further movement away from the partner (see (4))

TABLE 1—*contd*

Term	Concept	Operation
6 "Omission of gaze" *or* "unreciprocated gaze"	One partner does not look at the other	Assessed as in (1)
7 "Gaze avoidance" *or* "gaze aversion" *or* "cut-off"	A person avoids looking at the partner especially if being looked at, *and/or* moves the gaze away from the partner; distinguished from (6) by the presence of "intent". (In this case, (2) and (3) rarely or never occur)	Assessed as in (1) or (4)
8 "Mutual gaze avoidance" *or* "mutual gaze aversion" *or* "mutual cut-off"	Both partners avoid looking at the other	Assessed as in (1) or (4)

2 The accuracy of gaze assessment

2.1 METHODOLOGY

2.1.1 *Aspects of accuracy*

In discussing the accuracy of gaze assessment, it is important to distinguish between objectivity, that is inter-rater reliability of observation, and validity of judgement. Information on inter-rater reliability, that is the agreement of different observers on a judgement, is necessary but, as will be discussed later, is not sufficient for evaluating the accuracy of gaze assessment. Information about the objectivity of gaze assessment is only available in studies in which observers register the gaze behaviour. As far as recipients of gaze signals are concerned, such independent information cannot be obtained.

The assessment of judgement validity, that is the correspondence between signals which have been sent and received, is possible only in experiments in which the sent signals can be controlled. Validity is a necessary criterion in establishing the accuracy of gaze assessment.

2.1.2 Variables

Independent variables of spatial arrangement which are of relevance in the assessment of gaze behaviour are commonly as follows: (a) the *distance* between sender and recipient; (b) the *distance* between sender and observer; (c) the *angles* between sender–recipient and sender–observer. Independent variables of gaze behaviour usually are as follows: (a) the *gaze duration* (generally a relatively fixed temporal interval between 3 and 5 seconds); (b) the *gaze direction* (the fixation points selected); (c) the *head position* of the sender.

Usually the subject or observer is asked to give his judgement according to the criteria mentioned below. These criteria differ in their theoretical implications and in the degree of differentiation required for the judgement, and lead to diverse consequences for the subsequent statistical analysis and its interpretation.

2.1.3 Criteria

We assume that in judgement of gaze direction there is a continuum of possible gaze directions, judged by describing the points fixated at various times. Through statistical analysis information can be obtained about the degree and direction of misjudgements. Conclusions can then be made regarding the perception of gaze behaviour in general.

In most experimental situations used in assessing judgement ability, the recipient is asked to look constantly at the eye region of the sender. "One-sided gaze" and "mutual gaze" can in this case be considered operationally identical. In the case of judged "eye-contact" or "one-sided gaze" (sometimes identified in experiments as "positive reaction" or "face reaction") the judgement dimension is dichotomized while the signal dimension remains continuous. This operation is based on the assumption that only the presence or absence of eye-contact or one-sided gaze is relevant in interaction. The statistical analysis generally takes into account the distribution of positive reactions at the different fixation points. Assertions can be made about perception of eye-contact or one-sided gaze, that is the perception of a specific aspect of gaze behaviour.

2.1.4 Experimental paradigms

Studies on gaze behaviour are generally concerned with dyadic situations. The dyadic situation provides the best possibility for the control of the input signals. A characteristic experimental set-up usually shows the following features (cf. Fig. 1). The sender of gaze signals looks at

P

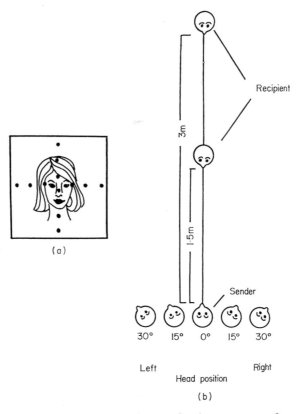

Fig. 1. Features of a typical experimental set-up for the assessment of recognition of gaze direction under different conditions.

(a) Typical distribution of target points.
(b) Schema of typical experimental arrangements.

points within or beyond the face of the recipient according to a previously determined random succession. The recipient and/or differently placed observers make their judgements. In some studies the gaze behaviour of the sender is oriented to a board with target points on it (Cline, 1967). In experiments with such a set-up the most important input variable, that is gaze direction, is controlled by instruction to the sender. In this way it is possible to make assertions about the validity of gaze recognition. The paradigm has been limited to a dyad of sender and recipient. An extension to several recipients by suitably controlling the behaviour of the sender is possible, but until now this has not been attempted.

The paradigm, however, is artificial, because it presumes a single direction of communication. The sender's signal must be decoded by the recipient. It is impossible for the recipient to address the other in turn with dialogic signals. No attention is paid to the fact that in real interaction the distinction between sender's and recipient's functions is difficult, if not impossible, for the investigator to make, as both partners are acting simultaneously as sender and recipient. Also, all additional contextual signals of a natural interaction are missing. The presence of earphones and the temporal succession of gaze signals determined in advance also contribute to the artificiality of these experiments.

In much of the remaining discussion we make no distinction between recipient and observer with reference to the accuracy of gaze signal assessment. This is justified because the conditions for the observer grow more and more similar to those for the recipient when the fixation points are at a greater distance from the face. The situation of the observer differs from that of the recipient because the conditions for perception are less favourable for the observer. In the most favourable case the observer is placed just left or right behind the recipient, necessarily further from the sender. Depending on the position of the observer, the accuracy of his observation will therefore be less than that for the recipient of gaze signals. However, the assumed gradual similarity between recipient and observer refers only to accuracy of gaze assessment in experiments made according to the above paradigm. In real interactions, with their associated contextual factors, a clear distinction must be drawn between recipient and observer judgements.

2.2 INTER-OBSERVER RELIABILITY OR OBJECTIVITY

The objectivity of gaze behaviour assessment is reported sometimes in percentage values and sometimes in correlation coefficients. The data reported for the assessment of eye-contact or one-sided gaze range from 66 per cent (Vine, 1971) to 98 per cent (Exline et al., 1965). Intercorrelations range from 0.50 (Mehrabian and Williams, 1969) to 0.98 (Exline, 1963). The evaluation of these figures is difficult: different criteria are used for the variables assessed; sometimes these are not clearly described; and they are sometimes missing. For example, Strongman and Champness (1968) report 95 per cent observers' agreement on registration of eye-contact although they do not provide more information. Generally, as was suggested above, the concepts "eye-

P*

contact" and "one-sided gaze" are not differentiated in objectivity or validity experiments; one-sided gaze is most frequently registered as eye-contact.

The effect of differentially strict criteria in the evaluation of agreement level between observers has been shown by Vine (1971) through observations of filmed interactions. He found an appreciable increase in the inter-rater reliability while registering the eye-contact, when, instead of his strict criterion of $t < 0.25$ s, Exline's criterion (1963) of $t < 2.0$ s discrepancy in the observer's judgements of the timing of senders' gazes was used. Different situations and conditions of observation may also influence the inter-observer reliability. With observations from video-tape recordings, Mehrabian and Williams (1969) obtained the lowest agreement between observers ($r = 0.50$) for eye-contact as compared with other categories of non-verbal behaviour. It is probable that film and video tape recordings do not offer optimal possibilities for the observation of these variables; the detection of agreement between observers working *independently* is, however, possible. In simultaneous direct observation of several persons during interaction, a further factor may influence the level of inter-rater reliability: in judging whether an eye-contact occurs, the observers can form shared strategies. Stephenson and Rutter (1970) showed that naïve observers in groups formed shared strategies, which were, however, different for the separate groups of observers. It is obvious that training observers together under similar conditions can lead to a high although not necessarily valid agreement. Presumably the frequently reported high inter-observer reliabilities are obtained partly because of these shared strategies after training (Vine, 1971).

Information on the objectivity of the agreement of several observers can obviously give only a very rough estimate of the accuracy of observation and therefore the possibility of observing gaze behaviour. More detailed results on the accuracy achieved in the observation of gaze behaviour can be expected from studies on validity in which the behaviour of the senders' is itself controlled.

2.3 VALIDITY

2.3.1 *Differentiation within the face*
Whether or not different visual target points within the face, and including eye-contact, can be differentiated has been studied in a

preliminary experiment by Krüger and Hückstedt (1969) and also by Ellgring (1970). In both cases the senders, at a distance of 80 or 200 cm, looked, in a random order, at 7 points of the eye region: forehead, bridge of the nose, tip of the nose, right and left eye, right and left face edge (on the axis of the eyes). The recipients were instructed to report which point the sender was fixating. Krüger and Hückstedt (1969) found in two sender–recipient couples 35 per cent correct judgements for the eye region at a distance of 80 cm and 10 per cent correct judgements at a distance of 200 cm.

With a homogeneous group of 17- and 18-year-old school-girls ($N=16$) Ellgring detected higher values: 41 per cent and 49 per cent correct judgements at a distance of 80 cm, 21 per cent and 29 per cent correct judgements at a distance of 200 cm, for the right and left eye respectively. These values fall above random expectation. Direct gazes at the eyes were no better assessed than were gazes towards other points within the face (Fig. 2).

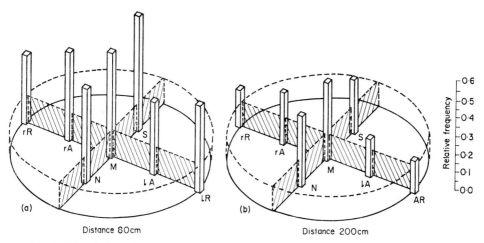

Distance 80cm   Distance 200cm

Fig. 2. The differentiation of directions of gaze to points within the face. Frequency of correct judgements are relative to the frequency of the senders' gazes to the different target-points. (From Ellgring, 1970.)

Target points:

S Forehead	rA right eye
M Middle (bridge of the nose)	lA left eye
N Nose	rR right border of face
	lR left border of face

The second level (– –, cross-hatched) corresponds to a frequency of 14.3 per cent (chance frequency).

However, responses were given with different frequencies for the various fixation points (which were fixated with equal frequencies). It is therefore concluded that the probabilities for the naming of each fixation point are not equal. Relating the number of correct responses to the total number of times a point was selected by the recipient, the resulting fraction reflects the bias associated with each point. Comparing the above scores with the corresponding scores obtained by relating the number of correct judgements to the total number of fixations, only small differences are evident for the points in the eye region. It can be seen in Fig. 3 that gazes towards the more rarely mentioned edge points are more often correctly assessed.

It is probable that the recipient tends to name the eyes when unsure of the fixation. The recipient only names less favoured points when convinced of the accuracy of his judgement.

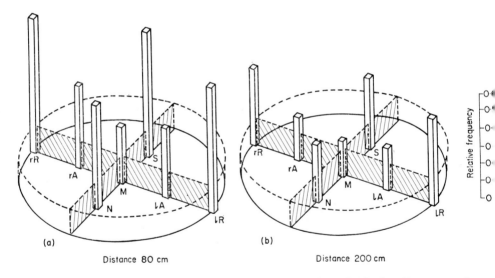

Fig. 3. The differentiation of directions of gaze to points within the face. Frequency of correct judgements relative to the frequency of the receivers' naming of the different target points. (From Ellgring, 1970.)

Target points:

S Forehead	rA right eye
M Middle (bridge of the nose)	lA left eye
N Nose	rR right border of face
	lR left border of face

The second level (– –, cross-hatched) corresponds to a frequency of 14.3 per cent (chance frequency).

The influence of distance between subjects on the recognition of gaze direction by observers is emphasized by the results of Stephenson and Rutter (1970). They found that with increasing distance (61 cm, 182 cm, and 305 cm), eye-contact is more frequently reported and that gazes, especially at the ear or shoulder, are increasingly recorded as eye-contact. They conclude that "work on eye-contact using observers behind one-way screens is of dubious value" (p. 392).

In spite of the evident difficulty in assessing eye-contact in normal interactions, participants are generally convinced of the presence of eye-contact. It is likely that additional signals other than the looking behaviour alone are operating (e.g. head position or other context factors). The more easily perceptible one-sided gaze to the face in general is probably sufficient for the subjective conviction that eye-contact is present. On the other hand, the possibly high probability of a gaze directed towards a partner during natural interaction actually being an eye-gaze cannot be dismissed. In the latter case, errors would only infrequently occur when judging a gaze towards the face as eye-contact (Argyle, 1970). However, this argument can only be supported by subjective evidence of observers and is circular in nature. A method for objective and accurate assessment of looking behaviour in natural interaction without observer errors is needed for the resolution of this problem.

To summarize, the results of the assessment of eye-contact show that even under the most favourable conditions eye-contact cannot be registered reliably by the receiver and/or observer. It is impossible for the recipient of gaze signals to distinguish between eye-contact and one-sided gaze at the general area surrounding the eyes.

2.3.2 *Gaze at the face*

In most publications, as in those of Gibson and Pick (1963) and Cline (1967), fixation of the bridge of the nose is considered eye-contact. However, in the way defined above, this is not eye contact but just a one-sided gaze towards the face. In references to eye-contact recognition the paper of Gibson and Pick is most commonly referred to. Their conclusion, "The ability to read the eyes seems to be as good as the ability to read fine print on an acuity-chart . . ." (p. 394), is used to justify the suitability of the variable "eye-contact". We will therefore discuss this paper in more detail. The main critical arguments apply to Cline's (1967) work as well; he repeated the experiment of Gibson and Pick with more elaborate variation of the sender–receiver conditions.

In the Gibson and Pick experiment a sender and six recipients of gaze signals were utilized. At a distance of 200 cm, the recipients judged whether they were looked at. The seven fixation points lay horizontally at intervals of 10 cm along the eye axis with the bridge of the nose as the mid-point. The head positions of the sender were as follows: pointing straight ahead, 30° to the right and to the left. Each point was fixated 25 times in the three head positions. To measure the accuracy of assessment, standard deviations of the three frequency distributions were used. On the basis of the equally high standard deviations, corresponding to 8–9 cm deviation from the mean of the distributions and to an angle of 2.8°, the authors concluded "that accuracy for the perception of gaze is independent of head pointing" (p. 391). Because of the constant errors (shifting of distributions in the direction of head pointing), however, they state that "evidently the perception of eye pointing is somewhat influenced by the perception of head pointing" (p. 391).

For at least three reasons the standard deviation is not in fact sufficient for measuring the accuracy of judgements.

1. The standard deviation provides no information about the mean. However, for the 30° head-turn conditions, the means differ by one unit (10 cm) in the direction of the head-turn and away from the central fixation point (the bridge of the nose). This means that the most frequent judgements in the turned-head conditions were wrong.
2. The standard deviation covers the area in which 64 per cent of the cases occur. But even within this area a considerable proportion of mistakes is included.
3. Extreme values are strongly weighted by the squaring procedure. The possibility cannot be excluded that the wrong positive reactions may consist of different types of errors. When the fixation point is close to the bridge of the nose, the mistakes may be due to the limited resolving power of the eyes. If the fixation point is more distant (20 cm or further) and false positive reactions are reported, then lack of attention or carelessness (as it occurs in vigilance tasks) might be the causal factor. This type of error is given a stronger weight if dispersion measures such as standard deviation are used. This weighting cannot be justified by the theory.

Information about the accuracy of gaze recognition by percentage of correct versus wrong responses for the different fixation points seems to be more adequate in this case. A re-examination of their data then shows the following results: Gazes at the bridge of the nose (the face) are correctly perceived in 84 per cent of the cases when head position is straight. However, 40 per cent (left) and 36 per cent (right) of fixations directed 10 cm out from the bridge of the nose, that is outside the face, are judged as glances at the face as well. When head position is turned to the right or left by 30°, only 52 per cent (right) and 36 per cent (left) of the glances at the face are judged correctly. There is an increase in face reactions for fixations at points 10 cm out from the bridge of the nose, in the direction of the head position: 56 per cent (right point, head to the right) and 68 per cent (left point, head to the left) of these gazes are judged as being directed to the face. For the corresponding fixation points opposite to the head turning, however, only 12 per cent (left lateral point, head turning to the right) and 8 per cent (right lateral point, head turning to the left) of the fixations are judged incorrectly as glances at the face. Here, the results for only three out of seven fixation points are reported. But the general trend holds for the others too, except that percentage of wrong face reactions decreases for points more distant from the bridge of the nose.

What conclusions are to be drawn from the data? We suggest the following:

1. The high proportion of incorrect as well as correct positive responses suggests a general reaction tendency towards "feeling that one is being looked at".
2. The head position has a strong influence on the perception of gaze behaviour. Gibson and Pick themselves draw attention to this; their emphasis on the "ability to read the eyes" (p. 394) is therefore all the more astonishing.
3. By reason of the considerable number of errors which occurred, it is difficult to understand the conclusion of this paper that gaze perception is not problematic and that the variable "eye-contact" can be assessed with satisfactory accuracy.

Cline (1967) repeated the experiment by Gibson and Pick with a more refined experimental set-up. His recipients observed the reflection of the sender, who fixated points located around the head of the recipient. One involved fixating the bridge of the nose as a central point. In all experiments, the deviations of the fixation points from the central point were between 4° (8.5 cm) and 12° (25.9 cm), with a distance of 122 cm between sender and recipient. In one condition the head position was varied (straight ahead versus turned to the right by 30°). The standard deviation of the frequency distribution of judgements over each fixation point was taken as a threshold and the mean discrepancy as a constant error. Cline's results correspond approximately to those of Gibson and Pick. Constant errors in the sense of an over-estimation of the deviation from the central point, which was higher for vertical deviations than for horizontal ones, were noticed. The constant errors were, however, not discussed in relation to assessment accuracy as was the case in Gibson and Pick's paper. As for Gibson and Pick, an influence of the head position on perception of gaze direction was noticed: "Head position and eye position interact to produce a perceived direction which falls between these positions." (p. 50.) When eye and head pointed in the same direction, a rather small constant error was obtained. When the head was straight ahead and the eye position was varied, the eye direction determined the constant discrepancy. With reference to the one-sided gaze, Cline states: "Accuracy for being looked at is quite high, and accuracy for other lines of regard are somewhat lower." (p. 50.) It is important to remember this limitation in the studies of Gibson and Pick and of Cline. These studies focus on the one-sided gaze and not on eye-contact, that is the gaze from eye to eye. (Also see note, p. 442.)

Anstis, Mayhew and Morley (1969) examined the recognition of gaze directions using senders, their television images, and a diaphragm (artificial eye), at a distance of 84 cm. The recipients judged the gaze direction as projected on a scale lying 6 cm above and 42 cm away from the eye level. Results showed that under all three conditions the mean of assessment of gazes towards the bridge of the nose corresponded to the actual gaze direction. Five degree to 20 degree gaze angles were over-estimated in the same direction as the gaze. Turning the head, and similarly the diaphragm, showed constant errors (which were much stronger for the diaphragm). Unfortunately, information on the range of judgements is lacking. The authors conclude that gaze direction assessment is mainly determined by the position of the pupil in the visible part of the eye. The small distance between the signal sources and the recipients only allow us to draw limited conclusions with respect to normal interaction; at a greater distance, less favourable visibility conditions need to be taken into consideration.

In two experiments, Krüger and Hückstedt (1969) examined the conditions in which recipient and observer consider the gaze of the sender to be directed at the recipient's face (one-sided gaze). Fixation points were the bridge of the nose and three points at intervals of 6, 16, and 26 cm in a vertical (experiment 1) or a horizontal direction (experiment 2). The head position of the sender was varied as follows: straight ahead, 20° (experiment 1) and 25° (experiment 2) to the left and to the right. In experiment 1, the gaze duration was varied between one second and three seconds. The observer was placed at an angle of 90° or 42° to the sender–receiver axis at a distance of 150 cm or 300 cm from the central point of the axis. The recipients and observers judged whether the senders looked at them. Two female senders, recipients, and observers took part in experiment 1, and 10 female senders, recipients and observers in experiment 2. The results show that at a distance of 300 cm a one-sided gaze is more frequently perceived as such than at a distance of 150 cm. Similarly, the number of misjudgements increases considerably; gazes at points outside the face are more frequently considered to be one-sided gazes. If the gaze duration is longer (experiment 1), a slight tendency towards more frequent "face" judgements is shown.

The head position influenced gaze perception since the recipients more frequently considered gazes oriented in the direction of the head position to be one-sided gazes. Therefore misjudgements were encountered more frequently. Generally, the observers discriminated much worse than did the recipients. A certain differentiation between the particular gaze directions was evident, but the proportion of correct judgements was small. The head position of the sender with regard to the recipient's position had a strong influence on the observer's judgement. When the head position of the sender was straight, twice as many face judgements were registered as with a lateral head position. Moving the head by 25°, the frequency of judging lateral targets as being fixated changed in favour of the direction of head turning. If the observer was at a right angle to the sender–receiver axis, a one-sided gaze was more often registered than if the angle was 42°. When the sender turned his head towards the observer, a one-sided gaze at the recipient was very rarely registered by the observer. The personality characteristic of extraversion (see Brengelmann and Brengelmann, 1960) had an influence on the behaviour of the observer, in that observers with high values of extraversion perceived more gazes to be orientated towards the face than do observers with lower values of extraversion.

Thus, the judgement of the one-sided gaze is not based on gaze direction only, but depending on the conditions for perception is strongly influenced by the distance between sender and recipient, the head position of the sender, the position of the observer (all location conditions), and also by personality characteristics. When the conditions for perception are not favourable, the influence of the gaze direction itself becomes weak compared with the above mentioned factors.

In the papers mentioned so far, the recognition of the gaze direction of the resting eye was sought. However, in normal interaction gaze and head movements can function as additional signals. The influence of these factors on the recognition of eye direction has been studied in several experiments by von Cranach, Hückstedt, Schmid and Vogel.[1]

The first of these experiments was similar to that of Krüger and Hückstedt; the same persons participated in the experiment. A distance of 150 cm between sender and recipient was selected. The fixation points were located on the eye axis, 6, 16 and 26 cm left and right of the bridge of the recipient's nose. For each fixation the senders gazed at one starting point and then looked to one of the fixation points, according to instructions given through earphones. In one session, the sender performed 780 fixations moving from each target point to all other target points, with five repetitions of each movement in random order. The fixations lasted 3 seconds. The recipients judged whether or not they were looked at. The experiment was repeated three times; in experiments 1 and 3 the tone signal announcing the fixation was suppressed, and in experiment 3 two observers sat on the left and right behind the recipient. The distribution of the "face" judgements was compared with that in the Krüger and Hückstedt (1969) experiment carried out under the same conditions (see Fig. 4).

No improvement in the discrimination performance was obtained as a result of additional gaze-turning. Increased face judgements were noticed, mainly with the outer fixation points. The additional gaze movement leads to the effect that people feel looked at more often. The increasing response tendency for the outer points is found mainly when a gaze movement in the direction of the face has taken place. With the observers this effect is much less evident. When the gaze is directed towards their standpoint, rather more face judgements are noticed.

[1] Unpublished experiments, Max-Planck-Institut für Psychiatrie, Munich, 1968.

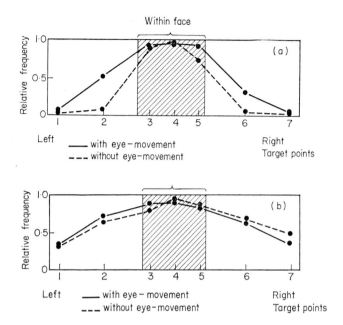

Fig. 4. (a) Relative frequency of the face reaction of the recipients. (b) Relative frequency of the face reaction of the observers.

When it is directed away from the observer fewer face judgements are given than without gaze turning.

These results show that gaze direction and gaze movement are to be considered independent factors in gaze recognition. An interaction effect of these factors in the sense of creating a stimulus configuration should have resulted in an improved discrimination; this, however, was not the case for the results observed.

In a continuation of this experiment the interaction between gaze direction and head position and head movement was examined under two distance conditions. Efforts were made to approximate "natural" behaviour in interactions. It was assumed that, depending on the distance between sender and recipient, the judgements of the recipients are based on a shared effect of these factors: gaze direction, head movement, and the sender's head position following this movement. Here, the distance between sender and recipient was 150 cm or 300 cm. The observer was placed 150 cm away at right-angles to the centre of the sender–recipient axis, which yields a distance to the sender of 168 cm or 212 cm. The subject looked at one of the seven fixation points on the

eye-axis of the recipient. The fixation points were located symmetrically at a distance of 5.5 cm, 16 cm and 26 cm from the bridge of the
nose (itself a fixation point). The head assumed five positions with 0°,
±15° and ±30° angles to the sender–recipient axis, with head movements between these positions. The sender was given instructions as to
the fixation point and the head movements via earphones.

The list of stimuli consisted of all combinations of the 20 possible head
movements with the 42 possible gaze movements in a random order
(840 instructions, in which each point was fixated six times). The
recipients and observers indicated by pressing a button when they felt
the sender's gaze to be orientated towards the recipient's face. Under
all conditions more than chance numbers of correct distinctions were
made between one-sided gaze and omission of gaze, when judgements
on the three facial points (bridge of the nose, right and left edge of the
face) were regarded as correct (see Fig. 5). Despite the statistical
significance achieved, Fig. 6 shows that the observers misjudged a considerable proportion of the gazes.

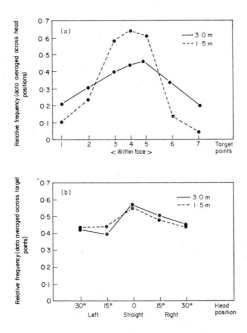

Fig. 5. Relative frequency of face reaction of recipients: (a) in relation to target
points; (b) in relation to head position.

The influences of gaze direction and head position are different for recipients and observers. With the recipients the influence of "gaze direction" prevails. At a greater distance the head position becomes

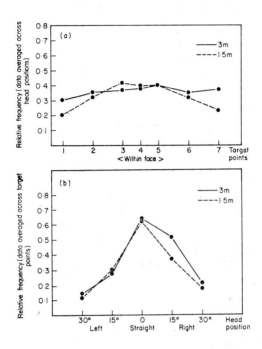

Fig. 6. Relative frequency of face reaction of observers: (a) in relation to target points; (b) in relation to head position.

more important in the assessment of the one-sided gaze, while the relevance of gaze direction decreases; the greater distance leads to more frequent positive judgements. Under both conditions, due to the unfavourable location of the observers, their judgement, even at a short distance, is determined to a great extent by the head direction. Therefore face judgements occur more frequently when the sender's head is straight or only slightly turned or when turning of the head into a straight position has preceded this. With the recipients, the greater distance from the sender leads to more frequent "face" judgements. Generally, under unfavourable perceptual conditions the importance of gaze behaviour in assessing the one-sided gaze, compared with other factors, especially the position of the head, decreases appreciably.

2.4 THE IMPROVEMENT OF GAZE RECOGNITION BY TRAINING

According to the above experiments, assessment of eye contact and one-sided gaze is, to say the least, problematic. To achieve greater accuracy of judgement, two procedures are possible. First, after a thorough study of the factors influencing the judgements of both observers and recipients, they can be informed about the possible sources of errors. Secondly, the extent to which the recognition of gaze signals can be positively influenced by learning procedures can be investigated. Mention of the importance of learning factors in the recognition of gaze signals is found in an unpublished study by von Cranach *et al.* Recipients who were first tested at the experimental distance of 300 cm from the sender then showed, at a distance of 150 cm, a slight tendency towards better discrimination of gaze direction itself and less dependence on the sender's head position than persons who had this distance as their starting condition. It should be noted that the subject did not receive any explicit feedback about the correctness of his judgement. After questioning the receivers, it seemed possible that their improved performance might be attributed to an increase in motivation, resulting from the improvement in conditions of perception between the first and second conditions.

To date, we are aware of only one experiment in which the subjects were given explicit feedback: Ellgring and von Cranach (1972) used a standard situation for gaze behaviour recognition, with the difference that, after each judgement, the point actually fixated was communicated to the participants. Senders and recipients sat facing each other at a distance of 300 cm. Outside the face of the receiver four fixation points were marked on the eye-axis at a distance of 20 cm and 40 cm horizontally to either side of the bridge of the nose (points 2, 1; 4, 5; and 3). Above the head of the sender was fixed a row of five small numbered lamps, which corresponded to the fixation points. The sender fixated for 2.5–3 seconds on each different point according to a formerly determined random order; each point was fixated 50 times in the experiment. On hearing a buzzing sound the recipient ($N=10$) decided which point the sender was fixating. The sender then gave the feedback specifying the point he was fixating, and the corresponding lamp on the ledge above his head flashed to give a more specific orientation.

With all subjects, a general learning effect in the direction of better discrimination of gaze signals (see Fig. 7) was evident. The effect, how-

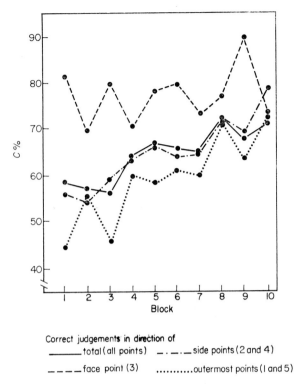

Correct judgements in direction of
——— total (all points)   _ . _ . _ side points (2 and 4)
_ _ _ _ face point (3)   ....outermost points (1 and 5)

Fig. 7. Correct judgements. Relative frequencies ($C\%$) averaged for different fixation points. $N=10$, Block$=50$ fixations.

ever, differed for the various fixation points. The learning effect increased with the distance between fixation points and bridge of the nose, while no clear trend was noticed in fixations of the bridge of the nose. In addition, the direction of errors changed during the learning experiment. For the analysis of this question only the lateral points 2 and 4 were taken into account. At the beginning, misjudgements in the direction of the face occurred more frequently; this type of error decreased continuously, approaching the frequency of errors in which fixations of the lateral points inside the face are perceived as fixation of the points outside the face (see Fig. 8).

This shows that a more accurate discrimination can be achieved through explicit feedback. This improvement in accuracy does, however, not occur for gazes orientated directly towards the face. We might assume that this discrimination has been over-learned in ontogenesis (see Vine, Chapter 5). For the points further from the face the condi-

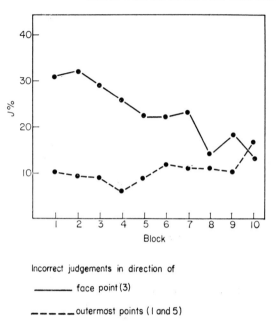

Incorrect judgements in direction of

————— face point (3)

— — — — outermost points (1 and 5)

Fig. 8. Incorrect judgements when targets are side points (2 and 4). Relative frequencies ($J\%$).

tions for perception are similar for receiver and observer. It is therefore to be expected that after a relatively short training period (the experiment lasted 45 minutes), a considerable improvement of the discrimination performance of observers might be achieved.

3 Discussion

Let us now consider the consequences of the findings we have reviewed for the use of gaze variables in empirical investigations.

All the studies considered imply an experimental paradigm that contains, as an essential element, a sender who distributes his gazes on and around the recipients' eyes and face. In a strict sense, the validity of the findings is restricted to this very kind of behaviour. In natural communication, should the sender behave differently (looking dichotomously either at the recipients' eyes or distinctly away from his face, as Argyle, 1970, and Vine, 1971, have argued), the above results would not apply. To our knowledge, however, no independent data exist on the true distribution of sender gazes in social situations. Possibly this data would be difficult to obtain, even using a modern eye-camera. In the meantime, the burden of proof of validity rests with those who use the variable.

It should also be pointed out that the assessment of vertical variations of gaze direction has not been sufficiently studied, although vertical gaze movement may carry considerable information in natural interaction.

Probably the most striking aspect of the empirical results is that it seems hardly justified to talk about a variable of "eye-contact" in the sense of a "mutual meeting of gazes, and being aware of the event". Objectively, the partner's gaze into the eyes cannot be accurately recognized, and it is no better recognized than the gaze at other points of the face. Thus it seems justified to replace this concept by the "mutual gaze". Subjectively, of course, "eye-contact" remains of importance.

But the assessment of the mutual and the one-sided gaze also turns out to be a difficult matter. With our few studies, using mainly one paradigm, a number of factors could be identified such as gaze movement, head direction, head movement, distance, duration and personality variables that impair the judgement of the receiver. The interaction of these factors is only partly clarified in that, especially for the observer, additional factors may influence the observations. The observer's judgement is further impaired by his location. Under some conditions its variance is almost completely determined by other factors than gaze direction. For this reason, the validity of the observer's judgement depends predominantly on the experimenter's choice of specific observational circumstances. Any experimenter would be wise to test his observer's accuracy of discrimination (the validity of their judgements); testing objectivity alone seems insufficient. It might be useful to re-define the variable, namely from "one-sided or mutual-gaze" towards a less specific term like "orientation". Finally, the possibility of improving the receiver's and observer's judgement by training, a simple and economic but as yet more or less unused device, should be stressed.

Considering these findings, we may try to achieve a better understanding of gaze communication in general (von Cranach, 1971a, 1971b). It is clear that the feeling of being looked in the eye or the face is a subjective experience embodying the decoded meaning of varying perceived signals, the specific patterns of which depend on situational factors. Thus the sender will always exhibit a pattern of movements and positions of the body, head and eyes, which may, when looking at a human partner, be accompanied by specific additional movements, such as eye blinks (von Cranach *et al.*, 1969), or eye-brow movements and smiles (Eibl-Eibesfeldt, 1967, pp. 410ff); while the recipient decodes only the sender's visual attention. Looking behaviour, its encoding and decoding, thus possesses its own syntax, and may therefore serve as an example of the properties of communicative behaviour in general.

Note

Vine (personal communication) recently drew our attention to an ambiguity in the published accounts of the constant error in perceived gaze direction when the sender's head is turned away from the recipient (cf. pp. 429–433). This ambiguity may be due to inconsistencies of terminology and description, but it appears that Cline (1967) may have found that perceived direction is *intermediate* between eye direction and head direction, whereas Anstis *et al.* (1969), Krüger and Hückstedt (1969), and apparently Gibson and Pick (1963), found that gaze deviation from the direction of head-turn was *over*-estimated rather than under-estimated. Although Cline's report is confusing (see Anstis *et al.*, p. 478; Vine, 1971, p. 323), a re-analysis of his data suggests there may be an actual conflict of results here. Further experiments are needed to discover whether procedural differences might be responsible.

References

Anstis, S. M., Mayhew, J. E. and Morley, Tania (1969). The perception of where a face or television "portrait" is looking. *Amer. J. Psychol.* **82**, 474–489.

Argyle, M. (1970). Eye-contact and distance: a reply to Stephenson and Rutter. *Brit. J. Psychol.* **61**, 395–396.

Argyle, M. and Kendon, A. (1967). The experimental analysis of social performance. *In* "Advances in Experimental Social Psychology" (Ed. L. Berkowitz), Vol. 3, pp. 55–98. Academic Press, New York and London.

Brengelmann, J. C. and Brengelmann, L. (1960). Deutsche Validierung von Fragebogen der Extraversion, neurotischen Tendenz und Rigidität. *Z. Exp. Angew. Psychol.* **17**, 291–331.

Cline, M. (1967). The perception of where a person is looking. *Amer. J. Psychol.* **80**, 41–50.

Cranach, M. von (1971a). The role of orienting behavior in human interaction. *In* "Environment and Behavior, The Use of Space by Animals and Man" (Ed. A. H. Esser), pp. 217–237. Plenum Press, New York.

Cranach, M. von (1971b). Die nichtverbale Kommunikation im Kontext des kommunikativen Verhaltens. *In* "Jahrbuch der Max-Planck-Gesellschaft", Göttingen.

Cranach, M. von, Schmid, R. and Vogel, M. V. (1969). Ueber einige Bedingungen des Zusammenhanges von Lidschlag und Blickwendung. *Psychol. Forsch.* **33**, 68–78.

Duncan, S., Jr. (1969). Nonverbal communication. *Psychol. Bull.* **72**, 118–137.

Eibl-Eibesfeldt, I. (1967). "Grundriss der vergleichenden Verhaltensforschung". Piper, Munich.

Ellgring, J. H. (1970). Die Beurteilung des Blickes auf Punkte innerhalb des Gesichtes. *Z. Exp. Angew. Psychol.* **17**, 600–607.

Ellgring, J. H. and Cranach, M. von (1972). Processes of learning in the recognition of eye-signals. *Europ. J. Soc. Psychol.* **2**, 33–43.

Exline, R. V. (1963). Explorations in the process of person perception: visual interaction in relation to competition, sex, and need for affiliation. *J. Pers.* **31**, 1–20.

Exline, R. V., Gray, D. and Schuette, Dorothy (1965). Visual behaviour in a dyad as affected by interview content and sex of respondent. *J. Pers. Soc. Psychol.* **1**, 201–209.

Gibson, J. J. and Pick, Anne D. (1963). Perception of another person's looking behaviour. *Amer. J. Psychol.* **76**, 386–394.

Krüger, K. and Hückstedt, Barbara (1969). Die Beurteilung von Blickrichtungen. *Z. Exp. Angew. Psychol.* **16**, 452–472.

Mehrabian, A. and Williams, M. (1969). Nonverbal concomitants of perceived and intended persuasiveness. *J. Pers. Soc. Psychol.* **13**, 37–58.

Stephenson, G. M. and Rutter, D. R. (1970). Eye-contact, distance, and affiliation: a re-evaluation. *Brit. J. Psychol.* **61**, 385–393.

Strongman, K. T. and Champness, B. G. (1968). Dominance hierarchies and conflict in eye contact. *Acta Psychol.* **28**, 376–386.

Vine, I. (1970). Communication by facial-visual signals. *In* "Social Behaviour in Birds and Mammals, Essays on the Social Ethology of Animals and Man" (Ed. J. H. Crook), pp. 279–354. Academic Press, London and New York.

Vine, I. (1971). Judgment of direction and gaze—an interpretation of discrepant results. *Brit. J. Soc. Clin. Psychol.* **10**, 320–331.

11

Some Non-verbal and Paralinguistic Cues as Mediators of Experimenter Expectancy Effects

Ernst Timaeus

1 An empirical definition of experimenter expectancy effects

At least since the study by Rosenthal and Fode (1963a), it has seemed probable that very simple experimenter manipulations can make prophesies about the outcomes of experiments come true. Their demonstration runs as follows:

1. Experimenters (Es) are instructed differently about the outcomes of a simple person perception experiment. Some of the Es are informed that their subjects (Ss) will, according to former studies, respond to the critical stimulus with positive responses; some are instructed the other way round, i.e. that negative responses are to be expected from former results. As a matter of fact, the dependent variable has quite a different

bias: the portrait photographs used as stimuli had all been located around zero on the rating scale.

2. All Es are motivated to accomplish the induced expectations by the promise that good data will be honoured by an extra pay.[1]

3. After these instructions and having acquainted themselves with the material under study, portrait photographs of people who are to be rated on a 20-point scale for success or failure in life, the Es go to work.

4. The Es did their work well: whether expecting negative or positive results, the data gathered by Es corroborated their expectations significantly.

2 How to communicate a hypothesis effectively: general strategies of mediating experimenter bias

The main question aroused by the Rosenthal phenomenon is: What are the specific behaviours emitted by the Es which can account for the effect? Knowing the answer would enable us to control effectively an important and ubiquitous artefact (Rosenthal, 1966, 1969) in behavioural research.

Three different classes of strategies can be discriminated:

1. The most direct one may be called "pushing the Ss". A nice demonstration of this class of strategy can be found in Skinner's (1948) "Walden Two". His hero Frazier says: "I remember the rage I used to feel when a prediction went wrong. I could have shouted at the subjects of my experiments, 'Behave, damn you, behave as you ought'." (cited by Skinner, 1959).[2] Fortunately Frazier refrains from doing so, thus he does not give us a real demonstration of the strategy because although he "could have done" he did not do so.

However, in one of the author's experiments, (Timaeus, 1973), involving a person perception task similar to that of Rosenthal (1966), the strategy appeared. One of the Es instructed to expect a negative bias when photographs were to be rated on a 20-point-scale for happiness or sadness, finished his instructions before administering the photographs with the remark: "Don't trouble too much about the photographs; they all look somewhat negative." All his Ss were treated in this way. This straightforward strategy happened very seldom; we observed only this one case.

---

[1] This is not a necessary condition for expectancy effects (Rosenthal, 1966).

[2] Having in mind another sentence by Skinner, "I never attacked a problem by constructing a hypothesis" (Skinner, 1959, p. 88), Frazier's standpoint is the more remarkable.

2. Verbal conditioning is a second possible class of strategy. The reinforcers are delivered by Es according to their induced expectancies, despite the fact that they are never taught to do so and that they have no psychological knowledge whatsoever about verbal conditioning.

It seems easy to control such reinforcing behaviour, but this can only be done if we can separate the Es from their Ss completely. As long as any contact between E and S is needed during the response phase of the experiment selective reinforcement can happen.

In one study we discovered (Timaeus, 1973) that our Es made intuitive use of verbal conditioning strategies, i.e. the Es had no scientific knowledge about those strategies. Four out of eight male Es verbally reinforced their Ss. The most frequent reactions to responses congruent to the expectations were repetitions of the Ss' ratings (80 per cent). More rarely used were reinforcers like "wonderful" etc. Verbal conditioning behaviour by only 50 per cent of all Es was sufficient to establish a significant overall effect (U-test, $p < 0.04$).

3. A rather subtle third technique of leading Ss the *right* way can be accomplished by non-verbal or paralinguistic cues emitted by the experimenter. Smiling, exchanging glances etc. are known to be effective variables for behaviour modification (see the chapters by Vine and by Kendon). In our research area these variables were suspected to be possible mediators from the beginning (see also some results of Rosenthal and Fode, 1963a, in the next section).

Non-verbal cues can operate in two different ways. First, such behaviour can play the role of a primary or secondary reinforcer. A smile after every positive rating from a male E could be enough to convince the female S to go on in this expected direction. Second, the transfer of a special hypothesis, and obedience to it by the S, could be established by stressing some points acoustically in the task instruction. These small hints may be effective in communicating to the Ss the special prophecy held by E.

3 Non-verbal cues spontaneously created by experimenters in different task areas for human subjects

3.1 PRELIMINARY REMARKS

Rosenthal (1969) quotes 94 independent experiments in his last summary of expectancy effects. But despite this impressive number there are only a few studies investigating the mediating variables for the effect.

In the next section only such studies are included as were planned beforehand with the idea of uncovering observable behaviour variables. Rating studies, where Ss or observers have made judgements on pre-scribed dimensions concerning Es behaviour, are not included (see for example Rosenthal *et al.*, 1960, 1966). Those studies are interesting and useful in some sense but they are of minor importance for purposes of eliminating expectancy effects in psychological research. Knowing that observer ratings for "sympathy" are correlated with the magnitude of expectancy effects ($r = +0.54$, Rosenthal *et al.*, 1966) does not help very much in controlling the biases of Es.

3.2 PERSON PERCEPTION

All studies in this section have used the photograph rating task. In the beginnings of expectancy research Rosenthal *et al.* (1964) were able to demonstrate that verbal conditioning is not a necessary condition for the effect. The rating of the *first* photograph of ten demonstrated the Es' effects of induced biases, which means that by definition rein-forcers were not responsible for the phenomenon.

This result hints at the suggestion that "task instruction" alone may be an effective mediator. This in turn raises the question as to which are the most effective communication channels; or stated differently: What sort of cues, optical or acoustical, can produce the effect?

The study by Rosenthal and Fode (1963a) is an investigation of this problem of communication channels. Three different treatments were applied: (1) the Es were visible to their Ss but the instructions were administered in written form; (2) the Es were acoustically present but not visible, i.e. they were hidden behind a screen and read out instructions to their Ss; (3) in the control condition Es were visible and had to read out the instructions. The results showed that the acoustical channel alone is sufficient to establish the effects. The optical condition alone demonstrated no effect. But the optical channel is not unimportant, because the optical plus acoustical treatment was stronger than the acoustical condition. Later experiments by Adair and Epstein (1968) give further support for one of the findings, namely that acous-tical cues alone are effective mediators. The orally given instructions of some Es in an earlier experiment were tape-recorded and played back to new Ss. In both experiments bias effects could be demonstrated.

Taking together all the results mentioned we have some knowledge about the preferred communication channels, but so far we do not know the specific cueing behaviour of the Es. Duncan and Rosenthal (1968) analysed sound recordings to solve this problem. They selected three Es who had fulfilled the induced biases. Their instructions, especially the portions where they read out the response alternatives available to the Ss, were coded with respect to supra-segmental phenomena (intensity, pitch level, voice openness, pitch range, tempo, drawl-clipping and vocal segregates). The precise procedure was undertaken using the transcription system developed by Trager and Smith (1957). By this technique for any instruction reading a differential emphasis score could be defined, indicating the emphasis an E has given to one or the other side of the rating scale ($+$ or $-$).

The correlation between differential emphasis scores and Ss' photo-ratings was $+ 0.72$ ($p < 0.01$). That means that when an E is stressing acoustically the plus side of the rating scale, he will get plus ratings from his Ss; and if an E is emphasizing the minus range over the plus, the Ss will react in accordance.

Another result is not so convincing. The correlation between expectancies induced and the differential emphasis scores was only $+0.24$ (n.s.). But this result may be confounded by a decreasing N, because for 3 of the 10 instruction readings there was no expectancy induced (stated by Duncan et al., 1970).

Somewhat earlier Friedman (1967) had analysed motion pictures to find mediating cues from the Es. One of his results interesting in this context refers to the exchange of glances between E and S. The astonishing finding was that the fewer glances exchanged, the greater the magnitude of expectancy effects became ($r = -0.31$, $p < 0.02$).

But this result is an artefact because Friedman (1967) analysed a sample where no main effect for expectancies could be demonstrated (Barber and Silver, 1968). The Es produced no significant effects in relation to their induced biases, but Friedman at least failed to report this finding. The general conclusion that Barber and Silver (1968) might have drawn is that if no main effects in a statistical sense can be established all further analyses can only produce invalid results. This sounds like statistical common-sense but the story shows that it is not always the case, as we shall see.

3.3 TONE DISCRIMINATION

Some data of Zoble (1968, cited by Rosenthal, 1969) support one result already mentioned (see Rosenthal and Fode, 1963a): if Ss had access to auditory stimuli this alone was enough to establish an expectancy effect. The task for the subjects was discrimination of tone-lengths. Unfortunately nothing can be said from this study about the specifity of the auditory cues.

Another result from the same study is, however, contrary to the findings by Rosenthal and Fode (1963a). The visual communication channel was more effective than the acoustical one in relation to the induced biases of Es. These different outcomes—either auditory cues are more effective than visual cues or the reverse relation holds—may be due to the incomparable tasks.

Two other results of Zoble's study are intriguing. Again, in contrast to Rosenthal and Fode (1963a), he found that restriction to one channel is more effective than the visual plus acoustical conditions: Rosenthal (1969) has interpreted these results as follows: ". . . when subjects are deprived of either visual or auditory information, they focus more attention and perhaps greater effort may enable subjects to extract more information from the single channel than they could, or would, from that same channel if it were only one part of a two-channel information input system". (p. 253.) Going one step further, the following can be supposed: if the more "informed" and more "effortful" Ss are at the same time more cue-aware, Rosenthal's suggestions could be proved questionnaires asking the Ss for cue-awareness.

3.4 STROOP-TEST PERFORMANCE

Experimenter expectancy studies which are interested in mediating variables are dependent on at least two possible outcome classes:

(1) whether or not an expectancy effect could be demonstrated;
(2) whether or not differential cues or cue-classes could be detected.

The combination of the possible outcomes allow four different results as indicated in Table 1.

Studies by Rosenthal and Fode (1963a), Adair and Epstein (1968), Duncan and Rosenthal (1968) and Zoble (see above) are demonstrations of the outcome combination denoted A in Table 1. For case B some

TABLE 1

Expectancy effects and cues

Cues or cue-classes detected	Expectancy effects	
	Yes	No
Yes	A	B
No	C	D

results of Friedman (1967) are apparently an example, but only at first sight. Another experiment involving case B will be discussed later on. Under C all those studies can be classified which have failed or not tried to find cues or cue-classes. One may look at D ambivalently. For researchers interested especially in bias effects those studies are failures. For the general advancement of psychology this class is naturally the most important one.

Returning to case B we remember that B is defined by the following conditions: (1) different expectancies have been induced; (2) the Es behaved systematically differently; (3) the outcomes are not affected by the cues delivered.

Timaeus and Lück (1968) used the colour-recognition task introduced by Stroop (1935). The Ss received an 8 × 11-in. sheet of paper on which 100 colour names were written. The colour names were written in coloured ink which differed from the colour named. Ss had to read out the names of the colours as fast as possible. The total time for completing the task was recorded. Each S had to perform the same task twice. In the first situation only an E was present; in the second situation an audience condition was used. For this reason E and his S changed rooms between trials. Under the audience condition the Ss worked in a laboratory where one-way screens were clearly visible, and in addition the Es instructed their Ss that they were under observation, pointing with head and arm in the direction of the screens. The expectancies for two different E-groups were contradictory: one group expected a facilitation effect under audience conditions, while the other group expected a relative inhibition effect.

As already mentioned, the Es were unable to fulfil their induced prophecies; but they tried very hard. The analysis of the tape-recorded instructions as read out by the Es demonstrated that those Es expecting relatively poor performance under audience conditions read the salient instructional passage mentioning screens and observers more slowly and emphatically. (The median time for this group was 7.3 s and for the other 8.05 s, $p < 0.06$ two tailed.) Casual observations of E's behaviour also showed that the same E-group pointed to the screens (i.e. gave head and hand signs) with greater motoric directness.

The inefficiency of the cues still has to be explained. One reason could have been the Ss' different interpretation of the cues, which need not necessarily have been congruent with Es' intentions. Data supporting the discrepancy between Ss' and Es' interpretations will be reported in section 5.

4 Non-verbal cues spontaneously created by experimenters in different task areas with animal subjects

4.1 LEARNING

Among the nine experiments with animals—worms and rats—summarized by Rosenthal (1969), only two are interesting for our purpose. Rosenthal and Fode (1963b) let their Es expect that they were working with either maze "bright" or maze "dull" rats. The induced prophecies were significantly proven. Though no direct cues are reported by the authors there are valid hints. The Es' self-ratings of their behaviour point to possible mediators. Es were undertaking more handling with "bright" rats than with "dull" rats. "Bright" rats were handled more gently than "dull" ones.

In another study with rats by Rosenthal and Lawson (1964) the more frequent handling again was with "bright" rats—or so the Es said.

These results are in agreement with the results of Bernstein (1957), who found that the learning behaviour of rats is sensitive to different handling procedures. In some sense one can say that the Es of the expectancy studies have unwittingly validated Bernstein's (1957) results.

4.2 THE "CLEVER HANS" PHENOMENON

The oldest study about experimenter expectancy effects was performed with only one subject. This was "Clever Hans", a horse. The more than clever E, amongst other Es, was Pfungst (1907). This experiment could well be incorporated in the area of expectancy effects. The story of Hans and Pfungst happened like this.

The teacher of Hans, Mr von Osten, probably believed he owned an extraordinary horse and wanted to make use of the animal's capacities. After some intense training the horse seemingly confirmed his trainer's opinion totally and became a first-class and frequently visited attraction. Psychologists became attracted too, and the German psychologists Stumpf and Pfungst, together with some other specialists in animal training, paid a visit to Hans to find out whether the horse was intentionally cued by von Osten.

They observed a full programme: Hans was able to read numbers and words, to perform arithmetic tasks like simple adding, subtracting, multiplying, and dividing. Questions about musical harmony also gave no difficulty to the horse. It is important that the critical responses of Hans were performed by tapping his right front foot. Most astonishingly the experts were unable to detect any intentional cueing while observing the interactions between von Osten and the horse. That was the occasion for Pfungst to start experimental work with Hans.

He asked himself: If the demonstrator (E) working with Hans did not know the solution of the task himself, was it then possible for Hans to accomplish correct results? For six different task areas he was clearly able to establish that if the Es were not aware of the solutions Hans produced incorrect responses. Only if the Es knew the right answers would the horse respond correctly. Having demonstrated this—the total dependency of Hans' performances upon the E's knowledge of the results—the next question was: What sort of cues are responsible for Hans' behaviour?

At first the acoustical channel was controlled. Using special caps for Hans' ears this channel was blocked. The manipulation had no influence on the performances, i.e. if the E knew the results Hans arrived at correct task solutions. But by blocking the Horse's vision, Hans was unable to solve any task correctly. So it had to be visual cues by the Es which created the cleverness of Hans.

Finally Pfungst *incidently* observed the critical cue which controlled the performance. Observing von Osten when interacting with his scholar, Pfungst (1907) discriminated a very small upward movement of the head at the same moment Hans had reached the correct number, for instance in an adding problem. In some further experiments Pfungst

(1907) varied only the critical head movement in order to validate his observations. All trials demonstrated that the head movement was the cue for Hans to stop tapping. By this last experiment the miracle was solved: the supposed intelligent performances could be reduced to discrimination abilities; or formulated in learning terms, the horse had been instrumentally conditioned by von Osten, but certainly von Osten was not aware of this kind of training.

One result has not yet been mentioned. Knowing the stop sign for tapping, what was the cue for beginning to tap? It was an easily discriminable gross movement: leaning the upper body forward.

To summarize, the following sequence of actions took place:

1. After introducing the problem, for instance $2+5=?$, the trainer gave a starting sign by leaning the upper body forward.
2. Contingent upon this the horse started tapping.
3. After the seventh tap the trainer moved his head upward and thereby stopped the horse. This movement was made while still staying in the starting position, i.e. upper body was still leant forward.
4. After the head movement the upper body of the trainer was again erected to the normal position.

The description of this sequence makes it easy to understand why the first critical observers were unable to detect the slight head movement, namely because the small movement was immediately followed by the gross movement of the upper body—the return to the normal position. From the viewpoint of *Gestaltists* a factor like "embeddedness" hindered detailed or part-oriented observation.

One main question is left for discussion. It relates to the invention of the cues. Pfungst (1907) explained it by a subjective theory of attention and tension he found by self-observation while working with Hans. Leaning forward with the upper body is an expression of close attention of the trainer, who is so curious to see what the horse will do. At the same moment the horse begins tapping, a psychological tension arises lasting for the whole time of tapping and suddenly decreases when the last tap is made. This tension release is expressed by the small head movement. If Pfungst's (1907) theorizing is valid and generalizable, everybody should experience such reactions of attention and tension, consequently followed by the observed movements, in similar situations. Later on we shall discuss Pfungst's (1907) laboratory experiments which give some proof of this theory.

5 Non-verbal cues in simulated bias experiments

5.1 PRELIMINARY REMARKS

All expectancy studies discussed so far have worked with similar strategies: the researchers introduced different outcome-expectancies for Es, let Es go to work, analysed the data and looked for behavioural differences associated with expectancies of different Es. Figure 1 demonstrates the sequence.

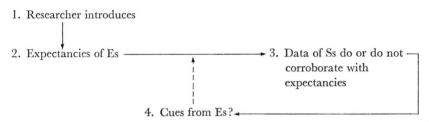

Fig. 1. Research strategy for E-expectancy effects.

All the parts of these strategies could be thought of as obligatory for expectancy effects. But at least one part seems more responsible than other parts. If there are no discriminative cues from the Es bias effects are improbable. The experiments discussed in this section are demonstrations involving the direct manipulations of the cues of Es, a procedure which changes the question mark for cues in Fig. 1 into hypothetical statements.

5.2 PERSON PERCEPTION

The first experiment in this area made use of photographs from persons judged to be around the zero-point on a rating dimension ranging from great sadness (-10) to great happiness $(+10)$ (Timaeus, 1970). The first problem involves the cues which have to be manipulated. The problem was solved empirically by asking experts in role playing. The role playing was restricted to the administering of the instructions because the results from Rosenthal and Fode (1963a) and Adair and Epstein (1968) demonstrated that the biases rest with cue-classes associated with the instruction-giving behaviour of their Es. Ten role players had to read two different versions of the instruction for the photograph-rating task, one designed to provoke negative, the other to provoke positive ratings. The performances were video-recorded and played back to the experts who had to judge which scenes should provoke positive responses. The analysis of the data revealed that the intentions of the role players could be correctly read by the judges (binomial test, combined $p < 0.001$).

Further content analysis of the video-recordings established that most of the experts had made use of the acoustical channel, by stressing the negative numbers when provoking negative results or stressing positive numbers when provoking positive results. This main strategy is identical to the results Duncan and Rosenthal (1968) arrived at after *post hoc* analyses from some Es' instruction readings.

Looking at the summarized results for expectancy effects (Rosenthal, 1969) with the person perception task one can conclude that it is not easy to establish bias effects in this task area. From 57 studies only seven demonstrated main effects for the expectancy variable. Thirteen studies produced no predicted biases and 30 studies indicated that expectancy interacted with another variable.

One reason for these results could have been the minimal cueing behaviour of the Es. So we decided for our first experiment to manipulate more than one cue-variable. In Table 2 all cues are listed which were manipulated simultaneously. All different cues were defined empirically by at least one expert from role players' readings of the same instructions. In a 2×2 design one factor was the cue-variables as indicated in Table 2. The other factor consisted of the frequencies of reading the task instruction for the Ss—one or two times. Despite all these elaborations no effects were attained: Ss' estimates were without systematic bias.

In order to draw more attention to the "cue-producing" E another experiment was run with the exposure time for the photographs limited to 1 s per portrait. We hoped by this manipulation to create more stimulus ambiguity and thereby it was hoped that the rather insecure Ss would look for help from the E. Again the instruction reading was given twice. The results now came out as predicted. Plus-cues lead to positive and minus-cues to negative ratings ($\bar{x}_+ = +0.12$, $\bar{x}_- = -1.42$, $p < 0.001$). This was valid for the mean of ten photograph-ratings per S.

Another analysis for the very first rating per S gave similar results ($\bar{x}_+ = -0.34$, $\bar{x}_- = -2.41$, $p < 0.05$). But this result was only accom-

TABLE 2

Cues for positive or negative photograph ratings

	Direction of bias			
	+		−	
Cues	Acoustical channel	1. Stressing all positive ratings and the word "happiness" 2. Whole instruction was read slowly in a friendly manner	Acoustical channel	1. Stressing all negative ratings and the word "sadness" 2. Whole instruction was read fast and staccato with a small pause after each sentence
	Optical channel	3. After reading positive ratings and the word "happiness" the S was smiled at	Optical channel	3. After reading negative ratings and the word "sadness" the S was looked at

plished when one S had been discarded from analysis. This can be justified by the very extreme and atypical score of the one subject (a score of −10 was given under plus-cues, the only such case out of a total of 88 Ss).

In a third experiment the time for stimulus presentation was further lowered to 1/4 s but this time the cues were only given in a single instruction reading. No cue-related effects could be demonstrated. Possibly the relationship between time of stimulus presentation and effectiveness of cues is inversely U-shaped with a maximum near the 1 s point.

The most recent study in this area has been carried out by Duncan *et al.* (1970). The experimental task for Ss consisted of the original photographs developed by Rosenthal and Fode (1963a). The paralinguistic cues were constructed in a similar way to that in the first experiment described (Timaeus, 1970). Three experts were requested to read the same task instructions in three different manners: (1) "objective and balanced"; (2 and 3) "slightly biased in either a positive or negative direction". No expectancies were given to the readers; instead they were instructed to "balance or attempt to bias the *readings*". The recorded speech samples were transcribed and scored for differential emphasis (method similar to that of Trager and Smith, 1957). Only that section of the instructions was transcribed which gave illustrations of the anchor points of the rating dimension ($+10$, -10, $+1$, and -1). In summary, the results demonstrated that all the experts more or less emphasized or de-emphasized plus or minus rating descriptions.

All the nine tape-recorded and scored instructions were played back to real Ss. The first hypothesis was that stressing the plus or minus direction of the scale would yield corresponding responses from the Ss. The second hypothesis referred to the concept of evaluation apprehension (EA) developed by Rosenberg (1965). EA may be looked upon as a special form of test anxiety. Rosenberg (1969) demonstrated that Ss coming to a psychological experiment are emotionally aroused with respect to the experimenter's evaluating them as psychologically normal and healthy or not. Formulated otherwise, Ss would prefer to be evaluated as normal, and in order to reach this goal would like to follow the wishes of the experimenter, probably expressed by the demand characteristics (Orne, 1959) of the situation or in our case by the cueing behaviour of the experimenter.

Duncan *et al.* (1970) hypothesized that arousing EA will facilitate the sensitivity of the Ss to the constructed cues, as well as the giving of appropriate responses. Three groups of Ss were run here. For two groups the EA was either high or low by pre-instruction manipulations, and the third group functioned as a control condition. High EA was aroused by informing Ss "that the purpose of the experiment . . . was to replicate prior findings indicating that the person perception task was extremely sensitive to, revealing of, emotional maladjustment and health in college students" (Duncan *et al.*, 1970, p. 213). Low EA was induced by giving the information that the Ss belonged to a control group and that their ratings would be used as a baseline for other experimental groups.

The result generally demonstrated that the effectiveness of the recorded readings, stressing plus or minus scale points, is dependent upon EA. Ss highly aroused on EA behaved differentially for plus or minus cues ($\bar{x}_+ = +0.8 = 4$, $\bar{x}_- - 0.39$, $p < 0.005$). Ss with low EA did not respond differentially to the cues. Ss in the control condition, where no EA had been manipulated, also demonstrated cue-directed behaviour ($\bar{x}_+ = +0.57$, $\bar{x}_- = -0.20$, $p < 0.0015$). This last result need not contradict the general statement that cueing behaviour in this experimental situation is a function of EA arousal. If we adopt Rosenberg's (1969) suggestion that EA is an ubiquitous phenomenon and that manipulating it means only strengthening or weakening this special motivation, then we might expect the Ss in the control-condition to operate on a medium level of EA.

5.3 STROOP-TEST PERFORMANCE

In the study quoted above (Timaeus and Lück, 1968), making use of a colour recognition test (Stroop, 1935) as dependent variable, the differently behaving groups of Es did not provoke different responses from their Ss.

Possibly the cues delivered were not perceived by the Ss because they lacked conspicuousness. In a replication of this experiment the same class of cues was varied, but with more stress and with the authors acting as role players. Under the condition of minimum cueing only a short lifting of the head towards the screens was produced while mentioning the one-way mirrors and observers—again without emphasis. Maximum cueing was defined by conspicuously pointing of hand and head towards the screens and by very slow reading of the critical passage of the instruction.

The time for reading the critical passage was checked by measuring the elapsed time after the performance. The result was as prescribed ($p < 0.001$). In spite of the unequivocal manipulation, the Ss did not react differentially to the cues, thus validating the already established results (see p. 452). All results suggest that under the experimental conditions involved, E-outcome bias is not likely. But another observation puts such an interpretation into question. In post-experimental interviews a fair proportion of the Ss tended to disbelieve that they had been observed ($p < 0.06$).

5.4 HYPNOTIC-LIKE SUGGESTIBILITY

The experiment by Barber and Calverly (1964) does not fall in the area of experimenter expectancy research; at least the authors arrived at their hypothesis from a different point of view. But the strategy they applied is similar to what we have called simulated bias experiments. Eight different test suggestions (arm lowering, arm levitation, hand lock, thirst hallucination, verbal inhibition, body immobility, post

Q

hypnotic-like response, and selective amnesia) were introduced to the Ss and measured objectively after the procedure from Barber and Calverly (1963).

The tone of voice used by Es when presenting the suggestions was varied in two directions: (1) "in a forceful tone which implies that positive responses are desired and expected"[1] (Barber and Calverly, 1964, p. 140); (2) in a tone of voice the authors called "lackadaisically", with the implication that it does not matter whether S responds (p. 140). The two versions were checked by raters who could easily discriminate both of them as being in the intended directions. The results were as predicted. A forceful tone of voice was associated with a higher mean score for suggestibility than the lackadaisical version ($\bar{x}_f = 3.9$, $\bar{x}_l = 2.4$, $p < 0.01$).

5.5 "CLEVER PFUNGST" REVISITED

There have been other animals besides Hans that have been studied for their miraculous performances, but until now Hans and Pfungst provide the best and most successful story (see Rosenthal's introduction to the new edition of Pfungst's book, 1965).

Having solved the field study with Clever Hans, Pfungst (1907) went back to the laboratory. Now Pfungst played the part of Hans and engaged Ss to take the role of the trainer. The simulation study may be explained by an example. The S had to choose a number between 1 and 20 and not to say the chosen number to Pfungst because he wanted to guess it. Guessing was done by finger tapping. Let us say the critical number was 15, then a correct answer by Pfungst would have been 15 finger taps. In addition to choosing the number, the Ss' tasks were to imagine the number during tapping, and to count the taps silently.

During tapping Pfungst paid special attention to his Ss, i.e. he was waiting for the famous head movement. In accordance with the tension hypothesis of Pfungst the Ss having 15 in mind will develop a psychological tension with the first tap of Pfungst and will stay in this psychic condition until the fifteenth tap has been given. Immediately after this occurrence, tension is released—to speak figuratively the S breathes again—and the expression of releasing tension should be the head movement upward.

---

[1] The term "expected" in this context supports the conclusion that this study is not free of expectancies and is well incorporated into our research area.

The main question was and is: Did it work? The answer was that it did. The naïve Ss produced the head movement in correct association with the nth tap. Clever Pfungst was perfectly able—as he reported—to read the special thoughts of his Ss. In addition Pfungst found that his Ss were unaware of their own cueing behaviour—a result similar to that of the horse's trainer.

Scientific psychology and the use of mechanical apparatus (today electronic devices) sound somewhat synonymous. The same was true for Pfungst. In order to make the head movement objectively visible, he constructed an apparatus sensible to any direction of head movements, which transcribed the movements onto a kymograph. With the help of the apparatus it was again shown that only the slight head movement upward was contingent on the critical nth tap. The ingenious laboratory experiments of Pfungst have, however, never been replicated. So we decided to do so. Because Pfungst did not give very much detail of his laboratory experiments our study can only loosely be called a replication. In two independent experiments (Timaeus and Schwebcke, 1970) male and female students unwittingly played the horse's part. In order to prevent an important deutero-problem (Riecken, 1962) on the part of Ss, a special cover story was invented. The task was introduced as a special man-machine set-up, i.e. while the S was imagining a chosen number (between 5 and 15) an EEG was registered and constantly fed into a computer. Besides this, optical and acoustical signals were delivered in series of 15, i.e. 15 signals, one after the other, were delivered (the maximum number the S could choose was 15). The task for the S was to imagine the number until the appropriate signal was delivered.

As far as the Ss were informed, the E was only an operator busy making all the apparatus work (mostly dummy equipment). In reality the E played Pfungst's role of observer. The E was counting the signals and observing the S. Because we were sceptical about the ubiquitousness of the head movement, the E attended to any conspicuous expressions. If the E had seen something, he noted the number together with the observed cue. Obviously our E had no knowledge about the number the Ss had chosen and were imagining. Every S had to fulfil 20 trials. In order to rule out chance, the E must be correct for at least 5 out of 20 trials ($p < 0.05$).

The results demonstrated that our E, like Pfungst, was able to read the special thoughts of his Ss. In the first experiment the E was better than chance for 15 out of 16 possible cases, with a range from 5 to 20 correct solutions ($\bar{x}=11.4$ correct solutions). The results of the second experiment were very similar in this and all other aspects investigated.

So far our results are in agreement with Pfungst's. But what happened with the cues? Our E very seldom observed the slight head movement upward (i.e. only 3 times). The most commonly seen cues belonged to the category of eye movements—eye-lid movements and changing the fixation point (48.1 per cent).

The different results obtained from Pfungst's and our own experiments regarding the cues used may be due to different positions of the Ss while doing their job. Our Ss were sitting with their arms on their legs and watching the signal detector in front of them. Unfortunately it is not known whether Pfungst's Ss were seated or standing upright.

6 Discussion

Generally one can say that Es expecting defined results can be very subtle in choosing non-verbal behaviour modifications to make their prophecies come true. But cueing alone does not always help, as we have seen (Timaeus and Lück, 1968). Especially the results of Duncan et al. (1970) point to an equally important part of any experimental psychological situation, namely the needs of the Ss. All Ss could be imagined as filters for any treatment, and thus for the cueing behaviour delivered by Es with their own, hypothesis-centred, motivation. Using evaluation apprehension as one possible operationalization, Duncan et al. (1970) are well in accord with their forerunners Riecken (1962) and Orne (1959), who stress the same point, conceptualized more generally as deutero-problems or, more specifically, as playing the "good subject" in fulfilling the special demands of the experimenter.

How should expectancy effects be controlled? It should be possible to solve the problem by making yesterday's artefact an independent variable (McGuire, 1969). Rosenthal (1966), most responsible for the recent history of expectancy effects, made several suggestions, some of which include the following:

a. Psychologists as inventors of testable hypotheses may run some pretesting, but should engage special firms for the process of data gathering. These firms—not in existence up to now—obviously should have no knowledge about the hypotheses stated.

b. Another solution of the dilemma is a more direct one. It demands expectancy control groups for any treatment under study and allows estimates about pure treatment effects as well as interaction effects.

This strategy seems to be not only elegant but efficient as well, but at the same time it is very expensive. Until now there has been only one empirical demonstration which approximates to the demanded multiple control design (Burnham, 1966, cited by Rosenthal, 1969).

Still another procedure is more to the core of expectancy effects. It relates to the cues emitted due to holding expectancies. Sometimes it will be easy to control cueing behaviour, as we have seen in our special area of non-verbal or paralinguistic hinting. In order to find such behaviour some sort of expectancy pretesting for any treatment is necessary, possibly by specialists such as actors, who should be more sensitive than other experts to efficient cueing of a wide range of behaviour. But in so far as the history of investigating cueing behaviour directly is so recent, any suggestion can at this stage have only a preliminary character.

References

Adair, J. G. and Epstein, J. S. (1968). Verbal cues in the mediation of experimenter bias. *Psychol. Rep.* **22**, 1045–1953.

Barber, T. X. and Calverly, D. S. (1963). "Hypnotic-like" suggestibility in children and adults. *J. Abnorm. Soc. Psychol.* **66**, 589–597.

Barber, T. X. and Calverly, D. S. (1964). Effect of E's tone of voice on "hypnotic-like" suggestibility. *Psychol. Rep.* **15**, 139–144.

Barber, T. X. and Silver, M. J. (1968). Fact, fiction, and the experimenter bias effect. *Psychol. Bull. Monogr.* **70**, 1–29.

Bernstein, L. (1957). The effects of variation in handling upon learning and retention. *J. Comp. Physiol. Psychol.* **50**, 162–167.

Duncan, S., Jr. and Rosenthal, R. (1968). Vocal emphasis in experimenters' instruction reading as unintended determinants of subjects' responses. *Language and Speech*, **11**, 20–26.

Duncan, S., Jr., Rosenberg, M. J. and Finkelstein, J. (1970). The paralanguage of experimenter bias. *Sociometry*, **33**, 207–219.

Friedman, N. (1967). "The social nature of psychological Research". Basic Books, New York.

McGuire, W. J. (1969). Suspiciousness of experimenter's intent. *In* "Artifact in Behavioral Research" (Eds R. Rosenthal and R. L. Rosnow). Academic Press, New York and London.

Orne, M. T. (1959). The nature of hypnosis: artifact and essence. *J. Abnorm. Soc. Psychol.* **58**, 277–299.

Pfungst, O. (1907). "Das Pferd des Herrn v. Osten". Barth, Leipzig.

Riecken, H. W. (1962). A program for research on experiments in social psychology. *In* "Decision, Values and Groups" (Ed. N. F. Washburn), Vol. 2. New York.

Rosenberg, M. J. (1965). When dissonance fails: on eliminating evaluation apprehension from attitude measurement. *J. Pers. Soc. Psychol.* **1**, 18–42.

Rosenberg, M. J. (1969). The conditions and consequences of evaluation apprehension. *In* "Artifact in Behavioral Research" (Eds R. Rosenthal and R. L. Rosnow). Academic Press, New York and London.

Rosenthal, R. (1965). Clever Hans: a case study of scientific method. Introduction to Pfungst, O., "Clever Hans". Holt, Rinehart & Winston, New York.

Rosenthal, R. (1966). "Experimenter Effects in Behavioral Research". Appleton-Century-Crofts, New York.

Rosenthal, R. (1969). Interpersonal expectations: effects of the experimenter's hypothesis. *In* "Artifact in Behavioral Research" (Eds R. Rosenthal and R. L. Rosnow). Academic Press, New York and London.

Rosenthal, R. and Fode, K. L. (1963a). Three experiments in experimenter bias. *Psychol. Rep.* **12**, 491–511.

Rosenthal, R. and Fode, K. L. (1963b). The effect of experimenter bias on the performance of the albino rat. *Behavl Sci.* **8**, 183–189.

Rosenthal, R. and Lawson, R. (1964). A longitudinal study of the effects of experimenter bias on the operant learning of laboratory rats. *J. Psychiat. Res.* **2**, 61–72.

Rosenthal, R., Fode, K. L., Friedman, C. J. and Vikan-Kline, L. (1960). Subjects' perception of their experimenter under condition of experimenter bias. *Percept. Mot. Skills*, **11**, 325–331.

Rosenthal, R., Fode, K. L., Vikan-Kline, L. and Persinger, G. W. (1964). Verbal conditioning: Mediator of experimenter expectancy effects? *Psychol. Rep.* **14**, 71–74.

Rosenthal, R., Persinger, G. W., Mulry, R. C., Vikan-Kline, L. and Grothe, M. (1966). A motion picture study of 29 biased experimenters. Unpublished data, Harvard University, 1962. (Cited by Rosenthal, 1966.)

Skinner, B. F. (1948). "Walden Two". Macmillan, New York.

Skinner, B. F. (1959). "Cumulative Record". Appleton-Century-Crofts, New York.

Stroop, J. R. (1935). Studies of interference in serial verbal reactions. *J. Exp. Psychol.* **18**, 642–662.

Timaeus, E. (1970). Zur nicht-verbalen Kommunikation von VI—Erwartungseffekten. Paper to 27th Kongress der Deutschen Gesellschaft für Psychologie, Kiel.

Timaeus, E. (1973). Zur Sozialpsychologie psychologischen Experimentierens. (In press.)

Timaeus, E. and Lück, H. E. (1968). Experimenter expectancy and social facilitation: II. Stroop-test performance under the condition of audience. *Percept. Mot. Skills*, **27**, 492–494.

Timaeus, E. and Schwebcke, A. (1970). Die Leistungen des "Klugen Hans" und ihre Folgen: ein experimenteller Beitrag zur Psychologie der Vp. *Z. Sozialpsychol.* **1**, 237–252.

Trager, G. L. and Smith, H. L., Jr. (1957). "An Outline of English Structure". American Council of Learned Societies, Washington, D.C.

Author Index

Subject Index

Terms in italics are behaviour elements in the category lists of Chapters 3 and 4. Latin species names are also italicized. Numbers in italics indicate definitions of other technical terms.

A

Abnormal stimulation of infants, 275–280
Accommodation, visual, 203–205
Accuracy of assessment of gaze direction, 422–442
  in recognition of facial expressions, 343–344, 353
Acoustical channel, 22, 448–450, 453, 456
Action implications, 199, 361, 364, 369–370
Acuity, visual, 203–205, 208
Adaptation, 5, 163–166, 299–300
  level, 254, 271
Additivity assumption, 351–352
Affect (*see also* Emotion),
  negative, 198, 243–245, 271, 371
  positive, 198, 220, 223, 243, 248–251, 266, 371, 383
  primary, 355
Affection by deaf-and-blind-born, 175, 184–185
Affective expression and recognition by infants and children, 196–200
Affiliation, 45, 305
Affinitity system of chimpanzee, 134, 137, 140–149
Aggression by deaf-and-blind-born, 173–174
Aggressive system of chimpanzee, 139–150
Air-raid judgements, 368–369
Allomanipulation by chimpanzee, 101–106
American Sign Language, 94
Anger of deaf-and-blind-born, 173–174, 179–180, 185
Anglo-Americans, 34
Animal studies, experimenter bias effects in, 452–454, 460–462
Anthropomorphism, 77, 85
Apes, 8–10, 75–157, 166, 302, 317
Appearance, 16–19, 31
Appeasement, 223, 317
Approval by deaf-and-blind-born, 184

Archer fish, 301
Armsway, 91
Arousal,
  and the Autonomic Nervous System, 306–310, 313
  of infants, 203, 254–256, 271, 277
Assimilation and accommodation, 260
Attachment of infants,
  abnormalities of, 275–278
  and caretaking, 263–269
  face schema development and, 259–280
  to mother, 253, 264–269, 279, 282
  theories of, 265–269
Attack face, 125
Attack system of chimpanzee, 132–134, 139, 149, 155
Attention of infants,
  to eyes, faces, and facial representations, 210–222, 246–263, 303
  and form perception, 205–210
  maternal influences on, 269–270
  measurement of, 203–222, 255–260
  organismic variables and, 202–203, 256–257
  perceptual abilities and, 199–210, 241, 251
  and schema development (*see* Schema)
  stimulus variables and, 207–210, 247, 256, 260
Attention signals, 60
Attitude, 43–46, 246, 314–316
Autism, 276–278, 285
Autistic activities of deaf-and-blind-born, 169–170
Autogroom, 96
Autonomic Nervous System, 299, 306–310, 316
Aversion of gaze (*see* Gaze aversion)
Avoidance, 89
  of faces
    by autists, 275–280, 316
    by infants, 214, 220, 242–243, 254–256